QUANTUM KEY

UNLOCKING SPIRITUAL INTELLIGENCE

GANESH KOLAMBAKAR

INDIA • SINGAPORE • MALAYSIA

ISBN 979-8-89026-906-5

Contents

Introduction

In today's fast-paced and competitive world, success is often measured in terms of material. We all crave external validation and recognition. However, as human beings, we are more than just our external accomplishments. Despite materialistic gains, we may begin to feel that the yardsticks applied to measure success are misleading. External achievements provide a sense of achievement, but a sense of fulfilment might still evade us, leaving that unexplained emptiness within, that yearning for a sense of connection to something greater than ourselves and a way to navigate the complexities and challenges of our modern world with clarity, compassion, and resilience. This can be attributed to the fact that we have an inner world that needs to be nourished and developed for us to live truly fulfilling lives, the key to which can be found in a balance between materialistic pursuits and spirituality. Therefore, it is absolutely essential to understand and connect with one's spiritual side.

The concept of intelligence has evolved over the years, and we now recognise different types of intelligence, beyond the traditional measures of intelligence quotient (IQ) and emotional intelligence or emotional quotient (EQ). One of these types is spiritual quotient (SQ) or spiritual intelligence—the ability to connect with and make sense of one's inner world.

The concept of spiritual intelligence has been gaining traction in recent years as a way of describing a distinct aspect of human intelligence that goes beyond our cognitive abilities and emotional intelligence. It encompasses our capacity for awareness, insight, intuition, empathy, and ethical decision-making, as well as our sense of purpose, meaning, and connection to the transcendent. It is this intelligence that enables us to ask fundamental questions about life, to gain answers by connecting with a higher power, and to develop values and beliefs that guide us as we navigate through life. Helping in the development of a sense of inner peace, contentment, and happiness that cannot be found in external accomplishments alone, SQ enables individuals to tap into their true potential and is critical to living a fulfilling life.

The journey towards spiritual intelligence begins with a spiritual orientation. I believe that spirituality serves as the foundation for spiritual intelligence. Some individuals may already possess spiritual embodiment, while others may need to bring it to the forefront of their lives. In either case, awareness and practice are crucial. The concept of spirituality is closely intertwined with that of spiritual intelligence; they are so interconnected that it is hard to discuss one without the other. Therefore, the nature of spirituality must be explored to fully grasp the concept of spiritual intelligence. Spirituality can be described as an individual's search for meaning, purpose, and transcendence in life. It is a personal journey that often involves a connection with something greater than oneself, such as a higher power or a sense of universal consciousness. On the other hand, spiritual intelligence is the ability to recognise and utilise this connection in everyday life. It encompasses skills such as empathy, compassion, and self-awareness, allowing individuals to navigate complex situations and make meaningful decisions. By exploring the nature of spirituality, we can gain a deeper understanding of the human experience and develop our spiritual intelligence to lead a more fulfilling life.

In this book, we will examine the importance of spiritual intelligence and how it can unlock the true potential of the human dimension. Drawing on a wide range of sources, including psychology, neuroscience, philosophy, spirituality, and personal experiences, this book delves into the nature of spiritual intelligence, its development and cultivation, and its relevance to personal growth, relationships, leadership, and society as a whole. We explore what spiritual intelligence is and how it can be developed and applied. We look at its key components, examine the vital role they play in our personal and professional lives, learn about the practices and techniques that help cultivate spiritual intelligence, and explore the benefits that come with this deeper understanding of our inner selves and our place in the world. We will also explore the relationship between spiritual intelligence and other forms of intelligence, such as EQ and IQ.

While I use eastern spirituality, mainly derived from Hinduism, in my book, individuals who are not comfortable with it can rely on their religious scriptures and traditions to understand themselves and enhance their spiritual intelligence. Within the framework of Hinduism, understanding *atman* (self) leads to knowledge of the ultimate reality—*brahman*—but spiritual intelligence is a universal concept that is not bound by any religion or faith. It only requires an open mind.

This book is a valuable tool designed to enhance your spiritual intelligence so that you can live a more meaningful and fulfilling life. Offering practical guidance and exercises for enhancing one's spiritual intelligence as well as inspiring stories and examples of individuals who embody this kind of intelligence in their lives, it's a handy guide that you can turn to whenever you need guidance or a deeper understanding of the fundamental principles. Whether you are a student, a professional, or a spiritual seeker, the insights and practices shared in this book will help you tap into your spiritual intelligence and live a life that is guided by your deepest values and purpose. Readers who appreciate its importance should encourage their children and family members to read it, too. This book is not just for personal use; it should have a place in every home as a reference book. Its teachings are universal and can help foster a culture of spiritual growth within families. Let it be a cherished possession that is passed down through generations, contributing to the enlightenment of future generations.

Above all, this book invites readers to explore the depths of their own being, and to discover the transformative power of spiritual intelligence in their own lives. It is my hope that this book will be a source of inspiration, guidance, and empowerment for all who seek to awaken to their true potential as spiritual beings. Embrace this book and share its wisdom.

Now, let's begin this journey of self-discovery and exploration.

Acknowledgements

I am immensely grateful to those who have unwaveringly believed in and motivated me. Their encouragement has allowed me to express my thoughts on an unfamiliar and profound concept. Without their support, this book would not have been possible. I feel deeply honoured to share my understanding on this subject and hope it inspires others to pursue their passions with dedication and enthusiasm.

I am deeply indebted to the inspiring people around me that have made this endeavour possible. Their contributions have fuelled my passion and provided me with the necessary tools with which to embark on this writing journey.

Furthermore, I want to acknowledge the impact of technological advancements and access to vast amounts of data. They made it possible for me to gather extensive information while delving into this subject. I want to express my gratitude to YouTube for its enlightening videos, which have greatly contributed to my exploration of spirituality. The platform has been invaluable, deepening my understanding and inspiring my journey. I am also thankful to platforms like Google and advancements in artificial intelligence, which have facilitated my research and writing on spirituality. Easy access to information and diverse perspectives have been instrumental in creating this book. I am sincerely appreciative of these technological tools for expanding my spiritual vista.

This book is dedicated to all those who have believed in me and have journeyed alongside me on my spiritual quest.

Chapter I

Understanding and Exploring Spiritual Intelligence

Spiritual intelligence, a relatively new concept in the field of psychology, refers to an individual's capacity to understand and utilise their spirituality in everyday life. Today, it is regarded by many as the ultimate faculty of human intelligence. Slowly but surely, the concept is gaining importance as a tool for human development and enrichment. While traditional intelligence assessments focus on cognitive abilities and emotional intelligence, spiritual intelligence aims to measure an individual's ability to connect with something greater than themselves, such as a higher power, nature, or the universe.

Naturally, spiritual intelligence flows from the spiritual side of an individual. People often draw parallels between religion and spirituality, but they are different concepts and it is important that we understand the difference between them. Religion may be dependent on the principles of spirituality, but spirituality is independent of religion. A spiritual person may not be religious. Even atheists can be highly spiritual. Religion is conditional, with rituals and dos and don'ts, and is thus fragmented and directive. It sets certain boundaries. Spirituality is holistic and has no boundaries. It emphasises looking inward and is experiential. Spirituality has at its core the principles of inclusiveness, connectedness, and tolerance, whereas religion can be intolerant. Spiritual people are those who have embarked on a transformative journey within, and this makes them fountains of wisdom. Their words are a balm for the soul, bringing solace and restoration. Their mere presence emanates a contagious positivity that uplifts and energises those around them.

Spiritual intelligence is not tied to any particular religion or belief system. Instead, it focuses on an individual's inner beliefs, values, and sense of purpose, as well as their ability to reflect on these aspects of their life. People with high levels of spiritual intelligence often possess a greater sense of meaning and purpose in life and are better equipped to handle the challenges that come their way.

The first person to propose the idea of multiple intelligences was Howard Gardner, a developmental psychologist and professor at Harvard University. According to him, intelligence is not a single, monolithic concept that can be measured by an IQ score; rather, there are multiple types of intelligence, each lending itself to the development of a unique set of skills and abilities. Gardner identified eight types of intelligence:

1. **Linguistic intelligence** is the ability to use language effectively, in the written and/or oral form/s.
2. **Logical-mathematical intelligence** is the ability to reason logically, solve problems, and think critically.
3. **Spatial intelligence** is the ability to think in three dimensions, visualise spatial relationships, and manipulate mental images.
4. **Bodily-kinesthetic intelligence** is the ability to use one's body effectively to accomplish tasks. Dancing, sports, and surgery require this kind of intelligence.
5. **Musical intelligence** is the ability to understand, appreciate, create and/or perform music.
6. **Interpersonal intelligence** is the ability to understand and interact effectively with other people.
7. **Intrapersonal intelligence** is the ability to understand oneself, one's emotions, and one's motivations.
8. **Naturalistic intelligence** is the ability to recognise and categorise different aspects of the natural world, such as plants, animals, and geological formations.

According to Gardner, individuals may possess varying degrees of each type of intelligence, and different cultures and contexts may value different types of intelligence. The theory of multiple intelligences has been influential in the field of education, as it suggests that teachers should use a variety of teaching methods to accommodate different types of learners.

Daniel Goleman, a psychologist who proposed the theory of emotional intelligence, complements Gardner's theory of multiple intelligences by focusing specifically on the role of emotions in intelligence. Goleman's theory of emotional intelligence incorporates some of the forms of intelligence identified by Gardner, such as interpersonal intelligence, intrapersonal intelligence, and even aspects of naturalistic intelligence. For example, self-awareness and self-management both involve aspects of intrapersonal intelligence, while social awareness and relationship management both involve aspects of interpersonal intelligence.

The concept of spiritual intelligence has been studied and developed by a number of scholars. It's worth noting that there are several established theories on spiritual intelligence, including those proposed by authors such as Danah Zohar, Cindy Wigglesworth, and Stephen Covey. Cindy Wigglesworth is an author, speaker, and consultant who has developed a model of spiritual intelligence that combines insights from various spiritual and psychological traditions. In her book *SQ 21*, she identifies four types of intelligence: physical intelligence (PQ), cognitive intelligence (IQ), emotional intelligence (EQ), and spiritual intelligence. However, she extensively explains and emphasises the significance of possessing spiritual intelligence. Her approach is based on the idea that spiritual intelligence helps individuals tap into their inner resources and live a more meaningful, purposeful life.

Cindy Wigglesworth's theory of spiritual intelligence involves four key components: self-awareness, universal awareness, self-mastery, and social-mastery/spiritual presence. She lays out a transformative path to becoming a better, more enlightened person. It's about understanding your values, showing compassion to others, and discovering your life's purpose. These skills empower you to rise above challenges, lead with integrity, and leave a positive impact on the world. In essence, SQ is the key to personal growth, deep connections, and leaving a lasting legacy of goodness and wisdom. Wigglesworth argues that developing spiritual intelligence can have a positive impact on one's personal and professional life and can help individuals navigate the complexities of modern society. She has also developed a number of tools and techniques for the development of spiritual intelligence, including meditation, mindfulness practices, and self-reflection exercises.

In *SQ: Spiritual Intelligence: The Ultimate Intelligence*, Danah Zohar and Ian Marshall define spiritual intelligence as 'the intelligence with which we address and solve problems of meaning and value, the intelligence with which we can place our actions and our lives in a wider, richer, meaning-giving context, the intelligence with which we can assess that one course of action or one life-path is more meaningful than another.' While this sounds like a lot, spiritual intelligence is in fact an innate ability that is present in all individuals, and it is closely linked to the concept of the soul. According to many spiritual and religious traditions, the soul is the eternal, divine essence that animates and sustains human life. It is the source of our consciousness, our sense of self, and our spiritual nature, of the wisdom and insight that will guide us on our spiritual journey. This wisdom is not necessarily something that can be learnt through external sources, but is something that arises from within us, as a result of our connection to the divine.

One of the key aspects of spiritual intelligence is the ability to connect with this inner source of wisdom and insight. This connection can be facilitated through practices such as meditation, prayer, and contemplation, which allow us to quiet the mind and cultivate a deeper awareness of our inner selves. Through these practices, we can access the wisdom and insight of the soul and gain a deeper understanding of our spiritual nature and purpose. What is also emphasised in the development of spiritual intelligence is the importance of cultivating virtues and values that are aligned with the soul, such as compassion, forgiveness, and gratitude. By living in accordance with these values, we can create a more harmonious and fulfilling life and cultivate a deeper sense of connection to the divine. This emanates from the understanding that it isn't enough to chase goals; we must take the time to reflect and mould ourselves in the process. We need to create space for ourselves to nurture our spiritual growth.

If we are constantly caught up in the pull and push of circumstances, we are not living a balanced life. We are allowing external factors to drive us instead of following our inner calling. This is one of the major reasons for conflict between the inner self and the external world. This phenomenon is complex and may lead to emptiness within, creating anxiety, despair, and frustration. In extreme cases, it leads to feelings of desolation and depression. This is why clarity about the purpose of life becomes crucial. When we have a clear understanding of our purpose, our passion drives us forward and we are able to navigate the challenges and opportunities that life presents.

In the pursuit of our goals, it's easy to lose sight of what truly matters. We get so caught up in the 'doing' that we forget about the 'being.' We forget to take care of ourselves and nurture our spiritual growth. Meaningful living cannot be approached casually, for it is a profound experience that requires us to connect with our innermost self, for which 'me time' is essential: time for self-reflection, self-care, and spiritual practice, the groundwork that will help align our goals with our life purpose.

Spirituality may look simple but isn't, for it is experiential and empirical. Some spiritual teachings are esoteric and difficult to grasp unless you have studied the relevant principles, methods, and practices, understood the fundamentals clearly, and experienced the resulting transformation. Attaining that level of realisation requires a disciplined approach to life and the adoption of certain practices. However, understanding and exploring spirituality at a fundamental level is an important starting point that will go a long way in germinating the spiritual intelligence that will ultimately evolve into a life of fulfilment.

Another key component of spiritual intelligence is the ability to practise mindfulness and meditation. These practices allow individuals to connect with their inner selves and reflect on their values and beliefs. Additionally, they help individuals develop a sense of awareness and presence in the moment, which can lead to greater self-understanding and self-awareness. Awareness is key. Unless we focus the beam of our attention on awareness, our true self will not be revealed to us, for we will get caught up in the external world, firefighting the chaos around us, locked in survival mode, failing to live life beyond the body–mind complex. Reflection, mindfulness, and meditation help us take control of ourselves and unlock our creativity to upgrade life.

A third important aspect of spiritual intelligence is the ability to develop and feel empathy and compassion for others. People with high levels of spiritual intelligence are often more attuned to the emotions and needs of those around them and are able to connect with others on a deeper level. This allows them to build stronger relationships and foster a sense of community and interconnectedness.

In addition to mindfulness and empathy, individuals with high levels of spiritual intelligence often possess a strong sense of intuition and a creative impulse. They are comfortable with themselves and are therefore able to think outside the box and see things from different perspectives, which can lead to more innovative and inspired solutions to problems. People with high levels of spiritual intelligence are thus often more resilient in the face of challenges and adversity. Their sense of purpose and connection to something greater than themselves provides them with a strong sense of inner strength and motivation.

While IQ and EQ are both important facets of human intelligence, spiritual intelligence transcends both. Unlike IQ, which is primarily a function of the brain, and emotional intelligence, which is connected to the heart, spiritual intelligence is an innate quality of the soul that needs to be awakened, and once it is awakened, it is the master of all intelligence faculties, flowing from our core and not overshadowed or influenced by external factors. Spiritual intelligence is free from the ego and the 'I' sense—rather, it is the true identity of the self, constructed in accordance with values one arrives at through reflection.

At the heart of emotional intelligence are five core components—self-awareness, self-regulation, empathy, motivation, and social skills—which form the foundation of our ability to connect with and relate to others. But beyond these five components lies a deeper wisdom that allows us to access the consciousness of the soul through spiritual intelligence.

The term 'VUCA', which stands for Volatility, Uncertainty, Complexity, and Ambiguity, is often used to describe the challenges that we face in today's world. The human mind tends to seek simplicity, clarity, and certainty, which can make it difficult to adapt to a VUCA world. However, by developing spiritual intelligence, we can learn to embrace the VUCA phenomenon and thrive in the face of uncertainty. Through the cultivation of inner awareness and presence, we learn to observe our thoughts and emotions without judgement and develop a greater sense of clarity and understanding about ourselves and our place in the world. This, in turn, can help us become more comfortable with uncertainty and ambiguity, as we develop a deeper trust in our own intuition and inner guidance, and this is the foundation of a growth mindset. Rather than seeing challenges and setbacks as failures, we learn to view them as opportunities for learning and growth. This mindset allows us to embrace the VUCA world not with fear and anxiety but with curiosity and wonder.

In addition to inner awareness and a growth mindset, spiritual intelligence also involves the development of strong values and ethical principles. By aligning our actions with our values, we can create a sense of purpose and direction in our lives, which can help us navigate the complex and ambiguous world around us. This can also help us build trust and credibility with others, as we demonstrate our commitment to living a meaningful and authentic life.

Tolerance and inclusivity are hallmarks of the mindset of spiritually intelligent people. They recognise that nothing in life is permanent, that everything—physical objects, relationships, emotions, or any other aspect of life—is constantly changing and evolving, that life is a journey, and that change is a necessary part of that journey. They are able to accept this impermanence without fear or anxiety, and they are more likely to embrace change as an opportunity for growth and transformation. This means that they are open-minded and accepting of others, regardless of their differences. They understand that every person's journey is unique and that we all have something valuable to contribute. Spiritually intelligent people are not dogmatic or rigid in their own beliefs; they are willing to listen to and consider alternative viewpoints. They know that there are many paths to spiritual growth and fulfilment and that no single path is right for everyone. This awareness reflects a deep understanding of the nature of life and the interconnectedness of all beings and it allows spiritually intelligent individuals to navigate life with a greater sense of peace, purpose, and compassion.

Individuals who possess spiritual intelligence do not search for happiness in the external, material world. They recognise that the mind is restricted in its ability to create genuine happiness because it is influenced by past experiences and deeply ingrained beliefs, which can lead to illusory, materialistic attachments. They are capable of distinguishing between their needs and wants, based on the understanding that their needs are minimal while their wants are infinite. They consciously strive to balance the two and are sensitive to the disparities between those who possess and those who lack material resources. Spiritual individuals are aware that happiness is a state of mind that can only be achieved by freeing the mind from attachment. They understand that it is the soul which has the capacity to generate a permanent state of bliss.

Another hallmark of a person with high spiritual intelligence is the ability to connect with others at a deep level. They have an aura that attracts others to them, and they radiate positive energy and compassion wherever they go. They are caring, loving, and empathetic and are able to forge strong bonds of understanding with those around them.

Spiritual intelligence is the ultimate intelligence, as it allows us to access the true wisdom of the soul and live a life that is grounded in authenticity, integrity, and purpose. Through the practice of spiritual intelligence, we can unleash our full potential and become the best version of ourselves.

The misconception that a spiritually intelligent individual must also be a philosophical individual is quite common. Spiritually intelligent individuals prioritise personal growth, subjective experiences, and emotional intelligence. They are in tune with their inner wisdom, intuition, and connection to a higher power. On the other hand, philosophical individuals lean towards objective analysis, logic, and reason, exploring ideas related to knowledge, reality, and existence. While spiritually intelligent people value qualities like compassion, empathy, and mindfulness, philosophical individuals may focus more on seeking objective truth over subjective experiences or personal beliefs.

While there may be some overlap between spiritual intelligence and philosophy, they are distinct approaches to understanding the world and one's place in it. The term 'philosophy' comes from the Greek word *philosophia*, a combination of two Greek words: *philo*, meaning love, and *sophia*, meaning wisdom. Thus, philosophy is often understood as the pursuit of wisdom or knowledge through rational enquiry, reflection, and critical thinking. The roots of philosophy can be traced back to ancient civilisations such as those of Greece, India, and China, where scholars and thinkers sought to understand the nature of reality, the purpose of human existence, and the principles of ethics and morality. Over time, philosophy has evolved into many different branches and subfields, including metaphysics, epistemology, ethics, logic, political philosophy, and aesthetics. Each of these branches explores different aspects of human experience and enquiry and contributes to a deeper understanding of the world and our place in it.

Across all these branches, the practice of philosophy involves critical thinking, logical reasoning, and the exploration of fundamental concepts related to knowledge, reality, and existence. While a philosophical person may also have spiritual beliefs and practices, his or her primary focus is likely to be on analysing and understanding the world through reason and logic. A spiritually intelligent person may be philosophical, but not necessarily. While a spiritually intelligent person may have a philosophical perspective on life, they may also draw on their personal experiences, intuition, and emotions to navigate the world.

Having said that, it is important to acknowledge that philosophy and spirituality are intertwined when it comes to the cultivation of spiritual intelligence. They each play a critical role in supporting and enhancing one another. Together, they form a powerful partnership, with philosophy providing a rational and analytical approach to understanding the world while spirituality offers a more experiential and intuitive way of connecting with the divine. This integration of the intellectual and the spiritual can lead to a more holistic and integrated approach to personal growth and transformation. Therefore, as I draw on eastern spirituality in this book, I will also draw on philosophical concepts to provide additional context and insight.

It is very important to understand that Indian spirituality means wisdom through *darshan*. *Darshan* can mean more than just physically seeing a deity or divine image. It can also refer to the experience of perceiving something beyond what is immediately visible or tangible. *Darshan* is the vision of true knowledge. In Advaita Vedanta, for example, *darshan* is a term used to describe the direct perception of the ultimate reality or *brahman*. This perception is said to transcend ordinary sensory experience and is attained through deep meditation and contemplation. As we proceed, we shall delve further into the nature of self to understand the ultimate reality or *brahman*. Similarly, in some schools of *tantra*, *darshan* is understood as a form of energetic exchange between the practitioner and the divine. This exchange involves opening oneself up to the energy and presence of the divine and can be experienced through various practices, such as mantra recitation, visualisation, and ritual worship. In Jainism, *darshan* is also understood as a form of spiritual insight or intuition. It involves seeing the world and one's place in it from a deeper, more compassionate perspective and is often associated with the practice of non-violence and ethical behaviour. Overall, *darshan* in Indian philosophy can refer to a wide range of experiences and practices, all of which involve seeing and experiencing something beyond what is immediately visible or tangible.

The essence of spirituality, which is the foundation of spiritual intelligence, lies in the understanding that we are not merely human beings who occasionally have spiritual experiences but spiritual beings that are temporarily experiencing a human existence. This shift in perspective can be transformative, as it allows us to recognise that our true nature is not limited by our physical bodies but is instead boundless and eternal. When we embrace this truth, we can begin to view our time on earth as an opportunity for growth and learning, rather than just a fleeting moment in the grand scheme of things.

There is a strong connection between spiritual intelligence and morality, as both frameworks are concerned with developing a deeper understanding of ourselves and the world around us. Spiritual intelligence can, in fact, provide a framework for moral reasoning and decision-making. Someone who has developed spiritual intelligence may be more likely to consider the ethical implications of their actions and to act in ways that are in line with their sense of purpose and values. They may also be more likely to practise empathy and compassion towards others, recognising the interconnectedness of all beings. There is research to suggest that individuals who score higher on measures of spiritual intelligence are more likely to demonstrate ethical behaviour, including honesty, fairness, and respect for others. Similarly, individuals who have a strong sense of purpose and meaning in life are more likely to act in ways that are consistent with their values and beliefs.

Comparative Analysis of the Three Forms of Intelligence

Aspect	IQ	EQ	SQ
Definition	Intelligence quotient, a measure of cognitive intelligence	Emotional quotient or intelligence, the ability to recognise, understand, and manage one's own emotions and the emotions of others	Spiritual intelligence, the ability to access higher meanings, values, and purposes
Main components	Reasoning, logic, analytical and problem-solving skills	Self-awareness, self-regulation, empathy, motivation, social skills	Awareness, practice, consciousness, purpose, passion
Primary focus	Analytical and logical thinking	Emotional and social awareness	Spiritual development and awareness through intuitive processes and mindfulness
Associated skills	Problem-solving, memory, critical thinking	Effective communication, intra- and interpersonal conflict resolution	Disciplinary practices, morality, ethics, understanding the self, belief in interconnectedness
Role in life	Useful in academic and professional pursuits	Important for personal and professional relationships	Essential for personal growth, fulfilment, and well-being

Aspect	IQ	EQ	SQ
Process of cultivation or development	Can be improved through learning and practice	Can be developed through self-reflection and communication training	Can be cultivated through spiritual practices, meditation, and self-enquiry
Measurement	Measured using standardised intelligence tests	Measured through self-reporting, observation, and assessments	Currently not standardised; measured through self-assessment or expert evaluation

Note: It's important to keep in mind that these three intelligences are not mutually exclusive and work together to shape an individual's personality and behaviour.

The concept of 'survival of the fittest' was first introduced by Darwin to explain how different species survived by evolving and adapting to the environment. However, today's world is vastly different. The stress is not on physical survival but on intellectual, emotional, and spiritual development. As human beings, we are constantly hungry for growth and evolution in these areas. The concept of survival of the fittest is still relevant, mainly in the context of competition, with a focus on being the best, the strongest, and the fastest. While competition can be healthy and lead to growth, it can also lead to stress, anxiety, and burnout. Spiritual intelligence empowers people to shift from competition to contribution, which is the need of the hour. When we focus on contribution, we are looking out not just for ourselves but for the greater good of society. It is a win-win situation for all. Darwin suggested that it's not the fittest alone who survives but the one who is adaptive and responsive to change. 'Survival of the fittest' becomes a redundant axiom when we shift our focus from competition to contribution. When we contribute, we use our unique talents, skills, and abilities to make a positive impact on the world, empowering ourselves to enter a creative mode rather than a mere survival mode. Spiritual intelligence is essential to our evolution as human beings. By cultivating awareness of our inner selves, turning our attention inward, and practising mindfulness, we can tap into our intuitive power and wisdom and lead a life of choice.

Striking a Balance Between Materialism and Spirituality

The pursuit of material wealth and success is common in today's society. However, this materialistic mindset can often lead to a sense of emptiness. Therefore, combining this pursuit with a spiritual understanding can bring balance to one's life and lead to a more meaningful existence. The first step towards achieving this balance is understanding that spirituality cannot be imposed from the outside. It must come from within, as a result of an individual's desire to satisfy their inner calling. This may involve exploring different spiritual practices until one finds what resonates with them.

As one's spiritual understanding deepens, one will gain the wisdom to relate to one's purpose in life. This understanding can lead to a shift in priorities, such that material success is not the only goal but rather a means to a greater end. To pursue only material success is to inhabit the lower self, while the complementary pursuit of spiritual self-knowledge grants one access to the higher self. The higher self allows individuals to connect with something beyond the material world and experience inner peace. This is achieved by understanding and connecting with the self at a deeper level, leading to a sense of purpose and direction in life. It also enables individuals to live in harmony with the world around them.

Balancing materialism with spirituality is essential for a fulfilling life. A person with a high SQ is a realised individual who has dwelt in the awareness within and unfolded the self to discover their true identity and thereby possesses experiential knowledge of the fact that they are beyond the body and mind and are in fact on a journey to access their consciousness or soul. They have mastered the art of living in a materialistic world yet remaining non-attached to people and situations. They deal with and handle what is in their control and avoid resisting what is not. They are unaffected, fearless, positive, peaceful, and purposeful in all situations.

Spiritual intelligence is a remarkable manifestation of inner wisdom that lies dormant within us, waiting to be awakened. This wisdom cannot be created, as it already exists within us. However, it is often obscured by the clutter of our minds, which is composed of compulsive thinking patterns known as *vritti*. The dominance of our ego, known as *ahankara*, influences our thought process and actions. To unlock this inner wisdom, we must first learn to clear away the clutter of our minds. This is a challenging task that cannot be accomplished overnight. It necessitates the cultivation of mindfulness, frequent meditation, and relentless perseverance. Through meditation, we can begin to dissolve the *vritti* and *ahankara* that block our path to spiritual intelligence, making way for greater clarity, understanding, and insight.

Challenging our perceptions and dismantling our beliefs is also a vital aspect of this journey. When we are open and receptive to new ideas, we can expand our understanding of ourselves and the world around us. This openness allows us to see beyond our preconceived notions and biases, enabling us to embrace new perspectives and experiences. In essence, spiritual intelligence is about cultivating a deep sense of inner wisdom and understanding. By clearing away the clutter of our minds and being open to new experiences and ideas, we can unlock the doors of realisation and gain a greater sense of clarity and purpose in our lives.

A spiritually intelligent individual is characterised by an insatiable hunger for knowledge and a willingness to explore diverse ideologies. Although they may not always agree with or share the same viewpoints as others, they approach these differences with respect and an appreciation for diversity. These individuals strive to build meaningful connections with others by attending workshops, seminars, and reading enriching books. Their passion for knowledge drives them to seek out deeper truths, and they look to scriptures as a source of wisdom and inspiration. While they may not necessarily agree with everything written in religious texts, spiritually intelligent individuals hold them in high esteem and approach them with reverence. They recognise their own limitations and acknowledge that there is always more to learn, which fuels their desire to continue exploring and seeking knowledge. In order to dispel their own ignorance, they believe it is important to remain open to all perspectives, reflect on their experiences, and engage in deep contemplation. They view this ongoing process of self-reflection as a crucial part of their journey towards greater understanding and enlightenment.

A spiritually intelligent person possesses an innate quality: introspection. They believe in the importance of self-knowledge, which ultimately leads to the realisation of the ultimate reality, known as *brahma gyan*. This journey of self-discovery is considered a way of life for spiritually intelligent individuals, as it enables them to gain a deeper understanding of the purpose of their existence and live a fulfilling life in accordance with that purpose. To a spiritually intelligent person, the journey of self-discovery is not a one-time event but an ongoing process that requires constant effort and attention. They view this journey as a life of momentum, with each step forward bringing them closer to their ultimate goal. Any interruption or disruption to this flow is viewed as stagnation, hindering their progress towards greater self-awareness and the realisation of the ultimate reality.

Here are five vital characteristics that can be attributed to spiritually intelligent people:

1. They are willing to step out of their comfort zone and explore the unknown. This may involve taking risks or trying new things, even if it feels uncomfortable or unfamiliar.
2. They are open-minded and curious, and they actively seek out different perspectives and viewpoints. They are not afraid to challenge their own assumptions or beliefs, and they are committed to finding their own truth.
3. They are skilled at communicating with others and are able to speak the language of the person they want to become. This means that they are able to connect with others on a deep level and inspire them to see the world in a different way.
4. They make decisions with both their head and their heart. While they may use logic and reason to make small decisions, they listen to the voice of their soul when making big, impactful decisions. They are attuned to their intuition and are guided by their inner wisdom.
5. They are committed to making a positive impact on the world around them. They are constantly contemplating how they can use their skills and talents to help others and create positive change. They are compassionate, empathetic, and focused on making a difference in the lives of as many people as possible.

These qualities make spiritually intelligent people highly sought-after and respected by others. They are able to navigate complex challenges and inspire those around them to live more fulfilling, meaningful lives.

Spiritual individuals have a strong belief in the importance of establishing a connection with others before attempting to convey their point of view. They understand that people have complex psychological needs and desires and need to feel seen, heard, and valued before they extend their trust and goodwill to others. The process of forming a connection typically involves three key steps: connecting, conveying, and convincing.

1. In the first stage, spiritual individuals focus on establishing a genuine connection with the other person. This may involve actively listening to their concerns, asking questions, and showing empathy for their situation.
2. Once a connection has been established, the next step is to convey their own perspective or point of view. This may involve sharing insights or information that could be helpful to the other person, or offering guidance and support based on their own experiences.
3. The final step is convincing, which involves presenting their point of view in a way that is respectful and non-threatening. This could involve using persuasive language or providing evidence to support their position, but it is always done with the goal of maintaining the connection that has been established.

Spiritual individuals recognise that building meaningful connections with others requires a deliberate and intentional approach. By focusing on understanding the needs and desires of others and approaching conversations with empathy and respect, they are able to establish a foundation of trust and understanding that can lead to deeper, more fulfilling relationships.

Integrating AI and Spiritual Intelligence: Illuminating the Future of Human Existence

Artificial intelligence (AI) has captured the world's attention in recent times. It is a remarkable tool that has simplified our lives and provided us with an abundance of knowledge and information. It is imperative that we understand AI, embrace it as a powerful ally, and cultivate a mutually beneficial partnership with it. However, amidst all the fascination with AI, what remains ignored is the extraordinary potential that can be unleashed if it is combined with spiritual intelligence. This combination has the potential to enrich our lives holistically, bringing us physical, mental, emotional, intellectual, and spiritual well-being.

With AI seamlessly assuming the functions traditionally attributed to the left brain, humans can now harness their full potential by focusing on the expansion of their right-brain capabilities. This entails honing critical analytical skills, fostering compassion, empathy, inclusiveness, and more. As AI takes the reins of our IQ-related work, our attention can turn towards nurturing and enhancing our emotional intelligence. The advent of AI can thus bring into prominence the roles of emotional and spiritual intelligence. While AI caters to our intellectual curiosity, spiritual intelligence ignites our thirst for wisdom and deeper understanding, fostering personal growth and transformation. Furthermore, the integration of spiritual intelligence with technology can facilitate the development of AI applications and systems that prioritise human values, ethics, and empathy. By infusing technology with the principles of compassion, connection, and holistic growth, we can ensure the harmonious coexistence of humans and machines and bring into view a more sustainable future.

AI has undeniably revolutionised our world. However, the dormant power of spiritual intelligence within us holds the promise of a deeper and more fulfilling existence. By embracing and harnessing this inner wellspring of wisdom, we can complement and supplement the wonders of technology, creating a more holistic and enriching life. As we venture into the future, let us remember that true fulfilment lies not only in the capabilities of AI but also in the nurturing and expansion of our own consciousness, which is our essence.

Components of Spiritual Intelligence

While there is no universally agreed-upon set of components of spiritual intelligence, several scholars and researchers have identified a number of key elements that are often associated with this construct. Some of the main components of spiritual intelligence are:

1. **Self-awareness**: The ability to reflect on one's own beliefs, values, and experiences, and to understand how they shape one's sense of self and connection to the world.
2. **Transcendence**: The capacity to go beyond the limitations of one's own ego and connect with something larger and more profound. This might involve experiencing a sense of awe or wonder in the face of nature, art, or spiritual practices.
3. **Compassion**: The ability to empathise with others and to feel a sense of concern for their well-being. This component of spiritual intelligence is closely related to the concept of empathy in emotional intelligence.
4. **Consciousness**: Consciousness is another important component of spiritual intelligence, as it involves being fully present in the moment and experiencing a deep sense of awareness and connection to the world around us. By cultivating consciousness, individuals can become finely attuned to their own inner landscapes, as well as the emotions and experiences that shape others' lives.
5. **Meaning and purpose:** Meaning and purpose are also key components of spiritual intelligence, as they involve understanding the larger context and significance of one's existence and seeking out a sense of direction and purpose in life.
6. **Gratitude**: The ability to appreciate the gifts and blessings in one's life and to feel a sense of thankfulness for the people and experiences that have shaped us.

7. **Inner peace**: Inner peace is also a key component of spiritual intelligence, as it involves finding a sense of calm and tranquillity amidst the chaos and challenges of life. By cultivating inner peace, individuals can become more resilient in the face of adversity and more competent at navigating the ups and downs of life with grace and equanimity.
8. **Forgiveness**: The capacity to let go of resentments and grudges and cultivate a sense of compassion and understanding towards those who have hurt us.
9. **Integrity**: Integrity is also a key component of spiritual intelligence, as it involves acting in accordance with one's own values and beliefs and living a life that is aligned with one's deepest convictions.
10. **Service**: Service can be understood as the capacity to contribute to the well-being of others and to make a positive difference in the world.

It's worth noting that these components are not mutually exclusive or exhaustive, and different scholars and researchers may use slightly different terminologies or conceptual frameworks to describe spiritual intelligence. However, they do provide a useful starting point for understanding some of the key elements that are often associated with this construct.

Chapter 2

Developing Spiritual Intelligence Through the Cultivation of Its Essential Attributes

Spiritual intelligence is the ability to connect with something greater than oneself and to use this connection to guide one's thoughts, actions, and overall sense of purpose. A person with high spiritual intelligence is characterised by certain essential attributes and qualities that enable them to live a more fulfilling and purposeful life. Each of those qualities has the potential to transform our lives in profound ways. Compassion, forgiveness, empathy, resilience, curiosity, gratitude, generosity, mindfulness, and non-attachment are among the most critical of these attributes.

The traits of humility, compassion, empathy, grace, and authenticity are commonly associated with spiritual intelligence. However, it's important to note that these characteristics can also be present in individuals with other types of intelligence. One doesn't need to be spiritually oriented to exhibit some of these positive traits. Some people may not even be aware that they exhibit these innate traits; being that way comes naturally to them.

Spiritual intelligence is a multifaceted and intricate concept. It can be challenging to distinguish between IQ, EQ, and SQ, as they are interrelated and used in conjunction with each other. However, individuals who exhibit purpose-driven lives, characterised by empathy, genuineness, appreciation, tolerance for differences, interconnectedness, mindfulness, meditation, reflection, and contemplation, all of which combine to produce heightened states of awareness, are believed to possess spiritual intelligence.

Enhancing one's spiritual intelligence requires commitment, consistent practice, and persistence. To illustrate this, I would like to share a story.

A man went up to a teacher and asked how he could attain spiritual enlightenment.

The teacher replied, 'Before I tell you how to reach enlightenment, let me tell you a story.

'There was once a king who was very proud of his luxurious palace. One day, he asked his ministers if they could identify an object that would fit in the palm of his hand but also fill the entire palace.

'All of his ministers were stumped, except for one. He brought a small seed to the king and placed it in his palm. "Plant this seed in the palace grounds," he said, "and give it time to grow. Eventually, it will become a mighty tree that will fill the entire palace with its branches and foliage."

'The king, impressed with the minister's advice, planted the seed. Years went by, and eventually the tree grew tall and strong, filling the entire palace with its beauty and grace.

'Enlightenment is like that seed,' the teacher said to the man. 'It starts small, but with time and attention, it can grow into something much greater. Just as you must tend to the seed and give it the space it needs to grow, so too must you nurture your spiritual intelligence through meditation, reflection, and self-awareness. With patience and dedication, you can achieve true spiritual enlightenment, which will fill your life with meaning and purpose.'

The story of the seed and the palace is relevant because it highlights the importance of patience, dedication, and tending to our spiritual growth. Just as the seed needed time, care, and attention to grow into a mighty tree, so too must we cultivate our spiritual intelligence through persistent effort and self-reflection.

In the pursuit of spiritual intelligence, we seek to develop qualities such as compassion, wisdom, and a deep sense of purpose and connection to the universe. However, these qualities cannot be achieved overnight. They require consistent practice and a willingness to reflect on our thoughts, feelings, and actions. Nurturing our spiritual intelligence in much the same way as the king nurtured the seed will have a positive impact on our lives, relationships, and the world around us.

The story reminds us that spiritual intelligence is a journey, and, like any journey, it begins with a small step. It encourages us to be patient, persistent, and dedicated to the path of self-improvement and spiritual growth, even though the journey may be long and challenging. With these thoughts in mind, we will explore some of the essential qualities that are commonly associated with spiritual intelligence.

Transforming the Self with Compassion

A person with high spiritual intelligence is compassionate towards themselves and others. They have a deep understanding of the interconnectedness of all things and recognise that everyone is doing their best, given their individual circumstances. They are able to put themselves in another person's shoes and see things from their perspective, which helps them respond with kindness and understanding. They strongly believe that everyone around them has the potential to evolve and grow through enrichment.

Compassion is a fundamental principle of spiritual intelligence, one that speaks to the very essence of our human experience. It is the ability to deeply connect with the suffering of others and to take action to alleviate that suffering. Compassion is a profound expression of the spiritual qualities of love, kindness, and wisdom. When we show kindness towards others, we in turn also gain a sense of personal fulfilment and purpose. Improving our spiritual intelligence requires that we develop greater empathy and understanding for others. Compassion helps us to do just that. It allows us to see beyond our own needs and desires and focus on the needs of others. By letting go of our own selfish desires and focusing on the needs of others, we can free ourselves from the burdens of our own ego. We become less concerned with our own problems and more aware of the suffering of others. This helps us develop a greater sense of inner peace. In addition, compassion helps us cultivate greater levels of forgiveness. When we are able to understand the suffering of others, we become more forgiving of their mistakes and shortcomings. This makes us tolerant towards others, even in the face of adversity and conflict.

Furthermore, spiritually intelligent individuals do not discriminate based on superficial characteristics such as race, gender, or socioeconomic status. They understand that these traits are merely societal constructs that do not define a person's worth. Instead, they focus on treating everyone with kindness and respect, recognising the inherent potential within each individual. A spiritually intelligent person views every human being as possessing unique strengths and weaknesses that make them valuable. By embracing compassion and empathy, we can create a more inclusive and accepting world, in which every person can thrive and reach their full potential.

In the Buddhist tradition, compassion is seen as one of the Four Immeasurables, along with loving kindness, joy, and equanimity. In the Hindu tradition, the principle of *ahimsa*, or non-violence and equanimity, is closely linked to the practice of compassion. *Ahimsa* involves a commitment to avoiding harm and to promoting the well-being of others through acts of kindness and service. Central to this is the quality of equanimity, an important concept in the Bhagavad Gita. It is often defined as a state of evenness, balance, and calmness in the face of life's ups and downs. It is the ability to remain unaffected by the dualities of life, such as pleasure and pain, success and failure, praise and criticism, and so on. According to the

Gita, equanimity is essential for spiritual growth because it helps free the mind from the disturbances of the ego and the senses and enables it to turn inward, towards the higher self.

In the Christian tradition, compassion is closely linked to the principle of agape or divine love. Agape is a selfless and unconditional love for all beings and a commitment to serving others and promoting their well-being. Jainism also emphasises the practice of non-violence and compassion towards all living beings. At the core of Jainism's teachings on compassion and love is the principle of *ahimsa*. Jainism teaches that compassion and love are essential virtues that help individuals attain spiritual growth and enlightenment. By practising non-violence, empathy, forgiveness, equality, and selflessness, individuals can develop a deeper understanding of the interconnectedness of all living beings and cultivate greater compassion and love towards them. Practising these virtues can help individuals overcome negative emotions, such as anger and resentment. The cultivation of compassion and love is seen as essential for spiritual growth and enlightenment in Jainism.

In addition to the spiritual benefits of compassion, there is also a growing body of scientific research that supports the positive impact of compassion on our physical and emotional well-being. Studies have shown that practising compassion can reduce stress and anxiety, increase feelings of social connection, and promote positive emotions such as joy, gratitude, and awe.

Compassion is a core principle of spiritual intelligence. By cultivating compassion, we can develop greater self-awareness, empathy, and wisdom, and can awaken to the deeper spiritual truths of existence. We can also make a positive difference in the lives of others and contribute to a more compassionate and loving world.

Unlocking the Power of Love Through Spiritual Intelligence

Love is a universal human experience that has been explored and celebrated in many cultures and traditions throughout history. From the ancient Greek philosophers to the poets of the Romantic era, love has been a source of inspiration, wonder, and transformation to all. In the context of spiritual intelligence, love is seen as a powerful force that can help us connect with the divine, transcend our individual selves, and cultivate a sense of inner peace and harmony.

Love is a central component of spiritual intelligence, as it helps us cultivate qualities like empathy, compassion, self-awareness, intuition, and a sense of interconnectedness with all things and tap into the deeper dimensions of our being. The Bhagavad Gita teaches that love is the highest form of devotion and that it can help us transcend our ego and connect with the divine. In Christianity, love is seen as a central tenet of the faith, with Jesus teaching that the greatest commandment is to love God and love your neighbour as yourself. Buddhism emphasises that cultivating compassion and loving kindness towards all beings is a way of transcending the illusion of separateness and achieving enlightenment.

Love is not a tangible substance but an abstract and intangible feeling that originates from within a person's heart. Love is not limited by physical boundaries and or by time, age, race, or religion. Love is universal and can transcend cultural, linguistic, and physical barriers. It is an emotion that is infinite and eternal. Unlike matter, which is finite and limited, love has no boundaries, and it cannot be destroyed or depleted. Furthermore, love is not a product of conscious design or effort. It is a natural phenomenon that arises deep within a person's heart, and it is experienced through the heart. The heart is the only medium for experiencing love, and it is the source of all emotions, including love.

There are many different types of love, each with its own qualities and characteristics. In the context of spiritual intelligence, three types of love are often discussed: eros, philia, and agape. Eros is the passionate, romantic love that we typically associate with couples. It is often described as a physical and emotional attraction between two people. Philia is a deep, platonic love that is based on mutual respect, admiration, and shared interests. It is often associated with friendship and can be a source of great support and encouragement. Agape, which has been discussed, is a selfless, unconditional love that is directed towards all beings, regardless of their actions or circumstances. It is often seen as the highest form of love, as it is not based on personal desire or attachment.

Love can help us transcend our individual selves and tap into a deeper, more expansive sense of being that enables us to navigate the challenges of life with greater resilience, empathy, and compassion. It is also an essential ingredient of physical and emotional health. Research has shown that people who experience more love and connection in their lives also experience lower levels of stress, anxiety, and depression and are more likely to live long and healthy lives.

Practising love in the context of spiritual intelligence involves cultivating a sense of compassion and empathy towards all beings, including ourselves. It involves being kind, generous, and supportive, even in the face of difficult circumstances. It also involves being open and receptive to love, both from others and from the divine. Some practices that help us cultivate love include meditation, prayer, journalling, and acts of kindness.

Kabir Das, the 15th-century Indian mystic poet and saint, believed that love was the true essence of spirituality and that it was the path to ultimate liberation. He wrote extensively on the subject of love, and his writings have inspired countless people over the centuries. According to Kabir, love is the ultimate reality and the true essence of spirituality. He believed that the love for God was the only true love and that all other forms of love were merely a reflection of this divine love.

'Prem bhakti ka madhva piya, hari sey hai sanchi

Jo hari bhajan kare, uska kuchh na bigadta, kabir sun lijiye nich'

(The nectar of love and devotion is sweet, it is the true way to God

Those who worship God, nothing bad ever happens to them, listen to me Kabir, you are a nobody.)

According to Kabir, this love formed the basis of all relationships—it was only through love that true friendships and partnerships could be formed. Indeed, it was only through love that humanity could progress and evolve.

'Prem na chahiye, kuchh aur chahiye

Prem hi sab kuchh hai, yehi hai bigar, yehi hai nirali'

(You don't need anything else but love

Love is everything, it is unique and unparalleled.)

Kabir believed that love was the path to unity and that it was only through love that people of different religions, castes, and creeds could come together and true peace and harmony could be achieved.

'Sab jagat ke vyavhar, prem ka sagar,

Jo tis mein doobae, so uski pauri paar'

(The ocean of love is the essence of all dealings in the world,

Those who immerse themselves in this ocean, cross to the other shore.)

Kabir believed that external rituals and ceremonies were of no use if they did not lead to inner transformation. He criticised the practice of blindly following religious rituals without understanding their true meaning.

'Pothi padh padh kar jag mua, pandit bhayo na koye,

Dhai akshar prem ke, jo padhe so pandit hoye'

(Reading books and scriptures, the world has perished, and none became wise,

But the one who reads and understands the essence of love, becomes truly wise.)

Kabir emphasised the importance of compassion and love towards all living beings.

'Prem gali ati saanchi, ta te dharo tan jeevan bhar,

Jahan tah tah prem ki, mukhe rahe iccha haar.'

(In the street of love, keep your body and soul throughout your life,

Wherever you go, let love be on your lips, and desires shall fade away.)

Love all, hate none. This is the message of Kabir, and the essence of all religions. Kabir Das' teachings on love are an inspiring reminder of the power of love to transform individuals and societies. Love is a multifaceted emotion that is fundamental to the human experience but can be difficult to define. Cultivating the feeling of love requires a lifelong commitment to being vulnerable, empathetic, and compassionate towards oneself and others.

The key to building loving relationships with others is to first learn to love yourself. This involves accepting yourself for who you are, acknowledging and embracing both your strengths and weaknesses, and treating yourself with kindness and compassion. When you truly believe that you are capable of being whole and complete, your entire perspective shifts. You begin to look inward, discovering your unique strengths and abilities. This realisation ignites a fire within you, driving you to seek and fulfil your potential. You become aware of the incredible gifts that have been bestowed upon you by a higher power, and you love yourself for it. As you develop this newfound self-love, you also begin to see the world around you through a different lens. You view everyone and everything as interconnected and realise that the growth and success of others is just as important as your own. This realisation inspires you to play a vital role in the growth and development of those around you, shifting your focus from competition to constructive contribution.

This transformation is powerful and authentic. It empowers you to step up and play a socially impactful role in the world. With your newfound confidence and passion, you become a catalyst for positive change, inspiring others to recognise their potential and fulfil their own destinies.

Gratitude and the Joy of Giving

A person with high spiritual intelligence is grateful for the blessings in their life. They recognise that everything they have is a gift and that they are not entitled to anything. They express gratitude for the people in their life, their health, their material possessions, and all the other things that make life worth living. In this context, one aspect of spiritual intelligence is the practice of giving.

Giving is the best form of love and kindness. The joy of contributing to the growth of others is irreplaceable. The act of giving can bring about a sense of satisfaction and joy that cannot be matched by any other experience. It is a way of connecting with the world around us and sharing our resources, talents, and time with others. When we give to others, we are sharing the abundance that we have received. This is the essence of the prosperity mentality. And it is important to remember the law of abundance, which states that when we give, we receive more in return, for we are helping not only others but also ourselves. We are creating positive energy that will help attract more abundance and prosperity to our lives.

The American businessman John Rockefeller is a person who exemplified the transformative power of giving. When Vivekananda met Rockefeller, he saw beyond the exterior of Rockefeller's wealth and status and recognised the potential in him to become a powerful force for good in the world. Vivekananda said to Rockefeller, 'You are the custodian of wealth. It is given to you to use for the welfare of humanity. The transformation of the world will come through the heart, not through the external means of material life.' This advice resonated deeply with Rockefeller, who then realised the importance of giving back to society.

Rockefeller was moved by Vivekananda's words and began to think deeply about how he could use his wealth to help others. He had already been involved in philanthropy for many years, but Vivekananda's message inspired him to take his giving to a new level. Rockefeller went on to establish the Rockefeller Foundation, one of the world's largest charitable organisations and one that has made significant contributions to medical research, public health, and education. He also supported the establishment of the University of Chicago, which has become one of the most prestigious universities in the world.

The meeting between Rockefeller and Vivekananda had a profound impact on both men. Vivekananda's message about using wealth for the betterment of humanity resonated deeply with Rockefeller and it inspired the latter to become one of the world's greatest philanthropists. Rockefeller discovered that the power of giving was the greatest joy that he had ever experienced. He learnt that true prosperity is not just about accumulating wealth, but about sharing it with others. Vivekananda, in turn, saw in Rockefeller a potential ally in his quest to spread the message of universal brotherhood and upliftment.

The attitude of only taking is a poverty mentality. It is the belief that the world's resources are limited and that one must take as much as possible in order to survive. This way of thinking can lead to feelings of scarcity, fear, and anxiety. In contrast, a prosperity mentality is about sharing and giving, about recognising that there is enough for everyone. Taking without giving is a manifestation of greed, which can harm relationships and lead to a self-centred and unsatisfying life. Thus, giving is not just a moral obligation but a way to connect with the world around us.

Giving is an essential aspect of spiritual intelligence. By cultivating a prosperity mentality, we can shift our focus from scarcity to abundance and begin to experience true joy and fulfilment. As John Rockefeller discovered, the power of giving is the greatest joy that one can ever experience.

Forgiveness: The Pathway to Healing and Reconciliation

A person with high spiritual intelligence is able to forgive themselves and others. They recognise that holding onto anger and resentment only creates negative energy that weighs them down. They are able to let go of past hurts and move forward with a sense of peace and acceptance. *Daya* (kindness or mercy), *kshama* (forgiveness), and *karuna* (compassion) are tools that enhance our spiritual intelligence.

Daya, or kindness, is a quality that involves acting with compassion and empathy towards others. It involves seeing the good in others and recognising the interconnectedness of all things. When we practise kindness, we not only help others but also cultivate a sense of inner peace and fulfilment. Kindness can be expressed through acts of service, generosity, and compassion.

Kshama, or forgiveness, involves letting go of resentment and anger towards others and recognising our own role in creating conflicts. When we practise forgiveness, we free ourselves from the negative emotions that weigh us down and prevent us from moving forward. Forgiveness allows us to cultivate more positive and harmonious relationships with others and a greater sense of inner peace.

Karuna, or compassion, involves extending empathy and understanding towards others, especially those who are suffering or in need. Compassion involves recognising the interconnectedness of all beings and acting with a sense of kindness and generosity. Compassion can be expressed in many ways—through acts of service, by volunteering, or by simply listening to others with empathy and understanding.

Incorporating these qualities into our lives can enhance our spiritual intelligence and bring more meaning and purpose to our lives. Practising kindness, forgiveness, and compassion can help us connect more deeply with others and with ourselves and can lead to a greater sense of inner peace and fulfilment. By cultivating these qualities, we can develop a more positive and constructive mindset and create a more positive and harmonious world around us.

Forgiveness is a universal virtue that is celebrated by many religious and philosophical traditions, including Hinduism, Buddhism, and Jainism. In each of these traditions, forgiveness is considered an essential attribute of a peaceful and fulfilling life. In this chapter, we will explore what each of these traditions has to say about forgiveness.

In Hinduism, forgiveness is seen as a key aspect of *dharma* or righteous living. The concept of forgiveness is closely related to the idea of *karma*, which holds that every action has consequences. Hindus believe that forgiveness is a way to break the cycle of *karma* and attain spiritual liberation. According to Hindu scriptures, forgiveness is an attribute that should be cultivated by all. Lord Krishna teaches in the Bhagavad Gita, 'Forgiveness is the quality of the brave, the one who is not afraid to let go of anger and resentment.' The teachings of Hinduism emphasise the importance of forgiveness not only for one's own spiritual growth but also for the benefit of society as a whole.

Forgiveness is a central theme in Buddhism, too. It is known as *kshanti* or *khanti*, which means forbearance, patience, and tolerance, and is considered essential to personal growth, inner peace, and spiritual development. Forgiveness is not about forgetting or condoning harmful actions but rather about accepting events without judgement, resentment, or anger and letting go of negative emotions and attachments that can cause suffering, and it is therefore seen a vital aspect of the Eightfold Path, which is the path to enlightenment and liberation from suffering. By forgiving others, one can release oneself from the grip of negative emotions and find inner peace. The Buddha himself taught the importance of forgiveness, stating, 'Holding onto anger is like drinking poison and expecting the other person to die.' The Buddhist conception of forgiveness is closely related to the idea of compassion, which is the foundation of Buddhist practice. The Buddhist practice of *metta*, or loving-kindness meditation, is a powerful tool for cultivating forgiveness and compassion.

The Buddha taught that forgiveness can be developed by practising mindfulness, compassion, and loving kindness. By cultivating these qualities, one can develop a greater capacity for forgiving oneself and others. Equal importance is given to the readiness to seek forgiveness and make amends for one's past actions. This means acknowledging one's mistakes, apologising for any harm caused, and taking steps to rectify situations. In Buddhism, forgiveness is viewed as a continuous process rather than a one-time event. It requires ongoing effort and dedication to maintain a state of forgiveness towards oneself and others.

Jainism teaches that forgiveness is critical to achieving spiritual liberation and attaining enlightenment. Jains believe in the principle of *ahimsa*, or non-violence, of which forgiveness is a key aspect. According to Jain teachings, forgiveness is a way to let go of negative *karma* and cultivate positive energy. Jainism, too, emphasises the importance of forgiveness not only for personal spiritual growth but also for the benefit of society.

Samvatsari is a powerful annual Jain festival of forgiveness. On the day of Samvatsari, Jains engage in a practice called *pratikramana*, which involves reciting prayers and seeking forgiveness from others for any wrongs they may have committed during the past year. The followers take a vow of repentance and ask for forgiveness from those they may have hurt, intentionally or unintentionally, through their thoughts, words, or deeds; they seek forgiveness from parents, teachers, elders, friends, relatives, and all living beings, including animals and plants. The ritual involves a period of introspection and prayer and seeking forgiveness from family, friends, and the community at large. The participants also grant forgiveness to those who have wronged them, releasing any negative emotions and grudges.

The goal of Samvatsari is to promote peace, harmony, and compassion within the community and to purify oneself of negative *karma*. The phrase '*Micchami dukkadam*' (May my misdeeds not cause pain to anyone) is often recited while seeking forgiveness from others and is a way of expressing remorse for any harm caused, intentionally or unintentionally. All in all, this practice is a powerful reminder of the importance of self-reflection, forgiveness, and compassion in Jain philosophy and practice.

Taoism, an ancient Chinese philosophy and religion that emphasises harmony with nature, simplicity, and the balance between opposites, also considers forgiveness essential to achieving inner peace and harmony. The fundamental Taoist belief is that the universe is constantly in motion and that its natural flow ensures perfect functioning. This is founded on the concept of *wu-wei*, which means 'non-action' or 'effortless action.' *Wu-wei* is not a passive but an active state of being. It is a state of consciousness that is deeply connected to our intuition and the present moment. It is about being fully engaged with the world while being detached from outcomes. By embracing *wu-wei*, Taoists aim to live more authentically, reduce stress and anxiety, and cultivate a sense of inner peace. The concept of *wu-wei* teaches us to trust the natural ebb and flow of life and to move through it with ease and grace. People can achieve harmony with the universe by submitting to its natural flow, not by trying to manipulate it or impose their own will upon it. The principle is, in other words, to let things unfold naturally and not interfere with them, to achieve your goals by doing nothing or by doing only what is absolutely necessary.

Within Taoism, forgiveness is viewed as a natural part of the flow of life. Taoists believe that everything is interconnected and forgiveness is necessary to maintain harmony within oneself and with others. Forgiveness is seen as a way of releasing negative emotions and attachments, allowing individuals to move forward with a clear mind and heart. Taoism teaches that forgiveness requires a shift in perspective, from a focus on personal gain and ego to a more compassionate and empathetic outlook. Forgiveness is not about condoning harmful actions or behaviours but about understanding the motivations and circumstances that lead to them. Moreover, the principle of *wu-wei* requires that forgiveness not be forced or contrived but that it arise naturally from a state of calm acceptance. Taoism emphasises the importance of self-forgiveness as well. Taoists believe that holding onto guilt and shame can create negative energy within oneself.

The Teachings of Christianity

Forgiveness is a central teaching in Christianity, a religion based on the life and teachings of Jesus Christ. Christians believe that forgiveness is essential for spiritual growth, healing, and reconciliation. In Christianity, forgiveness is seen as an act of grace, which means that it is freely given and not earned or deserved. Christians believe that forgiveness is a choice that requires humility, compassion, and love.

The Bible teaches that forgiveness involves letting go of anger, resentment, and the desire for revenge. Christians are called upon to forgive others as God has forgiven them, which means extending mercy and compassion to those who have wronged them. Jesus taught his followers to love their enemies and pray for those who persecute them. This means that forgiveness is not just about forgiving those who have hurt us but also about seeking reconciliation and restoration with them.

Christianity also encourages its believers to seek forgiveness from God for their own sins, acknowledge their own mistakes, ask for forgiveness, and sincerely repent and make amends. The Bible teaches that forgiveness is a continuous process that requires ongoing effort and dedication. Christians are called upon to forgive others as many times as necessary and to seek forgiveness whenever they fall short of God's standards. Overall, forgiveness is an essential aspect of Christian teachings. Cultivating forgiveness in one's daily life is seen as a way of living a compassionate, loving, and fulfilling life and contributing to a more peaceful and just world.

According to the Bible, the last words of Jesus Christ when he was crucified were, 'Father, forgive them, for they do not know what they are doing.' This statement is a powerful example of forgiveness in action. Even amidst intense physical and emotional suffering, Jesus shows compassion and forgiveness towards those who are responsible for his crucifixion. By asking God to forgive his executioners, Jesus establishes the importance of forgiveness for all Christians. He teaches that forgiveness is not only about letting go of anger and resentment but also about extending mercy and compassion to those who have wronged us. Jesus' words also highlight the importance of understanding the motivations and circumstances that lead people to harm others. He acknowledges that his executioners are acting out of ignorance rather than malice and offers them forgiveness as a way of breaking the cycle of violence and hatred.

Jesus' last words on the cross serve as a powerful reminder of the transformative power of forgiveness and the importance of extending compassion and mercy towards others, even in the face of adversity.

Islamic Teachings

Islam encourages forgiveness as a virtue and a means of earning rewards from Allah, and there are many examples from the Quran that illustrate this. The Quran states, 'And whoever pardons and makes reconciliation—his reward is [due] from Allah.' Muslims are encouraged to forgive those who have wronged them, whether over small or large issues. The Prophet Muhammad (peace be upon him) said, 'Whoever suffers an injury and forgives (the person responsible), Allah will raise his status to a higher degree and remove one of his sins.'

Muslims are also encouraged to seek forgiveness from Allah for their own sins and mistakes. The Quran states, 'And seek forgiveness of Allah. Indeed, Allah is Forgiving and Merciful.' Islam encourages forgiveness in all types of relationships, including within families, between friends, and between colleagues. The Prophet Muhammad (peace be upon him) said: 'The best of people are those who are the most beneficial to others, and the best of deeds is to reconcile between people.' Islam teaches that sincere repentance is a prerequisite for forgiveness from Allah. The Quran states, 'But indeed, I am the Perpetual Forgiver of whoever repents and believes and does righteousness and then continues in guidance.'

Mindfulness: The Key to Being Aware

A person with high spiritual intelligence practises constant mindfulness. They are able to stay present in the moment and fully engage with the world around them. They are aware of their thoughts and emotions and are able to observe them without judgement. This helps them cultivate a sense of inner peace and calm. Mindfulness is a key practice in developing spiritual intelligence. It involves being present in the moment and paying attention to our thoughts, feelings, and bodily sensations. Through mindfulness, we can develop greater awareness of our inner selves and connect more deeply with our spiritual nature.

Reflection and meditation are powerful tools that can help us cultivate mindfulness and awareness. By taking time to reflect on our thoughts and experiences, we can gain greater insight into ourselves and our inner world. Meditation is a practice that helps us quieten our minds and focus our attention on the present moment, allowing us to connect more deeply with our spiritual nature.

'If you are depressed, you are living in the past.

If you are anxious, you are living in the future.

If you are at peace, you are living in the present.'

The above quote from the *Tao Te Ching* is often cited by those who provide guidance on cultivating spiritual intelligence. The quote can be interpreted as a reminder to focus on the present moment and not get caught up in thoughts and emotions related to the past or future. When we dwell on the past, we may feel regret or guilt, which can lead to feelings of depression or sadness. Similarly, when we worry about the future, we may feel anxiety or fear, which can prevent us from fully engaging with the present moment.

By cultivating mindfulness and awareness of our thoughts and emotions, we can learn to recognise when we are dwelling on the past or worrying about the future and bring our attention back to the present moment. This can help us develop greater inner peace, acceptance, and gratitude for what we have in our lives right now. By focusing on the present moment, we can also cultivate greater clarity and insight into our own values, priorities, and goals, which can help us make wiser decisions and lead a more fulfilling life. The *Tao Te Ching* quote about living in the present moment can be a powerful reminder to cultivate spiritual intelligence by developing greater mindfulness, awareness, and acceptance of the present moment.

Spiritual intelligence is often developed over the course of personal experiences that give us a deep understanding of ourselves and the world around us. While some people may naturally possess a higher level of spiritual intelligence, it is a skill that can be developed and enhanced through intentional practice. One of the best primary tools that can be used is mindfulness, as it makes one aware of one's thought process and emotions and helps one filter them to align with one's values. Mindfulness is the practice of paying attention to the present moment with an attitude of openness, curiosity, and non-judgement. It provides clarity to one's purpose and gives direction to one's actions. This ancient practice has been shown to have numerous benefits for mental health, physical health, and overall well-being, reducing stress, improving cognitive function, and enhancing overall well-being.

Because of its benefits, mindfulness has been emphasised by various spiritual traditions, including Buddhism, Jainism, and Hinduism. Buddhism is perhaps the most well-known spiritual tradition that emphasises mindfulness. The Buddha taught that mindfulness is one of the key elements of the Eightfold Path. The practice of mindfulness is grounded in the concept of impermanence, which refers to the idea that all things are constantly changing and that clinging to things as if they were permanent causes suffering. In other words, mindfulness, according to Buddhism, is a way of cultivating an awareness of the impermanent nature of all things and letting go of attachments that cause suffering.

According to Jainism, the practice of mindfulness is a key aspect of achieving liberation from the cycle of birth and death. The Jain concept of mindfulness is also grounded in the idea of non-attachment, which involves detaching oneself from material possessions and desires. Through the practice of mindfulness, one can cultivate an awareness of the true nature of reality and become free from the cycle of suffering.

Hinduism also has a rich tradition of mindfulness practices. In Hinduism, mindfulness is closely tied to the practice of yoga. The ultimate goal of yoga is to achieve union with the divine, and mindfulness is seen as a way of cultivating the awareness and concentration necessary to achieve this goal. The practice of mindfulness in Hinduism involves focusing one's attention on the present moment and becoming aware of one's thoughts, feelings, and bodily sensations. Through this practice, one can develop a deeper understanding of the self and the nature of reality.

From the perspective of spiritual intelligence, mindfulness can be seen as a way of cultivating self-awareness, compassion, empathy, interconnectedness, and wisdom. By enabling us to be more attuned to the impermanent nature of reality and let go of attachments, mindfulness can lead to a greater sense of peace and well-being. Whether one approaches mindfulness from a religious or secular perspective, the practice can have profound benefits for both individuals and society as a whole.

How Mindfulness Can Enhance Spiritual Intelligence

By practising mindfulness, we can develop greater awareness of our thoughts, emotions, and physical sensations, as well as our awareness of the world around us. Here are some ways that mindfulness can help enhance spiritual intelligence.

Greater self-awareness: Practising mindfulness by observing our thoughts, emotions, and physical sensations without judgement helps us develop greater self-awareness. By becoming more aware of our inner world, we can gain insight into our deepest desires, fears, and values. Being aware of our thought patterns allows us to filter out and let go of what is not serving us. In addition, awareness can help us manage our emotions and thoughts more effectively, leading to greater peace of mind and overall well-being. This in turn can help us understand our place in the world and our connection to something larger than ourselves.

Improved emotional regulation: Mindfulness can help us regulate our emotions more effectively by allowing us to observe them without getting caught up in them. By developing the ability to observe our emotions without judgement, we can learn to respond to them in a more thoughtful, rational, and intentional way, thereby not getting caught up in the autopilot mode of compulsive thinking and emotional swings. Rather, one develops a purpose-driven thoughtful state. This can lead to greater understanding of the self and the world.

Increased connection to the present moment: Mindfulness helps us connect more deeply with the present moment, which is where we can find a sense of inner peace and tranquillity. Being aware allows us to switch off from those thoughts that are not empowering and elevating. By cultivating a greater sense of presence, we can begin to see the beauty and interconnectedness of all the things around us. This can lead to a greater sense of purpose and meaning in our lives.

Key Practical Tips

If you're interested in enhancing your spiritual intelligence through mindfulness, here are some practical tips for incorporating it into your spiritual practice:

Be a non-judgemental observer. A principle that is at the heart of the ancient Indian texts known as the Vedas is the idea of each person being a *sakshi*, which means witness or observer. This principle emphasises the concept of self-awareness and detachment from one's thoughts and experiences, and it encourages individuals to be aware of their thoughts without getting attached to or caught up in them. This allows us to gain a better understanding of our mental processes and helps us detach from negative or harmful thoughts. By observing our thoughts, we can learn to respond to them in a calm and rational manner, rather than reacting impulsively or emotionally.

We should not struggle and become tense or agitated in our attempts to control our thoughts. The idea here is to not get emotionally affected by these thoughts, to let go of the need to control them. Trying to control our thoughts can lead to stress, anxiety, and tension, which can have negative effects on our mental and physical well-being. Instead, we should strive to cultivate a sense of inner peace and detachment from our thoughts. We must bear in mind that we are separate from our thoughts. They do not define who we are. We have the power to control them, a power that emerges with deep reflection and practice. If we recognise this, we can learn to detach from negative thoughts and focus on positive thinking patterns through regular practice.

Start small. Begin by incorporating just a few minutes of mindfulness into your daily routine. You can start by simply observing your breath for a few minutes each day or by taking a mindful walk in nature. Over time, you can gradually increase the amount of time you spend in mindfulness practice.

Practise non-judgement. As you begin to observe your thoughts and emotions, practise doing so without judgement. Simply observe them with curiosity and openness and allow them to pass by without getting caught up in them.

Cultivate gratitude. As you become more mindful of the present moment, take time to cultivate gratitude for the blessings in your life. This can help you develop a greater sense of inner peace and contentment.

Harnessing the Power Within: The Impact of Internal Dialogue

Spiritual intelligence is a crucial aspect of our lives that can lead to a profound understanding of the world and our place in it. One of the most important attributes of a person with high spiritual intelligence is their ability to control their thoughts and internal dialogue. Our internal dialogue is a constant companion that shapes our thoughts, beliefs, and attitudes. It reflects our self-image and influences our behaviour, decisions, and actions. Therefore, it is essential to be mindful and aware of our internal dialogue and make sure it is positive and constructive.

People with high spiritual intelligence have a deep understanding of the power of their thoughts and the impact they have on their lives. They believe that thoughts create reality and that what we focus on expands. They know that negative self-talk can be damaging and that it can lead to self-limiting beliefs, which prevent us from reaching our full potential. They are aware that our unconscious mind is always listening to our internal dialogue and recording our thought patterns, performing a kind of linguistic programming that can condition us and shape our behaviour. Therefore, it is crucial to be mindful of our thoughts and internal dialogue. People with high spiritual intelligence take responsibility for their thoughts and beliefs and make a conscious effort to shift their negative self-talk into positive affirmations. They replace self-criticism with self-love and acceptance, recognising that they are worthy and deserving of love, respect, and success. They also understand that external criticism can trigger internal dialogue and reinforce negative self-talk. They know that it is important to detach themselves from negative feedback and not let it affect their self-image. They focus on their strengths and positive qualities, knowing that these are the attributes that define them.

One of the key principles underlying spiritual intelligence is the idea that everything in the universe is matter and energy that vibrates at different frequencies. This includes our thoughts and emotions, which also vibrate and resonate with the world around us. What we think and feel has a profound impact on our lives, as these vibrations attract or repel energies that are resonating at similar frequencies. In this context, it is essential to cultivate positive thoughts and emotions through mindfulness and other intentional practices. By doing so, we can create a state of harmony and coherence within ourselves, which can lead to greater happiness, fulfilment, and success in all aspects of our lives.

The critical mind and the deliberative mind both play a crucial role in shaping our thoughts and emotions. The critical mind is often associated with self-doubt, confusion, apprehension, and fear. It tends to analyse and critique everything, which can lead to a sense of paralysis or overwhelm. The critical mind is dominated by the subconscious and tries to overpower the conscious mind. On the other hand, the deliberative mind is decisive and operates with clarity and confidence. It is focused on finding solutions and making progress towards our goals. By cultivating the deliberative mind, we can expand our thought process and increase our vibrational intensity, which will attract positive outcomes and experiences.

When the critical mind is dominant, it is essential to counter it with positive affirmations that demonstrate complete faith and trust in the vibrational power of the universe. By doing so, we can shift our internal dialogue and align ourselves with higher frequencies of energy.

Refreshing the Mind: Embarking on the Journey of Mental Cleansing

Just as we sanitise our bodies to maintain hygiene, we must keep our minds sanitised and clean. We have seen above how the critical mind dominates and tries to influence the deliberative mind. However, our mind also has discretionary and determinative faculties. These, along with the deliberative faculty, can be constantly used to tame and train the mind to filter its thoughts and maintain a positive outlook, which is comparable to sanitising the mind. When we bring these primary faculties into our awareness and consciously commit ourselves to them through mindfulness, the outcome is a healthy mind, one that is not running on autopilot but in self-driven mode. Mindfulness is nothing but the effective use of these three faculties, i.e., discretion, deliberation, and determination.

Spirituality is a holistic approach to life that emphasises the significance of the mind-body-spirit connection. The practice of spirituality involves various tools and techniques that cleanse and purify the body and mind. Our mind is a powerful tool that can control our thoughts, emotions, and actions. However, just like any other organ in our body, the mind also needs maintenance and care to function at its optimal level. Through mindfulness, the mind's discretionary, deliberative, and determinative faculties can be effectively used to sanitise the mind as described above.

Discretion

Discretion is the ability to make judgements and decisions based on sound reasoning and good sense. This is a filtration process for thoughts. In the context of spirituality, discretion refers to the ability to discern between right and wrong, good and evil, and positive and negative thoughts. Practising discretion will enable us to filter out negative thoughts and focus on positive ones. This helps create a positive mindset and promotes a sense of well-being and contentment.

Deliberation

Deliberation is the process of carefully considering and weighing options before making a decision. In the context of spirituality, deliberation refers to the ability to think deeply about our thoughts and actions. Practising deliberation enables us to analyse our thoughts and emotions and determine if they are aligned with our values and beliefs. This helps us identify negative patterns of thinking and behaviour and make positive changes.

Determination

Determination is the ability to persevere and remain steadfast in the face of challenges and obstacles. In the context of spirituality, determination refers to the ability to stay committed to our values and beliefs despite difficulties and distractions. Through resolve, regular practice, and commitment to what's empowering and serving us best and aligned with our values, we can leverage this faculty of our mind. By practising determination, we can overcome negative thoughts and emotions and stay focused on positive ones. This helps create a sense of purpose and meaning in life.

'Conscious' vs. 'Aware': Embracing the Difference

The law of attraction suggests that we attract into our lives what we focus on, whether positive or negative. If we want to change our reality, we must consciously change our vibrations by focusing on positive thoughts and emotions. By doing so, we can manifest the experiences and outcomes that we desire.

To truly experience something, it's essential to have awareness. Although one can be conscious and awareness only operates in the conscious state, simply being conscious is not equivalent to having awareness. One can be conscious without being fully aware of their surroundings, emotions, or thoughts. Awareness is a heightened state of consciousness that entails being conscious of our surroundings, thoughts, and emotions, being present in the moment, and having a clear perception of what's happening. Awareness is what underlies our experiences. Without it, we might fail to notice the details of our experiences or fully appreciate them.

The impact of awareness is significant. By cultivating awareness, we become more present in our lives and better at enjoying our experiences. We can develop a greater appreciation for the world around us and for the people in our lives. In addition, awareness can help us manage our emotions and thoughts more effectively, leading to greater peace of mind and overall well-being. Overall, awareness is a crucial aspect of experiencing life fully, and we can all benefit from cultivating it in our daily lives.

Our everyday consciousness allows us to perceive our environment and react to it, but true awareness requires a mindful focus on our thoughts, beliefs, and actions. By directing our attention in a deliberate and intentional manner, we can regulate these mental processes and align them with our goals and values. This kind of awareness also enables us to identify and distance ourselves from harmful patterns and behaviours that don't serve our best interests. Mindful awareness is the practice of deliberately paying attention to the present moment without judgement or distraction. By doing so, we can observe our thoughts and feelings without being overwhelmed by them and we can choose how we respond to them instead of reacting on autopilot. This kind of self-awareness empowers us to make conscious choices and take intentional action instead of being driven by unconscious impulses or external pressures. Cultivating mindful awareness can have a profound impact on our lives.

Our emotions are often driven by our thoughts, which are triggered by our ego and intellect. These emotions, in turn, create an experience that gets embedded as a set of memory impressions in our subconscious mind. Once these impressions are embedded, they will surface time and again to cause similar emotions and experiences, creating a loop in which we get trapped unless we consciously leverage our ego and intellect to change our thoughts. A person's consciousness is influenced by four faculties of mind:

manas (the conscious, thinking mind), *buddhi* (the intellect), *ahankara* (the identity or ego), and *chitta* (storehouse of memories and subtle impressions). These four faculties work together to shape our thinking patterns, behaviours, and emotional responses.

The company we keep and the components we interact with can also influence our thinking patterns. Technology is an aspect of modern life that affects our subtle thinking patterns. Our habits and behaviours are now triggered by technology, which influences our buying preferences, lifestyle, content choices, social circles, and resultant emotional connections. A significant portion of our time is spent surfing through technological aids that create different experiences, unconsciously forming thought patterns and causing mood swings. While technology is a boon and an effective tool that can be empowering and can expand the consciousness, users of it need to be mindful of its side effects if it is not leveraged for positive impact on the *chitta*. One's consciousness must be the master and technology its servant.

Developing spiritual intelligence involves engaging in practices that help us gain greater control over our thinking patterns and emotional responses and infuse our experiences with meaning. Spiritual intelligence is the awareness that we are all vessels of consciousness and that our focus determines our reality. When we direct the light of our awareness, or consciousness, onto a certain area of our being, it becomes illuminated and more present within us. Our body, mind, and intellect are simply objects or instruments of perception for our consciousness. However, when we allow our thoughts to run on autopilot, we become trapped and manifest that energy. This makes it essential for us to cultivate a positive internal dialogue and practise positive affirmations, as they vibrate with the *pranic shakti* or vital energy within us. When we activate our energy centres and focus our thoughts on positive outcomes, we manifest what we intensely wish for.

You are a subject and a subject can be understood through subjects and not objects. Beyond our instruments of perception, there is a self that can be understood only in terms of itself, not in terms of any external objects. This self should focus its awareness on the mind through a beam of attention and willpower. By directing the mind rather than allowing it to direct us, one takes ownership of oneself as a subject, and one's life takes on a new meaning.

When we practise this level of mindfulness, we begin to transform our lives in meaningful ways. We become more aware of our thoughts and emotions, and we can choose to direct them towards positive outcomes. We manifest what we focus our awareness on, so by focusing on positive thoughts and outcomes, we attract more positivity into our lives. Spiritual intelligence teaches us that we are in control of our reality, and that by directing our awareness, we can create the life we desire.

From Mind to Body: Strengthening the Psychosomatic State

The word 'psychosomatic', which combines the Greek words *psyche* (meaning mind) and *soma* (meaning body), refers to the connection between a person's mental state and their physical health. This connection speaks to the fact that emotional and psychological factors can influence physical well-being and cause symptoms and illnesses to manifest.

The Bhagavad Gita provides guidance on various aspects of life, including spirituality, ethics, and self-realisation. While it does not explicitly mention the term 'psychosomatic state', it offers insights related to the mind-body connection and psychosomatic well-being. In this regard, it emphasises controlling the mind, practising yoga, cultivating detachment and equanimity, being mindful of the present moment, and seeking self-realisation. By applying these principles, we can enhance our psychosomatic state, achieving balance, harmony, and well-being in the mind and body.

Mindfulness is a practice that can be used to improve the psychosomatic state, as it helps individuals become more aware of their thoughts, feelings, and bodily sensations. Research has shown that mindfulness can have a positive impact on a range of psychosomatic conditions, including chronic pain, anxiety, depression, and other stress-related disorders. If you want to elevate your overall well-being, then practising mindfulness can be a game-changer, not only diminishing the negative impact of stress, anxiety, and depression on your mind and body, but also inspiring you to shift from a survival mode to a creative mode of thinking and thereby enabling you to harness your full potential. This way, you can make more conscious and fulfilling decisions in your life.

The Power of Metacognition: Enhancing Spiritual Intelligence Through Mindfulness

Meta thinking, also known as metacognition, is the ability to think about one's own thinking. It involves being aware of one's own mental processes, including one's thoughts, beliefs, and emotions. In the context of mindfulness and spiritual intelligence, meta thinking can be a powerful tool for self-reflection and self-awareness.

When we engage in meta thinking, we become more mindful of our own mental processes. We begin to notice patterns in our thinking and emotions, and we develop a greater understanding of how our thoughts and feelings impact our behaviour. This increased self-awareness can help us identify and address negative patterns in our thinking, allowing us to cultivate a more positive and spiritually fulfilling mindset. To begin practising meta thinking as a tool for mindfulness and spiritual intelligence, start by setting aside time each day for self-reflection. During this time, observe your own thoughts and emotions without judgement or criticism. Simply notice how you are feeling, what thoughts are passing through your mind, and how these thoughts and emotions are affecting your behaviour.

As you become more familiar with your own mental processes, you can begin to ask yourself questions that promote deeper self-reflection:

- *What thoughts or emotions are most prominent or dominant in me right now?*
- *Are these thoughts and emotions serving me or holding me back?*
- *How do my thoughts and emotions impact my behaviour and interactions with others?*
- *What patterns do I notice in my thinking or behaviour, and how can I address them?*
- *Are these patterns aligned with my goal, vision, and purpose?*

As you continue to practise meta thinking, you will likely notice a greater sense of self-awareness and control over your thoughts and emotions. You may find that you are better able to identify and address negative patterns in your thinking and cultivate a more positive and spiritually fulfilling mindset.

In addition to promoting self-awareness and mindfulness, meta thinking can also be a valuable tool for problem-solving and decision-making. By thinking about our own thinking, we can identify biases and assumptions that may be impacting our ability to make good decisions. We can also consider different perspectives and potential outcomes, helping us make more informed and spiritually aligned choices.

Humility: An Essential Quality for Personal and Social Growth

Humility is a trait that has been celebrated throughout history and across cultures. It is often described as the quality of being modest, unassuming, and respectful towards others. Humility is also closely linked to the ability to recognise one's own limitations, accept feedback and criticism, and acknowledge the contributions of others. A person with high spiritual intelligence is humble. They recognise that they are a small part of something much greater than themselves and that they have much to learn from the world around them. They are open to new experiences and perspectives and are willing to admit when they are wrong.

The Significance of Humility

Humility offers numerous benefits to individuals and society as a whole:

Improved relationships. Humility is essential for strong and healthy relationships with others. When we are humble, we are more approachable and open-minded, making it easier to connect with others at a deeper level.

Learning enhancement. Humility helps us recognise our own limitations and seek out opportunities for growth and development. This leads to increased learning and personal growth, which can benefit us in every sphere of our lives.

Better decision-making. Humility allows us to look at situations from multiple perspectives, helping us make more informed and thoughtful decisions.

Greater resilience. Humility helps us bounce back from setbacks and failures. When we are humble, we are better able to accept feedback and criticism, which can help us learn from our mistakes and become more resilient in the face of adversity.

Improved mental health. Humility can also improve our mental health. When we are humble, we are less likely to compare ourselves to others or feel pressured to achieve unrealistic goals. This can reduce stress and anxiety and improve our overall well-being.

How to Cultivate Humility

Cultivating humility is not always easy, but it is an essential skill to develop. Here are some tips for cultivating humility:

Acknowledge your limitations. Recognise that you don't know everything and that there is always room for growth and improvement.

Practise active listening. Listen to others without judgement and try to understand their perspectives.

Accept feedback and criticism. Instead of becoming defensive, view feedback and criticism as opportunities for growth and improvement.

Celebrate others' achievements. Acknowledge the contributions of others and celebrate their achievements. Appreciate people for even small accomplishments.

Practise gratitude. Take time each day to reflect on what you are grateful for and how others have contributed to your success.

Seek out diversity. Engage with people from different backgrounds and perspectives. This can help broaden your own perspective and increase your empathy and understanding.

Humility is a crucial trait in the context of spiritual intelligence. It requires us to recognise our own limitations, cultivate empathy and compassion, and develop a sense of interconnectedness with others and the world around us. By cultivating humility, we can access deeper levels of wisdom and consciousness, leading to greater personal and collective growth and development.

Purpose: The Key to Unlocking the True Meaning of Existence

A person with high spiritual intelligence has a sense of purpose. They have a clear idea of what they want to achieve in life and are committed to making a positive impact on the world around them. They are able to align their thoughts and actions with their purpose, which gives them a sense of direction and focus.

Living life without purpose and passion is like living within boundaries. When we don't have a clear direction or sense of purpose, we simply go through the motions, driven by the forces of life without any real direction. This often leads to a sense of emptiness and a lack of fulfilment, which can produce depression, anxiety, and a host of other mental health issues. Living life without purpose is simply surviving, and it is not an energetic, enthusiastic, or creative mode of living.

When we are inspired by a great purpose or an extraordinary project, we can transcend our limitations and unlock our true potential. Our minds break free from the bonds of limited thinking, and we become aware of our dormant faculties, talents, and abilities. We begin to see ourselves as greater than we ever imagined, and we are motivated to work towards our goals with enthusiasm and energy. This is the power of inspiration, and it is a critical aspect of spiritual intelligence.

Setting a goal or finding one's purpose in life is not an easy task and requires a deep understanding of oneself. It's not just about reaching a certain milestone or accomplishing a specific task; rather, it is about a deeper calling or desire that resonates with one's soul. The process of finding one's purpose can involve a process of elimination whereby we identify the things we don't like or aren't passionate about. This can help us narrow our focus and begin exploring the things that we are truly enthusiastic about.

When we find something that stimulates a drive in us, it can lead to a sense of enthusiasm and curiosity, which can in turn create a sense of passion. This passion can be a powerful force that drives us to pursue our goals and achieve great things. It's important to remember that finding one's purpose is not a one-time event, but rather an ongoing process of self-discovery and growth. As we move through life, our passions and interests may change, and it's important to remain open to new experiences and opportunities that will help us uncover new passions and goals. Finding our purpose in life can help us live in a way that is true to our values and therefore rewarding and fulfilling.

Exploring the purpose of life is not a rational process alone. It is driven by emotions and a value system. To connect with our core purpose, we must connect with our emotions and values and let them spontaneously surface. It is a journey of self-discovery that requires us to look within ourselves and connect with our innermost being. It involves asking fundamental questions about our existence, our beliefs, and our values. When we explore the purpose of life, we find meaning and direction that guides our actions.

Ikigai: A Road Map to Finding Purpose and Meaning in Life

Ikigai is a Japanese concept that roughly translates to 'a reason for being.' It is a powerful tool for personal growth and self-discovery that can be used to enhance spiritual intelligence by helping individuals identify their purpose in life and align their actions and goals with their deepest values and desires. By aligning their actions and goals with their *ikigai*, individuals can create a sense of fulfilment and satisfaction that is not based on external circumstances or material possessions.

Figure 1

The concept of *ikigai* is based on four key elements: what you love, what you are good at, what the world needs, and what you can be paid for. When these four elements are combined, they create a sense of purpose and direction that can guide individuals towards a more fulfilling and meaningful life.

The first element of *ikigai* is what you love. This refers to the things that bring you joy and happiness and that you are passionate about—hobbies, activities, certain kinds of work, anything really. By identifying what you love, you can begin to create a life that is more aligned with your deepest desires and values.

The second element of *ikigai* is what you are good at. This refers to your skills, talents, and abilities. By identifying what you are good at, you can begin to create a life that utilises your strengths and allows you to excel in your chosen field.

The third element of *ikigai* is what the world needs. This refers to the needs and desires of the world around you and how you can use your skills and passions to make a positive impact. By identifying what the world needs, you can begin to live a life that is focused on making a positive difference in the lives of others.

The fourth element of *ikigai* is what you can be paid for. This refers to the practical aspect of life—how you can use your skills and passions to make a living. By identifying what you can be paid for, you can begin to create a life that is financially stable and allows you to support yourself and your loved ones.

By combining these four elements, individuals can identify their *ikigai* and create a life that is aligned with their deepest values and desires. This can help individuals live a more fulfilling and meaningful life and enhance their spiritual intelligence by creating a sense of purpose and direction in their lives. In addition to helping individuals identify their purpose in life, *ikigai* can also be a powerful tool for personal growth and self-discovery. By focusing on the things that bring you joy and happiness and by aligning your actions and goals with your deepest values and desires, you can begin to cultivate a greater sense of self-awareness and inner peace.

Furthermore, by focusing on the needs of the world around you, you can cultivate a sense of compassion and empathy for others. This can help you see the interconnectedness of all things and recognise that we are all part of a larger whole, thereby enhancing your spiritual intelligence.

Ikigai is based on the belief that every person has a unique purpose in life, and that by identifying and pursuing that purpose, one can achieve a sense of fulfilment and happiness. Through the practice of *ikigai*, you can enhance your spiritual intelligence and cultivate a greater sense of self-awareness, compassion, and oneness with all things. The concept of *ikigai* is similar to many spiritual doctrines in other religions, such as Hinduism, Jainism, Buddhism, Christianity, etc. In these religions, the search for meaning and purpose is often seen as a central aspect of spiritual growth.

The concept of *purushartha* in Hinduism is different from that of *ikigai*, but they share some similarities. *Purushartha* is a Hindu concept that describes the four primary aims or goals of human life, which are *dharma* (righteousness), *artha* (finance), *kama* (desires), and *moksha* (liberation). These aims are interconnected and interdependent and they represent the different aspects of a well-rounded and fulfilling life. Both *purushartha* and *ikigai* emphasise the importance of leading a balanced and purposeful life and entail a recognition of the fact that the different aspects of life, such as material wealth, personal passions, and spiritual growth, are all interconnected.

The Jain understanding of concepts like *jiva* and *atma* is evocative of the non-dualistic nature of *ikigai*. *Jiva* is the individual soul, and *atma* is the universal soul. In Jainism, it is believed that recognising the non-dualistic nature of *atma* and *jiva* can help individuals see the interconnectedness of all things and cultivate a sense of oneness. The ultimate goal in Jainism is to transcend *jiva* and embrace *atma* in order to attain *moksha*.

In Buddhism, the concept of the Eightfold Path is similar to the idea of *ikigai*. The Eightfold Path is a set of guidelines for living a meaningful and purposeful life, and it includes concepts such as right intention, right action, right livelihood. Combining the Eightfold Path with the concept of *ikigai* can result in a more holistic approach to living a purposeful life.

In Christianity, the concept of vocation is similar to the idea of *ikigai*. Vocation refers to one's calling or purpose in life, and it is believed that by following one's calling, one can achieve a sense of spiritual fulfilment and purpose. By recognising the spiritual aspect of their purpose, individuals can also cultivate a greater sense of compassion and empathy for others and see the interconnectedness of all things.

Understanding the principles of these religions and infusing them with an understanding of *ikigai* can further enhance one's spiritual growth and self-discovery. By identifying what one loves, what one is good at, what the world needs, and what one can be paid for, individuals can pursue their spiritual purpose and calling in a way that gives them and those around them the greatest value.

The Importance of Purpose and Intention

Upanishadic teachings emphasise that a meaningful life is a journey and not a destination. At the heart of spiritual intelligence is the concept of purpose. When we live a purpose-driven life, we are constantly seeking to connect with something greater than ourselves. We recognise that life is not just about achieving external goals but about the purposeful journey we take to get there. Living a meaningful life is an unending journey in search of the infinite. As seekers, we are in a constant state of enquiry, always questioning and exploring our beliefs, values, and actions. This is where the 'why' comes in. Every thought and every action begins with 'why.' The 'what,' 'when,' 'where,' and 'how' are all outcomes of that 'why.'

The primary question is not 'What do I need to do?' but rather 'Why do I need to do it?' When we focus on the 'why,' we tap into our sense of purpose and intention. We connect with the deeper meaning behind our actions and make choices that align with our values and beliefs.

Living a purpose-driven life requires us to be mindful of our intentions. We must be aware of the motivations behind our actions and ensure that they align with our values. When we act with intent, we are more likely to achieve our goals and feel fulfilled in the process. Intentionality also involves being present in the moment. When we are fully engaged in what we are doing, we are more likely to make choices that align with our purpose. This is where mindfulness practices can be helpful. By cultivating present-moment awareness, we can tap into our intuition and make choices that align with our deepest values and beliefs.

The Search for Truth

Kabir believed that the search for truth was the primary purpose of human existence. He believed that truth was the highest value and that all other values were subordinate to it. He encouraged his followers to seek truth through meditation, introspection, and self-enquiry and to reject all forms of dogma and blind belief.

Here is a powerful and pertinent couplet by Kabir on the purpose of life:

'Jeevat samjhe jeevat bujh, jeevat he kar le sach

Jeevat karam ki fan par, jeevat he phal deh'

(Understand the purpose of your life, extinguish your ego, and realise the truth

Live for the greater good, and let your actions bear fruit.)

This emphasises the urgency and importance of understanding the purpose of one's life and living a life of purpose and service. It encourages us to let go of our egos and selfish desires and focus on making a positive impact on the world through our actions.

The purpose of life is to experience a complete sense of fulfilment. All our thoughts, activities, and actions can be defined as steps towards fulfilling this purpose. Our own sense of fulfilment is our life purpose, and supporting others in their efforts to experience the same is our mission. When we comprehend this, we begin to live meaningfully.

The Value of Priorities: Embracing the Preferable over the Pleasurable

There is a fundamental difference between pleasure and joy. What we experience as pleasure is temporary, a transitional phenomenon. True and lasting happiness comes from joy. This joy multiplies through our actions when we consciously choose between *shreyaskar* (preferable) and *preyaskar* (pleasurable). 'Pleasurable' describes the things we do to suit our convenience. 'Preferable' describes what we need to be doing, as per our conscience and values, to create a lasting state of joyfulness. In other words, joy is a result of living in alignment with our deepest values and purpose.

In the context of spiritual intelligence, it is important to distinguish between pleasure and joy. To experience true and lasting happiness, we must cultivate joy in our lives. One way to do so is by making conscious choices between what is pleasurable and what is preferable. Preferable actions are aligned with our conscience and values. By choosing the preferable path, we create a lasting state of joyfulness that can multiply through our actions.

Unleashing the Power of Authenticity

'When you do things from your soul, you feel a river moving in you, a joy.' - Rumi

Authenticity is a vital trait in the context of spiritual intelligence. It refers to the ability to be true to oneself, to be able to express one's beliefs, values, and feelings without pretence or artifice. Being an authentic person means living in alignment with one's deepest sense of purpose and meaning and cultivating a sense of integrity and honesty in all aspects of life.

When you act from a place of authenticity and connection with your inner self, you experience a deep sense of happiness and fulfilment. Authentic people are true to themselves and are not afraid to express their true feelings and emotions. They recognise that authenticity is the key to building strong relationships and connecting with others at a deep level.

In the context of spiritual intelligence, authenticity is crucial because it requires us to engage in deep self-reflection and introspection, which leads to the development of a strong sense of self-awareness and connection with our innermost selves. By cultivating authenticity, we can develop a deeper understanding of our values, beliefs, and priorities, and align our actions and behaviours accordingly. Authenticity is also linked to empathy and compassion, as it requires us to be honest and genuine in our interactions with others. When we are authentic, we create an environment of trust and openness, allowing others to feel comfortable expressing themselves and sharing their own experiences and perspectives.

One common challenge that people face in their personal and professional lives is the dilemma of whether to say or not to say what they feel. Often, this indecisiveness arises from a conflict within themselves rather than external factors. They may feel torn between their values and their desire to avoid conflict or maintain peace. This indecision can lead to stress, frustration, and even depression. To overcome this dilemma, individuals must focus on developing their spiritual intelligence by aligning themselves with values such as honesty, transparency, sensitivity, and fairness. By living in accordance with these values, individuals can build character and gain the clarity they need to speak and act with confidence and conviction. Being non-judgemental and respectful of others' perspectives can also help individuals navigate complex situations with ease.

Self-reflection and mindfulness are critical components of developing spiritual intelligence. Through introspection, individuals can gain a deeper understanding of their thoughts, emotions, and behaviours. By being mindful of their thought patterns, individuals can begin to identify and challenge limiting beliefs that may be holding them back from speaking or acting in a way that aligns with their values.

One of the fundamental aspects of spiritual intelligence is the willingness to reflect on and realise oneself. It is through this process of reflection and realisation that we can identify and let go of the parts of ourselves that are not serving us. By allowing these parts of ourselves to 'die,' we create space for growth, transformation, and evolution. This process of reflection and realisation can be challenging, as it often requires us to confront our fears, doubts, and limiting beliefs. However, by facing these challenges head-on, we can begin to let go of the things that are holding us back and move towards a more authentic and fulfilling life.

In addition to reflection and mindfulness, spiritual intelligence also involves a willingness to embrace uncertainty and change. It requires us to be open to new experiences and to approach life with a sense of curiosity and wonder. By embracing uncertainty, we can learn to trust ourselves and our ability to navigate whatever challenges come our way. By cultivating a regular practice of self-reflection and mindfulness, we can begin to let go of the parts of ourselves that are not serving us and move towards a more authentic and fulfilling life.

The following are some ways to nurture authenticity and to cultivate spiritual intelligence:

Practise self-reflection. Take time each day to reflect on your values, beliefs, and priorities. Reflect on what behaviours and actions are desirable and undesirable in terms of what is preferable and what is merely pleasurable. Consider how your actions and behaviours align with your innermost qualities. Reflect on whether there is a mismatch between your behaviours, actions, and values.

Embrace vulnerability. Being authentic involves being vulnerable and exposing your true self to others. Do not wear a personality mask. Be true to your character. Embrace this vulnerability as an essential component of personal growth and development.

Live in alignment with your values. Identify the areas of your life that you may be approaching inauthentically, such as your relationships or your career. Take steps to align your actions and behaviours with your deepest sense of purpose and meaning.

Engage in dialogue. Foster open and honest communication with others, engaging in dialogue that encourages authenticity and vulnerability. Be open to feedback and criticism.

Practise mindfulness. Engage in mindfulness practices such as meditation or yoga, which can help cultivate self-awareness and deepen your connection to your innermost self.

Embrace imperfection. Authenticity involves embracing imperfection and recognising that growth and development are ongoing processes.

Enhancing spiritual intelligence is a transformational journey. By nurturing authenticity and cultivating spiritual intelligence, we can deepen our understanding of ourselves and others. We develop greater empathy and compassion and live in alignment with our deepest sense of purpose and meaning. By embracing vulnerability and living authentically, we can create a more open and honest world, fostering trust, understanding, and growth.

Creativity is the Key to Development and Growth

A person with high spiritual intelligence is creative. They are able to tap into their imagination and use their creativity to solve problems and find new ways of looking at the world. They are not afraid to take risks and are willing to explore new ideas and possibilities. Creativity is often considered one of the most important attributes of spiritual intelligence. If spiritual intelligence is the capacity to use spiritual and emotional resources to solve problems and achieve a higher level of consciousness, creativity is a vital aspect of this capacity, as it allows individuals to tap into their spiritual resources and bring forth new, innovative ideas.

The Connection Between Creativity and Spiritual Intelligence

Creativity is the ability to generate new and valuable ideas or products. This ability is closely tied to spiritual intelligence, as it involves the use of intuition, imagination, and inspiration. These are all qualities that are associated with spiritual growth and development. In many ways, creativity can be seen as a manifestation of our spiritual potential. When we tap into our creative energy, we are accessing a deeper level of consciousness and awareness. This allows us to see beyond our limitations and connect with something greater than ourselves.

There are several ways in which creativity can be seen as an attribute of spiritual intelligence:

Creativity involves tapping into our intuition. Intuition is often seen as a key aspect of spiritual intelligence, as it allows us to access a deeper level of knowing. When we are creative, we are often working from our intuition, tapping into a deeper level of consciousness to generate new ideas.

Creativity involves connecting with our emotions. Emotions constitute another key aspect of spiritual intelligence, as they allow us to connect with ourselves and others at a deeper level. When we are creative, we are often drawing on our emotions to create something meaningful.

Creativity involves connecting with something greater than us. When we are in a state of flow and creativity, we are often connecting with something beyond our individual selves. This can be understood as a spiritual connection, as we are tapping into a larger, collective consciousness.

Here are a few suggestions for developing creativity:

Practise mindfulness. Mindfulness is a powerful tool for developing our spiritual intelligence and creativity. When we are mindful, we are fully present in the moment, which allows us to tap into our intuition and connect with our emotions. This can help us access our creative energy and generate new ideas.

Engage in creative activities. Engaging in creative activities, such as writing, painting, or dancing, can help us develop our creativity and connect with our spiritual selves. These activities allow us to tap into our intuition and connect with something larger than ourselves.

Seek out inspiration. Inspiration can come from many sources, such as nature, art, music, or literature. Seeking out sources of inspiration can help us tap into our creative energy and connect with something greater than ourselves.

Cultivate an open mind. An open mind is essential for developing our creativity and spiritual intelligence. When we are open to new ideas and experiences, we are more likely to tap into our intuition and connect with something greater than ourselves.

Embrace vulnerability. Vulnerability is often seen as a weakness, but it is actually a key aspect of spiritual growth and development. When we embrace vulnerability, we open ourselves up to new experiences and perspectives, which can help us tap into our creative energy and connect with something greater than ourselves.

Remember, vulnerability in the context of creativity is not about being weak or helpless but about being authentic, courageous, and willing to explore uncharted territories. When people embrace their vulnerability, they often become more open to taking risks and exploring new ideas. Here are a few examples:

Personal expression. Artists, musicians, and writers often draw inspiration from their own vulnerabilities and use them as a foundation for creating impactful works. By expressing their inner struggles, fears, and joys, they connect with audiences at a deeper level. By tapping into common human emotions and vulnerabilities, they create content that evokes empathy, sparks conversations, and fosters a sense of connection.

Innovation and problem-solving. In fields such as science, technology, and business, vulnerability can drive creative solutions. When individuals acknowledge their limitations and uncertainties, they are more willing to experiment, think outside the box, and explore unconventional approaches to problem-solving.

Collaboration and connection. Vulnerability can foster meaningful collaborations by creating an atmosphere of trust and empathy. When team members openly share their ideas, concerns, and doubts, it allows for a more inclusive and supportive environment, encouraging diverse perspectives and innovative solutions.

Growth and learning. Embracing vulnerability promotes personal growth and learning. When individuals are open to feedback, admitting their mistakes, and seeking new knowledge, they can continuously evolve their creative skills, leading to innovative breakthroughs.

The Spark of Curiosity: Igniting Enthusiasm for Exploration

Curiosity is a trait that is often associated with intelligence and creativity. It is therefore, unsurprisingly, an essential aspect of spiritual intelligence. A spiritually intelligent person is curious about the world around them and seeks to understand the deeper meaning and purpose behind things. They are not content to simply accept things at face value; instead, they ask questions and explore different perspectives. They are curious to know all they can about existence and explore the higher self. They are seeking the essence of life. Through mindfulness, meditation, and contemplation, they try to unravel the mysteries of their inner and outer worlds.

Curiosity is what drives individuals to seek out new experiences, engage with new ideas, and discover new truths about themselves and the world. When we are curious, we are open to new possibilities, and we are willing to explore areas beyond our comfort zone. This willingness to explore and experiment is an essential quality of spiritual growth, as it allows us to expand our understanding of ourselves and the world around us.

The Significance of Cultivating Curiosity

While some people may be naturally curious, others may need to work on cultivating this trait. Cultivating curiosity involves a willingness to ask questions, explore new ideas, and embrace uncertainty. It requires us to step outside of our comfort zone and to be open to new experiences. One way to cultivate curiosity is to approach life with a childlike sense of wonder. Children are naturally curious and have a boundless love of exploration. They approach the world with an open mind and an eagerness to learn. By embracing this childlike wonder, we can tap into our innate curiosity and begin to explore the world around us with fresh eyes.

Another way to cultivate curiosity is to practise mindfulness. When we practise mindfulness, we become more aware of our thoughts, feelings, and sensations. This heightened awareness can help us become more curious about ourselves and the world around us, as we become more attuned to our inner experiences.

Curiosity is an essential part of spiritual intelligence. By cultivating curiosity, we can open ourselves up to new possibilities and expand our understanding of the world. So if you are on a journey of spiritual growth, remember to nurture your curiosity and embrace the wonder and awe that the world around you can make you feel.

Rising Strong: Cultivating Resilience in Adversity

People with high spiritual intelligence are resilient. They are able to recover from setbacks and challenges and see them as opportunities for growth and learning. They are able to maintain a positive outlook even in difficult situations, which helps them stay focused on their goals. By cultivating these qualities, we can develop a deeper connection with ourselves, others, and the world around us.

Resilience allows us to weather any storm that life throws our way. When we develop resilience, we develop an unshakeable inner strength that enables us to stay centred and grounded, no matter what is happening around us. To develop resilience, we must first cultivate self-awareness. By becoming aware of our thoughts and emotions, we can recognise when we are feeling stressed, anxious, or overwhelmed. This awareness allows us to take a step back, assess the situation objectively, and respond in a way that is calm and rational.

We must also cultivate acceptance and non-attachment. Acceptance means acknowledging and letting go of any negative feelings that arise. Non-attachment means being open to all possibilities, without getting too attached to any particular outcome. These qualities enable us to stay present and focused, even when things are not going according to plan.

Developing resilience is not always easy. We must be willing to face our fears, confront our limitations, and embrace the unknown. But the rewards are immense. When we develop our resilience, we become more adaptable, more flexible, and more capable of navigating the ups and downs of life with ease. Moreover, when we develop our resilience, we also develop our spiritual intelligence. We become more attuned to our inner wisdom and more connected to our higher purpose. We begin to see the world with greater clarity and compassion, and we are better able to connect with others at a deeper level.

Resilience unlocks our full potential as human beings. It enables us to grow, learn, and thrive in the face of adversity and to live a life that is rich, meaningful, and fulfilling. So if you want to develop your spiritual intelligence, start by cultivating your resilience. The journey may be challenging, but the destination is worth it.

'Walk a Mile in Their Shoes': The Transformative Power of Empathy

Empathy is a powerful tool that can be used to build and reinforce relationships with others. It allows us to connect with others in a way that is genuine and authentic and to truly understand and appreciate their feelings and experiences. Unlike sympathy, which can be overwhelming and all-consuming, empathy allows us to remain anchored to our own centre of wisdom while still relating to others. Empathy is also empowering and can help others emerge as stronger individuals. When we are able to truly understand and connect with others, we can help them tap into their own resilience and inner strength. This can be a powerful force for healing and growth, both for ourselves and for others.

In fact, empathy is a key component of emotional intelligence, which is the ability to understand and manage our own emotions as well as the emotions of others. Those with high levels of emotional intelligence are able to relate to others at a deep emotional level and are skilled at handling difficult emotions with wisdom and compassion. It is important to note that empathy and sympathy are two distinct emotional responses, and an empathetic person is different from a sympathetic person. Empathy is the ability to understand and share the feelings of others, while sympathy is a feeling of pity in response to someone's situation. An empathetic person is someone who can comprehend and connect with another person's emotions without necessarily going through what the other person has gone through. Empathetic people can stay grounded in their own feelings and thoughts while still being present and receptive to the other person's perspective. In contrast, a sympathetic person may become emotionally involved and overwhelmed by the other person's emotions, often losing their own sense of self in the process.

Empathy requires emotional intelligence and the ability to put oneself in someone else's shoes while maintaining a sense of personal boundaries. It is essential to building meaningful relationships, fostering understanding and trust, and resolving conflicts effectively. By staying anchored, an empathetic person can provide support and comfort to others while also taking care of themselves.

To develop our spiritual intelligence and empathy, it's important to cultivate a sense of mindfulness and presence in our daily lives. This can involve practices like meditation, yoga, or simply taking time each day to reflect on our thoughts and feelings. It's also important to practise active listening and to truly engage with others in a way that is genuine and authentic.

The Heart of Empathy: Active and Deep Listening

In the context of spiritual intelligence, active listening plays a vital role in building meaningful and empathetic relationships with others. As has been established, spiritual intelligence involves understanding and connecting with the inner self and others at a deeper level, which requires the ability to listen and understand others' emotions and perspectives.

As human beings, we have a natural tendency to give advice and solutions to others without truly understanding their issues.

This behaviour can hinder our spiritual growth and limit our ability to connect with others at a deeper level. Instead, we should aim to practise active listening, which involves paying attention to others without interrupting or judging them.

Empathetic listening can have a great healing effect, as it can help individuals feel understood and validated. By practising empathy and actively listening to others, we can build stronger relationships and deepen our spiritual connections with ourselves and others.

Spiritual intelligence goes beyond emotional intelligence in that it involves a deeper understanding of the interconnectedness of all beings and a heightened awareness of the universal consciousness. Active listening is an essential part of spiritual intelligence, as it requires the individual to be fully present in the moment and to let go of their ego-driven desire to be heard.

Active Listening—Building Trust and Empathy in Relationships

As a primary level of listening, active listening requires a certain level of mindfulness and self-awareness. It requires the individual to be fully present in the moment and to let go of their own personal biases and beliefs. When we listen actively, we are listening not just to the words being spoken but also to the emotions, body language, and tone of the speaker. We are observant and mindful of nonverbal expressions too. We are open to understanding their perspective without judgement or preconceived notions.

To become an active listener, we must first develop our emotional intelligence. This involves being aware of our own emotions and how they impact our interactions with others. It also requires us to put ourselves in the shoes of the speaker and to try to understand their experience. By doing so, we are showing them that we respect and care for them and that we are willing to listen to their concerns without judgement. This creates a sense of trust and respect in the relationship, which is crucial for effective communication and problem-solving. When we are able to understand and connect with the emotions of others, we are better able to listen actively and respond in a way that is supportive and respectful.

Deep Listening: A Catalyst for Transformation and Empowerment

Deep listening, on the other hand, involves a more profound level of engagement and focuses on the speaker's underlying intentions, emotions, and beliefs. Like active listening, it involves listening without judgement, being fully present in the moment, and seeking to understand the speaker's perspective at a deeper level. However, deep listening requires individuals to be more introspective and reflective, to attune themselves to the speaker's nonverbal cues and emotions as a way of understanding their message better. Active listening is focused on the surface-level content of a conversation, while deep listening involves a more profound level of engagement with the speaker's underlying intentions and emotions. Both are important components of effective communication, but deep listening requires a greater degree of intentionality, introspection, and focus.

Benefits of Active and Deep Listening

The following are some of the benefits of active and deep listening:

Greater self-awareness: Active and deep listening requires individuals to engage in deep introspection and self-reflection and develop a greater sense of self-awareness and an understanding of their own emotions, thoughts, and behaviours.

Improved communication: Active and deep listening fosters open and honest communication, allowing individuals to express themselves more authentically and create deeper connections with others.

Enhanced empathy: By listening actively and deeply, individuals can develop a greater sense of empathy and compassion, understanding others' experiences and perspectives at a deeper level.

Increased understanding: Active and deep listening enables individuals to gain a more comprehensive understanding of complex issues, helping them navigate challenges and make more informed decisions.

Strengthened relationships: By engaging in active and deep listening, individuals can build deeper, more meaningful relationships based on trust, empathy, and understanding.

Heightened spiritual awareness: Listening actively and deeply can lead to a greater sense of spiritual awareness, allowing individuals to connect more deeply with themselves and the world around them.

Personal growth and development: By cultivating active and deep listening skills, individuals can gain insights that help them understand themselves and the world around them better, thereby enabling them to grow and develop personally.

While active listening is an important foundation for effective communication and relationship-building, deep listening takes it a step further by fostering a deeper connection with and understanding of the speaker's perspective, emotions, and experiences. It requires advanced skills and a willingness to be vulnerable and open to new perspectives. By developing deep listening skills, we can build stronger relationships, promote empathy and mutual respect, and navigate conflicts more effectively.

A story that illustrates the importance of deep listening:

Once upon a time, there was a wise elder in a small village. The villagers often came to the elder, seeking advice and guidance on various matters.

One day, a young man came to the elder with a problem. He said, 'Elder, I have a friend who always talks about me behind my back. I'm so frustrated and angry with her, and I don't know what to do.'

The elder listened attentively to the young man's story, nodding thoughtfully and asking clarifying questions along the way. When the young man was done speaking, the elder remained silent for a moment, deep in thought.

Then the elder said, 'I hear that you're feeling frustrated and angry with your friend. That must be very difficult for you. However, I wonder if there might be another way to approach this situation.'

The young man was surprised by the elder's response and asked, 'What do you mean?'

The elder replied, 'Instead of focusing your anger and frustration on your friend, I invite you to try to see things from her perspective. Perhaps she is going through a difficult time and is struggling to cope. By listening deeply to her and seeking to understand her perspective, you may be able to offer her support and strengthen your relationship in the process.'

The young man was taken aback by the elder's wisdom and insight. He realised that he had been so focused on his own emotions that he had failed to consider his friend's perspective. From that day onward, the young man made a conscious effort to listen deeply to his friend, seeking to understand her struggles and offer support. Over time, their relationship grew stronger, and they became closer friends than ever before.

This story highlights the importance of deep listening, which involves seeking to understand others' perspectives and emotions. By listening deeply and empathetically, we can build stronger relationships, gain new insights, and foster greater compassion and understanding in our lives.

The subtle but significant distinctions between active and deep listening have been listed in the following table:

Aspects	Active Listening	Deep Listening
Definition	The process of fully focusing on and understanding what someone is saying, both verbally and nonverbally. It is crucial for effective communication and building relationships.	The process of listening to understand the meanings and emotions underlying what someone is saying. It involves developing a deep understanding of the speaker's perspective, emotions, and experiences.
Focus	Active listening focuses on paying attention to the speaker's words, tone, and body language, with the goal of gaining information and facilitating communication.	Deep listening goes beyond words, focusing on the speaker's emotions, context, and nonverbal cues. The goal is to develop a deeper understanding of the speaker's perspective and experiences.
Presence	Active listening requires being present and attentive to the speaker's message, avoiding distractions, and demonstrating respect.	Deep listening demands full presence, mindfulness, and non-judgemental openness to the speaker's perspective. It requires a willingness to challenge one's own assumptions and biases.
Response	Active listening involves asking questions and summarising what the speaker has said. Feedback is often given to show understanding and validate the speaker's feelings.	Deep listening involves reflecting on the speaker's words, validating their emotions, and responding with empathy.

Aspects	Active Listening	Deep Listening
Importance	Active listening is essential for effective communication and building relationships. It improves communication, strengthens relationships, and builds trust.	Deep listening is important for deeper connections, empathy, and understanding between people, whereby it can help resolve conflicts more effectively.
Skills Required	Active listening skills include attentiveness, questioning, summarising, and feedback-giving. These skills can be learnt and practised to improve communication.	Deep listening requires advanced skills such as presence, mindfulness, empathy, and non-judgemental listening. These skills require more practice and a deeper understanding of oneself and others.
Challenges	Active listening requires focus and making an effort to maintain attention and avoid distractions. It can be challenging to maintain focus for extended periods of time, especially when the message is complex.	Deep listening demands vulnerability, openness, and a willingness to challenge one's own assumptions and biases. It can be difficult to let go of preconceived notions and truly listen to the speaker's perspective.
Applications	Active listening can be useful in job interviews and therapy sessions. It can help establish rapport and trust between the speaker and the listener.	Deep listening is crucial in conflict resolution or during difficult conversations with loved ones. It can help build deeper connections and understanding and promote empathy and mutual respect.

The Power of Letting Go: Understanding the Cruciality of Non-attachment

Non-attachment is a central principle of spiritual intelligence that emphasises the importance of letting go of our attachment to material possessions, relationships, and outcomes. It is an essential component of many spiritual traditions, including Buddhism, Hinduism, and Taoism, and is considered a powerful tool for the cultivation of inner peace, wisdom, and spiritual growth. Non-attachment involves a shift in perspective from valuing external objects and outcomes to valuing internal qualities such as love, kindness, and wisdom. This shift is achieved through a process of detachment, which involves recognising the impermanence of all things and letting go of our attachment to them. By practising non-attachment, we can cultivate a sense of inner freedom and liberation from the cycle of desire and suffering.

Practising Attachment with Detachment

Attachment is the root cause of pain, as it creates possessiveness and expectations. It restricts the freedom to explore life and creates barriers to freedom. Attachment can lead to negative emotions such as insecurity, fear, confusion, worries, jealousy, and even self-glorification. Detachment, on the other hand, is the freedom that we give ourselves and others to live life as we see fit. It is made up of compassion, devotion, and letting go. Detachment doesn't mean caring less; rather, it entails selfless caring with devotion.

Human beings are blessed with a heart that is full of love; it seeks love and wants to give love. This seeking and giving of love causes attachment. The mind and ego fabricate possessiveness, expectations, insecurities, fear, confusion, worries, and jealousy and even glorify these feelings. The purity of love is therefore found in detachment. While attachment is an accomplishment, detachment is fulfilment. Attachment sets boundaries; detachment removes barriers to freedom. Detachment is a function of mindfulness. When we attach ourselves to a higher purpose and our higher self, we evolve to such a level that we are able to understand this more deeply.

In the Buddhist tradition, non-attachment is one of the Four Noble Truths and is considered a key component of the Eightfold Path to enlightenment. The Buddha taught his disciples that all suffering arises from attachment and that the path to liberation from suffering involves developing a sense of detachment from the external world. The practice of mindfulness meditation is one of the primary methods of cultivating non-attachment in the Buddhist tradition, as it involves learning to observe our thoughts and emotions without becoming attached to them.

In the Hindu tradition, non-attachment is closely linked to the principle of detachment or *vairagya*. *Vairagya* is a process of renunciation in which we let go of our attachment to external objects and outcomes and focus on cultivating inner qualities such as devotion, wisdom, and self-discipline. The practice of yoga is one of the primary methods for cultivating non-attachment in the Hindu tradition, as it involves physical and mental practices that help purify the body and mind and develop a sense of detachment from the external world.

In the Taoist tradition, non-attachment is closely linked to the principle of *wu-wei*, which has already been discussed. Practising meditation and mindfulness is one of the primary methods for cultivating non-attachment in the Taoist tradition, as it involves learning to observe the natural flow of our thoughts and emotions without becoming attached to them.

One of the best-known teachings in the Bhagavad Gita on the topic of non-attachment is found in Chapter 2, verse 47:

'Karmany evadhikaras te

ma phalesu kadachana

ma karma-phala-hetur bhur

ma te sango stv akarmani'

(You have a right to perform your prescribed duty, but you are not entitled to the fruits of action.

Never consider yourself to be the cause of the results of your activities, And never be attached to inaction.)

This verse highlights the importance of performing one's duty without attachment to the outcome of the action. It encourages us to focus on the present moment and to act selflessly, without any personal motive or desire for a specific result. In the Bhagavad Gita, non-attachment is not seen as a renunciation of action or duty, but rather a way to perform our duties with greater clarity and purity of intention. By focusing on the task at hand without being attached to the outcome, we can work towards a greater goal with a sense of purpose and direction. Additionally, by cultivating non-attachment, we can avoid being swayed by the ups and downs of life. We can remain calm in the face of success and failure, pleasure and pain, and praise and criticism. This detachment allows us to remain focused on our spiritual goals and to live in a state of inner peace and contentment.

Kabir Das believed that the material world was illusory and that true reality lay beyond it. He preached that attachment to material possessions and desires was a major obstacle to spiritual progress and that detachment was necessary for spiritual growth. He believed that the true nature of the self was beyond the material world and that one must realise this truth in order to attain liberation.

'Maya mari na man mara, mara gaya sharir

Maya ta mohi mohi kari, mithya jagat sab bir'

(*Maya* (illusion) did not die, but my mind has died, and the body has also died *Maya* has deceived me by creating an illusory world.)

The principle of non-attachment reminds us that our actions and duties are important, but their results are not in our control. By surrendering attachment to outcomes and focusing on the present moment, we can enhance our spiritual intelligence and move closer to realising the true nature of the self.

Non-attachment can be challenging to practise, especially in a world that values material possessions, achievements, and success. However, it is still possible to cultivate non-attachment in your daily life through daily practices such as mindfulness, letting go of that which is not serving you, focusing on experiences rather than things, letting go of expectations, expressing gratitude, etc. Remember that cultivating non-attachment is a journey and it may take time to fully embrace this practice. Be patient with yourself and celebrate small victories along the way.

Vasudhaiva Kutumbakam: The Universal Brotherhood of Humanity

Vasudhaiva kutumbakam is a Sanskrit phrase that means 'the world is one family.' It is an ancient Indian concept that highlights the interconnectedness of all living beings and promotes a sense of universal brotherhood and mutual respect. The idea behind *vasudhaiva kutumbakam* is that all people, regardless of race, nationality, or religion, are part of the same global family and should treat each other with compassion and kindness. This concept encourages people to work together for the greater good and to strive for a more peaceful and harmonious world. In fact, the idea of the world being one family extends beyond just human beings to include all living beings as well as the planet itself, emphasising the need for environmental sustainability and the preservation of the natural world.

In today's rapidly evolving world, the concept of *vasudhaiva kutumbakam* is more relevant than ever. As we become more connected through technology and travel, it is important to recognise our shared humanity and to work together to address the many challenges facing our planet, including climate change, poverty, and conflict. It's a powerful reminder that we are all in this together and that, by fostering greater cooperation and understanding between individuals, institutions, and diverse communities, we can create a brighter and more harmonious world. Just imagine what we could achieve if we all saw ourselves as part of the same family—a family that transcends borders, cultures, and beliefs. Embracing this idea would lead to bridges being built across cultural, religious, and geographic divides and the creation of a more inclusive, compassionate, and sustainable society.

Sarve jano sukhino bhavantu is a related Sanskrit phrase that is often used as a prayer, blessing, or an invocation of peace and harmony. In English, it translates to 'May all people be happy and prosperous.' This phrase also conveys the idea of universal welfare and goodwill towards all living beings. It does not originate in any specific Upanishad or scripture. However, the sentiment behind the phrase is in line with the teachings of various Hindu scriptures, such as the Upanishads, Bhagavad Gita, and Yoga Sutras. These texts emphasise the importance of compassion, kindness, and universal welfare.

Love for humanity is unconditional and healing. Both of the above phrases propagate the fundamental unity and interconnectedness of all life. They call for the cultivation of compassion, empathy, and kindness towards all living beings and for the recognition that we are all part of the same global family. They remind us of our shared humanity and our responsibility to care for each other and the planet we live on. In terms of spiritual intelligence, it is crucial to internalise these concepts and incorporate them into our daily lives.

In this context, Kabir's concept of the unity of all humanity is very relevant. He rejected all forms of social and religious discrimination. He believed that all people were equal in the eyes of God and that no one could be considered superior or inferior based on their caste, religion, or social status.

'Jati na poochho sadhu ki, poochh lijiye gyan

Mol karo talwar ka, padhi rahne do myaan'

(Don't ask about the caste of the saint, ask about his knowledge

Value the sword for its sharpness, don't bother about its sheath.)

From a spiritual intelligence perspective, embracing the concept of *vasudhaiva kutumbakam* can have several benefits. Spiritual intelligence involves the ability to see beyond the surface-level differences and recognise the interconnectedness of all things. It includes qualities such as empathy, compassion, and a sense of purpose that is larger than oneself. By recognising that the world is one family, we can cultivate a sense of empathy and compassion for others, even those who may seem different from us. This can help us develop a greater understanding of the world around us and connect more deeply with other people, regardless of their background or beliefs.

Chapter 3

Understanding Human Anatomy: We Are Beyond Body and Mind

The integration of body and mind is a fundamental aspect of spiritual intelligence, and somatic yoga is a powerful tool for the achievement of this integration. This technique is based on neuroscience and involves a series of physical movements and mental exercises that promote both physical and mental well-being. By practising somatic yoga regularly, we can slow down the wear and tear of our body and prevent illness and disease. Moreover, this technique also helps establish a deeper connection between our body and mind, leading to a sense of inner peace, harmony, and bliss.

Spiritual alignment and resultant spiritual intelligence may appear very simple as concepts, but they are in fact quite profound. Spiritual alignment is possible only through perseverance, discipline, and practice—what is called *sadhana*. Spiritual intelligence is an integral part of our being, and it encompasses all aspects of our being, including the body, mind, ego, memory, intellect, and soul.

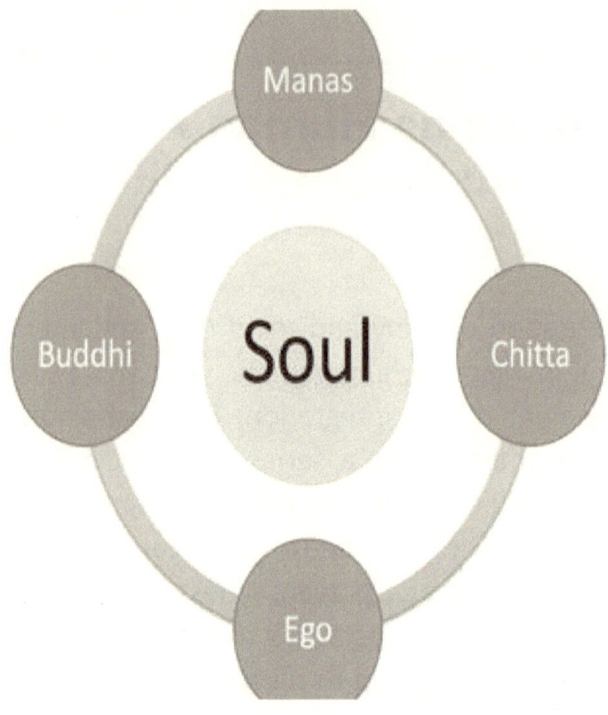

Figure 2

To enhance our spiritual intelligence, it is essential to understand and work with each of these aspects of our being. Let's take a closer look at each of these elements and explore ways to strengthen our spiritual intelligence.

Body

Living organisms are made up of different levels of complexity. At the highest level, beings like humans consist of biochemicals, including cells and organs. These biochemicals are made of atoms, which are made of even smaller particles like electrons, protons, and neutrons. These tiny particles are the basic elements that constitute the entire universe. So everything in the universe, living or not, is essentially made of the same small parts at the atomic level. While the human body is physical and finite, our spiritual essence, referred to as *atma*, resides within it.

Our body is the temple of our soul, and it is the vehicle through which we experience the world. It is essential to take care of our body through healthy habits, such as exercise, proper nutrition, and adequate rest. These practices not only improve physical health but also contribute to mental and emotional well-being, which in turn enhances our spiritual intelligence.

Mind

Our mind is the gateway to our consciousness, and it is responsible for our thoughts, beliefs, and perceptions. It is essential to cultivate a positive and open mindset, free from judgement and preconceived notions. Meditation, mindfulness, and self-reflection are powerful tools to quiet the mind and enhance our spiritual intelligence.

Ego *(Ahankara)*

Ahankara is our sense of self, and it is what gives us our individuality. However, when it is overdeveloped, it can lead to a false sense of identity and limit our ability to connect with our higher self. The 'I' sense arises from the *upadhi*. In the Vedic Hindu tradition, *upadhi* refers to the various limiting conditions or attributes associated with an individual's identity. These attributes include factors like the body, mind, emotions, and societal roles. The concept of *upadhi* suggests that these attributes act as veils, obscuring one's true self or inner consciousness.

The influence of *upadhi* on the self is such that it tends to create a sense of attachment and identification with these external attributes. This attachment can lead to the misconception that these attributes define one's true nature, causing individuals to perceive themselves as separate from others and the broader universe. Consequently, the ultimate goal in many spiritual practices within the Vedic tradition is to transcend the limiting conditions of *upadhi* in order to realise the true self or *atman*. This true self is considered eternal, unchanging, and interconnected with all existence.

It is essential to cultivate humility, self-awareness, and a sense of detachment from the ego to enhance our spiritual intelligence.

Memory *(Chitta)*

Our *chitta* is the storehouse of our memories and experiences, and it influences our thoughts, emotions, and behaviour. To enhance our spiritual intelligence, we must release any negative or limiting beliefs and patterns that we have accumulated over time. We should be mindful of what's reflected in our *chitta*. Forgiveness, gratitude, and detachment can help us heal and free our *chitta*.

Intellect *(Buddhi)*

Our *buddhi* is the faculty of discrimination and discernment, and it allows us to make wise choices in life. It is essential to cultivate our *buddhi* by seeking knowledge, wisdom, and understanding of the universal principles that govern our existence. Reading spiritual texts, seeking the guidance of wise teachers, and engaging in deep contemplation are effective ways to enhance our spiritual intelligence.

Soul

Our soul is our true essence, the spark of divinity that resides within us. To enhance our spiritual intelligence, we must connect with our soul and align with our higher purpose. Practices such as prayer, meditation, and service to others can help us awaken our spiritual potential and live a life of meaning and fulfilment. As has been stated, we are essentially spiritual beings experiencing human existence, rather than the other way around. In the words of Corinne McLaughlin, 'Although we might initially say that we "have" a soul, it is more accurate to say that we are a soul who "has" a personality, and this self-centred personality is our instrument of expression in the world. The soul reveals that we are not separate from each other or from all life, whether visible and invisible. To experience the soul is to experience a deep sense of oneness with all that is—a profound sense of inspiration and joy.'

In Hinduism, the soul is known as *atma*. *Atma* is understood as the eternal, unchanging, and non-material essence of a person that is beyond the physical body, mind, and intellect. It is considered the true self and identical with *brahman*, the ultimate reality.

The five faculties, i.e., body, mind, ego, intellect, and memory (*chitta*), are different aspects of a person's being that interact and influence each other. They are not considered comparable to *atma*, for *atma* is not a faculty or component of the body–mind complex. Vedanta refers to *atma* as *atman* (self). It is the underlying reality that exists beyond these components and is often described as the witness or observer of these faculties. Therefore, *atma* is not the sixth faculty after *chitta* but is distinct from all the five faculties.

Enhancing our spiritual intelligence requires a holistic approach that involves nurturing all aspects of our being. By cultivating healthy habits, a positive mindset, humility, self-awareness, forgiveness, discernment, and a connection with our soul, we can tap into our higher wisdom and live a life that is in harmony with the universe. In various spiritual traditions, the path to realising the self involves going beyond the limitations of the body, mind, ego, and intellect. The Upanishads as well as the spiritual texts of Buddhism, Jainism, and other traditions teach us about the nature of the self and how we can realise it. The self is the pure consciousness that underlies all of our experiences. The Upanishads propose that we can realise the self by transcending the limitations of the body, mind, and intellect through spiritual practices such as meditation and self-enquiry.

The self is the subject. The external world is considered objective and only exists in our thoughts. By detaching ourselves from our thoughts and emotions, we can go beyond the illusions of the external world and connect with our innermost being, which is free and independent, and gain wisdom. In other words, the true self is not bound by external circumstances and can be discovered through introspection and meditation. This understanding can have a profound impact on how we see ourselves and the world around us.

However, according to Buddhist teachings, the self is not a permanent, unchanging entity but rather a constantly changing process or stream of consciousness. Buddha taught that there is no permanent self or soul that exists independently of the body and mind. This concept is known as *anatta* or 'non-self'. Buddha believed that the self is an illusion created by our desire for permanence and attachment to worldly things. He taught that we are made up of five aggregates or five *skandhas*, which are form (*rupa*), feelings or sensations (*vedana*), perception (*sanna*), mental formations (*sankhara*), and consciousness (*vinnana*, which refers to our awareness of the world around us). According to Buddhist teachings, these five *skandhas* are the building blocks of individual existence, and the interplay between these five *skandhas* creates the illusion of a self, which is subject to suffering and impermanence. Therefore, to attain liberation, one must transcend the limitations of the self and the *skandhas* and reach a state of pure consciousness and awareness. When the five *skandhas* dissolve or are seen as empty, the sense of a fixed, permanent self also dissolves. What remains is a state of pure awareness, often referred to as *nirvana* or enlightenment. This state of being is free from the suffering that arises from attachment to the impermanent self and the world of sensory experience. It's important to note that this state of pure awareness is not experienced by a separate self, as there is no separate self to experience it. Rather, it is a state of non-dual awareness in which the distinction between subject and object dissolves and there is a direct realisation of the nature of reality.

In Buddhism, the state of *shunya*, also known as emptiness or voidness, refers to a state of profound silence and stillness that arises from the cessation of all mental activity, including the sense of self or ego. It is a state of complete inner stillness and openness, a state in which the mind is free from any kind of attachment, craving, or conceptualisation. It is not a state that is experienced by a self but rather a realisation of the true nature of reality beyond the limitations of the self, beyond one's own perspective and conditioning and the world of sensory experience. It is the state of experiencing the emptiness of all phenomena that arises from the cessation of all mental activity and the realisation of the interdependent and impermanent nature of all things. The goal of Buddhist practice is to attain a state of pure awareness or enlightenment that transcends the limitations of the self and the cycle of rebirth.

For a layperson, the experience of the state of emptiness can have profound implications for their spiritual development. One gains a deep understanding of the interconnectedness of all things, a great sense of compassion and wisdom, a more balanced and harmonious relationship with the world around them, the ability to let go of attachment and craving, and a sense of inner peace and contentment. This can lead to a more meaningful and fulfilling life, free from the suffering caused by attachment to things that are impermanent and constantly changing.

In Hinduism, *ahankara* or the ego or 'I' sense is also seen as a source of suffering, as it creates a sense of separateness and attachment to material things. However, while Buddhism emphasises the impermanence and emptiness of the self, Hinduism sees the self or *atma* as eternal and unchanging, and ultimately identical to the ultimate reality, *brahman*. The idea of self or *jiva*, as mentioned earlier, is also central to Jain philosophy. The term *jiva* refers to the individual living being or the consciousness that animates the body and is considered to be eternal, beginningless and endless, and trapped in a cycle of birth and death due to karmic bonds. On the other hand, the term 'soul' in Jainism refers to the pure and perfect state of consciousness that is free from all karmic bondage and the cycle of birth and death. This state of consciousness is also known as *moksha* or liberation. Therefore, while both *jiva* and soul are related to the concept of consciousness in Jainism, they refer to different states of consciousness—*jiva* being the individual living entity bound by *karma* and soul being the pure and liberated state of consciousness. *Jiva* is eternal and goes through cycles of birth and death, and its ultimate goal is to achieve *moksha* or liberation from the cycle of rebirths.

According to Jainism, all *jivas* are equal and possess the potential to achieve liberation or *moksha*, regardless of their caste, gender, or social status. This is in line with the Jain idea of *ahimsa*, or non-violence, which requires all living beings to be treated with respect and compassion and implies that no living being is considered superior to another. Jainism does acknowledge that there are beings who have progressed further along the path of spiritual development and have attained a higher level of consciousness. Those beings who are believed to have achieved enlightenment are known as the Tirthankaras or 'ford-makers', and they serve as guides and role models for spiritual aspirants. However, even the Tirthankaras are not considered superior to other *jivas* in the ultimate sense, as all *jivas* have the potential to attain the same level of spiritual progress and liberation.

Jainism teaches that the self is pure consciousness and is obscured by the karmic matter that accumulates on it as a result of our actions but can be accessed through the practice of truthfulness, self-discipline, and non-violence. Understanding oneself is crucial to this process. By understanding oneself—one's thoughts, emotions, and actions—one can identify one's strengths and weaknesses and work on improving oneself. This self-improvement can help one develop virtues such as compassion, humility, and non-violence, which are central to Jainism.

Jainism also emphasises the idea of detachment from material possessions and worldly desires. By detaching oneself from these external factors, one can focus on one's internal spiritual growth and journey towards self-realisation. Through meditation and contemplation, one can gain a deeper understanding of one's self and the true nature of reality. This idea of self in Jainism can be leveraged to gain wisdom by focusing on self-realisation, self-discovery, and detachment from worldly desires. By understanding oneself and working on self-improvement, one can develop virtues and achieve spiritual growth, ultimately leading to liberation.

The following table compares viewpoints on the 'self' in Hinduism, Buddhism, and Jainism:

Aspect	Hinduism	Buddhism	Jainism
Concept of self	*Atma* is the eternal, immortal, transcendent, unchanging, and divine self/soul that is identical to *brahman* (ultimate reality).	The concept of *anatta* or no-self is a rejection of the concept of a permanent, unchanging, and independent self/soul. It emphasises the impermanence and interdependence of all things.	*Jiva* is the individual self, constantly changing and transmigrating. It is intrinsically pure and possesses infinite knowledge, bliss, and power.

Aspect	Hinduism	Buddhism	Jainism
Ultimate goal	Union with *brahman*, realisation of the true self.	*Nirvana*, the state of complete liberation from suffering.	*Moksha*, release from the cycle of birth and death.
Path to liberation	Possible paths include Karma Yoga (path of selfless action), Bhakti Yoga (path of devotion), Jnana Yoga (path of knowledge), and Raja Yoga (path of meditation and control of the mind).	The Noble Eightfold Path, which requires mindfulness, wisdom, and meditation.	Meditation and purification of the soul. Paths include 'right perception', 'right knowledge', and 'right conduct'. The practice of asceticism and non-violence (*ahimsa*) is emphasised.
Relationship with the world	The world is illusory, a manifestation of *brahman*.	The world is characterised by suffering and attachment to it causes suffering.	The world is full of suffering and is to be renounced.
Ethics	*Dharma*: duty and righteousness, *karma* and reincarnation.	Five precepts: Non-violence, non-stealing, refraining from sexual misconduct, false speech, and consuming intoxicants.	*Ahimsa*: non-violence, non-attachment, purification of the soul.

Aspect	Hinduism	Buddhism	Jainism
Reincarnation	Based on the law of *karma*, the eternal self/soul (*atma*) undergoes repeated cycles of birth, death, and rebirth (*samsara*) until it achieves liberation (*moksha*).	Emphasises the continuity of consciousness and rebirth but denies the existence of an eternal self/ soul. Existence is viewed as a series of interconnected, momentary phenomena.	Believes in the cycle of birth, death, and rebirth (*samsara*) for the eternal soul (*jiva*) until it achieves liberation (*moksha*).
God(s)	*Brahman*: many deities and *avatars*.	No belief in a supreme being or creator God.	No belief in a supreme being or creator God.
Liberation/ Enlightenment	*Moksha* is the ultimate goal, attained by realising the identity between the individual self (*atma*) and the universal self (*brahman*). It ends the cycle of birth and death.	*Nirvana* is the ultimate goal, achieved by realising the nature of reality and extinguishing desires. It entails liberation from the cycle of rebirth and suffering.	*Moksha* is the ultimate goal, achieved by liberating the soul (*jiva*) from karmic bondage. It brings an end to the cycle of birth, death, and rebirth.

Note that these are generalisations and there can be variations within each of these traditions depending on the specific school of thought or philosophical interpretation under consideration.

Comprehending the principles of Hinduism, Buddhism, and Jainism ultimately entails recognising that our being transcends the limitations of the physical body and mind, realising the true nature of our existence, and living in alignment with it. This is essential for personal growth, spiritual development, and leading a fulfilling life. Enhancing spiritual intelligence involves grasping the true nature of our existence and the essence of life itself. This understanding is crucial to living a purposeful life that promotes our well-being and fulfilment.

The ego, in particular, is an obstacle to self-realisation. The ego creates a false sense of self that is attached to the body, mind, and intellect. The ego is rooted in the illusion of separation between the self and the world. This sense of separation prevents us from recognising the unity and interconnectedness of all things. Spiritual practices such as meditation, self-enquiry, and mindfulness are powerful tools with which to transcend the ego and realise the self. Through meditation, we can quiet the mind and access a state of pure awareness that is beyond the limitations of the body, mind, and ego. By focusing our attention on our breath, a mantra, or an image, we can turn our attention inward and access a deeper level of consciousness.

Self-enquiry is another powerful tool. By questioning our thoughts, beliefs, and assumptions, we can begin to see beyond the limitations of the ego and connect with the deeper truth of our being. Asking questions such as 'Who am I?' or 'What is the nature of the self?' can help us uncover the illusions created by the ego or mental construct and access a deeper level of awareness. The spiritual teachings of the Upanishads, Buddhism, Jainism, and other traditions provide guidance on how to access the pure consciousness that lies within us all. Our endeavour should be to transcend the ego and realise the true nature of the self through spiritual practices. The rewards of this realisation are a sense of peace, joy, and fulfilment that transcend the limitations of the physical world.

The chariot analogy is a powerful metaphor used in the Katha Upanishad to explain the relationship between the body, senses, mind, intellect, and the soul. The analogy begins with the comparison of the body to a chariot, the senses being the horses that pull it and the mind being the reins that guide it. The intellect, or *buddhi*, is likened to the charioteer who steers the chariot in the right direction. Finally, the soul is compared to the passenger who is ultimately responsible for the journey.

This analogy teaches us that our body, mind, and senses are all essential components of our being and must work together in harmony to achieve spiritual growth. However, it is the soul that must be in control, directing the other components towards the ultimate goal of spiritual realisation.

The body is often seen as the vehicle for the soul's journey, providing the necessary tools and experiences for growth. The senses, which are often driven by desires and cravings, can either aid or hinder our spiritual progress, depending on how they are controlled. The mind, which is responsible for processing and interpreting sensory input, must be trained to focus on spiritual goals and not get caught up in distractions.

The intellect or *buddhi* is the aspect of our being that allows us to make conscious choices and guide our actions towards spiritual growth. It is the *buddhi* that must be trained to make decisions based on spiritual values and not just on temporary pleasures or desires.

Finally, the soul is the ultimate goal of our spiritual journey. The soul is beyond the limitations of the body, mind, and senses, and is the source of true joy and fulfilment. The soul is eternal and cannot be harmed by any external force, including death.

The Interplay of the Gross, Subtle, and Causal Bodies in the Pursuit of Wisdom

In several Hindu schools of thought, the concept of the human body is divided into three levels of existence: the *sthula* (gross), *sushma* (subtle), and *karana* (causal) bodies. These bodies are said to underlie the physical body.

The *Sthula* (Gross) Body

The *sthula* body is the physical body that we can see, touch, and feel. It is made up of the five gross elements (*mahabhutas*): earth, water, fire, air, and ether. These elements combine to form the physical body and its various organs, tissues, and cells. This body is the most tangible and material aspect of our existence.

The *Sushma* (Subtle) Body

The *sushma* body is the subtle body that underlies the physical body. It is composed of the five subtle elements (*tanmatras*): sound, touch, form, taste, and smell. These subtle elements cannot be perceived by the senses; rather, they are experienced through the mind. The *sushma* body is also associated with the *prana* (life force) and the *nadis* (energy channels). It is believed that the *sushma* body connects the physical body with the mind.

The *Karana* (Causal) Body

The *karana* body is the causal body, which underlies both the gross and subtle bodies. It is composed of the seeds of past actions, thoughts, and desires, which are stored in the form of *samskaras* (impressions) and *vasanas* (tendencies) in the unconscious mind. These *samskaras* and *vasanas* are said to determine our future actions and experiences. The *karana* body is also associated with the universal consciousness and the source of all existence.

The causal body is also referred to as the 'seed body' because it contains the potential for all aspects of the individual's being, including their physical body and their subtle body. It is considered the cause of the individual's existence in the physical and subtle realms. This means that everything that we experience in our lives, including our thoughts, emotions, and actions, arise from the causal body.

If the ultimate goal of human existence is to realise one's true nature, which is beyond the limitations of the physical and subtle bodies, then this realisation involves transcending the limitations of the causal body as well and connecting with the ultimate reality or consciousness that underlies all existence. To do this, one must practise various spiritual disciplines, such as meditation and self-enquiry, to purify the mind and gain insight into the nature of reality.

The concept of the causal body is also found in other ancient philosophical and spiritual traditions—*brahman* in Hinduism, 'Buddha-nature' in Buddhism, and the 'soul' in Platonic philosophy. All of these traditions emphasise the importance of transcending the limitations of the individual self and connecting with a higher reality that underlies all existence.

In Hinduism, *brahman* or the Supreme Spirit is the ultimate reality that underlies all existence. It is an all-pervading, eternal, and infinite consciousness that transcends all dualities and limitations. According to Hindu philosophy, all individual beings are ultimately manifestations of this ultimate reality but are limited by their physical, subtle, and causal bodies. The goal of spiritual practice in Hinduism is to realise one's true nature as an expression of the Supreme Spirit and to transcend the limitations of the individual self.

'Buddha-nature' refers to the potential for awakening or enlightenment that exists within all sentient beings. It is considered the fundamental nature of all beings but is obscured by the veils of ignorance, attachment, and aversion. The goal of Buddhist practice is to cultivate awareness and insight into the true nature of reality and to remove these veils, allowing the Buddha-nature to shine forth. In this way, one can realise their true nature as a Buddha or an awakened being and live a life of compassion, wisdom, and freedom.

In Platonic philosophy, the concept of the soul refers to the immortal and incorporeal aspect of the human being. According to Plato, the soul is a divine and eternal essence that is distinct from the physical body. It is the source of human consciousness, reason, and morality, and it is capable of transcending the limitations of the physical realm. In Platonic philosophy, the goal of human life is to attain knowledge of the true nature of reality, which includes the knowledge of the soul's immortal nature. Through this knowledge, one can attain a state of harmony and balance and live a life of wisdom and virtue.

Thus, the *sthula*, *sushma*, and *karana* bodies are three levels of existence in philosophy that underlie the physical body and are progressively more subtle. Each body is associated with different aspects of our being and can be cultivated through various yoga practices to promote physical health, mental clarity, and spiritual growth.

The Relevance of the Vedic Concept of the Five *Koshas* (Sheaths)

The concept of the Five *Koshas* is associated with the Vedanta school of Hinduism, which is one of the six main schools of Hindu philosophy. The *koshas* or sheaths are the five layers or levels of existence that make up the human body, mind, and spirit. These *koshas* are believed to be interconnected and to work together to create a holistic understanding of the self. Each *kosha* represents a different aspect of the self and is related to a specific layer of existence.

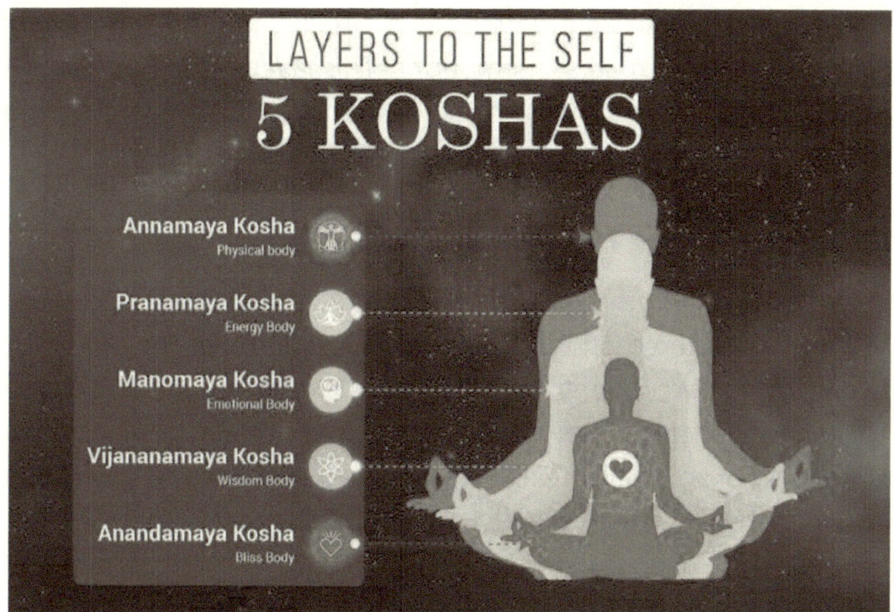

Figure 3

Understanding the *koshas* is a key aspect of developing spiritual intelligence, as it helps individuals to cultivate a deeper understanding of themselves and their place in the world.

***Annamaya Kosha* (The Physical Sheath)**

The first *kosha* is the physical sheath, which represents the outermost layer of the human body—the bones, muscles, organs, and skin. This layer is closely connected to the physical world and is responsible for sensory experiences such as touch, taste, and smell. Developing physical health and wellness is a crucial aspect of spiritual intelligence, as it helps individuals create a strong foundation for personal growth and self-awareness.

***Pranamaya Kosha* (The Energy Sheath)**

The second *kosha* is the energy sheath, which represents the layer of energy that flows through the body. This layer is responsible for vital functions such as breathing and circulation, and it is closely connected to the mind and emotions. This layer can be developed through practices such as *pranayama* and meditation, which help balance the flow of energy and promote overall wellness.

Manomaya Kosha (The Mental Sheath)

The third *kosha* is the mental sheath, which represents the layer of the mind and emotions. This layer is responsible for thoughts, feelings, and perceptions, and it is closely connected to the physical and energy sheaths. Developing mental health and wellness is a key aspect of spiritual intelligence, as it helps individuals cultivate a greater sense of self-awareness and emotional stability.

Vijnanamaya Kosha (The Wisdom Sheath)

The fourth *kosha* is the wisdom sheath, which represents the layer of intuition and insight. This layer is responsible for higher-level thinking, creativity, and spiritual awareness. Developing the wisdom sheath requires practices such as meditation and contemplation, which help individuals connect with their inner wisdom and intuition.

Anandamaya Kosha (The Bliss Sheath)

The fifth and final *kosha* is the bliss sheath, which represents the layer of pure joy and happiness. This layer is responsible for feelings of connection, love, and spiritual fulfilment. Developing the bliss sheath requires practices such as selfless service, meditation, and devotion, which help individuals connect with their inner joy and the greater spiritual reality.

Anandamaya kosha or the bliss sheath is the highest level or layer of our being, according to the ancient Indian scriptures. It is said to be the essence of all the other layers or *koshas* that make up our whole self. It is also known as the spiritual self and is the aspect of our being that experiences pure joy, unconditional love, and complete contentment. The idea that the bliss state exists within you implies that this ultimate state of happiness, contentment, and fulfilment cannot be activated by external factors like a good job, material possessions, or other people's approval. It is already present within you, waiting to be uncovered and experienced.

As human beings, we are born to be joyous. However, we tend to get caught up in the other *koshas*. These layers often cause distractions and disturbances, making it difficult for us to experience the joy and contentment that lie within us. Therefore, it is important to manage and overcome these other *koshas* in order to access and experience the blissful state within us. We need to maintain a healthy physical body (*annamaya kosha*) by exercising, eating well, and being mindful of our overall health. The life force (*pranamaya kosha*) needs to be balanced through practices like *pranayama*, meditation, and yoga. We need to keep our thoughts positive and under control (*manomaya kosha*) and develop our intellect (*vijnanamaya kosha*) through acquiring knowledge, reading, and studying. By managing and overcoming these *koshas*, we gradually peel away the layers that cover and obstruct the bliss sheath, allowing us to finally access and experience the joy and contentment that lies within us. It is important to understand that the journey towards experiencing *anandamaya kosha* or the blissful state takes time, effort, and dedication. But the reward of finding inner peace and true happiness is worth the journey.

Understanding the *koshas* can help us leverage spiritual intelligence in different ways. Firstly, it helps us understand the various dimensions of our personality and how they interact with each other to make us what we are. Secondly, it allows us to identify and overcome the various obstacles that may exist in these different layers, which may hinder our self-growth. Through spiritual practice, we can go beyond each *kosha* to reach our higher self, experience bliss, and connect with the divine. This insight into the *koshas* can help us develop a deeper sense of self-awareness, mindfulness, and compassion towards ourselves and others. Comprehending the *koshas* is a key aspect of developing spiritual intelligence, as it helps individuals cultivate a deeper understanding of themselves and their place in the world. By developing each *kosha* through practices such as yoga, meditation, and contemplation, individuals can cultivate a holistic approach to self-discovery and personal growth. Ultimately, the goal of understanding the *koshas* is to achieve a state of spiritual wholeness, wherein each aspect of the self is balanced and in harmony with the greater spiritual reality.

The concept of the *koshas* is not exclusive to Hinduism; rather, it is a universal concept found in many religions and spiritual traditions. In Buddhism, for example, the *koshas* are represented by the five *skandhas*. Similarly, in Jainism, the *koshas* are referred to as the *pancha kashayas*, which represent the five sources of inner impurities or passions. They are anger, ego, deceit, greed, and attachment.

In Christianity, the concept of the *koshas* can be related to the idea of the tripartite nature of man, which refers to the belief that human beings are composed of three parts: body, soul, and spirit. Developing each aspect of the tripartite nature is considered important for spiritual wholeness. According to this concept, the body is the physical aspect of a human being, consisting of flesh, bones, and organs. The soul is the immaterial component of a person, consisting of the mind, will, and emotions. Finally, the spirit is the part of a human being that connects with God, enabling individuals to experience spiritual life.

In Islam, the concept of the *koshas* can be related to the idea of the *nafs*, which represents the human soul and is divided into various levels of consciousness. It is the innermost part of a person's being that determines their thoughts, actions, and desires. From an Islamic perspective, the *nafs* can be either pure or corrupted, depending on how it is influenced by external factors such as ego, desires, and temptations. Developing the *nafs* is considered important for spiritual purification. The goal of the Islamic spiritual practice is to purify and detach oneself from the negative influence of the *nafs*, in order to achieve a higher level of spirituality and closeness to Allah.

According to Islamic teachings, the *nafs* is the inner self of a person, which contains both positive and negative qualities. The Quran mentions that the *nafs* has the potential to command evil as well as good. It can be inclined towards negative traits such as anger, greed, envy, and arrogance or positive qualities such as kindness, generosity, and humility. Therefore, it is the responsibility of a person to purify their *nafs* and strive towards spiritual excellence.

Islamic scholars have identified three types of *nafs*, based on the level of spiritual development. The first is the *nafs al-ammara*, which is the lowest level of the *nafs*, characterised by the inclination towards evil and worldly desires. The second level is *nafs al-lawwamah*, which is a self-accusing soul that is aware of its shortcomings and strives to correct them. The third and highest level of *nafs* is *nafs al-mutmainnah*, which is a soul at peace with God, content with His will and commands, and fully submitted to Him.

In all of these traditions, the underlying message is that the human experience is multifaceted, and that achieving spiritual intelligence requires a holistic approach to self-discovery and personal growth. By developing each aspect of the self, whether it be the physical body, the energy body, the mind and emotions, the wisdom body, or the bliss body, individuals can cultivate a deeper sense of self-awareness, spiritual connection, and fulfilment. Ultimately, the goal of understanding the *koshas* is to achieve a state of spiritual wholeness, where each aspect of the self is balanced and in harmony with the greater spiritual reality.

Understanding *Purusha* (Pure Consciousness): Connecting with Your Inner Self

Purusha is a Sanskrit term used by the Sankhya school of philosophy to describe the pure, conscious self or spirit that underlies all of existence. It is an important concept in the spiritual traditions of India and is closely related to the concept of *atma*, which refers to the individual soul or self. The term *purusha* comes from the Sanskrit word *puru*, which means 'to fill', 'to pervade', or 'to be abundant'. The concept of *purusha* is also closely connected with the idea of *brahman*. While *brahman* is an infinite, eternal, and unchanging reality that transcends all distinctions and dualities, *purusha*, on the other hand, is seen as a reflection or manifestation of *brahman* in the individual soul or self—the pure, unchanging consciousness that underlies all mental activity. The mind is seen as a reflection of *purusha*, and the goal of yoga is to quiet the mind and turn it inward, so that the individual can experience the true nature of *purusha*.

In the context of spiritual intelligence, the concept of *purusha* is important because it emphasises the importance of self-awareness and self-realisation. By recognising the true nature of *purusha* (pure consciousness or soul) within ourselves, we can free ourselves from the limitations of the ego and connect with the larger spiritual reality that underlies all of existence. This can help us develop wisdom as well as a deeper sense of purpose and meaning in life.

Beyond *Prakriti* (the World of Matter): Understanding the True Nature of Reality

Prakriti is a term used in Sankhya philosophy to refer to the cosmic nature or the material world. According to Sankhya philosophy, *prakriti* is the fundamental principle of the universe, which manifests in three primary qualities or *gunas*: *sattva* (purity and intelligence), *rajas* (activity and passion), and *tamas* (inertia and darkness). It is the fundamental principle of the universe and is responsible for the creation, preservation, and destruction of all things.

Sankhya philosophy views human beings as composed of *prakriti* in various proportions. The individual self or the soul is believed to be distinct from *prakriti*, but it becomes bound to *prakriti* (the material world) due to ignorance and desires, resulting in the cycle of birth and death. The influence of *prakriti* on human beings is believed to be significant. The three *gunas* of *prakriti* affect human behaviour, emotions, and thoughts. For instance, *sattva guna* is associated with a calm and peaceful mind, *rajas guna* is associated with desire and activity, and *tamas guna* is associated with lethargy and ignorance.

The way out, according to Sankhya philosophy, is to achieve liberation or *moksha* by realising the true nature of the self, which is distinct from *prakriti*. This can be achieved through the practice of meditation, yoga, and self-enquiry, which lead to the purification of the mind and the removal of ignorance. By transcending the influence of *prakriti*, one can attain the state of pure consciousness and liberation.

Purusha is the individual self or consciousness, distinct from *prakriti*. It is pure, unchanging, and unaffected by the qualities of *prakriti*. *Purusha* is the observer or witness of the world, not bound by the cycle of birth and death. *Prakriti* is the cause of all material phenomena, while *purusha* is the cause of consciousness. Furthermore, *prakriti* is the object of perception, while *purusha* is the subject of perception. In other words, *prakriti* can be perceived through the senses, while *purusha* cannot be perceived as an object. Therefore, *prakriti* and *purusha* are two distinct entities, and it is important to differentiate between them to understand the nature of the universe and the individual self.

According to this philosophy, we mortal beings are a combination of both *purusha* and *prakriti*. Understanding these two concepts is relevant to our lives because it provides a framework for understanding the nature of existence and the purpose of life. It teaches us that our true nature is that of the unchanging and eternal *purusha* (pure consciousness) and that our mortal existence is temporary and subject to change. It also allows us to detach from the material world, focus on spiritual growth and self-realisation, and develop a greater appreciation for the interconnectedness of all things and the importance of living in harmony with nature. It reminds us that we are all part of a greater whole, and that our actions have an impact not just on ourselves but on the world around us.

The Sankhya school, like Vedanta, proposes that souls become bound when they are influenced by *prakriti*, leading to delusion and ignorance. Upon realising that the cause of their bondage is nature and not themselves, they strive for liberation, attaining freedom from the cycle of births and deaths.

While *purusha* and *atma* share some similarities in that both are considered to be the individual self or consciousness, they are not identical concepts. *Purusha* is considered distinct from *prakriti*, *atma*, and *brahman*. Both *atma* and *purusha* represent a spiritual or transcendent aspect of the self; however, they come from different philosophical traditions and have slightly different connotations and goals. Meanwhile, *brahman*, *purusha*, *ishwara*, and *paramatma* are all concepts in Hindu philosophy that refer to the ultimate reality or the absolute truth; however, there are some differences in their meanings and usage.

Brahman

Brahman is the supreme and eternal consciousness that underlies and permeates all existence. It is the ultimate reality and source of all creation, sustenance, and dissolution. *Brahman* is often described as formless, limitless, and indivisible. It is beyond human comprehension and can only be realised through direct experience or self-realisation. It is said in the Brihadaranyaka Upanishad that, 'The man who realises that it is the Supreme Life that shines in and through all life does not waste words. His pleasure and his love are then all in the soul. He becomes the most enlightened among the philosophers. Truth, penance, understanding and purity are essential for this revelation of the *brahman*.'

The above quote highlights that there is a supreme life force that permeates and illuminates all life. Realising this leads to a deep understanding that everything is interconnected and that there is a higher purpose to life. Words are not necessary to convey this truth, as the realisation itself is beyond words. The focus is on the soul and inner being, and pleasure and love are found in that realm. Those who understand this are the most enlightened among philosophers, as they have transcended the limitations of intellectual knowledge and accessed a deeper level of understanding. However, achieving this requires certain qualities, such as truth, penance, understanding, and purity. These qualities help remove the obstacles that block one's perception of the underlying unity of all things. The key is to recognise the unity of all life and the need for certain qualities to reveal this unity within oneself. The idea of *brahman* encourages us to cultivate these qualities and seek the realisation of the supreme life force within.

Atman

'In the depth of the soul is the Atman, the oversoul. And that oversoul is really love and compassion, peace, joy and wisdom.' - Ram Das

Atman is a concept from Hindu philosophy, specifically from the Advaita Vedanta tradition. It refers to the individual self or soul (*atma*), which is seen as identical to the ultimate reality or *brahman*. According to Advaita Vedanta, the ultimate goal of spiritual practice is to realise the identity of *atman* and *brahman* and thus achieve liberation from the cycle of birth and death.

Purusha

As explained above, *purusha* is a concept from the Sankhya and Yoga schools of Hindu philosophy. It refers to the pure consciousness or spirit that is distinct from the material world and from *prakriti*. *Purusha* refers to the individual self or consciousness that is present in each living being. In some schools of Hindu philosophy, *purusha* is seen as being identical to *brahman*, while in others it is seen as being distinct from *brahman*. According to Sankhya philosophy, *purusha* is considered the seed and *prakriti* the womb that together gave rise to the universe.

Within the framework of Advaita Vedanta, *purusha* can be called *atma* and *brahman* in the sense that the individual self (*atma/purusha*) is considered to be a manifestation or expression of the ultimate reality (*brahman*).

Ishwara

Ishwara refers to a personal god or deity that is worshipped by devotees. It is often seen as a manifestation of *brahman* that is accessible to humans in a more tangible form. *Ishwara* is often depicted with human qualities and is worshipped through various rituals and practices.

Paramatma

Paramatma refers to the supreme or ultimate self that is present in all beings. It is often contrasted with the individual self or *jivatma*. *Paramatma* is said to be present in all beings as a witness or observer and is often associated with the concept of consciousness or awareness.

Both *atma* and *paramatma* are interconnected. *Atma* is the individual soul that resides within a specific living being, while *paramatma* is the universal soul that exists beyond individual identities and encompasses the entirety of creation. *Atma* retains its individuality and experiences the world through the mind and senses of its respective body. It undergoes the cycle of birth and death, seeking liberation (*moksha*) from the cycle of rebirth. On the other hand, *paramatma* is eternal, unchanging, and unaffected by the material world. It is the supreme consciousness and the ultimate goal of spiritual realisation.

While *atma* and *paramatma* are distinct in terms of their individual and universal aspects, they are also considered interconnected. Hindu philosophy emphasises the concept of *advaita*, which means non-duality. It suggests that *atma* and *paramatma* are fundamentally one and the same, with the apparent separation between them being an illusion caused by ignorance. Realising this unity through spiritual practices leads to self-realisation and the experience of oneness with the divine.

In Hindu philosophy, different terms are used to describe the ultimate reality or the supreme soul by different schools. *Brahman* can be referred to as *paramatma*. *Brahman* is often used to denote the absolute reality that transcends all distinctions and is the source of all existence. *Paramatma* is another term used to describe the universal soul, the divine essence that pervades and sustains all creation. Both *brahman* and *paramatma* represent the highest and most expansive understanding of the divine in Hinduism.

While these terms may vary in their usage, they ultimately point to the same underlying truth of the divine reality. The distinction lies in the perspective or focus: *brahman* or *paramatma* represents the all-encompassing, universal aspect, while *atma* represents the individual, personal aspect. However, at the deepest level of realisation, these distinctions are transcended and the ultimate truth of oneness is recognised.

The Relevance of *Tanmatras* in the Study of Human Anatomy and Psychology

The fundamental building blocks of matter as we currently understand them are atoms and subatomic particles such as protons, neutrons, and electrons. Before the Big Bang, the universe was thought to have been in a state of extremely high energy and density, with all matter and energy concentrated into a single point or singularity. The nature of what existed before the Big Bang is still a topic of scientific enquiry and debate, and there are various theories and hypotheses about what might have been present in this pre-Big Bang state. However, there is currently no scientific evidence or theoretical framework that supports the existence of subtle elements or any other non-physical entities in the pre-Big Bang state or in the current universe. Scientific explanations of the universe are based on empirical evidence and are subject to ongoing refinement and revision based on new observations and discoveries.

In the Vedic theory of creation propounded by the Sankhya school, the *tanmatras* play an important role in explaining the origins of the universe and how the physical world was formed from subtle elements. According to this theory, the universe arises from a state of unmanifested potential and the subtle elements gradually become gross matter, giving rise to the physical world, known as *prakriti* (matter), made up, as has been mentioned, of the three *gunas* (qualities): *sattva* (purity), *rajas* (activity), and *tamas* (inertia). It is from *prakriti* that the five subtle elements or *tanmatras* arise. These subtle elements are *shabda* (sound), *sparsha* (sound), *rupa* (sight), *rasa* (taste), and *gandha* (smell), which then combine to form the five gross elements or *mahabhutas*—ether, air, fire, water, and earth—that make up the physical world. Each of the *mahabhutas* consists of the *tanmatras* combined in specific ratios. Thus, *tanmatras* are seen as the subtle building blocks of the physical world.

There are 24 *tanmatras*, out of which five are considered basic, primary, or fundamental, each corresponding to a sense perception and its corresponding motor functions, while the other 19 are considered supplementary or secondary, associated with more subtle aspects of our being, such as the mind, ego, intellect, and consciousness. The 24 *tanmatras* (including *prakriti*) that form the basis of the material world consist of:

- Ten sensory *tanmatras* associated with the five senses (sound, smell, taste, touch, and sight) and their corresponding sense organs (ear, nose, tongue, skin, and eyes).
- Three subtle *tanmatras* associated with the internal faculties: mind (*manas*), intellect (*buddhi* or *mahat*), and ego (*ahankara*).
- Five motor *tanmatras* associated with the motor organs (mouth, hands, feet, anus, and genitals), which allow us to interact with the physical world.
- Five gross elements (*mahabhutas*), which form the physical universe: space (*akasha*), earth (*prithvi*), fire (*tejas*), water (*apas*), and air (*vayu*).

The table below describes *tanmatras* in chronological order of their appearance in the universe:

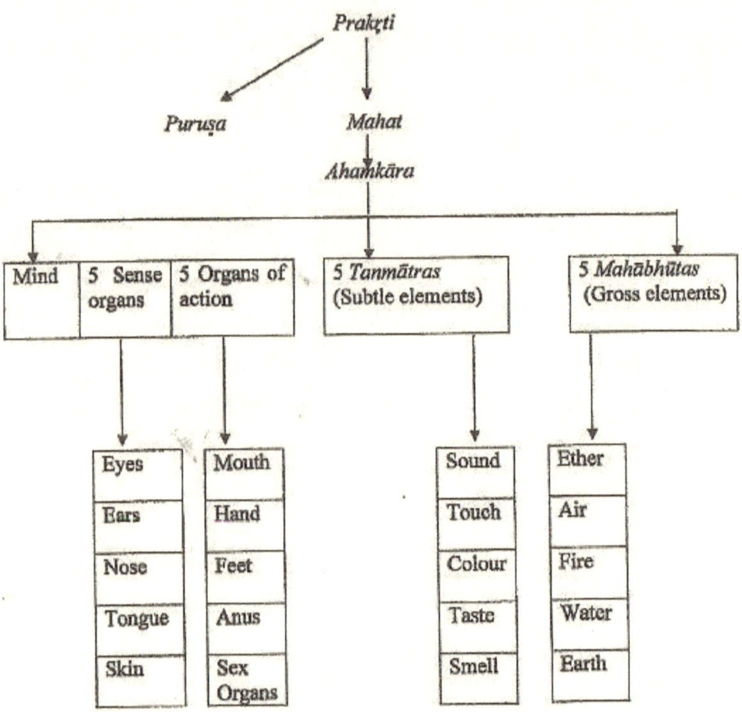

Figure 4

Note: *Purusha* is not considered a *tanmatra*. *Purusha* is beyond the realm of matter and is considered pure consciousness, whereas *tanmatras* belong to the subtle realm of matter. Furthermore, *purusha* is regarded as the observer or witness of the material world, while *tanmatras* are the subtle elements that make up the material world.

By combining and recombining in various ways, the 24 *tanmatras* generate the gross elements—ether, air, fire, water, and earth—that form the universe we perceive through our senses. When our senses come in contact with objects, they gather impressions and transfer them to the mind (*manas*), which then sorts and organises them into precepts. It is important to note that all 24 *tanmatras* are considered interdependent and equally important. They are all part of the same system of subtle elements that form the physical universe and our experience of it. Vedic philosophy describes the universe as a cyclical process of creation, maintenance, and dissolution, with the subtle and gross elements forming the basis of this cycle.

Creation encompasses not just the material world but also living beings, including human beings. In this context, the role of motor organs, or *karmendriyas*, becomes significant. Living beings, including humans, are not only passive recipients of sensory experiences but also active participants in the world. We interact with the environment and engage in various actions using our motor organs. The *karmendriyas* (motor organs) enable us to express ourselves, communicate, move, carry out daily tasks, and engage in other physical actions. The *tanmatras*, as the subtle essences associated with our senses, provide us with the experiences and stimuli that drive our actions. Our sensory perceptions, processed through the *tanmatras*, inform and influence our physical responses through the *karmendriyas*.

According to this theory of creation, all material forms in space and time, including living bodies, arise from the countless combinations of these substantial elements. The association between *tanmatras* and *karmendriyas* (motor organs) lies in the concept that our actions in the material world are driven by our sensory experiences. The *karmendriyas*, which are responsible for performing physical actions, are stimulated and directed by the *tanmatras*. For example, when we see an object (stimulation of the visual *tanmatra*), our hands (*karmendriya*) may reach out to touch or grasp it. Similarly, when we hear a sound (stimulation of the auditory *tanmatra*), our vocal cords (*karmendriya*) may respond by speaking.

While the concept of *tanmatras* in Hinduism and the idea of atoms in quantum mechanics may seem similar in terms of both being regarded as building blocks of the physical world within their respective frameworks, they are fundamentally different in terms of their nature and origin. Atoms are physical particles that are studied and described by science, and they have been observed and measured experimentally. The existence of atoms and our understanding of their behaviour is not a matter of belief or tradition. On the other hand, the concept of *tanmatras* is a part of the philosophical and spiritual traditions of Hinduism, and its origins lie in the ancient texts and scriptures of the religion. *Tanmatras* are not physical particles that can be observed or measured; rather, they are subtle aspects of existence that are believed to underlie the physical world.

Understanding the concept of *tanmatras* can provide insights into the nature of the physical world and the human experience. By recognising the subtle building blocks of the universe and the ways in which the physical body interacts with the external environment, one can gain a deeper understanding of the interconnectedness of all things, the relationship between the physical world and consciousness, and the nature of perception and how we experience the world around us through our senses.

Sankhya philosophy proposes that the ultimate goal of human life is liberation from the cycle of birth and death, which can be achieved through the realisation of the true nature of the self and the world. Understanding the role of *tanmatras* and *karmendriyas* in the creation and experience of the physical world can aid in this pursuit of self-realisation and ultimate liberation.

Furthermore, *tanmatras* help us understand how the material world can influence our body, mind, and intellect. At the core of this understanding is the knowledge that our pure consciousness or self can become clouded by *prakriti*, the material world. We use *naam* (name) and *rupa* (form) to identify and categorise the things we see. *Tanmatras* provide the raw material for our perception of the physical world. However, our mind and intellect play a significant role in shaping how we interpret this raw material. Our understanding of the world is based on the impressions we receive from our senses, and our intellect helps us process these impressions to form a coherent picture of the world around us. Our perception is subjective and therefore what we see is not necessarily the ultimate reality, but rather our interpretation of it. Thus, the material world that we experience is illusory. It is essential, in the journey towards the realisation of our true nature, to avoid getting caught up in the illusions of *prakriti*. Through the concept of *tanmatras*, we can recognise our connection and relationship with the universe, as our composition is the same as that of the universe.

The influence of *tanmatras* on human anatomy and personality is complex and multifaceted. According to Vedic philosophy, each individual has a unique combination of *tanmatras* that determines their physical and psychological makeup. Let's look at the five basic or fundamental subtle elements or *tanmatras* and understand their impact on human personality.

***Shabda* (Sound)**

The first *tanmatra* is *shabda* or sound, which represents the element of ether or space. Ether is considered the subtlest and most pervasive element. Think of it as the canvas on which creation begins. It is associated with the sense of sound—through the subtle vibrations of sound, the process of creation unfolds.

This *tanmatra* is closely associated with the auditory sense, making it particularly relevant for individuals with an auditory personality. These individuals may be more attuned to sound, enjoying music, speech, and other audio-based experiences. They may be particularly sensitive to the tonal quality of voices, as well as the mood or atmosphere created by sounds in their environment.

***Sparsha* (Touch)**

Sparsha or touch represents the element of air. Air manifests after ether. It is the subtle energy that allows us to perceive, touch, and feel things. It is the medium through which sound waves travel, enabling us to hear and experience the world through the sense of touch.

This *tanmatra* is associated with the sense of touch, making it particularly relevant for individuals with a tactile personality. These individuals may be particularly sensitive to the sensations of touch and may tend to enjoy physical activities such as massages, yoga, and sports. They may also enjoy tactile experiences in their environment, such as the feeling of a cool breeze on their skin or the textures of different fabrics.

Rupa **(Sight)**

Rupa or sight represents the element of fire. Fire is generated through the interaction of air with friction. It embodies the qualities of sound, touch, and illumination. When we see something, it is the result of light reflecting off objects and entering our eyes. This is made possible through the *tanmatra* of *rupa*.

The *rupa tanmatra* is associated with the visual sense, making it particularly relevant for individuals with a visual personality. Such individuals may be more attuned to the appearance of their surroundings and may tend to enjoy beautiful landscapes, artwork, or architecture. They may be particularly sensitive to the colours and shapes in their environment and may find visual symmetry and balance to be particularly pleasing.

Rasa **(Taste)**

Rasa or taste represents the element of water. Water arises from the condensation of fire. It encompasses the qualities of sound, touch, sight, and fluidity. It is through the *tanmatra* of *rasa* that we experience the flavours and sensations associated with different foods and drinks.

This *tanmatra* is associated with the sense of taste, making it particularly relevant for individuals with a gustatory personality.

These individuals may be more attuned to the flavours of food and drink and may enjoy experimenting with different taste sensations. They may find pleasure in the textures and sensations of food and may enjoy the process of cooking and creating their own dishes.

Gandha (Smell)

Gandha or smell represents the element of earth. Earth is the densest and most solid element. It arises from the cohesion of water. The *tanmatra* of *gandha* encompasses the qualities of sound, touch, sight, and taste and the ability to emit various smells. It is through this *tanmatra* that we perceive different scents and fragrances in our environment.

The *gandha tanmatra* is associated with the sense of smell, making it particularly relevant for individuals with an olfactory personality. Such individuals may be particularly sensitive to different scents and aromas and may tend to enjoy the rich sensory experience that comes with experiencing new and different smells. They may enjoy exploring natural environments, such as forests and gardens, and may find pleasure in the scents of fresh flowers, herbs, and other botanicals.

Understanding the relationship between the *tanmatras* and different sensory experiences can be helpful in:

Building stronger relationships. By understanding someone's sensory preferences, we can tailor our interactions with them to establish stronger connections. For instance, if we know someone has a visual personality, we can choose visual aids or imagery to help convey messages to them. If someone has an olfactory personality, we can incorporate scents into our interactions to make them more enjoyable and memorable.

Creating more engaging experiences. Understanding the different sensory experiences associated with each *tanmatra* can help us create more engaging experiences for ourselves and others. For instance, we might create a visually stimulating environment for someone with a visual personality or incorporate a variety of flavours and textures for someone with a gustatory personality.

Developing self-awareness. Understanding our own sensory preferences can help us become more self-aware and better at managing our emotional and physical well-being. For instance, if we know we have a tactile personality, we might seek out physical activities or tactile experiences to help us feel more grounded and connected.

Enhancing creativity. By exploring different sensory experiences, we can stimulate our creativity and come up with new ideas and approaches. For instance, we might use visual imagery or different scents to spark our imagination and help us generate new ideas.

Overall, understanding the relationship between the five subtle elements and different sensory experiences can help us better appreciate the rich diversity of human experience and create more meaningful connections and experiences for ourselves and others.

The *tanmatras* are believed to interact with the three *gunas* (*sattva*, *rajas*, and *tamas*) to give rise to the gross physical world and all its manifestations. According to Sankhya philosophy, an imbalance in the interaction of the *tanmatras* with the *gunas* can lead to physical and mental health issues. For example, an excess of *tamas* can lead to lethargy, depression, and other mental health issues, while an excess of *rajas* can lead to agitation, anxiety, and stress. Therefore, understanding this relationship will help ensure our well-being and allow for a meaningful and purposeful life.

Unlocking the Power Of Nature: The Influence of the Five Gross Elements on Our Body and Mind

In many spiritual traditions, including those of the Indian subcontinent and China, human beings are believed to be made up of five fundamental elements: ether (or space), wind (or air), fire, earth, and water. These elements are seen as representing different aspects of the natural world. In Sanskrit, these elements are known as the *pancha bhutas* or *panchamahabhutas*. They are the building blocks of the universe; every person, animal, plant, and thing is made up of various combinations of the *pancha bhutas*.

The *Pancha Bhutas*

Earth (*Prithvi*): Earth represents stability, support, and solidity. It is associated with the sense of smell, and the corresponding sense organ is the nose. Earth is said to provide a sense of grounding and stability and is often associated with the physical body.

Water (*Ap*): Water represents fluidity, adaptability, and change. It is associated with the sense of taste, and the corresponding sense organ is the tongue. Water is said to have a cleansing and purifying effect and is often associated with emotions and the flow of energy.

Fire (*Tejas*): Fire represents transformation, illumination, and energy. It is associated with the sense of sight, and the corresponding sense organs are the eyes. Fire is said to provide warmth, light, and energy, and is often associated with the power of transformation.

Air (*Vayu*): Air represents movement, flexibility, and expansion. It is associated with the sense of touch, and the corresponding sense organ is the skin. Air is said to provide movement and expansion and is often associated with the power of communication and expression.

Space (*Akasha*): Space represents expansion, openness, and emptiness. It is associated with the sense of hearing and the corresponding sense organs are the ears. Space allows all things to exist and is often associated with the power of consciousness and awareness.

According to the *pancha bhuta* philosophy, everything in the physical universe is made up of these five elements in various proportions. Each element has its own unique qualities and characteristics, and they work together in harmony to create and sustain the world we live in. Ayurveda uses the *pancha bhuta* framework to understand the nature of different substances and how they affect the body and mind. It is believed that balancing the five elements within the body can help promote health and well-being, while an imbalance can lead to disease and illness. In Hinduism and Buddhism, the *pancha bhuta* philosophy is used as a tool for spiritual growth and enlightenment. By understanding the nature of the five elements and their role in the physical universe, individuals can gain a deeper understanding of their own true nature and the nature of the world around them.

In the context of spiritual intelligence, the recognition of these five elements can be helpful in understanding the interconnectedness of all things and in developing a deeper sense of connection with the natural world. For example, by recognising that we are made up of the same elements as the earth, water, and sky, we can begin to see ourselves as part of a larger web of life rather than as separate individuals. By comprehending our profound interconnectedness with the *pancha bhuta* or gross elements, we transcend the confines of conditioned thinking that limit our perception of the universe. Instead of perceiving ourselves as finite beings, we recognise the infinite nature of our existence. This expanded awareness brings a sense of liberation, allowing us to tap into our boundless potential.

By using the framework of these five elements, we can gain insights into different aspects of our inner experiences, emotions, thoughts, desires, and how they interact and shape our overall well-being. It allows for a holistic perspective on our inner world and can be used as a tool for self-reflection, growth, and understanding. Each element represents something about us: earth is our physical body, water is emotion, fire is passion, air is thought, and ether is awareness. This framework highlights the fact that emotions and thoughts affect each other and helps us reflect on ourselves to achieve personal growth.

Earth, water, fire, air, and ether or space are believed to be the building blocks of all matter, including the human body. The human body is composed of approximately 60–70% water, depending on factors such as age, sex, and overall health. However, the concept of the five gross elements in ancient Indian philosophy is not based on scientific measurements or percentages, but rather on a metaphysical understanding of the universe and the interdependence of its elements. Modern science also holds that the human body is also made up of these five elements, but they are known by different names and are described in terms of molecules and atoms. For example, the metaphysical element earth corresponds to the chemical element carbon, which is a major component of the human body's organic molecules, such as proteins, fats, and DNA. Water corresponds to hydrogen and oxygen, which make up the majority of the body's fluids, while fire corresponds to energy and metabolism, and air corresponds to the respiratory system. However, unlike in metaphysics, modern science does not assign specific proportions to these elements in the human body. Instead, the body is described in terms of its chemical and physical properties and its functions are explained through biological processes and systems.

In the context of eastern philosophy, the five gross elements are believed to be present in all living beings and natural phenomena, including the human body. Each element is associated with certain qualities and characteristics that contribute to the physical and metaphysical aspects of life. According to ayurveda, the proportion of each element in the human body varies depending on an individual's constitution or *dosha*. The three *doshas* are *vata* (air and ether), *pitta* (fire and water), and *kapha* (earth and water), and each person has a unique balance of these elements that affects their physical, mental, and emotional characteristics.

By working with these elements in a conscious way, we can begin to cultivate a deeper sense of balance and harmony in our lives. For example, if we feel ungrounded or scattered, we might focus on earth energy, perhaps by spending time in nature, practising yoga, jogging, or eating foods that grow in the ground. If we feel stuck or stagnant, we might focus on water energy, perhaps by spending time near bodies of water or by practising emotional release techniques. Ultimately, the recognition of the five elements can be a powerful tool for developing spiritual intelligence, as it can help us see ourselves and the world around us in a more holistic and interconnected way. By recognising the beauty and complexity of the natural world and by working to harmonise our own inner world with the rhythms of the universe, we can cultivate a deep sense of peace, purpose, and fulfilment in our lives.

The three *doshas* (defects)—*vata*, *pitta*, and *kapha*—are believed to be the three basic energies that govern the body and mind. Each person has a unique combination of these *doshas*, which determines their physical and psychological characteristics, as well as their vulnerability to certain health issues. The *vata dosha* is associated with the elements of air and ether and is responsible for movement, creativity, and flexibility. An imbalance in *vata* can lead to anxiety, fear, and restlessness. The *pitta dosha* is associated with the elements of fire and water and is responsible for digestion, metabolism, and energy production. An imbalance in *pitta* can lead to anger, frustration, and irritability. The *kapha dosha* is associated with the elements of earth and water and is responsible for structure, stability, and nourishment. An imbalance in *kapha* can lead to lethargy, depression, and attachment.

According to ayurveda, an imbalance in any of these *doshas* can lead to mood swings and other mental as well as physical health issues. For example, an excess of *pitta* can lead to irritability and anger, while an excess of *kapha* can lead to depression and lethargy. During times of stress and uncertainty, our *doshas* may become imbalanced. The goal is to bring attention to our *doshas* and to understand how they affect us so we can work to restore balance. Balancing the *doshas* through diet, lifestyle, and other therapies is believed to promote physical and mental health and prevent imbalances that cause mood swings and emotional disturbances. Spiritually aligned people are aware of this phenomenon and achieve the optimal balance through mindfulness, yoga practices, and food habits.

Leveraging Health, Creativity and Well-being Through Prana, Tejas, and Oja

Prana, *tejas*, and *ojas* are the counterparts of *vata*, *pitta*, and *kapha*. Unlike the *doshas*, which in excess cause diseases, these three energies are believed by ayurvedic practitioners to promote health, creativity, and well-being when they are kept in balance, which can be achieved through yoga, a proper diet, exercise, meditation, control over the senses, devotion, and herbal remedies. Ayurveda seeks to reduce disease, particularly chronic diseases, and increase positive health in the body and mind through these three vital essences that aid in renewal and transformation.

Prana

Prana refers to the life force or vital energy that sustains all living beings. It is said to be the force that animates all physical and mental processes in the body and is essential for maintaining good health and vitality. Increased *prana* is associated with enthusiasm, adaptability, and creativity, all of which are considered necessary when pursuing a spiritual path in yoga and in enabling one to perform various physical and mental practices with heightened focus and energy. It is believed that a balanced and abundant *prana* flow can deepen the practitioner's connection to the inner self, enhance self-awareness, and foster a sense of inner peace and harmony, thus supporting their journey towards spiritual growth and self-realisation.

Tejas

Tejas is the subtle essence of fire or heat in the body. It is responsible for digestion, metabolism, and the transformation of food into energy. It is also associated with mental clarity, sharpness, intelligence, courage, fearlessness, and insight and is particularly important when one is making decisions.

Ojas

Ojas is the subtle essence of the body's fluids, particularly those that nourish the reproductive and nervous systems. It is said to be the source of physical and mental endurance, immunity, and overall vitality. Lastly, *ojas* is said to impart peace, confidence, and patience, thereby enabling continued effort and consistent development. Eventually, the most important element to develop is *ojas*, as it is believed to strengthen physical and psychological endurance.

***Dosha* (Defects)**	***Bhuta* (Elements) Composition**	***Manasa Dosha* (*Guna*)**	**Characteristic**
Vata	*Vayu, akasa*	*Sattva*	*Prana*, the life force and the healing energy of *vata* (air)
Pitta	*Agni, jala/apas*	*Rajas*	*Tejas*, inner radiance and the healing energy of *pitta* (fire)
Kapha	*Prithvi, jala/ apas*	*Tamas*	*Ojas*, the ultimate energy reserve of the body, derived from *kapha* (water)

Unlocking Your Vital Energy: Exploring *Chakras* and Energy Channels

In order to tap into spiritual intelligence, we need to understand the various aspects of our being, including our physical and subtle bodies, and the role that our thoughts, emotions, and beliefs play in shaping our experiences.

The *chakras*, according to Hindu and yogic traditions, are energy centres located along the spine that correspond to different aspects of the body, mind, and spirit. According to Vedic science, there are over 100 *chakras* in our *sukshma sharira* or subtle body, but seven *chakras* are the most prominent and influential in shaping our personality and character. These seven *chakras* are located along the spine and correspond to different aspects of our being, such as our physical, emotional, mental, and spiritual states.

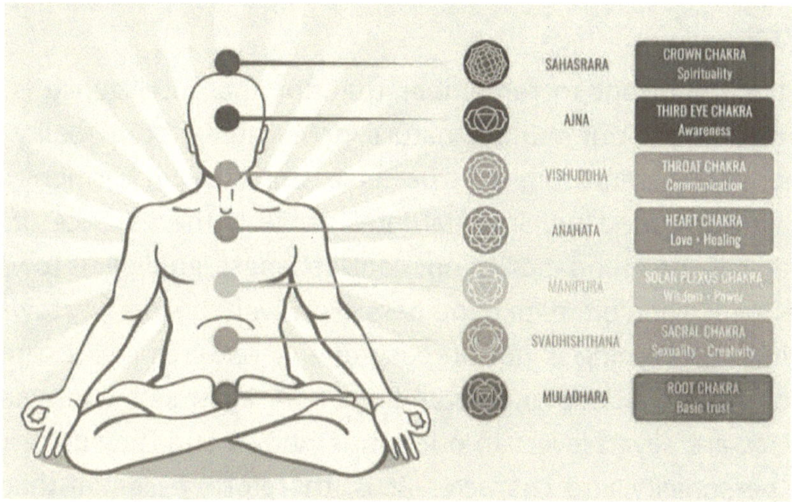

Figure 5

The first three *chakras*—*muladhara* (root), *swadhisthana* (sacral), and *manipura* (solar plexus)—are located in the lower part of the body and are associated with our survival instincts, emotions, and personal power. When these *chakras* are overactive, they can lead to negative qualities such as anger, greed, lust, and ignorance.

To connect with our true identity and higher consciousness, we need to focus on the higher *chakras*, such as *anahat* (heart), *vishuddhi* (throat), *ajana* (third eye), and *sahasrara* (crown). These *chakras* are associated with qualities such as love, communication, intuition, and wisdom and are essential to the development of spiritual intelligence. When we activate and balance these *chakras* through practices such as visualisation, meditation, and *kundalini* awakening, we experience a profound transformation in our lives. We become more aware of our true nature and our connection to the cosmos and are able to tap into our innate wisdom and spiritual power. However, in order to fully tap into our spiritual intelligence, we need to overcome the vices that are enemies of human beings, such as anger, greed, and lust. These vices emerge as a result of focusing too much on the lower *chakras* and can be overcome through practices such as mindfulness, self-awareness, and self-control.

It is important to remember that spiritual intelligence is not about denying our human nature or escaping from reality but rather about embracing our true selves and living in harmony with the world around us. Spiritual intelligence is the essence of our being. It is the foundation of our consciousness, guiding us towards inner peace and ultimate happiness. However, the journey towards spiritual awakening is not an easy one. It requires self-discipline, devotion, and a deep understanding of our inner self. These seven *chakras* are seven levers in our subtle bodies and they determine our personality and character. It is, therefore, essential that we remain conscious of and focus on these *chakras* to define who we are.

Leveraging the Five Gross Elements to Balance the *Chakras*

Each *chakra* is associated with one of the five elements, and balancing the elements can help balance the *chakras*.

Earth (*Prithvi*): The earth element is associated with the root *chakra*, located at the base of the spine. To balance this *chakra* and the earth element, try grounding practices such as walking barefoot in nature, gardening, or yoga postures that focus on the lower body.

Water (*Ap*): The water element is associated with the sacral *chakra*, located in the lower abdomen. To balance this *chakra* and the water element, try practices that promote emotional awareness and flow, such as journalling, dancing, or hip-opening yoga postures.

Fire (*Tejas*): The fire element is associated with the solar plexus *chakra*, located in the upper abdomen. To balance this *chakra* and the fire element, try practices that promote transformation and energy, such as breath work, physical exercise, or core-strengthening yoga postures.

Air (*Vayu*): The air element is associated with the heart *chakra*, located in the centre of the chest. To balance this *chakra* and the air element, try practices that promote connection and expansion, such as loving-kindness meditation, social activities, or heart-opening yoga postures.

Space (*Akasha*): The space element is associated with the throat *chakra*, located in the throat. It is also associated with the third eye and crown *chakras*. To balance this *chakra* and the space element, try practices that promote communication and expression, such as chanting or singing, public speaking or writing, or throat-opening yoga postures.

By leveraging the five elements in these ways, individuals can balance the *chakras* and promote overall health and well-being. It is important to note that this is a holistic approach, and individuals should also seek out medical advice and care as needed.

The Power Within: *Kundalini Jagruti Kundalini* and Inner Awakening

One of the most powerful tools for spiritual awakening is *kundalini jagruti*. This process involves awakening the dormant *kundalini* energy that resides at the base of the spine in a serpentine form and then raising it up through the central energy channel, called the *sushumna nadi*, that runs from the base of the spine to the crown of the head. This process is facilitated by the activation of the *ida* and *pingala nadis*, which help to purify and balance the flow of energy in the body.

The activation of the *ida* and *pingala nadis* is accomplished through various techniques, such as *pranayama* (breathing exercises), *asanas* (postures), and meditation. These practices help to stimulate the flow of energy through the *nadis*, allowing the *kundalini* energy to rise up through the *sushumna nadi* and activate each of the *chakras* in turn.

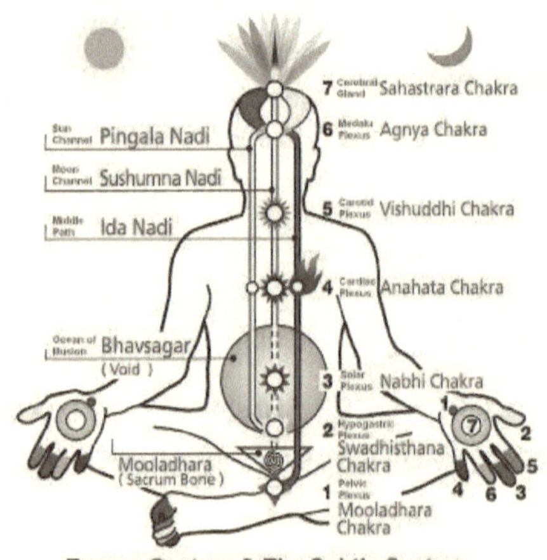

Figure 6

The impact of the *kundalini jagruti* process can be profound and transformative. Some of the reported benefits of this practice include:

Increased spiritual awareness. The awakening of the *kundalini* energy is said to lead to a profound sense of spiritual awareness and connection to the divine.

Greater physical health. The *kundalini* energy is believed to have a positive impact on physical health, helping to release tension and blockages in the body and promoting overall well-being.

Enhanced creativity and intuition. As the *kundalini* energy rises through the *chakras*, it is believed to activate our creative and intuitive abilities, leading to insights and inspiration.

Greater emotional balance. The *kundalini jagruti* process can help us achieve emotional balance and stability, leading to a sense of inner peace and well-being.

This energy is often described as a coiled serpent, hence the name *kundalini*. The concept of *kundalini* awakening has roots in Hinduism and is also found in other spiritual traditions, including Buddhism and Taoism. In Hinduism, *kundalini* is associated with the goddess Shakti, who represents the feminine creative energy of the universe. *Kundalini* awakening is said to bring about a range of experiences, including feelings of intense heat or energy, vibrations, and visions. These experiences are often described as being transformative and life-changing. Some people report feeling a sense of unity with the universe or a deep connection to a higher power. However, *kundalini* awakening can also be accompanied by negative experiences, such as physical discomfort, emotional turmoil, and even psychosis. This is why it is important to approach the awakening process with caution and to seek guidance from a qualified spiritual teacher or practitioner. It is important to approach these practices with respect and a willingness to surrender to the process. It is also important to note that *kundalini* awakening is not an end in itself. Rather, it is a natural part of the spiritual journey that can lead to greater awareness and understanding.

Pancha Prana

The concept of *prana* is also central to many spiritual and philosophical traditions, including yoga, ayurveda, and *tantra*. In the context of spiritual realisation, *prana* is seen as an essential component of our existence and an important tool for accessing higher states of consciousness. The five *pranas*, or *pancha prana*, are regarded as the different aspects or expressions of *prana* that govern various bodily functions and processes.

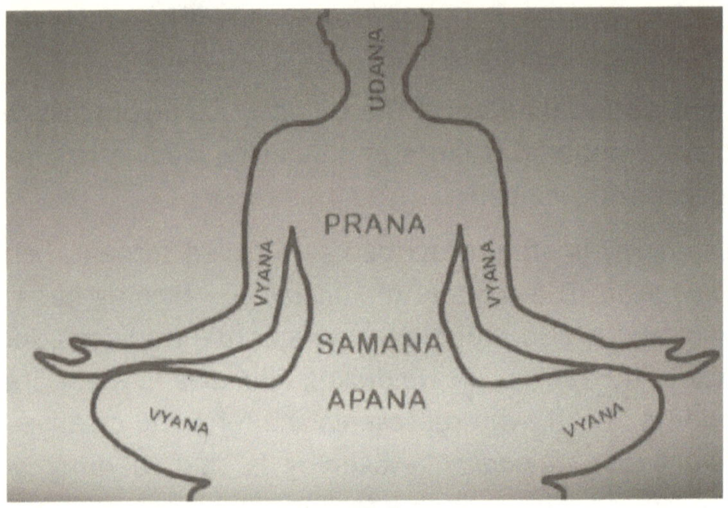

Figure 7

The five elements of *prana* (vital energy) are:

1. ***Prana***: The upward-moving energy that governs inhalation and is responsible for taking in oxygen and other vital substances.
2. ***Apana***: The downward-moving energy that governs exhalation and is responsible for eliminating waste products from the body.
3. ***Samana***: The energy that governs digestion and assimilation of food and is responsible for maintaining balance in the body.
4. ***Udana*:** The energy that governs speech, expression, and upward movement in the body, such as in the process of standing up.
5. ***Vyana***: The energy that pervades the entire body and is responsible for circulation, coordination, and movement.

Each of these five *pranas* has a specific role and function in the body, and when they are balanced and functioning properly, they can support spiritual realisation and growth. For example, the practice of *pranayama*, or breath control, can help to balance the *pranas* and bring about greater awareness and control over the mind and body. By regulating the breath and directing the flow of *prana*, one can access deeper levels of consciousness and connect with the divine. The five *pranas* are also associated with the five elements—earth, water, fire, air, and ether. By working with the *pranas*, one can also connect with and harness the power of these elemental energies for spiritual growth and transformation. Overall, the five *pranas* are seen as essential components of the spiritual path, providing a foundation for physical health, mental clarity, and spiritual intelligence.

Activating *Pranas* to Stimulate *Chakras*

The five *pranas* are closely related to the seven *chakras*, which are the energy centres in the body that correspond to specific physical, emotional, and spiritual functions. Each *chakra* is associated with one or more of the five *pranas*, and activating these *pranas* can help balance the flow of energy in the *chakras*.

1. ***Apana prana-muladhara chakra.*** *Apana prana* is associated with the *muladhara* or root *chakra*, which is located at the base of the spine. This *chakra* governs our sense of stability, security, and being grounded. Activating *apana prana* can help stimulate the root *chakra* and promote a sense of stability and security in the body. This is responsible for all excretory and reproductive functions and governs the large intestine, kidneys, anus, and genitals. It is associated with the element of water.
2. ***Madhyana/samana prana-manipura chakra.*** *Madhyana* or *samana prana* is associated with the *manipura chakra*, which

is located near the navel. It is responsible for all digestive and metabolic functions and the circulatory system and governs the heart, liver, small intestine, stomach, and pancreas and their secretions. It is associated with the element of fire.

3. ***Prana–anahata chakra.*** *Prana* is associated with the *anahata* or heart *chakra*. This governs the lungs, larynx, and chest region. It is the force by which air is drawn into the body. It is associated with the element of air.
4. ***Udana prana–vishuddha chakra.*** *Udana prana* is associated with the *vishuddha* or throat *chakra*, which is located in the throat. This *chakra* governs our ability to communicate, express ourselves, and speak our truth. Activating *udana prana* can help stimulate throat *chakras* and promote healthy communication and self-expression.
5. ***Vyana prana*–all *chakras.*** *Vyana prana* is associated with all of the *chakras*, as it governs the overall flow of energy in the body. However, it is particularly associated with the *manipura chakra*, which governs our sense of personal power, confidence, and self-esteem. Activating *vyana prana* can help balance the flow of energy throughout the body and promote a sense of personal power and confidence.

The activating process for each *prana* involves various yoga practices, such as specific *asanas* (yoga poses), *pranayama* (breathing exercises), and meditation techniques. For example, to activate *apana prana*, you might practise grounding yoga poses such as the tree pose, the mountain pose, or the warrior poses, as well as gentle twists to stimulate the digestive organs. To activate *udana prana*, you might practise inverted yoga poses, such as the shoulder stand or headstand, as well as visualisation techniques that focus on the crown *chakra*. To activate *prana*, you might practise yoga poses that open the chest and throat, such as the cobra pose or the fish pose, as well as chanting or singing to activate the voice and connect with the energetic qualities of *prana*.

Prana and *Kundalini* Awakening

The concept of *prana* is closely related to *kundalini* awakening. In fact, the awakening of *kundalini* is said to be accompanied by a surge of *pranic* energy that rises up through the *chakras* and activates various psychic centres in the body. As the *kundalini* energy rises, it can trigger various physical and energetic phenomena, such as intense heat, vibrations, and waves of energy. These experiences are often associated with the movement of *pranic* energy through the body.

The balance and flow of *prana* are also seen as essential to the process of *kundalini* awakening. When the *pranic* channels, or *nadis*, are blocked or imbalanced, the flow of *kundalini* energy is impeded, and this can cause discomfort or even harm. Practices such as *pranayama*, meditation, and yoga are often used to balance and purify the *pranic* channels and prepare the body for the awakening of *kundalini*.

Kundalini awakening is an important step towards spiritual intelligence, as it awakens the cosmic intelligence within us. It triggers the release of stagnant energy and blockages, which in turn enables us to experience divine power and knowledge. It enables us to overcome our vices, recognise our true identity, and connect with the cosmos.

The Cosmic Awakening: The Power of Yoga to Expand Your Consciousness

While all forms of yoga can be beneficial for overall health and well-being, there are certain schools of yoga that are particularly useful and effective for awakening the *kundalini*.

Kundalini Yoga

As the name suggests, this school of yoga is specifically designed to awaken the *kundalini*. It involves a combination of physical postures, breathing exercises, chanting, and meditation techniques that are specifically aimed at activating the energy centres in the body and move the energy thus produced up through the *chakras* to the crown of the head.

The *kundalini* yoga school was founded by Yogi Bhajan in the late 1960s. Yogi Bhajan was a Sikh spiritual teacher who took *kundalini* yoga from India to the United States. He believed that this comprehensive approach to spiritual practice that integrates physical, mental, and spiritual aspects of the self could help people in the modern world cope with the stresses and challenges of daily life and help them connect with their higher selves.

The practice of *kundalini* yoga involves a series of physical postures and movements, called *kriyas*, which are designed to stimulate the body's *chakras*. Each *kriya* is designed to address a specific aspect of the body, mind, or spirit and may include movements, breathing exercises, and chanting. *Kundalini* yoga also involves the use of mantras, or sacred sounds, which are chanted to help focus the mind and open the heart. These mantras are believed to have powerful vibrations that can help transform the practitioner's consciousness.

Another important aspect of *kundalini* yoga is the use of *pranayama* or breathwork. The breath is seen as a powerful tool for connecting with the body and the mind and for stimulating *kundalini* energy. Various techniques are used to control and regulate the breath, including deep breathing, 'breath of fire', and alternate nostril breathing. Meditation is also an integral part of *kundalini* yoga practice. Through meditation, practitioners can learn to quiet the mind, focus their attention, and connect with their inner selves. Many different meditation techniques are used in *kundalini* yoga, including mantra meditation, breath meditation, and visualisation.

Hatha Yoga

This is the most commonly practised form of yoga and involves a series of physical postures (*asanas*) and breathing techniques (*pranayama*) that aim to balance the body and mind. Many of the *asanas* in *hatha* yoga are designed to activate the energy centres in the body and stimulate the flow of *prana* throughout the body. *Hatha* yoga is a branch of yoga that focuses on physical postures, breathing techniques, and meditation to achieve a healthy and balanced mind and body. It is one of the most popular forms of yoga and has gained popularity in recent years due to its emphasis on improving flexibility, strength, and overall health.

The word *hatha* comes from two Sanskrit words: *ha*, which means sun, and *tha*, which means moon. As this name indicates, *hatha* yoga aims to balance the two opposing energies within us—the active energy of the sun and the calm and restful energy of the moon. The practice of *hatha* yoga involves a series of physical postures or *asanas* that are designed to stretch and strengthen the body as well as improve flexibility, balance, and endurance. These postures are often held for several breaths and are meant to be practised slowly and with focused attention.

Pranayama is also an essential part of *hatha* yoga practice. *Pranayama* techniques help increase the flow of oxygen to the body, reduce stress, and calm the mind. Some common *pranayama* techniques include deep breathing, alternate nostril breathing, and breath retention.

Meditation is another integral part of *hatha* yoga practice. It involves sitting quietly and focusing the mind on a single point, such as the breath or a mantra. This helps reduce stress, increase focus and concentration, and promote a sense of inner peace and calm. *Hatha* yoga is suitable for practitioners of all levels, from beginners to advanced practitioners. It is a gentle form of exercise that can be adapted to suit the needs and abilities of the individual practitioner. Regular practice of *hatha* yoga has been shown to have numerous health benefits, including improved cardiovascular health, increased flexibility, and reduced stress and anxiety.

While *hatha* yoga and Patanjali's nine *lingas* share some similarities, such as the use of *asanas* and *pranayama*, they differ in their approach and focus. *Hatha* yoga is more focused on the physical aspect of yoga and its effects on the body and mind, while Patanjali's nine *lingas* provide a holistic framework for spiritual growth and self-realisation through the practice of yoga.

Tantra Yoga

Tantra yoga is a branch of yoga that originated in ancient India and is based on the principles of *tantra*, a spiritual and philosophical system that seeks to unite the polarities of the universe and achieve a state of oneness or unity with the divine. It is closely associated with Shaivism. *Tantra* yoga is a holistic approach to yoga that combines physical postures, breathing techniques, meditation, and the use of mantras and other spiritual practices to achieve spiritual growth and self-realisation.

Tantra yoga, which involves a variety of *asanas* designed to balance the energy in the body, improve flexibility, and strengthen the muscles, is often associated with the practice of *kundalini* yoga. However, these *tantric* postures are often held for longer periods of time than in other forms of yoga. Breathing techniques (*pranayama*) also constitute an important part of *tantra* yoga. These techniques are designed to control the flow of *prana* or life force energy in the body and can help reduce stress, increase focus and concentration, and promote a sense of inner peace and calm.

Meditation in *tantra* yoga practice involves sitting quietly and focusing the mind on a single point, such as the breath or a mantra. Through the practice of meditation, one can develop a deeper understanding of the self and cultivate inner peace and harmony. The use of mantras or sacred sounds is also an important aspect of *tantra* yoga. Mantras are chanted or recited in a rhythmic manner to focus the mind and cultivate a sense of inner peace and harmony. These mantras are often associated with different *chakras* or energy centres of the body and can be used to balance the energy in the body and achieve spiritual growth.

Pancha Makara

There are five symbolic items used in certain *tantric* practices, known as the *pancha makara* or five Ms.

1. ***Madya* (Wine)**. This represents the liquid aspect or fluidity in the universe. It is a symbol of the nectar of spiritual bliss or divine ecstasy.
2. ***Mamsa* (Meat)**. This represents the solid aspect or physicality in the universe. It is a symbol of the nourishing power of the universe.
3. ***Matsya* (Fish).** This represents the aspect of movement in the universe. It is a symbol of the life force energy that animates all beings.
4. ***Mudra* (Grain)**. This represents the aspect of subtle energy in the universe, the energy that sustains life and connects all beings.
5. ***Maithuna* (Sexual Union).** This represents the aspect of creation or procreation in the universe. It is a symbol of the union of opposites and the merging of the individual self with the divine.

The use of the five Ms in *tantra* yoga is meant to be taken not literally but symbolically. These concepts are used to tap into the energy and symbolism associated with them and thereby achieve spiritual growth and transformation. They are typically used only in certain *tantric* practices and are not a part of mainstream *tantra* yoga practice. It is important to note that the use of the five Ms should only be undertaken under the guidance of a qualified teacher, as they can be potentially dangerous if not used correctly.

Tantra vs. Yoga

Tantra and yoga are seemingly two sides of the same coin; the contrasts between them draw attention to the pros and cons of indulgence and suppression respectively. *Tantra* advocates indulging desires, greed, and ego with awareness. It encourages people to be mindful and fully present when they engage with their desires. According to *tantra*, acting with complete awareness ensures that one will never make a mistake. When someone desires something with awareness, they may come to realise that their desire was trivial. *Tantra* provides the freedom to act with the understanding that freedom comes with responsibility.

On the other hand, other schools of yoga advocate the suppression of desires, greed, and ego with awareness. Suppression is not seen as negative but rather as a way of bringing discipline to the elements that govern one's life. Two of the eight limbs of yoga—*niyama* (self-discipline) and *pratyahara* (the withdrawal of senses)—focus on the skill of suppression. When people are conscious that they are suppressing their senses, they can undergo a transformation.

Sexual energy is also addressed in both *tantra* and yoga. *Tantra* suggests that sexual energy is a powerful force that dominates human awareness more than any other energy. Rather than seeing it as a taboo or negative force, *tantra* encourages individuals to channel this energy in a positive way and use it for spiritual awakening. Although some may struggle to comprehend this approach, understanding how to transform sexual energy can lead to a profound transformation. *Tantra* does not advocate promiscuity but encourages individuals to transcend the physical realm and move beyond sex. Additionally, *tantra*'s teachings on sexuality can promote healthy understanding and prevent sexual abuse.

On the other hand, yoga advocates the suppression of sexual energy, advancing the view that sexual energy can disrupt our senses and prevent us from experiencing higher states of consciousness. However, yoga views sexual suppression not in a negative way but as a way of calming and ceasing sexual energy. Practising yoga correctly can offer insights into this process, and advanced practitioners can guide others in this practice.

While these are two distinct approaches to spiritual practice, both yoga and *tantra* can lead to the same destination. Individuals can meditate or seek guidance from a divine source to determine which path they are best suited to. Ultimately, both practices have a lot in common and can help individuals build a disciplined spiritual path.

Kriya Yoga

Kriya yoga is a form of yoga that focuses on the internal practices of *pranayama* and meditation. It aims to purify the energy channels in the body and awaken *kundalini* energy to achieve spiritual enlightenment. *Kriya* yoga shares some similarities with *hatha*, Patanjali, and *tantra* yoga, but it also has its own unique practices and approach. Here are some ways that *kriya* yoga differs from these other forms of yoga:

1. **Techniques**. While *kriya* yoga incorporates elements of breath control (*pranayama*), meditation, and self-reflection like other forms of yoga, it also includes a specific set of techniques that are unique to *kriya* yoga. These techniques are designed to awaken the dormant spiritual energy within the body and to purify the mind and emotions.

2. **Emphasis on spiritual growth.** While other forms of yoga may focus on physical health and well-being, *kriya* yoga places a strong emphasis on spiritual growth and transformation. The practice of *kriya* yoga is intended to help practitioners connect with their true nature as spiritual beings and to overcome negative patterns of thought and behaviour.
3. **Lineage**. *Kriya* yoga is associated with a specific lineage of teachers that can be traced back to the Indian yogi Mahavatar Babaji, who is said to have taught the techniques to his disciple Lahiri Mahasaya in the 19th century. This lineage is often seen as an important part of the practice of *kriya* yoga.
4. **Emphasis on the importance of teachers.** While all forms of yoga benefit from the guidance of a qualified teacher, *krlya* yoga places particular emphasis on the role of the teacher in guiding students through the techniques and ensuring that they are practised correctly.

Raja Yoga

Raja yoga, as outlined in Sanskrit texts, serves as both the ultimate aim of yoga and a means to attain it. In the 19th century, Swami Vivekananda's interpretation of Patanjali's Yoga Sutras led to the term being associated with the practice of yoga, and it became known as *raja* yoga. Over time, it also gathered alternative names like *ashtang* yoga, royal yoga, royal union, *sahaja marg*, and classical yoga.

Raja yoga involves a combination of physical postures, breathing exercises, and meditation techniques that aim to control the mind and achieve spiritual awakening. Many of the practices in *raja* yoga are designed to awaken *kundalini* energy and raise it through the *chakras*. The practice of *raja* yoga involves developing self-awareness, self-discipline, and mental focus to achieve spiritual enlightenment and inner peace. It is a challenging but rewarding path that requires commitment, practice, and guidance from an experienced teacher.

Raja yoga and Patanjali yoga are two terms that are sometimes used interchangeably, as they both refer to the classical yoga system outlined by Patanjali in the Yoga Sutras. However, there are some subtle differences between the two. Patanjali yoga, also known as classical yoga, is a comprehensive system of yoga that includes a wide range of practices, such as ethical guidelines, physical postures, breath control, meditation, and self-realisation. Patanjali's Yoga Sutras outline the eight limbs, or steps, of yoga, which include *yama* (ethical principles), *niyama* (self-discipline), *asana* (physical postures), *pranayama* (breath control), *pratyahara* (withdrawal of the senses), *dharana* (concentration), *dhyana* (meditation), and *samadhi* (enlightenment). *Raja* yoga, on the other hand, is a specific path of yoga that emphasises the practice of meditation and self-discipline as a means of achieving self-realisation and spiritual enlightenment. The reason *raja* yoga is sometimes referred to as 'royal yoga' is that it is said to be the highest and most comprehensive form of yoga.

While both Patanjali yoga and *raja* yoga share the same foundational principles and practices, the latter places a greater emphasis on the practice of meditation and mental discipline, while Patanjali yoga encompasses a wider range of practices and techniques.

Raja yoga, as explained in the Bhagavad Gita, combines the principles of self-discipline, detachment, meditation, and devotion to achieve a state of inner calm, spiritual insight, and union with the divine. It is a holistic approach that integrates various paths of yoga to lead individuals towards self-realisation and liberation. Lord Krishna describes the concept of *raja* yoga as the path to spiritual enlightenment and union with the divine through meditation that enables one to control the mind. Lord Krishna explains that, to practise *raja* yoga, one should first find a quiet and peaceful place where one can sit comfortably and meditate. Then, one should focus their mind on a single object, such as the flame of a candle or the image of a deity, and let go of all distractions.

Lord Krishna also emphasises the importance of detachment in *raja* yoga. He explains that one should practise detachment from both material objects and the fruits of one's actions. This means that one should focus on the present moment and the task at hand without worrying about the outcome or result. He also stresses the importance of discipline in *raja* yoga. He advises practitioners to exercise moderation in their eating and sleeping habits, to practise self-control, and to maintain a steady and consistent practice of meditation.

Integral Yoga

Integral yoga is a comprehensive spiritual and transformative path developed by combining various yogic practices, philosophies, and psychological insights to facilitate the evolution of the consciousness and the realisation of the divine consciousness on earth. The origin of integral yoga can be traced back to the teachings and practices of Sri Aurobindo, an Indian philosopher, yogi, and spiritual leader of the early 20th century. Sri Aurobindo developed integral yoga as a comprehensive system that aimed to harmonise and integrate all aspects of human existence, including the physical, mental, emotional, and spiritual dimensions.

Integral yoga draws inspiration from various traditional yogic practices, such as *hatha* yoga, *raja* yoga, and *bhakti* yoga, as well as other spiritual and philosophical traditions from around the world. Sri Aurobindo emphasised the evolution of consciousness and the pursuit of spiritual transformation as key elements of integral yoga. The practice of integral yoga involves not only the individual's personal transformation but also a broader aspiration for the transformation of humanity and the world. It seeks to unite the divine and the earthly aspects of life, with a view to unlocking a higher state of consciousness and a more integral and harmonious way of being.

Integral yoga encompasses the following key elements:

1. **Evolutionary perspective**. Sri Aurobindo's integral yoga is built on the conceptual premise that human existence is part of a larger evolutionary process. It aims to go beyond individual spiritual liberation and seeks the transformation of human consciousness to contribute to the evolutionary progress of the entire world.
2. **Psychic being.** Central to integral yoga is the concept of the psychic being, which is regarded as the divine essence or spark within each individual. The psychic being represents the true self and the connecting link to the divine. The goal of the practice is to awaken the psychic being and align oneself with the psychic being's guidance and influence.
3. **Self-mastery and transformation.** Integral yoga emphasises self-mastery and the transformation of the various dimensions of human existence, including the physical, vital (energetic/emotional), mental, and spiritual aspects. The aim is to bring about integral and harmonious development that transcends limitations and inner conflicts.
4. **Integral *sadhana*.** *Sadhana* refers to spiritual practice or discipline. Integral yoga incorporates various yogic practices and disciplines, such as meditation, concentration, mantra repetition, *pranayama*, *asanas*, self-observation, and self-discipline. These practices are designed to purify and harmonise the different aspects of the being and facilitate spiritual progress.
5. **Supramental consciousness.** Sri Aurobindo envisioned the emergence of a supramental consciousness as the next

stage of human evolution. This consciousness surpasses the limitations of the individual ego and operates from a higher truth. The aim of integral yoga is to open oneself to this supramental force and facilitate its descent into the individual and collective consciousness.

Integral yoga does not advocate renunciation of or withdrawal from the world. Instead, it encourages active engagement in daily life, with an aspiration to manifest the divine consciousness in all aspects of human existence, including work, relationships, and social responsibilities. It is important to note that practising integral yoga requires dedication, discipline, and a sincere desire for spiritual growth and transformation. Sri Aurobindo's writings and teachings provide detailed guidance for those interested in pursuing this path.

Although *chakra* activation is not the primary focus of integral yoga and Sri Aurobindo did not extensively discuss *chakras* in his teachings, the techniques of integral yoga can potentially help activate and harmonise the *chakras*, for they encompass the physical, vital, mental, and spiritual dimensions and can help purify and harmonise the various levels of being, including the energy centres associated with the *chakras*. Practices such as meditation, concentration, breathwork, and self-discipline can promote a deeper awareness and balance in the subtle energy system. By cultivating inner stillness, concentration, and a spirit of surrender before the divine, practitioners of integral yoga may experience the activation and harmonisation of the *chakras* as a natural outcome of their spiritual progress. However, as emphasised before, it is important to approach *chakra* work with proper guidance and understanding. It is advisable to study under and learn from experienced teachers or practitioners who have expertise in both integral yoga and the *chakra* system. They can suggest specific techniques and provide guidance and insights to support the activation and harmonisation of the *chakras* in a safe and effective manner.

In spite of their different names and approaches, all the schools of yoga fundamentally originate in the ancient Vedic practices of India. They share common elements but they emphasise different aspects or techniques of yoga. So, while the different schools of yoga share a common goal of cultivating spiritual growth and awareness, they have different methods and approaches that cater to different needs and preferences. For example, *hatha* yoga focuses primarily on *asanas* and *pranayama* to prepare the body for meditation and spiritual growth, while *kundalini* yoga emphasises the awakening of the *kundalini* through a combination of *asanas*, *pranayama*, and meditation. The Eight Limbs of Patanjali yoga include ethical guidelines, *asanas*, *pranayama*, concentration, and meditation. *Raja* yoga, on the other hand, emphasises the cultivation of mental and emotional balance through meditation and self-reflection, and *kriya* yoga is a synthesis of various yoga practices, including *asanas*, *pranayama*, and meditation, designed to accelerate spiritual growth and awakening.

The Flow of Energy: A Comparative Study of *Prana* and *Chi*

Chi (also spelled *qi* or *ki*) is a concept that originates in traditional Chinese medicine and martial arts. It is often translated as 'life force energy' or 'vital energy' and is believed to flow through all living things. While there are some differences between the specific concepts of *prana* and *chi*, both are based on the idea of a vital energy that flows through living things and plays a role in maintaining health and well-being.

Chi is believed to be in every cell, tissue, and organ. It is considered essential to physical, mental, and emotional health. According to traditional Chinese medicine, when the flow of *chi* in the body is balanced and unobstructed, the body is healthy. Conversely, an imbalance or blockage of *chi* can lead to illness or disease. In the world of martial arts, practitioners use the concept of *chi* to develop their physical and mental abilities, such as strength, flexibility, balance, and focus.

Much ongoing scientific research is dedicated to investigating the concept of *chi*, and while there is no conclusive evidence to support its existence, some studies suggest that certain practices, such as meditation and acupuncture, may have positive effects on the body that could be related to the concept of *chi*.

Spiritual intelligence is the foundation of our consciousness, guiding us towards inner peace and ultimate happiness. To achieve spiritual intelligence, we must focus on the higher *chakras*, and *kundalini* awakening is one of the most powerful tools for this. It is a journey that requires self-discipline, devotion, and a deep understanding of our inner self, but the rewards are immeasurable.

Chapter 4

Human Potential in the Context of Quantum Physics

The concept of spiritual intelligence has been gaining popularity in recent years, as more people have sought a deeper understanding of themselves and the world around them. Spiritual intelligence also involves understanding and using the laws of the universe to manifest our desires and achieve our goals.

The relationship between creation theory and human potential in the context of quantum physics has been explored by many scientists, theologians, and philosophers. While the relationship is complex and multifaceted, the fundamental concept behind the exploration of creation theory and human potential within the realm of quantum physics is the interconnectedness of the universe and all living beings. It suggests that human beings have boundless potential since we encompass everything within us, and whatever is beyond us exists in the universe. This potential can be harnessed through meditation and spiritual practices to manifest our desires.

The theory of the origin of the universe highlights the incredible potential that exists within the universe. It suggests that, from a state of nothingness, energy and matter were created, leading to the formation of everything we know, and that, before the universe came into being, all that 'existed' was quantum vacuum. However, this quantum vacuum was not empty. It was full of energy, also known as singularity. A part of this energy became agitated, causing turmoil within the quantum vacuum, which then created matter. This matter gradually cooled down, leading to the formation of the universe, with all its galaxies, stars, and planets. Similarly, the human mind is often described as having the potential to manifest anything we desire or imagine. This potential stems from the power of our thoughts and beliefs, which can shape our perceptions and influence our actions. This theory speaks to the notion that everything we see and experience is the result of a deeper, underlying energy that lies within us all.

Like the universe, the human mind is a vast and complex system that can create and transform reality. It is capable of harnessing the power of thought to bring about positive change and transformation in our lives. Through visualisation and positive affirmations, we can tap into our inner potential and create the reality we desire. This process of manifestation is based on the principle that our thoughts and beliefs shape our reality, and we can use this vibrational power to attract the experiences we want.

The marriage of quantum physics and the study of human potential holds the promise of unlocking new frontiers of knowledge and transforming our understanding of what it means to be human. Practical applications of concepts such as superposition and entanglement may be useful in fields such as psychology, education, and personal development. By incorporating quantum principles in these domains, we can develop innovative approaches to enhance cognitive abilities, promote mental well-being, and tap into the latent potential of the human mind. Techniques like meditation, visualisation, and intention-setting can be re-examined through the lens of quantum physics, potentially yielding new insights and practices to optimise human performance and personal growth.

Just as the universe created matter through the agitation of energy, we can create our reality by channelling our energy and focus towards our goals. By aligning our thoughts and beliefs with our desires, we can activate our creative potential and manifest our dreams. This process requires discipline, focus, and commitment, but, with practice, we can unlock the infinite potential within us and create a life of abundance and fulfilment. Ultimately, the similarity between human potential and the creation of the universe lies in the power of the mind to shape reality and bring about transformation.

The emptiness out of which the universe was created was not in fact emptiness, but energy in the form of waves. These waves contained subatomic energy that manifested as matter, causing creation. The same metaphysical principle applies to us, as the energy within us can manifest as creation. The state of emptiness (thoughtlessness) is the highest point of our internal energy. It is a transcendental state of awareness. As has been mentioned previously, Buddha referred to it as *shunya* (zero), a state of complete emptiness. A deep meditative state is a prerequisite for this.

The goal of spirituality is to connect the self and the cosmos, which leads to integration. When this integration happens, we crack the code that allows us to access the knowledge space. Everything that we need is available within us, and what's not available within us is available in abundance in the universe. The key is to believe, accept, and surrender to the process (suggestibility). Meditative power is a tool that allows us to match the various vibrational frequencies of the universe and thereby manifest what we want. This process is not a miracle but a science that is empirical and experiential. It involves understanding the laws of the universe, such as the law of attraction, the law of vibration, and the law of abundance. These laws state that like attracts like, everything is energy and vibration, and there is an abundance of everything we desire in the universe.

One implication of Einstein's theory of relativity, which describes the relationship between space and time, and how they are intertwined, is that all objects in the universe are in motion relative to one another and nothing is truly static. This is also an allusion to the idea of vibrations and frequencies in the universe. Everything in the universe, from the smallest subatomic particle to the largest galaxy, has a vibrational frequency. This frequency is a measure of how fast an object is vibrating, and it can be influenced by a variety of factors, such as temperature, pressure, and electromagnetic fields. Our perceptual limitations, however, prevent us from sensing the vibrations of most objects in the universe. We are only able to sense a limited range of frequencies with our five senses. However, scientists have developed tools and instruments that allow us to detect and measure frequencies outside our sensory range, such as x-rays, radio waves, and infrared radiation. This suggests that our thoughts have a vibrational frequency, just like everything else in the universe. Therefore, our thoughts and emotions can influence the vibrational frequency of our bodies and the world around us. If we focus our thoughts and intentions on a specific outcome, we can create a vibrational energy that attracts that outcome to us. This is the basis for the idea of manifesting what we want through vibrational energy.

Spiritual intelligence is the science of manifestation that involves connecting to our inner self and the cosmos. It involves using the above-mentioned laws to manifest our desires and achieve our goals. It involves understanding our thoughts and emotions and how they affect our vibrational frequency. Positive thoughts and emotions raise our vibrational frequency and attract positive experiences into our lives. Negative thoughts and emotions lower our vibrational frequency and attract negative experiences.

Meditation: The Magic of Manifestation

As we have seen above, creation is the manifestation of potential energy within the quantum vacuum. This potential energy is an unknown and unconscious force that rests within us, too, also in the form of vacuum. It is worth remembering that this vacuum is not empty; it contains transformational potential energy. Through meditative practice, we can access this energy and manifest it in our lives. This requires a deep understanding of the power of silence and emptiness, as it is through these states that we are able to access our potential energy. When we achieve a state of peace and stillness, we are able to tap into the zero point of silence, the highest form of potential energy within us and the one that gives us access to the power of creation. By connecting with the energy of creation, we can tap into a deeper level of consciousness and understanding that allows us to connect with the world on a more profound level and to see the interconnectedness of all things. Through spiritual practice, we can transcend the limitations of the physical world and connect with the infinite potential that lies within us all.

Emptiness can be understood in different ways, depending on the context. In the context of Buddhism, emptiness refers to the idea that all phenomena lack inherent existence or essence. This means that everything that exists, including each of us, is empty of a fixed, unchanging essence or self. In the context of deep meditative states, emptiness can refer to the experience of a profound sense of openness, spaciousness, expansion, and freedom from the usual mental chatter and clutter. In this state, one may perceive a profound sense of interconnectedness and a lack of separation between oneself and everything else. This experience of emptiness can lead to the realisation of wisdom, because it can help break down the habitual patterns of thought and perception that prevent us from seeing things as they truly are. By experiencing emptiness, we can gain insight into the nature of reality and our place in it, which can lead to a greater sense of clarity, compassion, and understanding.

In the context of attracting energy to fulfil aspirations, the experience of emptiness can be seen as a way of clearing the mind of obstacles and distractions that may be preventing us from manifesting our intentions. By cultivating a state of emptiness, we can create a space for new possibilities to arise and allow our intentions to take root and manifest in our lives. Additionally, the practice of meditation and the cultivation of emptiness can help cultivate a sense of inner peace and harmony, which can attract positive energy and support from the universe.

However, in today's fast-paced world, peace has become a rare commodity. Many people spend their lives searching for peace, often seeking it in external things such as material possessions, relationships, or achievements. However, peace is not something that can be created. It is already present within us, buried deep under the layers of stress and anxiety that come with modern life. To experience peace, we need to silence the agitation within us. Peace is nothing but the absence of agitation. This can be achieved through reflection, awareness, and meditation. By taking the time to be still and quiet, we can access the peace that already exists within us. Meditation is a powerful tool for the cultivation of inner peace. It helps us calm our minds and enter a state of deep relaxation. Through meditation, we can learn to let go of negative thoughts and emotions and connect with the peace and stillness that lies within us. It is a way of cultivating mindfulness and focusing on the present moment. The silence that arises from the absence of mental agitation has many benefits. It allows us to connect with our inner wisdom, enabling us to find answers to life's most challenging questions. It provides a sense of clarity, helping us see things from a different perspective. And it can help us connect with our inner selves to discover our true purpose and meaning in life.

The idea of homogeneity refers to a state of oneness and interconnectedness, wherein all people and things are united and in harmony. However, our reality is one of heterogeneity, where diversity is a significant obstacle to achieving this ideal. The enormous variation observable in our world can make it difficult to find common ground and work together towards a common goal. To overcome this challenge, we must first accept and embrace diversity as a valuable and natural aspect of life. We must recognise that our differences are what make us unique and contribute to the richness of our world. By doing so, we can start to see how our diverse perspectives and experiences can work together to create something greater than the sum of its parts.

However, accepting diversity is not enough on its own. To truly achieve homogeneity and create a more impactful world, we must internalise this idea and engrave it into our attitudes and actions. It requires consistent effort and meditative practice to cultivate a mindset of openness, empathy, and compassion towards others. As we work towards this goal, we may find that our minds are cluttered with the external thickness of diversity, which can hinder our progress towards homogeneity. To overcome this, we must empty our minds completely through meditation. By doing so, we can develop greater clarity, focus, and mindfulness, which can help us see beyond our differences and work towards a common goal. Achieving homogeneity is not an easy task, but it is a worthy one. By accepting diversity and working towards interconnectedness and oneness, we can create a more harmonious and impactful world.

People with high spiritual intelligence understand the importance of inner peace. They recognise that it cannot be attained through external means; it can only be found within. They cultivate practices such as mindfulness, meditation, prayer, and reflection to connect with this inner peace and access the wisdom and clarity it provides. Being mindful of our awareness enables us to reflect on our thoughts and emotions and to recognise their psychological, emotional, and physical impacts on us. This allows us to make conscious choices about how we respond to our experiences instead of being driven by habitual reactions.

We have seen how Patanjali has provided a structured and well-organised explanation of the process of meditation through *ashtanga* yoga, which is made up of the eight limbs or practices that lead to the attainment of a meditative state. Deep meditation is a practice that involves calming the mind, focusing on the present moment, and cultivating a sense of inner stillness and awareness.

Deep Meditation: How to Achieve It and What It Does For You

Find a quiet and comfortable place where you won't be disturbed. Sit on a cushion or a chair with your back straight. Close your eyes and take a few deep breaths. Let go of any tension or stress in your body. Focus your attention on your breath. Pay attention to the sensation of the air moving in and out of your nostrils or the rising and falling of your chest or abdomen. As thoughts arise, gently acknowledge them without judgement and bring your attention back to your breath. Keep focusing on your breath; allow yourself to relax deeper and deeper with each breath. With practice, you may notice your mind becoming quieter and your body feeling more relaxed. Keep meditating for a period of time that feels comfortable to you, whether it's five minutes or an hour.

The impact of deep meditation can be significant. It can help reduce stress, anxiety, and depression, improve concentration and focus, boost creativity and intuition, and promote a sense of inner peace and well-being. Regular practice can also lead to positive changes in the brain and body, including increased grey matter density, lower blood pressure, and improved immune function. Remember that meditation is a skill, and like any skill, it takes time and practice to develop. Be patient with yourself and keep coming back to your practice, even if you feel like you're not making progress. Over time, you'll find that deep meditation becomes easier and more natural and that the benefits continue to grow.

Manifesting Through Meditation

It is possible to manifest what you want through meditation. Start by settling on a clear idea of what you want to manifest. This could be a new job, a fulfilling relationship, improved health, or any other desire you have.

Visualise. Spend time each day visualising yourself already having achieved your desire. Use all of your senses to create a vivid mental image of what it feels like to have this desire fulfilled. Feel the emotions associated with it, such as joy and gratitude.

Practise gratitude. Practise gratitude for what you already have in your life and for the manifestation of your desire. This will help you stay focused on positive emotions and increase your vibrational frequency.

Let go of attachments. Release any attachments or resistances to the outcome of your desire. Trust that the universe will bring you what you need at the right time and in the right way.

Meditate regularly. Make meditation a daily practice to help you stay focused on and aligned with your desire. You can use guided meditations, visualisation techniques, or simply sit in silence and focus on your breath.

Take action. Take inspired action towards your desire. This could mean applying for a new job, reaching out to someone you're interested in, or taking steps to improve your health.

By combining these steps with regular meditation, you can begin to manifest what you want in your life. Remember to stay focused, stay positive, and trust the process. With time and persistence, you can create the life you desire.

Transformational change is possible only when we let go of what no longer serves us and introduce more elevating thoughts into our consciousness. This process of replacing negative thought patterns with positive ones creates new neural connections in the brain. The solution for embedding our subconscious with what serves us best is within us, and once we have uploaded this software and start updating it on a day-to-day basis, everything falls into place.

Our experiences are primarily constructed through our five senses, which serve as the basis for our representational system and our model of the world. However, there are things that cannot be sensed through our five senses, things that can only be perceived through silence. When we achieve the zero point of silence, we enter into a state of peace, which, as has been mentioned before, is the highest form of potential energy within us, like the energy-filled vacuum that created the universe and all living things. All of us have been created by this potential energy and therefore have the ability to tap into it and manifest it in our lives, too. Through meditative practice, we can access this vacuum and manifest it as a world of infinite possibilities.

Through *sadhana* (spiritual practices), we can develop this ability and realise our true potential. The power of emptiness and the ability to manifest something out of nothing is a profound force that can transform our lives and the world around us. One important aspect of spiritual intelligence is the recognition that human beings are not separate from the universe; rather, they are deeply interconnected with it. This interconnectedness can be seen in many ways, including through the recognition that we are made up of the same basic elements as the rest of the natural world and that we are constantly exchanging energy with our environment.

In particular, many spiritual traditions emphasise the importance of connecting with the vibrational energy of the cosmos, which is believed to be a powerful source of healing, inspiration, and transformation. This energy can be thought of as a kind of spiritual nourishment, which can help restore balance and harmony in our lives and guide us towards our highest potential.

Aristotelian Theory and the Power of Manifestation

Aristotle's theory of potentiality and actuality is one of his fundamental concepts and has been a cornerstone of philosophical thought for centuries, and it has significant implications for spiritual intelligence. Aristotle argues that everything in the world has both potentiality and actuality. Potentiality is the possibility that something will become what it has the potential to be, while actuality is the realisation of that potentiality. For example, an acorn has the potential to become an oak tree, but this potential is only actualised when the acorn is planted and grows into an oak tree. Similarly, humans have the potential to become their best selves, but they must work towards actualising that potential. This theory can be applied to the development of spiritual intelligence in individuals.

The practice of manifestation through meditation emphasises the power of visualisation and taking action to bring about our desired outcomes. This is similar to Aristotle's idea of potentiality and actuality, as both involve the idea of moving from a state of potential to a state of actuality. By using the power of our minds to envision the future we want and then taking concrete steps towards achieving it, we can transform our potential into reality. Aristotle's theory and the concept of manifestation through meditation both offer us a powerful message: that we have the ability to shape our own lives and achieve our full potential. Whether we are seeking personal growth, professional success, or spiritual enlightenment, these concepts remind us that we are not limited by our current circumstances but instead possess an infinite capacity for growth and transformation. The potential for greatness lies within each of us, and it is up to us to unlock it and achieve our full potential.

Going by Aristotle's theory, every human being has the potential to develop spiritual intelligence. Furthermore, Aristotle believed that actuality is always superior to potentiality. In the context of spiritual intelligence, this means that the actualisation of spiritual potential is more important than the mere possession of that potential. In other words, it is not enough to simply have the potential to be spiritually intelligent. Rather, one must actively strive to develop and actualise that potential through practice and experience. Aristotle's theory of potentiality and actuality also has implications for the concept of purpose within the framework of spiritual intelligence. According to Aristotle, everything in the world has a purpose, and fulfilling that purpose is the highest goal. This means that individuals must strive to fulfil their spiritual potential and purpose.

Overall, Aristotle's theory of potentiality and actuality provides a framework for understanding how things change and evolve over time, from potentiality to actuality. Quantum energy in the form of singularity represents potentiality, while its transformation into matter represents the process of actualisation: actualisation of the universe's potential to give form to galaxies, planets, and stars and Earth's potential to give rise to living beings. The human ability to manifest desire through meditation can also be understood in terms of potentiality and actualisation. In this case, the potentiality exists within the human mind, and the process of actualisation occurs through the practice of meditation. As one focuses on their desires and brings them into the present moment, they are actualising their potential to manifest those desires.

Influencing the Subconscious Through Neuroplasticity

Neuroplasticity refers to the brain's ability to change and adapt throughout a person's life. It is the mechanism by which the brain can create new neural pathways, modify existing ones, and reorganise its structure in response to environmental stimuli and experiences. The concept of neuroplasticity challenges the long-held belief that the brain is a static organ that cannot be changed once it has fully developed. Instead, research has shown that the brain is like plastic in that it has a remarkable capacity to adapt and change in response to new experiences, learnings, and developments.

The brain is an incredibly complex organ that contains an estimated 86 billion neurons. However, simply having a large number of neurons is not enough for optimal brain function. It is through the process of neuroplasticity that the brain is able to change and reorganise itself throughout life, allowing us to adapt to new experiences, learn new skills, and also overcome negative habits and behaviours.

Neuroplasticity is a powerful tool that can be harnessed through intentional and repeated practice of positive behaviours. One way to promote neuroplasticity is through a process called 'neural pruning,' whereby weak or unnecessary connections are eliminated while strong connections are reinforced. By actively working to deactivate connections associated with negative habits and reinforce those associated with positive behaviours, we can promote neural pruning and the growth of new neural connections. This process is facilitated through a variety of techniques, including cognitive-behavioural therapy, mindfulness meditation, and regular exercise.

The impact of neuroplasticity on our lives is immense. It allows us to continually learn and grow, even as we age. It gives us the ability to break free from negative patterns and habits and to cultivate new and positive ways of thinking and behaving. Through neuroplasticity, we can achieve a more fulfilling and meaningful life, both for ourselves and for those around us.

One of the most significant ways in which neuroplasticity helps us is by enabling the formation of new habits and memories in our subconscious. The subconscious mind is a powerful force that influences our thoughts, feelings, and behaviours. It is the part of the mind that operates below the level of conscious awareness and is responsible for many of our automatic responses and habits. These patterns are often deeply ingrained and difficult to change through conscious effort alone. However, through the process of neuroplasticity, it is possible to rewire the brain and change these patterns.

When we engage in a new habit or learn something new, our brains create new neural pathways, which become stronger and more efficient with repeated use. Over time, these neural pathways become entrenched, making the habit or skill easier to perform without conscious thought. For example, when you first start learning how to drive, the act requires a lot of conscious attention and effort. But with practice, the neural pathways associated with driving become stronger and more efficient and the skill becomes second nature. Similarly, if you are learning a new language, consistent practice can help embed the new language into your subconscious mind. As you become more fluent in the language, your brain creates new neural connections and strengthens existing ones related to the language, making it easier for you to recall words and phrases automatically and without much conscious effort. When we learn new information, our brains form new connections between neurons, which become stronger with repetition and can lead to long-term memory formation. With repetition and consistent practice, the brain develops a 'muscle memory', which is stored in your subconscious and can be accessed automatically. This allows us to recall information or perform desired activities. This same process of embedding new experiences in the subconscious can be applied to other skills and behaviours as well. By repeatedly experiencing something, we can create new neural connections in our brain that become deeply embedded in our subconscious, allowing us to perform that skill or behaviour with greater ease and automation.

This is why consistent and deliberate practice (*sadhana*) is so important when learning a new skill or behaviour, as it helps strengthen the neural connections associated with that experience and embed it more deeply in our subconscious. In the context of spiritual intelligence, neuroplasticity is a powerful tool that can be used to rewrite the subconscious and change deeply ingrained patterns of thought and behaviour and also to get rid of patterns that are not empowering us or helping us evolve and grow.

'Neurons that fire together wire together' is a phrase often used to describe the concept of Hebbian plasticity, which is a type of neuroplasticity that involves the strengthening of synaptic connections between neurons that are frequently active at the same time. The phrase is often used to explain the formation of neural networks and how learning and memory work in the brain. When we learn something new, for example, the neurons involved in that process fire together repeatedly. As a result, the connections between these neurons become stronger and the neural network associated with that learning becomes more robust.

Neuroplasticity can also help in recovering from brain injuries, such as a brain stroke. For example, consider a patient who has suffered a stroke and has lost the ability to walk or stand. Through physiotherapy and consistent practice, this patient can reactivate or form new neural pathways to relearn how to walk and stand. By repeating the same physical movements over and over again, the brain is able to create new neural connections that help the patient form new habits and regain lost skills. Over time, this repeated practice leads to the formation of new neural pathways, which allows the patient to regain strength and mobility. With continued effort and training, the patient may be able to walk and stand independently once again. This demonstrates the power of neuroplasticity and how the brain can adapt and change even after an injury. With the right treatment and support, individuals can recover lost abilities and improve their quality of life.

One way to harness the power of neuroplasticity to change the subconscious is through mindfulness practices. Through mindfulness, we can observe our thoughts and emotions and become more aware of the patterns and beliefs that are driving our behaviour. By being mindful of our thoughts and emotions, we can begin to identify negative patterns and replace them with more positive ones. Another way to utilise neuroplasticity is through visualisation techniques. Visualisation involves creating a mental image of a desired outcome or behaviour. By repeatedly visualising a new behaviour or outcome, we can create new neural connections in the brain that support this new pattern of behaviour. For example, if we want to overcome a fear of public speaking, we can visualise ourselves speaking confidently and articulately in front of an audience. By repeatedly visualising this, we can rewire our brain to support this new behaviour.

It is important to note that changing the subconscious through neuroplasticity is a gradual process that requires consistent effort and repetition. However, with dedication and practice, it is possible to rewire the brain and create new, positive patterns of thought and behaviour that support our spiritual growth and well-being.

Spiritual intelligence emphasises the importance of attitude and perspective, especially in the face of adversity. It is easy to feel victimised by difficult experiences and allow them to dictate our future actions and emotions. However, it is crucial to understand that we have the power to change the way we respond to these experiences and change the trajectory of our lives. There is a famous story of a man who, while experiencing excruciating pain, told a doctor that the pain was a reminder that he was alive and that it gave him the strength to fight. This attitude is a powerful example of the importance of perspective. Instead of focusing on the negative aspect of his experience, the man chose to find meaning in his pain and use it as a source of motivation.

It is easy to fall into the trap of victimhood and believe that past experiences determine our future. However, this is not necessarily the case. Two people can go through identical traumatic experiences, and one can be devastated while the other remains unscathed. This is because it is not the event itself that affects us but our emotional response to it. The reality is that we cannot change what has happened in the past, but we can change the way we respond to it. It is possible to edit and delete past experiences that no longer serve us by letting go of the emotions and beliefs that keep us stuck in a pattern of victimhood. This process of letting go requires reflection, awareness, and a willingness to cultivate a different perspective.

In essence, the ability to let go and edit past experiences requires a shift in attitude and perspective. It means recognising that we have the power to control our emotional response to past experiences and use those experiences as sources of growth and learning. The process of letting go and editing the past is not a straightforward one, but it is a necessary step towards spiritual growth and development. By letting go of the past, we free ourselves to create a better future.

Visualisation as the Process of Actualising Potentiality (Manifestation)

In the context of spiritual intelligence, the above section heading emphasises and highlights the role of imagination and visualisation in maximising our creativity. Spiritual intelligence involves developing our consciousness and inner self and using our creative abilities. Visualisation can be a powerful tool in achieving this goal. Human beings are the only species with the unique ability to use imagination and visualisation to break the rules they live by and expand their creative potential. By exploring our creative abilities, we can tap into parts of our subconscious mind that are underdeveloped and limiting our growth and development. This suggests that the creative part of our being can help us overcome limiting beliefs and the conditioning that prevents us from reaching our full potential.

Meditation is the best tool with which to maximise our creativity and heal ourselves. In the meditative state, our mind is open to new suggestions, which means that we can use positive affirmations to program our minds with new beliefs and ideas that support our spiritual growth. Ironically, the effectiveness of this process relies on the fact that the human mind is stupid; it cannot differentiate between visualisation and reality. When we imagine or visualise things, the mind accepts what it sees as events as well as experiences; they are then embedded in our subconscious. This is why we are told to watch our thoughts, as every thought has a vibrational energy with the capacity to create a reality. Once such thoughts are embedded in the subconscious, they keep surfacing as if in autopilot mode. This becomes *samskara*, which will reflect in our *chitta* in the form of *vritti* (compulsive tendencies). But the good news is, to change such undesired thought patterns, we can superimpose visualisations of desired and empowering thoughts on our subconscious.

Visualisation holds tremendous power, as it not only allows us to imprint positive thoughts into our subconscious minds but also sparks incredible ideas through the creative process of imagination. With the aid of modern technology, the ideas generated through visualisation can be harnessed to achieve even greater results. The act of visualising positive outcomes can have a profound impact on our lives. When we visualise achieving our goals, we create a mental image that is stored in our subconscious mind. This mental image then becomes a guiding force that influences our thoughts, feelings, and actions, ultimately leading us towards success. Furthermore, the act of visualisation is a highly creative process that can generate remarkable ideas. As we imagine new possibilities and explore different scenarios, we are engaging in a process of brainstorming and problem-solving. This process can lead to innovative and groundbreaking ideas that can revolutionise the world around us.

In the modern world, technology allows us to leverage the power of visualisation and imagination to bring our ideas to life and create realistic simulations of our visions. We can test, refine, and improve our ideas until they become viable solutions that can be implemented in real-world scenarios.

In short, the power of visualisation is immense and, when combined with the creative process of imagination, it can generate astonishing ideas. With the aid of technology, these ideas can be leveraged to create tangible solutions that can make a significant impact on our lives and the world around us.

Chapter 5

The Power of Awareness

What is Consciousness?

To begin discussing awareness, it is crucial to first comprehend the concept of consciousness and its relationship with awareness. From the standpoint of spiritual intelligence or wisdom, consciousness is the foundation upon which awareness arises. In other words, consciousness is what underlies awareness, allowing us to experience our surroundings and our own existence. It's important to recognise that this awareness is not a mere physical or cognitive experience but rather a fundamental force that guides us towards spiritual realisation. This guiding force is what ultimately determines the depth and extent of our spiritual understanding and awareness.

Consciousness is the state of being aware of one's surroundings, thoughts, feelings, and experiences. It is the subjective experience of being alive and present in the world. Consciousness enables us to perceive, process, and respond to the world around us. The exact nature of consciousness is still not fully understood, and it remains a topic of ongoing scientific and philosophical enquiry. However, it is clear that consciousness is intimately connected to the brain and the body. Specific regions of the brain are known to be involved in generating and modulating the conscious experience. Consciousness is also sometimes viewed as a fundamental aspect of the universe itself. In some spiritual and philosophical traditions, consciousness is seen as the ultimate reality or source of all existence.

In general, consciousness is an intricate and diverse phenomenon that is challenging to define. However, it plays a crucial role in shaping our daily existence, and studying it can enhance our comprehension of ourselves and the surrounding world. Consciousness can be thought of as the underlying awareness that enables us to experience the world around us, while awareness is the conscious recognition and understanding of this experience. Thus, awareness arises from consciousness and serves as a vital tool for our spiritual growth and development.

According to Vedic science, consciousness is the fundamental essence of all living beings and the universe itself. It is the pure awareness that underlies all mental and physical phenomena, and it is considered to be eternal and unchanging. In Vedic philosophy, consciousness is sometimes described as the 'ultimate reality' or *brahman*. *Chit* (also spelled as *chetana* or *chaitanya*) refers to pure consciousness or awareness. It is the essence of the individual soul or *atman*, which is said to be eternal, unchanging, and infinite. *Chit* is considered to be the source of all knowledge, experience, and perception. It is beyond the mind and the senses and is often described as pure light or pure awareness. In Vedic science, the consciousness is believed to be located within the heart rather than in the brain. The heart is seen as the seat of the soul and the source of consciousness, with the brain acting as an instrument through which consciousness is expressed in the physical world.

Neuroscience, on the other hand, defines consciousness as the state of being aware of one's surroundings, thoughts, and feelings. It is the state of being alive, conscious, and present in the world. Neuroscientists study consciousness by observing brain activity and neural processes that underlie it. Neurology views consciousness as being closely associated with brain activity. Specific regions of the brain, such as the prefrontal cortex and the parietal cortex, are thought to be particularly important to conscious experience.

One key difference between the two perspectives is that neuroscience tends to focus on the objective aspects of consciousness that can be measured and studied through scientific methods, while Vedic science emphasises the subjective experience of consciousness and the potential for individuals to directly experience higher states of awareness through spiritual practices.

Despite their different approaches, both Vedic science and neuroscience acknowledge the crucial link between consciousness and the brain and body. Moreover, while Vedic science emphasises meditation and other practices as ways of deepening one's awareness of consciousness, neuroscience aims to unravel the neural mechanisms that give rise to our conscious experience. However, Vedic science also acknowledges the existence of a deeper, non-material aspect of consciousness that is not limited to the physical body.

The study of consciousness is a multifaceted, complex field that spans multiple scientific and spiritual disciplines. By exploring this topic through different lenses, we can gain a deeper understanding of ourselves and the world around us.

We are All Consciousness (Awareness)

Awareness is the ability to perceive, know, or be conscious of something. It refers to the level of consciousness or alertness that an individual possesses in relation to their surroundings, themselves, or their experiences. Being aware involves being mindful of one's thoughts, emotions, and physical sensations, as well as the external environment, including people, objects, and events. Awareness can also refer to the knowledge or understanding of a particular issue, concept, or situation, and the ability to make informed decisions based on this understanding. It can be developed through various practices, such as meditation, introspection, and mindfulness.

Our ordinary state of awareness involves perceiving the world through our five senses and our mind, which can be influenced by our past experiences, beliefs, and biases. However, pure awareness is considered to be beyond this ordinary state of awareness. It is a state of heightened consciousness that transcends our mental and sensory experiences and provides us with a deeper understanding of ourselves and the world around us. Pure awareness is often associated with a sense of presence, peace, and clarity, and can be accessed through practices such as meditation, mindfulness, and self-enquiry. It is seen as a state of wisdom that arises from a deep connection to our inner self and the larger universe.

The idea that we are all consciousness or awareness suggests that, at the core of our being, we are not our physical bodies, thoughts, or emotions but the awareness that experiences those things. This means that the true essence of our being is not limited by the boundaries of our physical body; rather, it is infinite, boundless, and interconnected with all of existence.

The concept of pure consciousness refers to an advanced or transcendental state of consciousness that is free from all limitations and impurities. It is said to be free from the influence of our thoughts, emotions, or external circumstances. It is a state of being in which we are fully present in the moment and in harmony with the world around us. The source of this wisdom is said to be within each individual, and it is believed to be hidden by the illusions of the mind and ego. By transcending the limitations of the mind and ego, one is said to be able to tap into this inner source of wisdom and experience the true nature of reality.

In Vedic philosophy, this source of wisdom is often referred to as the *atma* or the true self. Through meditation, self-enquiry, and other spiritual practices, individuals can uncover this inner source of wisdom and live a life that is aligned with their true nature. The relevance of this concept to our lives is that it can help us shift our perspective and experience the world in a new way. By recognising that we are not limited by our physical bodies or external circumstances, we can begin to see the interconnectedness of all things and cultivate a deeper sense of compassion and empathy for others.

Spiritual intelligence involves freeing our consciousness from the clutter of our minds and egos, which allows us to access the incredible power of our awareness. The ancient sages were able to uncover profound knowledge of the universe through deep meditation, without relying on external instruments or technology. They were able to understand concepts like psychology, metaphysics, and even meteorology, and develop mathematical formulas through their awareness alone. In contrast, while we may be fascinated by artificial intelligence and modern technology, we often overlook the immense potential of the spiritual intelligence within us, which, if cultivated, can complement our other intelligences. Technology has become an inseparable part of our lives, transforming the way we work, live, and even connect with others at an emotional level. However, as we continue to rely on machines for every aspect of our existence, we must ask ourselves whether gadgets, material possessions, and modern lifestyles alone can provide the fulfilment and sense of contentment that we all desire.

As we become more self-centred and focus solely on our own needs, we risk losing the essence of what makes us human: our capacity for compassion, empathy, and sacrifice. While technological advancements are crucial for progress and development, they cannot replace the emotional security, love, and affection we receive from our fellow humans. To truly improve the quality of our lives, we must cultivate our consciousness and awareness, connecting with others at a deeper level to find true contentment and happiness. With compassion and empathy as our guiding principles, we can create a world where technology and humanity work hand-in-hand to transform our reality. The crux of the matter is that, to attain integration and a sense of fulfilment in life, it is necessary to strike a balance and create harmony between one's inner and outer worlds. Our liberation hinges on realising the incredible potency of consciousness. Whether we let it lie dormant, cluttered with the distractions of the world around us, or activate it to awaken our awareness and revolutionise our existence is up to us.

The pursuit of pure consciousness can help us find greater peace and fulfilment in our lives. By letting go of our attachments to our thoughts and emotions, we can find a sense of inner calm and clarity that allows us to approach life with greater ease and joy. The pursuits of material success and spiritual understanding are not necessarily mutually exclusive. In fact, understanding abstract concepts such as consciousness, awareness, and interconnectedness can actually help you in your pursuit of material success by providing a greater sense of purpose, meaning, and fulfilment.

Harnessing the Power Within and Embracing Inner Knowingness

True knowledge cannot be gained from external sources alone. It comes from within and is a collaborative effort of various aspects of the mind. When we pick up a thought and dwell or reflect on it, our mind starts contemplating it and provides us with many different perspectives. These perspectives are our own and are products of our unique experiences and thought processes. Our critical mind discards those perspectives that do not stand the scrutiny of our deliberations and insights. Our discretionary mind then firms up the perspectives that do stand up to our critical analysis. By approaching knowledge with an 'I know nothing' mindset, we empower our minds to connect with our inner knowingness.

Instincts and Intuitions: Our Inner Compass to Success

Our instincts and intuitions also play a crucial role in our understanding of spiritual intelligence. They help us connect with our inner selves and guide us towards the right path. When we follow our instincts and intuition, we become more aware of our spiritual needs and are better equipped to connect with the spiritual realm.

The Importance of Critical Thinking

Critical thinking is an essential aspect of spiritual intelligence. It allows us to question our assumptions and beliefs and to examine them in a critical light, thereby opening ourselves up to new ideas and perspectives that can help us to expand our understanding of the spiritual realm.

The Value of Contemplation and Reflection

Contemplation and reflection are also essential aspects of spiritual intelligence. They allow us to connect with our inner selves and to gain a deeper understanding of our spiritual needs and desires. By taking the time to reflect on our thoughts and experiences, we become more aware of the spiritual dimensions of our existence. Awareness within is the single biggest contributor to putting things in perspective. Due to our compulsive tendency to understand and fix everything in the outer world, we not only ignore our inner world but cause it to cloud over, as we keep countering and managing the outer world. Turning the mind inward to become aware of a phenomenon not only helps us understand ourselves but also helps us find the right perspectives that put everything in place.

The intelligence with which we can bring everything into our awareness is the source of our intuitive power and wisdom, guiding us with self-management and also helping us effectively manage the outer world. The process of being mindful and reflective through meditative practice can be instrumental in bringing things into our awareness.

Leveraging the Conscious, Subconscious, and Superconscious Realms of the Mind

Our mind is an intricate and complex structure that can be categorised into three main domains: the conscious, the subconscious, and the superconscious. Each of these domains plays a crucial role in shaping our thoughts, emotions, beliefs, and behaviour.

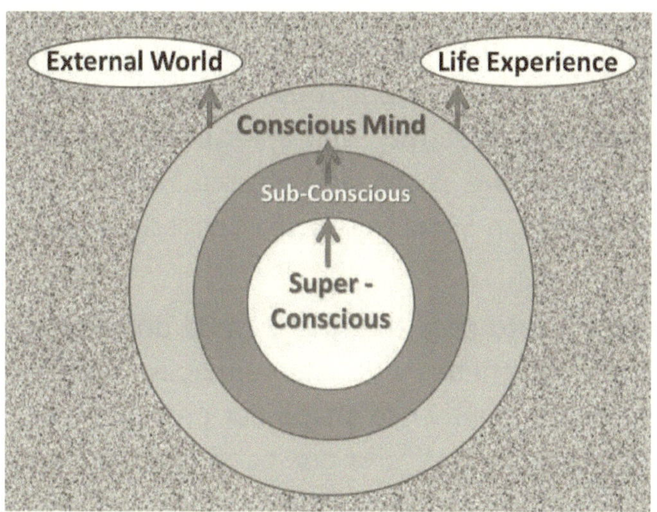

Figure 8

The conscious mind is the part of our mind that is responsible for our awareness and perception of the external world. It is the tip of the iceberg, the part of the mind that we are actively aware of and can control to a certain extent. It is where we process information, make decisions, and engage in rational thinking. This faculty of the mind is the smallest in size, and its capacity to process information is limited.

The subconscious mind is the part of our mind that is responsible for storing information, memories, and experiences that are beyond our conscious awareness. It is like the bulk of the iceberg—hidden beneath the surface, yet vast and powerful. It operates outside of our conscious control, influencing our emotions, beliefs, habits, and behaviour. It is estimated that the subconscious mind provides more than 75% of our total mental power. Our thinking is greatly influenced by experiences, memories, and beliefs that are embedded in the subconscious mind.

The superconscious mind is the highest level of consciousness, representing a realm of spiritual enlightenment, higher consciousness, and universal awareness. It is the rarest and least utilised of the three faculties, and only a few individuals are capable of accessing it. The superconscious mind is believed to be the source of intuition, creativity, and spiritual insight. It transcends the limitations of time, space, and physical reality. It is estimated that we use less than 5% of this state of consciousness during our lifetime.

It is important to note that these three domains of the mind are not separate entities but interconnected parts of a single whole. They work together to shape our perception of the world, our beliefs, our emotions, and our behaviour. The subconscious mind, in particular, plays a crucial role in shaping our personality and behaviour, as it is responsible for storing and processing our past experiences and emotions. Understanding the different states of the mind can help us gain greater control over our thoughts, emotions, and behaviour. By becoming aware of the power of our subconscious mind, we can begin to identify and change limiting beliefs, negative emotions, and destructive habits. Similarly, by tapping into our superconscious mind, we can access a higher level of consciousness and spiritual awareness, leading to greater insight, creativity, and fulfilment in life.

Mindfulness can help individuals become more aware of the workings of their conscious and subconscious minds, as it enables individuals to become more aware of their thoughts and emotions and to develop greater control over them. By paying attention to the present moment, individuals can become more aware of their habitual thought patterns and emotional reactions. This awareness can help individuals identify negative thought patterns and emotions and develop strategies to manage them.

Accessing the superconscious realm is a rare and challenging feat that requires a high level of spiritual development, discipline, and practice. It is believed that the superconscious domain can only be accessed by individuals who have achieved a state of spiritual enlightenment, who have transcended the limitations of the mind, ego, and the physical body. Meditation, spiritual practice, self-reflection, self-awareness, positive affirmations, visualisation, and mindfulness can help individuals access the superconscious state. Hypnosis is a technique that can also help individuals access the subconscious mind and reprogram negative patterns or beliefs. A trained hypnotherapist can guide individuals into a state of deep relaxation and suggest positive affirmations or visualisations that will reprogram the subconscious mind.

There are some similarities between the concepts of the conscious, subconscious, and superconscious and the Vedic principle of the four states of mind: *jagrat*, *svapna*, *sushupti*, and *turiya*. These concepts are all related to the different levels or layers of the human mind and consciousness; however, they are different in nature. In many spiritual traditions, a higher state of consciousness is considered a state of heightened awareness, wherein the individual transcends the limitations of the ego-mind and experiences a deeper sense of connection with the universe or divine consciousness. For example, in Buddhism, the concept of enlightenment or *bodhi* represents a state in which one has awakened to one's true nature and transcended the limitations of the ego-mind. This state is often described as a higher state of consciousness that brings about profound inner peace, clarity, and wisdom. Buddhists believe that achieving this state is the ultimate goal of spiritual practice and leads to liberation from suffering.

Similarly, in the mystical traditions of Christianity, Islam, and Judaism, the concept of 'mystical union' or 'communion with God' is considered a state of elevated consciousness that transcends ordinary perception and brings about a deep sense of spiritual connectedness and oneness with the divine.

In modern times, the concept of a higher state of consciousness has also been explored by various researchers and thinkers in the fields of psychology, neuroscience, and transpersonal studies. For example, psychologists such as Abraham Maslow and Ken Wilber have proposed models of human development that include higher states of consciousness beyond ordinary waking consciousness. Neuroscientists have also explored the neural correlates of higher states of consciousness, such as meditation-induced states of mindfulness or transcendence, and the effects of psychedelics on consciousness.

Understanding Consciousness Through Its Four States

The four states or layers of the human mind according to Vedic philosophy, as mentioned above, are *jagrat, svapna*, *sushupti*, and *turiya*. *Jagrat* is the waking state in which we are aware of our surroundings and engaged in daily activities. *Svapna* is the dream state in which our subconscious mind becomes active and we experience a world that is not present in the waking state. *Sushupti* is the deep sleep state in which our conscious and subconscious mind are at rest, and we experience a state of pure awareness without any thoughts or perceptions. *Turiya* is the fourth state, which transcends the other three states and represents a state of pure consciousness in which the individual self merges with the universal self. The understanding and exploration of these concepts can help us deepen our self-awareness and enhance our spiritual growth.

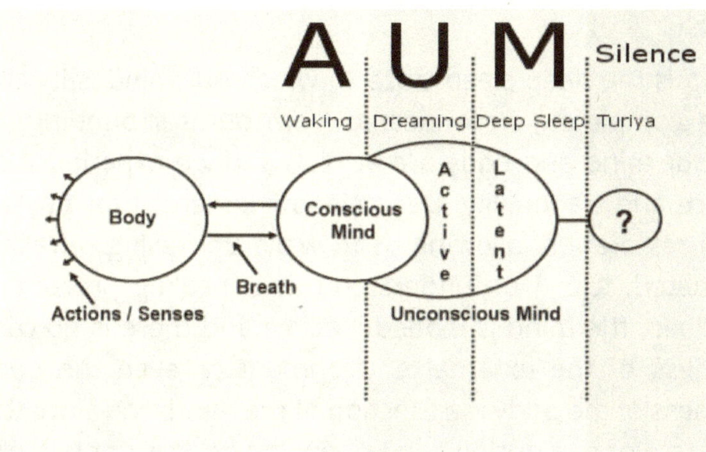

Figure 9

In the context of spiritual intelligence, understanding the four states of consciousness is very important because each state of consciousness plays a crucial role in our spiritual growth and well-being. The practice of spiritual intelligence involves developing an awareness and understanding of these four states of consciousness. By doing so, we can learn to access and utilise each state for our own growth and well-being.

Jagrat

Jagrat is the waking state, in which we are fully conscious and aware of our surroundings. In this state, our minds are active, and we are constantly processing information from the outside world. However, our thoughts can often be clouded by the noise of the external world, preventing us from accessing our deeper wisdom and insight.

Svapna

Svapna refers to the dream state, in which our mind is still active but we are disconnected from our physical surroundings. In this state, our mind creates its own reality, often reflecting our subconscious desires and fears.

Sushupti

Sushupti is the deep sleep state, in which our mind is inactive and we are completely disconnected from our surroundings. In this state, our mind and body are at rest, and we experience a sense of peace and tranquillity. Deep sleep is essential for physical and mental restoration, allowing us to wake up feeling refreshed and rejuvenated. It can be understood as a healing process. During deep sleep, the mind is indeed inactive and there is no conscious awareness of the external environment or even the body. The awareness of the body is a function of the mind, and since the mind is in a state of rest during deep sleep, the body is not perceived.

This lack of awareness is one of the reasons why deep sleep is often described as a state of unconsciousness. However, it is important to note that, even though there is no conscious awareness of the body during deep sleep, the body continues to function autonomously. The heart continues to beat, the lungs continue to breathe, and the various organs and systems in the body carry out their respective functions without any conscious effort or control.

While the state of *sushupti* may not directly contribute to the expansion of consciousness, it has several benefits:

1. **Physical restoration.** Deep sleep allows the body to repair and rejuvenate itself. It promotes healing, replenishes energy levels, and supports overall well-being.
2. **Mental rejuvenation.** Deep sleep helps to restore cognitive functions, improve memory consolidation, and enhance mental clarity upon waking up.
3. **Emotional balance.** Sufficient deep sleep contributes to emotional stability, reduces stress levels, and enhances mood regulation.
4. **Integration of experiences.** Deep sleep aids in integrating and assimilating information and experiences from waking and dreaming states. It facilitates the processing and organisation of memories and knowledge.

While deep sleep may not directly facilitate the expansion of consciousness in terms of spiritual or metaphysical growth, it plays a crucial role in maintaining physical and mental health, which can indirectly support personal development and overall well-being.

The *sushupti* state of consciousness and deep meditative states share some similarities, but they are not identical.

Similarities Between the Sushupti and Deep Meditation States

1. **Absence of awareness.** Both deep sleep and deep meditative states involve a reduced or suspended awareness of external stimuli.
2. **Restful state.** Both states promote relaxation and rest, allowing the mind and body to enter a state of profound calmness.
3. **Altered perception of time.** In both deep sleep and deep meditation, individuals may experience a distortion of time, perceiving it to be shorter or longer than it actually is.
4. **Healing and rejuvenation.** Both states can have restorative effects on the body and mind, aiding in physical healing and mental rejuvenation.

Differences Between the Sushupti and Deep Meditation States

1. **Consciousness vs. awareness.** In deep sleep, the consciousness is largely inactive, and there is no conscious awareness. In deep meditation, although the mind is focused and concentrated, there is an active awareness and presence.
2. **Purpose and intention.** Deep sleep is a natural physiological process necessary for rest and rejuvenation. Deep meditation, on the other hand, is a deliberate practice aimed at cultivating various qualities, such as mindfulness, insight, and spiritual growth.

3. **Cognitive engagement.** Deep meditation involves active mental engagement, such as focusing on an object, repeating a mantra, or observing thoughts and sensations. Deep sleep lacks such deliberate cognitive engagement.
4. **Expansion of consciousness.** Deep meditation is often associated with the expansion of consciousness, as it can lead to insights, expanded awareness, and a deepening of spiritual experiences. Deep sleep, while essential for overall well-being, does not typically involve the expansion of consciousness in the same way.

Turiya

Finally, *turiya* is the state of transcendence in which we are fully awake and conscious but no longer identify with our thoughts or physical body. In this state, we experience a sense of oneness with the universe and a deep understanding of our place in it. *Turiya* is a state of profound spiritual insight in which we can access our deepest wisdom and connect with our higher selves.

The *turiya* state and superconsciousness are related concepts but they are not exactly the same. While both involve transcending the limitations of the ordinary waking state, they are described in slightly different ways and may be understood differently depending on the specific spiritual or mystical tradition in question. *Turiya* is a Sanskrit term used in the Hindu tradition to refer to the fourth state of consciousness, beyond the waking, dreaming, and deep sleep states. In this state, the individual is said to experience pure consciousness, free from all mental activity and duality. This state is often described as a state of transcendental awareness, in which the individual is able to perceive reality beyond the limitations of the physical world. Superconsciousness, on the other hand, is a term used in various spiritual and mystical traditions to describe a higher state of consciousness that goes beyond the ordinary waking state. It is often associated with experiences of expanded awareness, higher perception, and connection with a higher power or universal consciousness.

Leveraging the Four States for Spiritual Growth

In the Hindu tradition, the four states of consciousness are often seen as different levels of awareness that can be used for spiritual growth and gaining wisdom. Here's how each state can be leveraged for this purpose:

1. ***Jagrat.*** In this state, the individual is fully awake and engaged with the physical world. This state is characterised by sensory perception, thinking, and action. To gain wisdom in the waking state, one can cultivate mindfulness and awareness of one's thoughts, emotions, and actions. By observing and reflecting on one's experiences, one can gain insight into the nature of reality and the workings of the mind.
2. ***Svapna.*** In the dream state, the individual is asleep but still experiences mental activity in the form of dreams. This state is characterised by imagination, creativity, and symbolic thinking. To gain wisdom in the dream state, one can learn to interpret and reflect on one's dreams. Dreams can reveal subconscious patterns and beliefs that may be affecting one's waking life. By exploring and understanding one's dreams, one can gain insight into the deeper workings of the mind and the psyche.
3. ***Sushupti.*** In the deep sleep state, the individual is in a state of complete rest and absence of mental activity. This state is characterised by a sense of peace, stillness, and inner silence. To gain wisdom in the deep sleep state, one can cultivate practices such as meditation and self-enquiry. By accessing inner stillness and silence through a deep meditative state,

one can connect with a deeper aspect of oneself and gain insight into the nature of consciousness itself.

4. ***Turiya.*** In the *turiya* state, the individual experiences a state of pure consciousness beyond the limitations of the physical world and the mind. This state is characterised by a sense of transcendence, unity, and wholeness. To gain wisdom in the *turiya* state, one can engage in practices such as meditation, self-enquiry, and devotion. By experiencing the state of pure consciousness, one can gain insight into the nature of the self, the universe, and the ultimate reality.

AUM: The Fundamental Sound of the Universe

The Mandukya Upanishad, which is part of the Atharva Veda and considered one of the major Upanishads, focuses on the nature of consciousness and the ultimate reality of existence. It introduces the AUM mantra as the fundamental sound of the universe and describes it as consisting of three syllables: A, U, and M. Each syllable represents a different aspect of existence: A stands for waking consciousness, U stands for dreaming consciousness, and M stands for deep sleep consciousness. The silence after the sound 'M' represents the fourth state of consciousness, *turiya*.

Therefore, chanting the AUM mantra is believed to help practitioners connect with all four states of consciousness and ultimately reach the state of *turiya*, which is regarded as the ultimate spiritual goal in Hinduism. The AUM mantra is also believed to have a profound effect on the mind and consciousness, helping provide access to wisdom and spiritual insight. The repetition of the mantra is a form of meditation and is believed to help quiet the mind, promote inner peace and clarity, and, over time, increase concentration, focus, and awareness, which can lead to a deeper understanding of oneself and the world. It is said that the sound vibrations of the AUM mantra have a purifying effect on the mind and body and can help remove negative thoughts and emotions. By purifying the mind, one can attain a state of inner peace and clarity, which can lead to the development of wisdom.

One way of leveraging the four states of consciousness for spiritual development is to use them as tools for self-exploration and personal growth. For example, by paying attention to our dreams and analysing their symbolism, we can gain insights into our subconscious desires and fears. This can help us identify areas of our lives that require attention. Similarly, by practising mindfulness and meditation, we can learn to quiet our minds and access deeper states of consciousness. This allows us to tap into our inner wisdom and connect with our higher selves.

Another way to leverage these faculties is to use them as tools for creativity and innovation. By accessing deeper states of consciousness, we can tap into our creative potential and generate new ideas and solutions. This is particularly relevant in today's fast-paced and constantly evolving world, where innovation and creativity are highly valued. By accessing deeper states of consciousness, we can connect with our shared humanity and develop a sense of oneness with the universe. This can help us become more compassionate and empathetic towards others and make a positive impact in the world. By leveraging these faculties through practices such as mindfulness, meditation, and self-exploration, we can align with our core values, improve our spiritual intelligence, and make a positive impact on the world.

Understanding the concepts of the conscious, subconscious, and superconscious mind and the Vedic principle of the four states of mind can have significant relevance on our day-to-day life. The latter provides a framework for understanding the different levels of our consciousness and the potential for spiritual growth and evolution. By developing an awareness of these different layers, we can gain insights into our thoughts, emotions, and behaviours and work towards personal growth and self-improvement. By exploring and practising the techniques associated with each state, we can deepen our understanding of our true nature, develop greater self-awareness, transcend our ego-driven desires, cultivate compassion and interconnectedness, work towards personal growth and spiritual evolution, and move towards a state of pure awareness and higher consciousness.

Exploring the Link Between Transpersonal Psychology and Vedic States of Consciousness

Abraham Maslow and Ken Wilber, renowned American psychologists, have established and developed models of human development, including expanded consciousness. There appears to be some connection between these models, more particularly Ken Wilber's integral theory and the Vedic four states of consciousness, including the mind's superconscious state, although they are not directly comparable. It's essential to note that these models come from different backgrounds and disciplines but they provide valuable insights into understanding human growth and consciousness from different perspectives.

Abraham Maslow was best known for his theory of human motivation, often referred to as Maslow's hierarchy of needs. His work revolutionised the field of psychology by shifting the focus from psychopathology to a more positive and holistic approach to understanding human behaviour. The hierarchy of needs suggests that individuals have needs that must be fulfilled in a specific order. At the foundational level, people require basic physiological needs to be met, such as the need for food, water, and shelter. Once these needs are met, individuals seek safety and security, then love and belonging, and self-esteem, and finally self-actualisation, which represents the realisation of one's full potential.

Ken Wilber is known for his groundbreaking work on integrating multiple disciplines and perspectives into a comprehensive human development framework known as integral theory. His work encompasses a wide range of subjects, including philosophy, psychology, spirituality, sociology, and ecology. Integral theory incorporates multiple dimensions of human experience and consciousness into various stages of development; egocentric (self centric), ethnocentric (group focused), world-centric(inclusive), to kosmos-centric(cosmic unity) with each stage representing a broader perspective and an increased capacity for empathy and understanding of reality. He believed in the evolution of consciousness, with the higher self being the ultimate goal, reaching a holistic, interconnected perspective. This framework recognises states of higher consciousness beyond ordinary waking consciousness. According to Wilber, human development encompasses not only the unfolding of psychological and cognitive capacities but also the potential for accessing higher states of consciousness.

Both Maslow's and Wilber's models acknowledge the existence of a state of higher consciousness beyond ordinary waking consciousness. For Maslow, this is manifested in self-actualisation, whereby individuals experience a profound sense of purpose, creativity, and fulfilment. This state of self-actualisation can be seen as a higher level of consciousness in which individuals transcend their limited self-identity and connect with a deeper, more expansive aspect of themselves. Similarly, Wilber's integral theory recognises the potential for individuals to reach higher states of consciousness, which he refers to as 'transpersonal' stages. These stages go beyond the individual ego and encompass a broader awareness and interconnectedness with the world. In these transpersonal stages, individuals may experience states of unity, expanded awareness, and connection with a larger cosmic or universal consciousness.

While Maslow's and Wilber's models do not directly map onto the Vedic concept of the four states of consciousness, they do converge in their acknowledgement of the potential for individuals to transcend ordinary waking consciousness and access higher states of awareness. These models offer valuable frameworks for understanding and exploring human development and the possibilities of personal growth and transformation, aligning with the idea of reaching a superconscious state in Vedic philosophy.

The Difference Between the Subconscious and the Unconscious

The terms 'subconscious' and 'unconscious' are often used interchangeably to refer to mental processes that occur outside of our conscious awareness. However, there are some differences between the terms. The subconscious mind is typically understood to be the part of the mind that lies just below the surface of our conscious awareness. It consists of mental processes that are not currently in our conscious awareness but can be easily brought to the surface with a little effort—examples include memories, thoughts, and feelings that we can access if we focus our attention on them. This layer of the mind is often associated with automatic behaviours and responses, as well as habits and patterns that we have developed over time.

On the other hand, the unconscious mind is typically understood to be a deeper level of the mind that is completely inaccessible to our conscious awareness. It includes mental processes that we are not aware of and cannot bring to the surface without the help of psychoanalysis or other therapeutic techniques. The unconscious mind is often associated with deep-seated emotions, fears, and desires, as well as repressed memories and traumas that we may not even be aware of. Some perspectives suggest that our unconscious mind may hold imprints from past lives that have been deeply engraved within us, potentially either catalysing personal growth or hindering it.

Thus, while the terms 'subconscious' and 'unconscious' are related and both refer to mental processes outside of our conscious awareness, the subconscious is more readily accessible and closer to our conscious mind, while the unconscious is a deeper level of the mind that is not accessible without specialised techniques. The unconscious mind is a vast and complex aspect of our mental functioning, and its full potential is not yet fully understood. However, there are some ways of tapping into the power of our unconscious mind and using it to our advantage.

One of the primary ways of using the unconscious mind is through the process of visualisation. This entails using visualisation as a tool to communicate with and influence deeper levels of consciousness. The process involves creating vivid mental images that represent our desired outcomes or goals. By repeatedly visualising these images, we are essentially sending messages to our unconscious mind, programming it to support and work towards achieving those goals. The idea behind this approach is that the unconscious mind is highly receptive to images, symbols, and emotions. By engaging in detailed visualisation and imbuing our visualisations with strong positive emotions, we can create a powerful and effective means of communication with the unconscious mind. Through consistent visualisation, we can help shape our beliefs, attitudes, and behaviours at the unconscious level, leading to the desired changes and outcomes in our lives.

Another way of using the unconscious mind is the process of suggestion. This involves making positive affirmations or suggestions to yourself that are designed to program your unconscious mind to achieve a specific goal. For example, you might repeat affirmations such as 'I am confident and successful' or 'I am capable of achieving my goals' to yourself on a regular basis. By doing so, you are reinforcing positive beliefs and attitudes in your unconscious mind, which can help you achieve your desired outcomes.

Finally, the unconscious mind can be accessed through practices such as meditation and hypnosis, which are designed to quiet the conscious mind and allow deeper levels of awareness to emerge. By accessing these deeper levels of awareness, we can gain insights and understanding that will help us overcome limiting beliefs and behaviours that may be hindering our progress.

Gaining access to the unconscious mind involves deep psychological exploration and understanding, which typically requires techniques like psychoanalysis, dream analysis, or hypnosis, among others. These methods aim to bring unconscious thoughts, desires, memories, and emotions into conscious awareness, helping individuals gain insight into their inner processes. It is important to remember that the nature of the unconscious mind is still a subject of debate among psychologists, and various theories exist regarding its functioning and accessibility. While visualisation techniques may indirectly facilitate insights or promote self-reflection, they are not direct pathways to accessing the depths of the unconscious mind as described in psychoanalytic theory.

The Hidden Realm: Understanding the Unconscious Through Freudian and Jungian Psychology

It is believed that more than 50% of the human brain is blocked and, therefore, inaccessible during our lifetime. This brain, a marvel of complexity, holds vast untapped capacities. Within this uncharted territory lie information, memories, and potential that cannot be accessed through cognitive processes. The unconscious harbours hidden memories, hurts, insecurities, and fears. Our hidden potential and abilities are hindered by these obstacles. This underscores the crucial importance of uncovering the unconscious. Once we recognise its significance, it is imperative to delve into its depths. Embarking on a journey of self-discovery opens the door to transformation. We empower ourselves to confront repressed memories, unresolved pain, and lingering fears. Through this process, we free latent abilities stifled by self-doubt and apprehension.

Essentially, our minds house a vast reservoir of untapped potential and unexplored emotions. By acknowledging and embracing the importance of delving into our unconscious, we embark on a journey of self-empowerment, healing, and growth. This unlocks dormant capabilities that can lead to a deeper understanding of ourselves and the world around us.

Freudian Psychology

Sigmund Freud is one of the most influential figures in the history of psychology, and his theory of the mind is known as psychoanalysis. According to Freud, the mind is made up of three parts: the conscious, the preconscious, and the unconscious. The conscious mind is the part of the mind that we are aware of at any given moment. It includes our thoughts, feelings, and perceptions. The preconscious mind is the part of the mind that contains thoughts, memories, and other mental content not currently in our awareness but easily accessible. The unconscious mind is the part of the mind that contains thoughts, feelings, and impulses that we are not aware of but which influence our behaviour and personality. Freud believed that the unconscious is the most important part of the mind, and that it is the source of many of our desires, fears, and conflicts.

Freud also believed that the mind is divided into three structures: the id, ego, and superego. The id is the primitive, instinctual part of the mind that seeks pleasure and avoids pain. The ego is the rational part of the mind that mediates between the id and the demands of reality. The superego is the moral part of the mind that internalises social norms and values.

As for consciousness, Freud believed that it is only a small part of the mind and that much of our mental activity occurs outside of our awareness. He believed that our conscious thoughts and behaviours are often influenced by unconscious processes, such as repressed memories and unconscious motivations. Freud often used the analogy of an iceberg to explain his theory of the mind. According to Freud, the mind is like an iceberg, with the tip of the iceberg representing the conscious mind and the vast bulk of the iceberg submerged beneath the surface, representing the unconscious mind, the source of our most basic drives and instincts. He also believed that unconscious conflicts and repressed memories could lead to psychological distress and mental illness.

According to Freud, the unconscious mind is not something that can be completely controlled or stopped, as it is an essential part of the human psyche. However, he asserted that the goal of psychoanalysis is to make the unconscious more conscious and to help individuals gain insight into the underlying causes of their thoughts, feelings, and behaviours. This process involves exploring past experiences, analysing dreams, and uncovering repressed memories and desires.

Despite the similarities in their basic structure, there are some fundamental differences between Freud's theory and the Vedic theory of mind. Freud's theory focuses primarily on the role of the unconscious mind in shaping human behaviour, while Vedic theory emphasises the importance of connecting with the superconscious mind to achieve enlightenment and spiritual growth. Vedic theory also talks of understanding our thoughts and emotional and behavioural patterns to enable us to reprogram our subconscious, while Freud believed that the key to gaining control over the mind was to gain insight into the unconscious and to bring unconscious thoughts and feelings to conscious awareness.

It's important to keep in mind that gaining insight into your unconscious mind is a gradual process, and it may take time and practice to become more aware of your thoughts, feelings, and behaviours. If you are experiencing significant psychological distress, it may be helpful to seek the assistance of a trained mental health professional.

Jungian Psychology

Jungian psychology, also known as analytical psychology, is a psychological theory and therapeutic approach developed by Swiss psychiatrist Carl Jung. This theory is also based on the idea of different levels of consciousness: the conscious, the unconscious, and the collective unconscious. Jung believed that the unconscious is a reservoir of repressed or forgotten experiences and emotions and that it is not just a personal construct but also has a collective aspect. This collective unconscious contains the shared experiences and symbols of human beings throughout history, which are passed down from generation to generation.

Jungian psychology is based on the idea that psychological problems arise when the conscious and unconscious aspects of the psyche are not in balance. This can lead to symptoms such as anxiety, depression, and a sense of meaninglessness. The goal of therapy in this approach is to help the individual achieve a greater understanding and integration of their unconscious material, thereby achieving a more balanced and fulfilling life. The Jungian concepts of the collective unconscious, individuation, and the shadow self are summarised below:

The collective unconscious. Jung's concept of the collective unconscious refers to the idea that there are inherited or universal patterns of thought, feeling, and behaviour that are present in all humans, regardless of culture or personal experience. These patterns are believed to be part of our shared evolutionary history and are represented by symbols and archetypes. By working with these archetypes, individuals can gain a deeper understanding of themselves and their place in the world and connect with a larger divinity or spirituality.

Archetypes are common themes or characters that exist in the shared unconscious of humanity. They are expressed in myths, literature, and stories from different cultures and times. One example is the archetype of the hero. Jung believed that the hero archetype is present in all cultures and represents the human desire to overcome obstacles and achieve greatness. Another example is the mother archetype. This archetype represents the nurturing and caring qualities that are associated with motherhood. It is present in the myths and stories of many cultures and is often symbolised by the image of a nurturing, protective mother. Some well-known mythologies that feature archetypes include Greek mythology (stories of gods and goddesses, heroes and monsters, and epic battles), Hindu mythology (rich with gods and goddesses, such as Shiva, Vishnu, and Kali, and tales of the Ramayana and the Mahabharata), Chinese mythology (dragons, immortals, and celestial beings, such as those in the story of the Monkey King in *Journey to the West*). These archetypes continue to resonate with people today and are often used in literature, film, and other forms of art because they reflect universal human experiences and emotions. According to Jung, by recognising and understanding these archetypes, we can gain insight into our own unconscious minds and the forces that shape our thoughts and behaviour.

According to Jungian psychology, the anima and animus are two archetypes that represent the feminine and masculine aspects of the human psyche, respectively. The anima is the unconscious feminine aspect within the male psyche, while the animus is the unconscious masculine aspect within the female psyche. In other words, they represent qualities that run contrary to the dominant traits of an individual's gender. For example, a man with a strong anima may exhibit qualities such as empathy, sensitivity, and intuition, while a woman with a strong animus may exhibit qualities such as assertiveness, independence, and rationality. According to Jung, the anima and animus archetypes play a crucial role in the process of individuation, as they represent the unconscious aspects of the human psyche. To achieve individuation, one must recognise and embrace these unconscious aspects. By acknowledging and integrating them into conscious awareness, a person can harmonise their personality and achieve a state of psychological wholeness. This process allows individuals to access and utilise their full potential, leading to personal growth and self-realisation. For example, a man may need to integrate his anima in order to develop greater sensitivity and appreciation for his emotional life, while a woman may need to integrate her animus in order to develop a greater sense of assertiveness and independence.

Anima and animus can manifest in a variety of ways—through dreams, fantasies, and relationships with others. Jung believed that these archetypes are innate, meaning that they are part of our psychological makeup from birth. To leverage Jungian psychology for greater understanding and intelligence, individuals can work to recognise and integrate their anima and animus, which may involve exploring their unconscious through techniques such as dream analysis, active imagination, or other forms of self-exploration. This process can help individuals gain a greater understanding of their own psychological makeup and increase their capacity for empathy, self-awareness, and personal growth. By embracing both the feminine and masculine aspects of our psyche, we can develop a more balanced and integrated sense of self.

In simple terms, using the collective consciousness in day-to-day life means exploring your own unconscious mind to understand the shared ideas, symbols, and archetypes that are present in all human beings. This can help you gain a deeper understanding of yourself and connect with others at a deeper level.

Individuation. Another important concept in Jungian psychology that can contribute to the development of spiritual intelligence is the process of individuation. Individuation involves becoming one's true self and achieving a sense of wholeness and integration. By integrating all aspects of the psyche, including the unconscious, individuals can discover their own unique destiny and purpose in life and connect with a larger sense of meaning and purpose. Individuation is a psychological process that involves the development of a person's unique personality and identity. It is an essential part of the journey towards psychological wholeness and self-realisation.

A person who has grown up in a strict, conservative household might swim against the tide of their upbringing by feeling drawn to creative pursuits such as art or music but, due to pressure from family members to pursue a more conventional career path, might end up surrendering their passion to pursue a career in the arts. As such people grow old and delve deeper into their unconscious, they explore new artistic aspects of their personality and identity that they may have previously suppressed or ignored. They may find that their inclination towards art and creative work allows them to express emotions and ideas that they had previously been unable to articulate and that they feel more connected to their inner self as a result. This journey represents a process of individuation.

Jungian psychology also emphasises the importance of dreams and active imagination in accessing the unconscious and working with symbolic material. By exploring and reflecting on their dreams and engaging in active imagination practices, individuals can gain insights into their own psyche and connect with deeper spiritual dimensions of their being. Over time, this process of creative exploration and self-discovery leads to a greater sense of psychological wholeness and a stronger, more authentic sense of self. The person may find that they are more confident and self-assured, more able to assert their own needs and desires, and more accepting of their own flaws and limitations. This process can be challenging and often involves confronting uncomfortable truths and facing difficult emotions. However, it is ultimately a transformative and empowering process that allows individuals to live more fully and authentically in the world.

The individuation process refers to the journey of self-discovery and the integration of one's conscious and unconscious aspects (in other words, all aspects of one's psyche), leading to a greater sense of wholeness and completeness. This can be achieved by practising self-awareness and self-reflection, exploring your own unconscious mind, identifying and working through your shadow aspects (the hidden or repressed parts of your psyche), and integrating your anima/animus, which can play a significant role in this process.

Some tools that can be helpful in implementing the process of individuation include journalling, dream analysis, and working with a trained Jungian analyst or therapist who can guide and support your journey towards self-discovery and personal growth. It is important to note that the process of individuation is a lifelong journey and unique to each individual.

The shadow self. The shadow self, according to Carl Jung, represents the hidden or repressed aspects of the psyche. It includes parts of ourselves that we may not be aware of or may choose to ignore, such as our fears, insecurities, negative thoughts, and impulses. The term 'self-shadow' refers to the parts of the psyche that a person has repressed or rejected, often as a result of social conditioning or cultural expectations. These self-shadow qualities are typically seen as negative or undesirable and are often projected onto others or repressed into the unconscious mind.

Jung believed that the shadow self is an integral part of the human psyche and that acknowledging and integrating it is essential for personal growth and self-awareness. He believed that the shadow self is often the source of negative emotions and behaviours that can hold us back from reaching our full potential. The importance of exploring the shadow self lies in the potential for personal growth and transformation. By acknowledging and integrating these hidden aspects of ourselves, we can gain a deeper understanding of our motivations, behaviours, and beliefs. This process of self-exploration can help us overcome negative patterns and achieve a greater sense of wholeness. For example, a person who has been raised in a culture that values stoicism and emotional restraint may repress their own feelings of vulnerability and sensitivity, seeing these qualities as weak or shameful. These repressed emotions may then manifest as projections onto others, with the person becoming overly critical or judgemental of those who display these qualities. Another person, who has internalised cultural stereotypes about gender or sexuality, may repress aspects of their own identity that do not conform to these stereotypes, such as same-sex attraction or non-binary gender identity. These repressed aspects of the self may then manifest in dreams, fantasies, or other unconscious expressions as the psyche seeks to integrate these repressed qualities into the conscious self. Jung believed that it is important for individuals to confront and integrate their self-shadow in order to achieve psychological wholeness and self-realisation. This process of shadow work involves acknowledging and accepting these repressed or projected aspects of the self and working to integrate them into the conscious psyche.

By embracing their self-shadow, individuals can gain a deeper understanding of their own motivations and behaviours and can develop a greater sense of empathy for others. This process, which may require the guidance of a therapist or trained professional, can ultimately lead to greater psychological health and well-being. However, exploring the shadow self can be challenging and uncomfortable, as it may involve confronting our fears, insecurities, and negative emotions. It is important to approach this process with patience, compassion, and a willingness to learn and grow. Therapy and other forms of self-reflection and introspection can be helpful in this process.

Jungian psychology provides a valuable framework for the development of spiritual intelligence by emphasising the importance of exploring and integrating all aspects of the psyche, working with archetypes and symbolic material, and connecting with a larger sense of meaning and purpose in life. This helps in the process of developing self-awareness and understanding and relating to others.

There are some similarities between Jungian psychology and the Vedic states of consciousness. Both systems recognise the importance of the unconscious and the insights that can be gained from exploring it, particularly through the examination of dreams. Jung believed that dreams are a reflection of the unconscious mind and that they contain symbolic representations of the individual's psyche. He saw dreams as a way for the unconscious to communicate with the conscious mind, and he believed that analysing and interpreting dreams could provide insights into the individual's personality, conflicts, and potential for growth. Similarly, in Vedic philosophy, the dream state is seen as a reflection of the individual's consciousness and a gateway to the unconscious mind. In both Jungian psychology and Vedic philosophy, there is an emphasis on the importance of exploring the unconscious and the insights that can be gained from doing so.

Carl Jung suggested several ways of exploring and integrating the shadow self. Here are a few of his suggestions:

Become aware of your projections. Jung believed that we tend to project our own unresolved issues onto others. By becoming aware of our projections, we can identify the hidden aspects of ourselves that we are projecting onto others.

Engage in active imagination. Active imagination is a technique whereby one engages in a dialogue with one's unconscious mind, often through creative expression such as drawing or writing. This can help us access and integrate the hidden aspects of ourselves.

Pay attention to your dreams. Jung believed that our dreams can provide insights into our hidden aspects. Keeping a dream journal and reflecting on the symbolism in our dreams can help us identify and integrate our shadow self.

Practise mindfulness. Mindfulness can help us become more aware of our unconscious patterns and behaviours.

Embrace the darkness. Jung believed that exploring the shadow self requires a willingness to embrace the darkness and the discomfort that comes with it. By accepting and integrating these aspects of ourselves, we can achieve a greater sense of wholeness and self-awareness.

Exploring and integrating the shadow self is a process that can take time and requires self-reflection, introspection, and, often, professional help. Here are some ways of exploring your shadow self, in addition to those suggested by Jung:

Self-reflection. Take time to reflect on your thoughts, feelings, and behaviours. Pay attention to any patterns that may be holding you back or causing negative emotions. Journalling can be a helpful tool in this process.

Identify your triggers. Identify situations or people that trigger negative emotions or behaviours. These triggers may reveal hidden aspects of your psyche that need to be explored and integrated.

Seek therapy. Working with a trained therapist or counsellor can be a helpful way of exploring your shadow self. A therapist can provide a safe and non-judgemental space in which to explore your emotions and help you identify patterns and behaviours that may be holding you back.

Practise self-compassion. It is important to approach this process with self-compassion and understanding. Recognise that exploring the shadow self can be challenging and uncomfortable and that it's okay to take things slowly.

Embrace imperfection. Remember that everyone has a shadow self and that it's a natural and necessary part of the human psyche. Embrace your imperfections and see them as opportunities for growth and self-improvement.

Yoga Psychology: The Five States of Mind

Yoga psychology is a branch of psychology that draws from the ancient wisdom of yoga to understand the human mind and its functioning. One of the key aspects of yoga psychology is the concept of the Five States of Mind. These states are known as *mudha*, *kshipta*, *vikshipta*, *ekagra*, and *niruddha*. Understanding these states can help individuals develop their spiritual intelligence and achieve greater self-awareness and inner peace.

Mudha is a state of total lethargy and dullness also called the donkey mind. In this state, the mind is completely inactive and lacks energy or motivation. This state is associated with deep sleep and is characterised by a lack of awareness or consciousness.

Kshipta is a state of agitation or restlessness. In this state, the mind is active but lacks focus or direction. This state is also called monkey mind. The mind is easily distracted and jumps from one thought or idea to another. This state is associated with waking consciousness and is characterised by a sense of restlessness or unease.

Vikshipta or butterfly mind is a state of scattered attention. In this state, the mind is more focused than in the *kshipta* state, but still lacks full concentration. The mind is easily distracted and is prone to wandering. This state is associated with dream consciousness and is characterised by a sense of scattered attention or lack of focus.

Ekagra is a state of one-pointed concentration. In this state, the mind is fully focused on a single object or idea. The mind is free from distractions and is able to maintain a state of deep concentration. This state is associated with meditation and is characterised by a sense of deep focus and inner calm.

Niruddha is a state of complete stillness and silence. In this state, the mind is completely free from thoughts and distractions. The mind is fully present in the moment and is characterised by a sense of pure awareness and inner peace. This state is associated with the state of *samadhi* and is the ultimate goal of yoga and spiritual practice.

By understanding the five states and cultivating a greater awareness of our own mental states, we can develop our spiritual intelligence and achieve a greater sense of inner peace and well-being. Through the practice of yoga, meditation, and mindfulness, we can learn to move from the lower states of mind, such as *mudha* and *kshipta*, to the higher states of *ekagra* and *niruddha*. With practice, we can learn to cultivate a state of inner peace and awareness that can help us navigate life's challenges with greater clarity and equanimity.

The concept of the Five States of Mind is not unique to yoga psychology but can be found in various other spiritual traditions and scriptures as well. In Buddhism, the five states are known as the Five Hindrances. These are states of mind that can hinder one's progress on the path of spiritual development. The Five Hindrances are sensual desire, ill-will, sloth and torpor (lethargy), restlessness and worry, and doubt. These states are seen as obstacles to clear thinking and inner peace and are to be overcome through mindfulness and meditation.

In Jainism, the five states are known as the Five *Kleshas*. These are mental states that lead to attachment, aversion, and ignorance. The Five Kleshas are anger, greed, delusion, pride, and envy. These states are seen as the root causes of suffering and are to be overcome through spiritual practices such as meditation, self-reflection, and self-control.

In Hinduism, the five states are also closely connected to the concept of the Five *Koshas*, which we have already discussed in the previous chapter. These are layers of the self that can be penetrated through meditation and self-awareness. The Five *Koshas* are the physical body, the energy body, the mental body, the intellectual body, and the bliss body. By transcending each layer, one can reach a deeper state of consciousness and connection with the divine.

By incorporating these teachings and principles, we can deepen our understanding of the Five States of Mind. Whether we call them the Five States of Mind, the Five Hindrances, the Five *Kleshas*, or the Five *Koshas*, the message is the same: by cultivating mindfulness, self-awareness, and inner peace, we can overcome the obstacles to our spiritual growth and experience a deeper sense of connection and purpose in life.

Unveiling the Link: Brain Waves and Mind Functionality

Brain waves refer to the patterns of electrical activity that can be measured in the brain using electroencephalography (EEG). These waves are categorised into different frequency ranges, each with its own associated functions. Brain waves play a crucial role in the meditative process, helping quieten the mind and regulate or direct it towards the desired outcome through attention and focus.

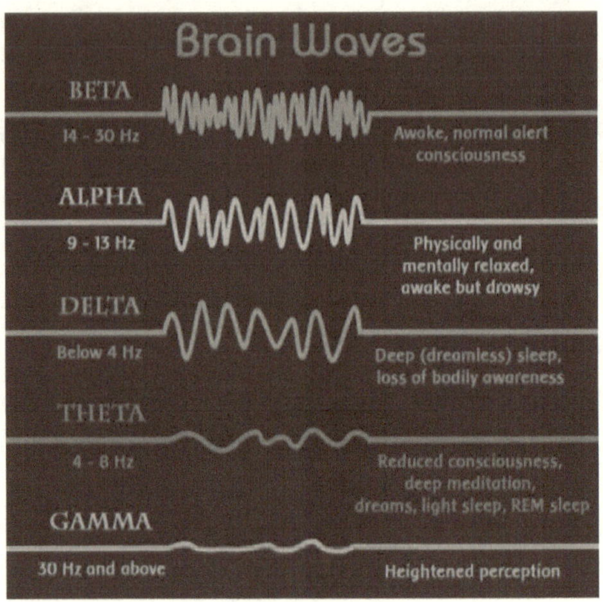

Figure 10

There are five commonly recognised brain waves:

Beta waves. Beta brain waves are a type of neural oscillation that occur within the frequency range of approximately 12–30 Hz. They are the most common brain waves observed in awake and alert individuals. Beta waves are associated with active and focused mental states as well as various cognitive processes. When the brain generates beta waves, it is typically engaged in activities that require active thinking, problem-solving, decision-making, and concentration. These waves are prevalent during normal waking consciousness, such as when we are actively working, studying, or engaging in conversation. Beta waves are often observed in the frontal and parietal lobes of the brain, which are associated with executive functions and higher-order cognitive processes.

Different levels of beta activity can indicate varying states of mental arousal. Lower beta frequencies (around 12–15 Hz) are associated with relaxed and focused states, while higher beta frequencies (around 18–30 Hz) are linked to more intense mental activity and increased alertness. While beta waves are generally beneficial for cognitive functioning, excessive beta activity or an imbalance in the beta frequencies can lead to issues such as anxiety, stress, and restlessness. For example, individuals with anxiety disorders may exhibit elevated beta activity, making it difficult for them to relax or calm their racing thoughts.

Alpha waves. Alpha brain waves are a type of neural oscillation that occur within the frequency range of approximately 8–12 Hz. They are most commonly observed when individuals are in a relaxed and calm state, with their eyes closed. Alpha waves are associated with states of wakeful relaxation, daydreaming, and light meditation. When the brain generates alpha waves, it typically indicates a state of mental and physical relaxation. These waves are often observed in the occipital and parietal lobes of the brain, which are involved in visual processing and spatial awareness. Alpha waves are also linked to increased creativity, mental imagery, and a sense of well-being.

Alpha waves are commonly observed during states of daydreaming or mind-wandering, when the mind is relaxed and not actively focused on external stimuli. They are also present during meditation, when individuals are trying to achieve a state of deep relaxation and inner stillness. Research has shown that alpha waves play a role in enhancing learning and memory processes. When alpha activity is increased, individuals tend to have improved access to their long-term memory and can retain and recall information better. Moreover, alpha waves have been associated with stress reduction and the alleviation of anxiety. Individuals who experience anxiety or excessive stress often exhibit lower levels of alpha activity. Meditation, deep breathing exercises, and relaxation techniques can help increase alpha waves and promote a state of calmness and mental balance.

Understanding the characteristics and functions of beta and alpha brain waves can help provide valuable insights into the different states of consciousness and cognitive processes experienced by individuals. Continued research in this field can further deepen our understanding of brain activity and its impact on mental well-being and cognitive performance.

Theta waves. Theta brain waves are a type of neural oscillation that occur within the frequency range of approximately 4–8 Hz. They are commonly observed during states of deep relaxation, meditation, and light sleep. Theta waves are associated with various cognitive and emotional processes, including creativity, intuition, deep learning, and emotional processing.

When the brain generates theta waves, it is typically in a state of reduced consciousness and heightened receptivity to internal experiences. Theta waves are prevalent during the early stages of sleep and are also present during periods of deep meditation or hypnosis and progressive muscle relaxation, indicating a state of calmness and tranquillity. They are commonly observed in the frontal and temporal lobes of the brain.

Theta waves have been linked to enhanced creativity and problem-solving abilities. They are associated with the integration of information from different brain regions, allowing for novel connections and insights to emerge. This state of relaxed and open awareness during theta activity can foster enhanced cognitive flexibility and the generation of innovative ideas. Moreover, theta waves are closely tied to emotional processing and memory consolidation. Research suggests that theta activity plays a crucial role in the formation and retrieval of memories, particularly episodic memories and emotional experiences. During theta waves, the brain consolidates and organises information, facilitating the transfer of experiences from short-term to long-term memory.

Delta waves. Delta brain waves are the slowest and lowest-frequency brain waves, occurring within the frequency range of approximately 0.5–4 Hz. They are primarily observed during deep sleep and are associated with restorative and regenerative processes in the body and brain. When the brain generates delta waves, it is in a state of deep sleep, unconsciousness, or extreme relaxation. Delta waves are predominant during the deepest stages of sleep, when the body is undergoing restorative processes such as tissue repair, hormone regulation, and memory consolidation.

Delta waves are believed to be essential for physical and mental rejuvenation. During deep sleep, the brain clears out metabolic waste products, replenishes energy stores, and strengthens immune function. Delta waves are crucial for the maintenance of overall health and well-being. In addition to deep sleep, delta waves can also be observed in certain meditative practices, such as yoga *nidra* or lucid dreaming. These states induce a relaxed and highly receptive mental state, allowing for profound self-exploration and spiritual experiences.

While delta waves are vital for deep sleep and rejuvenation, excessive delta activity during wakefulness can be associated with conditions such as brain injury or neurological disorders. It is important to maintain a proper balance of delta waves during appropriate sleep stages for optimal cognitive functioning and overall health.

Gamma waves. Gamma brain waves are a type of neural oscillation that occur within the frequency range of approximately 30–100 Hz. They are the fastest and highest-frequency brain waves observed in humans. When the brain generates gamma waves, it is believed to be in a state of heightened mental activity. These waves are commonly observed during tasks that require focused attention, concentration, and information processing. Research has shown that gamma waves play a crucial role in binding together different sensory inputs and integrating them into a coherent perception of the world. They are thought to facilitate communication between different regions of the brain, enabling the synchronisation of neural networks involved in complex cognitive functions.

One prominent theory suggests that gamma waves are involved in the formation and retrieval of memories. Studies have found that gamma activity increases when individuals encode new information or retrieve stored memories. Furthermore, gamma waves have been linked to states of heightened creativity and insight. Some studies have shown that individuals with high levels of gamma activity exhibit enhanced problem-solving abilities and creative thinking. Additionally, gamma waves have been associated with altered states of consciousness, such as meditation and deep relaxation. Experienced meditators often exhibit increased gamma activity, which is believed to reflect a state of heightened awareness and mental clarity.

Gamma brain waves are a fascinating area of study in neuroscience, offering insights into the functioning of the mind and its cognitive capabilities. Further research is needed to fully understand the precise mechanisms underlying gamma wave generation and the role of gamma waves in various cognitive processes.

Leveraging Brain Waves for Mindfulness and Meditation

Brain waves can be leveraged in mindfulness and meditation practices to help induce and maintain a specific mental state, such as relaxation or focused attention. By understanding the different brain wave states and their associated functions, practitioners can use various techniques to intentionally change the frequency of their brain waves to achieve their desired state. Each brain wave state can be associated with different mental and emotional states:

1. **Beta waves** are not typically associated with peace and harmony but can be useful in gaining wisdom by promoting focused attention and analytical thinking. By intentionally inducing beta waves, individuals can sharpen their cognitive abilities and analyse information with greater clarity and precision.
2. **Alpha waves** are often associated with peace and harmony. By inducing alpha waves, individuals can experience reduced stress and anxiety. Alpha waves can also be useful in promoting introspection and self-awareness, allowing individuals to connect with their inner wisdom and gain insights into their thoughts and emotions.
3. **Theta waves** are often associated with deep relaxation and a sense of inner harmony. When in a theta state, individuals may experience a sense of connection with their inner self and may be able to access deeper levels of intuition and creativity. In terms of gaining wisdom, theta waves can help access the subconscious mind and uncover deep-seated beliefs and emotions that may be hindering personal growth and development. Theta waves are also associated with heightened creativity. When in a theta state, individuals may experience vivid imagery and insights, making it an ideal state for creative exploration or problem-solving.
4. **Delta waves** are associated with deep sleep and unconsciousness, making them less relevant in the context of achieving inner peace and harmony. However, delta waves can be useful in gaining wisdom by promoting restorative sleep and allowing the body and mind to recharge and repair.
5. **Gamma waves** are associated with heightened awareness and focus, making them useful for gaining wisdom and enhancing cognitive abilities. By intentionally inducing gamma waves, individuals can increase their ability to

concentrate and process information, allowing them to gain insights and wisdom. It is the ideal state for activities that require intense focus, such as studying, writing, or creative work. This is a heightened state of awareness or expanded consciousness.

While each brain wave state has its own unique characteristics, all of them can be used to promote peace, harmony, and gain wisdom in different ways. By understanding the different brain wave states and how to induce them, individuals can develop practices and techniques that are tailored to their specific needs and goals.

Brain waves and Patanjali's Five States of Mind can both be used to describe the different states of consciousness that humans can experience. The *kshipta* state of mind, characterised by restless and scattered thoughts, is associated with beta brain waves. The *mudha* state of mind, characterised by dullness and lethargy, is not directly associated with any specific brain wave, but can be linked to low levels of alpha or theta waves. The *vikshipta* state of mind, characterised by a distracted or agitated mind, is associated with alpha brain waves. The *ekagra* state of mind, characterised by focus and concentration, is associated with theta brain waves. The *niruddha* state of mind, characterised by a state of deep meditation in which the mind is completely still and silent, is associated with delta brain waves. Lastly, gamma waves are also associated with advanced states of meditation and *samadhi*.

Nonetheless, these two systems are not directly related or dependent on each other. Brain waves are physical phenomena that can be measured using technology, while Patanjali's Five States of Mind is a philosophical framework for understanding consciousness and mental activity. Both offer different perspectives on the nature of consciousness and mental activity and can be used together to deepen our understanding of the human mind.

Chapter 6

Mastering the Mind

Our mind is a remarkable tool that holds the power to shape our experiences and reality. It is the driving force behind our thoughts, emotions, and actions, and it is important to understand how it operates to harness its true potential.

The first thing to note is that your mind functions and does things the way you directly or indirectly want it to. It responds precisely and specifically to your desires and intentions. It is attentive to the language that you use and pays close attention to the words that you speak and the mental images in your head. It is naturally inclined to steer you away from painful experiences and towards pleasurable ones. It is also programmed to seek out the familiar and therefore has a tendency to repeat familiar patterns and behaviours. This means that if you wish to do something different, you must engage in behaviours that are unfamiliar to your mind.

There is a strong connection between our internal dialogue and external communication. The words we speak and the actions we take reflect our beliefs, thoughts, and emotions, revealing the true nature of our inner world. Our thoughts have a direct impact on our internal dialogue, which in turn shapes our perception of the world. The language we use in our thoughts and conversations can have a profound effect on our experiences, shaping the way we interpret events and situations. However, the mind is also limited in its understanding of reality and imagination. This is where spiritual intelligence comes in, which is the ability to access and utilise a deeper level of consciousness to connect with the divine and to navigate life's challenges.

As has been discussed, neuroplasticity, or the ability of the brain to form new neural connections, can be used to enhance spiritual intelligence. By engaging in empowering activities and rewiring our experiences, habits, environment, and lifestyle, we can reprogram our brain to form new neural connections. By visualising and imagining empowering experiences, we can modify or edit beliefs and memories that are not serving us. Many successful athletes and performers use visualisation techniques to enhance their performance. This requires us to be mindful of our thoughts and experiences and to engage in empowering activities that support our growth and well-being. With practice, we can develop our spiritual intelligence and access the wisdom and guidance of our inner selves.

We do not know our capabilities until we put them to the test. The fourth window of our potentiality remains unexplored due to self-doubt, confusion, and fear of failure. It's okay to fail when we try something new but it's not okay to fail in the mind even before we try. Excellence is a constant process of doing your best. Every task or activity that we undertake in our personal or professional life is a challenge and an opportunity to learn to be a better version of ourselves. We have infinite potential, but our thinking, feeling, and willing patterns, if not properly aligned, may limit our actualisation.

This is why we should be mindful of emerging thoughts as well as behavioural patterns. Internal dialogue, self-talk, and self-coaching plays a great role in helping us explore our potential. Conscious thinking can be moulded into empowering patterns to elevate and accelerate our performance level.

Going Beyond the Mind

At a primary level, we often talk about mindfulness. It means being present in the moment and paying attention to our thoughts and emotions. When we are mindful, we can achieve a positive and happy state. However, mindfulness is not enough to connect with our true self. Just as the pole vault requires athletes to use a pole to jump over a horizontal bar, spiritual intelligence requires us to go beyond the mind and experience a state of mindlessness. When we do so, we connect with our true self, which is pure consciousness.

Figure 11

Understanding the State of Mindlessness

When we talk about a state of mindlessness, we mean a state in which there are no thoughts, a state in which we are free from the limitations of our mind and can connect with our true self. The idea of achieving a state of mindlessness can be confusing because it seems to contradict the concept of awareness. However, 'mindlessness' doesn't entail suspending awareness altogether. Instead, it refers to a state in which we let go of our attachments to our thoughts, emotions, and beliefs and allow our consciousness to expand beyond our usual mental constructs. In other words, mindlessness is not the same as unconsciousness. Rather, it is a state of heightened awareness that arises when we release our mental chatter and become more fully present in the moment.

One way to achieve a state of mindlessness is through meditation or mindfulness practice. By focusing our attention on our breath, sensations, or a simple object, we can quiet the mind and enter a state of deep relaxation and stillness. In this state, we become more aware of our thoughts, emotions, and physical sensations, but we don't identify with them or get caught up in them. Instead, we simply observe them without judgement or attachment and allow them to pass through us like clouds in the sky.

Another way to achieve mindlessness is through activities that promote a state of flow, such as art, music, dance, or sports. In these activities, we become fully immersed in the present moment and lose our sense of self-consciousness or self-judgement. We become one with the activity itself, and our awareness expands beyond our individual ego and into a larger field of consciousness. Ultimately, the goal of achieving a state of mindlessness is not to disconnect from the world or shut down our awareness but rather to expand our awareness and connect more deeply with ourselves, others, and the universe as a whole. By releasing our mental chatter and embracing a state of open and receptive awareness, we can tap into a deeper level of insight, wisdom, and creativity that can help us navigate life's challenges with greater ease and grace.

Clearing the Cloud of Thoughts

To enter a state of mindlessness, we need to clear our minds of the clutter of thoughts that clouds it. This is where *sadhana* (spiritual practice) comes in. *Sadhana* helps us clear our mind of thoughts and includes practices like meditation, yoga, and other spiritual practices.

Going Beyond the Senses

When we enter a state of mindlessness, we go beyond our senses. We realise that we are not our body or our mind, but pure consciousness.

The Role of Higher Intelligence

Our lower intelligence is often entangled in our senses and compulsive thoughts. However, our higher intelligence is always present within us, waiting to be activated. When we activate our higher intelligence, we become aware of the importance of a state of mindlessness. This awareness prompts us to practise mindfulness and creates heightened states of awareness. By activating our higher intelligence, we can become aware of the importance of a state of mindlessness and practise it to lead a more fulfilling life.

The Significance of Patanjali's States of Mind

One of the key aspects of spiritual intelligence is the ability to be present in the moment and aware of one's thoughts and emotions. This can be achieved through mindfulness or meditation practices, which help to cultivate a state of *ekagra*. In this state, the mind is still and clear, allowing us to connect with our deeper selves and the higher power that exists within us.

We have already learnt in the previous chapter how the five states of mind can influence our overall well-being and shape our intellectual, emotional, and spiritual growth. Of particular importance in this context are the fourth state, *ekagra*, characterised by one-pointed attention and relaxed focus, and the fifth and final state, *niruddha*, in which the mind is fully absorbed and not distracted by random thoughts. This state can be achieved after surpassing the state of *ekagra*, and signifies yoga, union with the highest consciousness. In *niruddha*, the mind enters a space of peace and vacuum, which is not empty but full of energy. This vacuum is a space of infinite potential, not known to the subconscious mind. It is here that we can tap into the power of manifestation, the ability to turn potentiality into actuality.

To manifest our potential, we must develop suggestibility, which involves believing, accepting, and surrendering to the infinite potential that exists within us. This means letting go of our doubts and fears and being open to the guidance and inspiration we receive. By cultivating a state of suggestibility, we become more receptive to the opportunities and insights that will help us manifest our greatest dreams and achieve our goals. This is commonly achieved through mindfulness or meditation, which can lead to the state of *ekagra*.

Regulation of Compulsive Thinking Through Patanjali Yoga

The inner wisdom that we seek in our efforts to develop spiritual intelligence is experiential in nature and cannot be fully comprehended through the lens of science alone. While science has made remarkable progress in understanding the physical world, the depth and complexity of spiritual intelligence is yet to be fully understood by scientific enquiry. Fields such as physics and quantum mechanics have contributed greatly to our understanding of the universe, but they are of limited use in exploring the profound depths of spiritual intelligence.

Yoga, which has been studied and documented for over 4,000 years, provides significant insights into human nature and the nature of existence. Modern psychology relies on this ancient knowledge to better understand the complexities of the human mind and its relationship with the world. By invoking our inner wisdom and drawing upon the ancient wisdom of traditions such as yoga, we can gain a greater insight into our place in the universe and the fundamental nature of reality.

Patanjali's Yoga Sutras is an ancient text on the practice of yoga and meditation. The text is divided into four chapters or books and serves as a comprehensive guide to the practice of yoga and spiritual development. The second chapter of the text, known as the Sadhana Pada, contains the famous verse, '*Yoga chitta vritti nirodha*,' which has become a cornerstone of yoga philosophy and a key principle for improving awareness and spiritual intelligence.

The phrase roughly translates to 'yoga is the cessation of the fluctuations of the mind'; in simple terms, it means, through yoga, we can bring compulsive thinking under control.

This statement captures the essence of the practice of yoga, which is designed to calm the mind and bring it to a state of stillness and clarity. The mind is often compared to a lake that is disturbed by ripples and waves, representing the various thoughts and emotions that constantly arise and distract us from our inner peace. When the water is still, we can see the bottom of the lake; the same is the case with the mind. When it is not in an agitated state, we can consider many aspects of our existence that are not known to us in our normal, conscious state.

Our mind (*chitta*) is prone to misconceptions, and we are often trapped by them without even realising it. By consistently practising yoga, we can liberate ourselves from these misconceptions and ultimately achieve true freedom. By calming the mind and stilling the fluctuations of our thoughts, we can cultivate a deeper awareness of our true nature and connect more deeply with the divine.

Western society regards the mind as a wellspring of intelligence, knowledge, and wisdom, a conscious entity that enables us to perceive and interpret the world around us. The ancient practice of yoga offers a different perspective on the nature of the mind. According to yoga, the mind's knowledge and intelligence are not inherent; instead, they are borrowed from past experiences, perceptions, and the ego. This borrowed knowledge is referred to as *vritti,* which is comparable to a wave of thoughts or perceptions. *Vritti* arises in response to external stimuli recorded by the mind's recording mechanism, *manas*. The ego then identifies with the *vritti*, labelling it as either 'good' or 'bad,' and consequently experiencing happiness or unhappiness.

Thus, yoga teaches us that the mind's intelligence is limited by its past experiences, perceptions, and ego, which colour our perceptions and influence our thoughts. However, through yoga, we can gain a deeper understanding of the mind and learn to detach from its limiting influences. By cultivating mindfulness and self-awareness, we can observe the *vrittis* as they arise and detach from the ego's identification with them. This detachment can lead to a greater sense of clarity, inner peace, and freedom from the mind's limiting influences.

The importance of the principle of *yoga chitta vritti nirodha* lies in the fact that the mind is the source of all our thoughts, emotions, and perceptions and thus has a profound influence on our experience of the world. Moreover, if *vrittis* are not controlled, they go on to become imprints of mind (*samskara*) that will keep surfacing repeatedly as patterns of thinking.

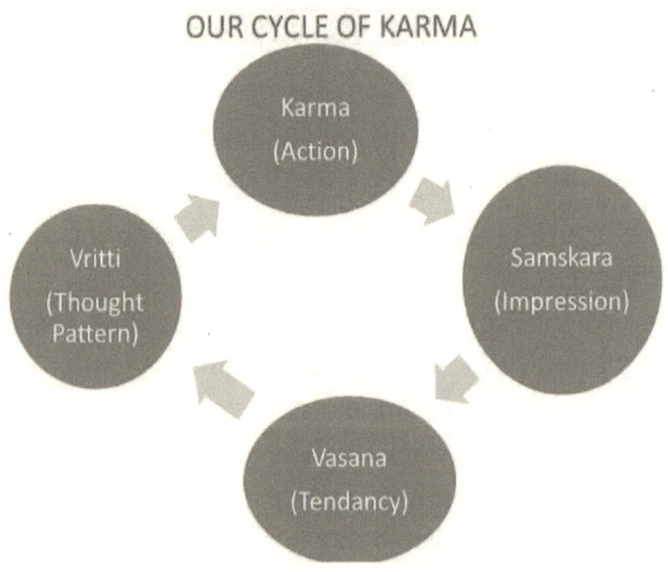

Figure 12

To begin with, let's delve into how we perceive the world we inhabit. Our senses, namely vision, sound, touch, smell, and taste, allow us to experience the external world. However, the information we gather from our senses is not always an accurate reflection of reality. We tend to generalise, delete, distort, and modify the information we receive based on our previous experiences and beliefs. As a result, the way we experience a particular thing or person is subjective and unique. The information we gather is stored in our memory bank, and we construct our own version of reality with this data. This internal model of the world that we create through the process of generalisation, modification, and deletion is our personal truth. However, it may not necessarily be an accurate representation of reality.

Thus, our perceptions are influenced by the memories and experiences stored in our subconscious mind. This concept is explained by the ancient Indian sage Patanjali, who described the mind as composed of five components or *vrittis*: *pramana* (valid knowledge), *viparyaya* (false knowledge), *vikalpa* (imagination), *smriti* (memory), and *nidra* (sleep). Understanding these components and their impact on the mind can help us improve our awareness and spiritual intelligence.

Figure 13

Pramana

Pramana refers to valid knowledge, which is acquired through perception, inference, and testimony. When the mind is in a state of *pramana*, it is clear and focused and we can see things as they are without being clouded by our biases and prejudices. This state of mind is essential for spiritual development because it allows us to see the truth and understand the nature of reality. *Pratyaksha vritti*, which is the direct perception of reality, can empower us with true knowledge and help us understand our own nature and the nature of the world. By cultivating mindfulness and being present in the moment, we can enhance our ability to perceive things as they are and recognise the true nature of our being.

Valid knowledge is the type of knowledge that helps eliminate ignorance and allows us to understand things in their entirety. It is known as *pramana* because it is based on facts and evidence. There are three types of evidence that give rise to *pramana*: direct experience, knowledge from authoritative sources, and inference. If you directly perceive something, it is called *pramana*. For instance, if you see smoke in the mountains, you can infer that a fire is causing it. However, if there is doubt or confusion, you can look for support from authoritative sources or some other evidence. Ultimately, when all the evidence is collected, and there is no hindrance to perception, you have arrived at valid knowledge.

Through the lens of *pramana*, we can analyse our thoughts and determine whether the knowledge we possess is reliable and true. This practice can prevent us from being overwhelmed by baseless anxieties, but it requires self-awareness and consistent effort. There are six types of *pramanas*. Understanding these six *pramanas* is crucial in calming the fluctuations of the mind and gaining a clearer sense of self and our place in the world. The six *pramanas* can be understood as faculties of the mind that are utilised to analyse and interpret information when we become conscious of an object or situation. To understand different kinds of knowledge, distinct faculties are required to ascertain what is true; *pramanas* can help us determine what is genuine and trustworthy by providing a framework for distinguishing between various kinds of knowledge.

The six *pramanas* are:

1. ***Pratyaksha*/Perception.** *Pratyaksha* is the most basic and primary means of acquiring knowledge. It refers to acquiring knowledge through direct experience. There are two types of *pratyaksha*: internal and external. External *pratyaksha* involves using the five senses to perceive the world around us, while internal *pratyaksha* relies on intuition and cognition of remembered feelings such as pain, love, danger, or anger. It is essential to rely on our own perceptions and not blindly accept someone else's experience as our own.
2. ***Anumana*/Inference**. *Anumana* is the process of applying reason and prior knowledge to one or more observations to reach a new conclusion. It is often used to draw conclusions about things that cannot be directly perceived. For example, inferring fire from observing smoke is a classic example of *anumana*. This method of knowledge acquisition relies on the ability to make logical connections and use past experiences to draw new conclusions.
3. ***Upamana*/Comparison and Analogy**. *Upamana* is a process by which conclusions are drawn from either observing similarities or understanding analogies between similar words, objects, or situations. Similes and metaphors can help us acquire knowledge through *upamana*. This method of knowledge acquisition relies on our ability to identify patterns and make connections between seemingly disparate things. An example of *upamana* would be comparing the speed of a cheetah to that of the wind to convey its extraordinary swiftness. This comparison helps convey an understanding

of the cheetah's speed to someone who might not have directly experienced it.

4. ***Arthapatti*/Postulation.** *Arthapatti* is the process of presuming or supposing a fact derived from circumstance or an already established fact. It is often used when there is a contradiction between what we observe and what we know to be true. In this sense, *arthapatti* can be considered the junction between common sense and conjecture. This method of knowledge acquisition relies on our ability to use our existing knowledge and make educated guesses based on circumstantial evidence. Also known as presumption, it involves assuming the existence of something that is not evident through any other means of knowledge. It is a way of inferring the presence of something based on the absence of something else that is necessary for its existence. In other words, if we observe a particular phenomenon and it cannot be explained by any other means, we presume the existence of something else that is necessary for that phenomenon to occur. For example, if we see a man carrying a heavy load with ease, we may presume that he is strong. In this case, his strength is not made evident through any other means, but we can presume that he is strong based on the fact that he is carrying a heavy load with ease. *Arthapatti* is considered a reliable means of acquiring knowledge, especially in cases where other means of knowledge fail to explain a particular phenomenon.

5. ***Anupalabdhi*/Non-apprehension.** This method of knowledge acquisition relies on our ability to use our existing knowledge and logical reasoning ability to draw conclusions. *Anupalabdhi*, also known as non-perception or absence, is a *pramana* that involves the knowledge of the absence of something. It is a way of inferring the non-existence of

something based on its absence from the realm of perception. In other words, if we do not perceive something that should be present, we infer its non-existence. For example, if we do not see a book on a shelf where we usually keep it, we infer that the book is not there. Similarly, if we do not hear any sounds coming from a room, we infer that there is no one in the room. *Anupalabdhi* is considered a reliable means of acquiring knowledge, especially in cases where other means of knowledge fail to explain the absence of something. It is also considered an important means of acquiring knowledge in Indian philosophical traditions, as it helps us understand the nature of reality by inferring the non-existence of certain things.

6. ***Sabda*/Verbal Testimony.** *Sabda* is the process of relying on the spoken or written word of past or present experts. This is considered an important and authentic means of acquiring knowledge, since we each have limited time and energy to learn truths directly. This method of knowledge acquisition relies on our ability to trust the expertise of others and understand the context and reliability of their testimony.

These six *pramanas* are essential means of acquiring knowledge. Each method has its strengths and weaknesses and can be used in different situations, depending on the context and the type of knowledge being sought. Understanding the six *pramanas* and their significance can help us evaluate the information we receive and make informed decisions based on our own perceptions and logical reasoning.

Pratyaksha is considered the most immediate and reliable means of acquiring knowledge. It involves direct sensory experience through the five senses and is often seen as the foundation for other *pramanas*. The remaining five *pramanas* can contribute to our understanding of the world, but they are not considered infallible and can be subject to error or limitations. For example, while *anumana* can lead to accurate conclusions, there is always the possibility of an error if the reasoning or observations are flawed. Similarly, while *upamana* can provide insights, analogies are not exact replicas, and, thus, the comparisons made can have limitations or be inaccurate; while *arthapatti* can be useful in explaining certain phenomena, it relies on presumptions that may or may not be entirely accurate; while *anupalabdhi* can be of value, the absence of evidence does not always guarantee the absence of the object or phenomenon in question; and lastly, *sabda* is dependent on the credibility and accuracy of the source, which may vary from source to source.

In conclusion, while the *pramanas* other than *pratyaksha* can contribute to our understanding of the world, they are not considered foolproof or completely reliable. They are subject to potential inaccuracies, limitations, and varying degrees of certainty.

Viparyaya

Viparyaya, on the other hand, refers to false knowledge, which is the result of a misperception or misunderstanding. When the mind is in a state of *viparyaya*, it is clouded by our biases and prejudices, and we see things as we want them to be rather than as they truly are. This state of mind can lead to delusion and prevent us from seeing the truth. *Viparyaya vritti* can create suffering and misery. It can arise due to past conditioning, biases, or misinterpretations of information. To overcome this, we need to practise self-awareness, critical thinking, and reflection.

Vikalpa

Vikalpa refers to imagination or conceptualisation. When the mind is in a state of *vikalpa*, it creates mental constructs or images that are not necessarily based on reality. While imagination is an essential aspect of creativity, when the mind is dominated by *vikalpa*, it can lead to confusion and distraction, preventing us from seeing the truth. *Vikalpa vritti* can also lead to suffering by creating unrealistic expectations or fantasies. However, it can be leveraged positively by using it for creative problem-solving or visualisation exercises.

Incorrect knowledge occurs when we hold a belief that is not based on reality. Our mind can create perceptions that are not rooted in actual fact, leading to delusions and fantasies (*vikalpa*) based on illusions (*viparyaya*). The majority of our thoughts are formed in this way, and we become immersed in these *vrittis* in our daily lives. It is important to base our actions on *pramana* and not be misled by *viparyaya* or *vikalpa*. As we practise yoga, we can establish correct knowledge through physical experience, awareness, observation, and self-correction during *asanas*.

Smriti

Smriti refers to memory, which allows us to recall past experiences and knowledge. This is also considered a *vritti* because recalling or remembering past experiences causes a modification of the mind. When the mind is in a state of *smriti*, it is focused on the past, which can be a source of comfort or a hindrance to our spiritual development. While memories can be useful for learning and growth, dwelling on the past can prevent us from being present in the moment and seeing things as they are. Positive memories can bring joy and happiness, while negative memories can create pain and suffering. We need to learn to let go of negative memories and cultivate positive ones to improve our mental well-being.

The relevance of *smriti* as a *vritti* lies in the fact that our memories shape our perception of reality and influence our behaviour, emotions, beliefs, values, and attitudes towards ourselves and others. Negative memories can create barriers that prevent us from realising our true nature by generating negative emotions such as fear, anger, and resentment. By practising self-awareness and mindfulness, we can identify and let go of negative memories and cultivate positive ones that support our journey towards realising our true nature. By becoming aware of the impact of our memories on our consciousness and regulating our thoughts and emotions, we can maintain balance in our *chitta* and cultivate positive memories that support our journey towards realising our true nature.

Nidra

Nidra refers to sleep or unconsciousness. *Nidra* is considered a *vritti* because it is a modification of the mind that occurs during a state of unconsciousness. Just like other *vrittis*, *nidra* can impact our consciousness and affect our mental well-being. During sleep, the mind is in a state of rest and is disengaged from the external world, but it continues to process information and experiences, and this can impact our mental state and consciousness.

While sleep is essential for physical and mental well-being, when the mind is dominated by *nidra*, it can prevent us from developing our awareness and spiritual intelligence. It is crucial to cultivate healthy sleep habits and regulate our sleeping patterns to maintain balance in our consciousness. Lack of sleep or poor-quality sleep can lead to imbalances in our *chitta*, resulting in fatigue, mood swings, and reduced cognitive function. On the other hand, adequate and restful sleep can rejuvenate our mind and body and enhance our mental and physical health. By regulating our sleep patterns and cultivating healthy sleep habits, we can maintain balance in our *chitta* and improve our mental well-being.

The Role of Yoga

The five *vrittis* can have a significant impact on our consciousness and can either help us realise our true nature or lead us towards suffering. Certain *vrittis* or mental modifications can be empowering, especially those related to *pratyaksha*, as they provide us with true knowledge. However, *viparyaya*, *vikalpa*, *smruti*, and *nidra* can corrupt our *chitta* if left unchecked. An imbalance caused by these *vrittis* can result in incorrect knowledge, leading to additional suffering and misery and can prevent us from realising our true nature and corrupt our consciousness. Therefore, the regulation and control of these *vrittis* is essential to maintaining a balance in our *chitta* and achieving a state of true knowledge and realisation. By doing so, we can avoid the pitfalls of incorrect knowledge and suffering and attain a higher state of consciousness. By practising yoga and meditation, we can develop a state of *pramana*, which allows us to see the truth and understand the nature of reality. We can also cultivate a state of mindfulness, which allows us to be present in the moment and avoid being dominated by *vikalpa* or *smriti*. By reducing our attachment to the past and the external world, we can cultivate a deeper sense of inner peace and connect more deeply with our true nature.

The practice of yoga, through the use of *asanas* (postures), *pranayama* (breathing exercises), and meditation, aims to stop these fluctuations and bring the mind to a state of tranquillity. But yoga, as outlined in the Yoga Sutras, is not just about physical postures and breathing exercises but also involves a comprehensive system of ethical and moral guidelines known as the *yamas* and *niyamas*. These guidelines include principles such as non-violence, truthfulness, non-stealing, purity, contentment, self-discipline, self-study, and surrender to a higher power. Yoga teaches us to control the mind so that the mind doesn't control us. By paying attention to our thoughts and choosing to focus on those that benefit us rather than those that bring us down, we can experience the power of the mind and a newfound sense of freedom.

According to the Yoga Sutras, the mind is composed of three parts, which have been discussed previously: *manas*, the part that records external stimuli; *buddhi*, the part that categorises and analyses these impressions; and *ahankara*, the ego that claims these impressions as its own. By learning to manage these three parts of the mind, we can cultivate a sense of inner peace and clarity. Learning to control the mind requires practice and patience, but the benefits are worth it. When we can calm the waves of our mind, we can experience a sense of 'smooth sailing' in life. The mind's nature is to think, but we can learn to control the mind and prevent it from controlling us.

Many of us experience suffering due to our attachment to our thoughts and desires. This attachment, or *vritti*, causes us to cling to pleasure and avoid pain. Fortunately, the *atma*—the unchanging and divine part of us—offers liberation from *vritti*. The *atma* is the witness and seer that resides within each of us, holding true wisdom and intelligence. Unlike the mind and ego, the *atma* is not identified with thought waves. This means that it is free from the suffering of the mind and ego.

The practice of yoga is centred around freeing ourselves from this suffering. The primary goal of yoga is to disengage from thought waves and to realise our true nature, which is not the same as the ego or mind's *vritti*. The process of achieving this is not about making the mind go blank, but about unlearning the conditioning that leads us to identify with our thoughts. Though this is a challenging process, various yoga practices can help us achieve it. By doing so, we can attain true self-realisation, which allows us to live in accordance with our core (soul) which ultimately leads to enlightenment. The *atma* is sometimes referred to as the liberator, as it frees us from the limitations of the mind and ego. By realising that the *atma* is our true nature, we can break free from the cycle of birth and death caused by our attachment to the material world. Ultimately, the goal of yoga is to achieve this liberation from suffering.

Patanjali identified the five *vrittis*, which can be imagined as whirlpools in a still and tranquil pool of water, causing ripples and waves. These fluctuations manifest in the form of thoughts that interrupt and interfere with our consciousness. Patanjali believed that the goal of yoga is to tame these *vrittis* and quiet the mind, freeing us from the suffering caused by incessant thoughts. The human mind is constantly acquiring knowledge, from the moment of birth onwards; the challenge is to distinguish between true knowledge and false information and trust our own thoughts. Hindu epistemology offers an answer to this question through the concept of *pramana*, which means 'proof' in Sanskrit.

It's truly remarkable that Patanjali identified the five *vrittis* that influence the consciousness and result in modifications of the mind over 4,000 years ago. These *vrittis* operate through our five senses, which receive information and relay it to the mind. However, the mind processes this information through the lens of these *vrittis*, which can sometimes lead to incorrect or distorted knowledge (except in the case of *pratyaksha vritti*). This concept is strikingly similar to the premise of modern psychology, which acknowledges that our perception of the world is filtered through our representational systems. These systems can sometimes generalise, distort, or delete information, leading to an internal model of the world that may not be entirely accurate. It is fascinating to note the similarities in views and understanding between these two schools of thought, despite the vast differences in their origins and time periods.

Patanjali's Eight Limbs of Yoga

Patanjali's Eight Limbs of Yoga, also known as *ashtanga* yoga, is a comprehensive system of yoga that aims to achieve harmony and balance in one's physical, mental, emotional, and spiritual well-being. The eight limbs are interconnected and practising them together can help one achieve a state of self-realisation and transcendence.

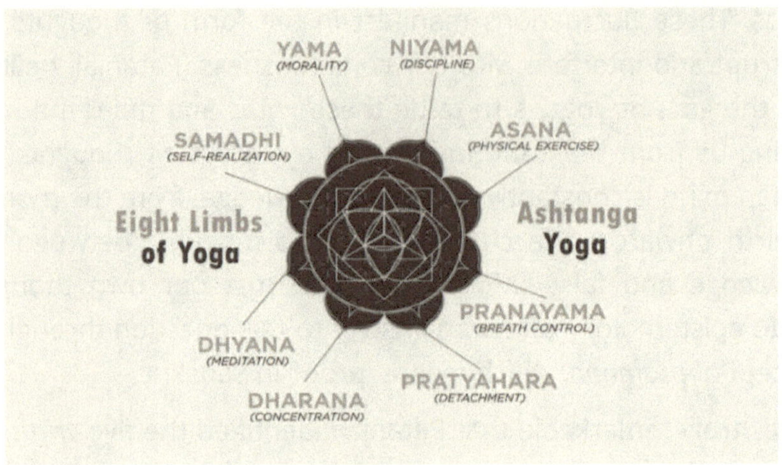

Figure 14

Here is an overview of each limb and how it can be leveraged for personal growth and evolution:

1. ***Yama* (Ethical Guidelines).** The first limb of Patanjali's Eight Limbs of Yoga is *yama*, which refers to ethical guidelines or moral restraints. It includes five ethical principles that guide individuals in their relationships with others and the world around them. These principles are *ahimsa* (non-violence), *satya* (truthfulness), *asteya* (non-stealing), *brahmacharya* (celibacy or moderation), and *aparigraha* (non-greed or non-possessiveness). By practising these principles, individuals can cultivate a sense of social responsibility and ethical behaviour. These principles can also help individuals develop a sense of inner peace and contentment, which is essential for personal growth.
2. ***Niyama* (Self-Discipline).** The second limb of Patanjali's Eight Limbs of Yoga is *niyama*, which refers to self-discipline or observances. It includes five principles that focus on individual practices promoting spiritual growth and self-awareness. These principles are *saucha* (cleanliness or purity), *santosha* (contentment), *tapas* (discipline or perseverance), *svadhyaya*

(self-study or self-reflection), and *ishvara pranidhana* (devotion to a higher power). By practising these principles, individuals can develop self-discipline, self-awareness, and inner strength. These principles can also help individuals cultivate a sense of gratitude and devotion, which is essential for spiritual growth.

3. ***Asanas.*** *Asanas* are physical postures designed to strengthen and stretch the body while promoting mental focus and relaxation. There are many different *asanas*, each with its own benefits, and they are often used as a foundation for the practice of yoga. The *asanas* also serve to establish a harmonious connection between the mind and body.

4. ***Pranayama***. *Pranayama* is the practice of controlling the breath. It involves various techniques such as deep breathing, alternate nostril breathing, and breath retention. The goal of *pranayama* is to increase the flow of *prana* (life force energy) throughout the body, which can lead to improved health and well-being. It removes the blockages in the energy channels and also helps activate the *chakras*.

5. ***Pratyahara***. *Pratyahara* is the withdrawal of the senses from external stimuli. It involves turning the attention inward and away from distractions. By practising *pratyahara*, we can begin to quiet the mind and cultivate a deeper sense of awareness. It is an effective tool with which to practise non-attachment and to remove obstacles like cravings, aversions, and delusions.

6. ***Dharana.*** *Dharana* is the practice of concentration. It involves focusing the mind on a single point, such as a mantra, a candle flame, or the breath. By developing the ability to concentrate, we can improve our mental clarity and focus.

7. ***Dhyana.*** *Dhyana* refers to sustained concentration on a single object or point of focus, such as the breath or a mantra, with

the goal of stilling the mind and achieving inner peace. This is a state of deep meditation.

8. ***Samadhi.*** The eighth and final limb is *samadhi*, which is the ultimate goal of yoga and refers to a state of complete absorption, union, and oneness with the object of meditation. According to Patanjali, *samadhi* is achieved when the mind becomes completely absorbed in the object of meditation and the practitioner experiences a state of union or oneness with the object. This state is beyond the realm of dualities and individuality, and it allows the practitioner to access a higher level of consciousness and spiritual insight. *Samadhi* is a subtle or formless representation of the divine or ultimate reality.

The teachings on the mind found in Patanjali's Yoga Sutras are unique, but some of the practices are shared by many spiritual and religious traditions. The Buddhist tradition also emphasises the importance of the mind in spiritual development. In particular, the Four Foundations of Mindfulness, which are central to Buddhist practice, teach practitioners to be aware of the present moment and to observe the mind and its various states, including those that are conducive to spiritual growth (such as mindfulness, concentration, and insight) and those that are obstacles (such as craving, aversion, and delusion). The Buddhist tradition is similar to Patanjali's Yoga Sutras in that it recognises that the mind can be trained and transformed through various practices, including meditation and ethical conduct.

Sikh teachings also emphasise the importance of the mind in spiritual development. In particular, the concept of *chitta* (mind) is central to Sikh philosophy, and Sikhs believe that the mind can be trained and transformed through the practice of *naam simran* (meditation on the divine name). The Sikh tradition recognises that the mind can be influenced by negative thoughts and emotions (such as ego, anger, and attachment), which can hinder spiritual growth. Therefore, Sikhs are encouraged to cultivate positive states of mind (such as love, compassion, and humility) and to engage in selfless service to others as a way of purifying the mind.

Unravelling the Veil of Ego *(Ahankara)*

Spiritual intelligence enables us to look beyond our ego and recognise the eternal essence that resides within us. It is this recognition that allows us to discover the true purpose of our life and to live with clarity, purpose, and passion. One of the fundamental requirements of spiritual intelligence is an understanding of the difference between nourishment of the soul and nourishment of the ego.

The mind is a complex system that consists of four faculties: *manas* (memory), *buddhi* (intellect), *ahankara* (identity), and *chitta* (cosmic intelligence). Of these four faculties, *ahankara*, or identity, is a crucial aspect of spiritual intelligence. It does not refer merely to our physical identity but goes beyond that to include our beliefs, values, opinions, and views. *Ahankara* is what drives our ego, which is a reflection of our identity. Our ego (the 'I' sense) shapes our perception of the world and influences our thoughts, emotions, and actions. It is the ego that creates boundaries and separations between individuals, leading to conflicts, misunderstandings, and other negative experiences. However, our identity and ego are not static. They can be transformed and shaped through conscious efforts.

The ego is the part of us that is driven by external validation, material wealth, and power. It is the voice in our head that tells us we need to be better, more successful, or more popular in order to be happy. It is the part of us that is never satisfied and constantly craves more. The soul, on the other hand, is the essence of our being. It is the part of us that is connected to something greater than ourselves and seeks meaning, purpose, and fulfilment in life.

The ego is a master of deception. It can easily cloud our judgement and lead us down a path that is not in alignment with our true purpose. It can make us believe that external validation, material possessions, and power are the keys to happiness, when in reality they are just temporary distractions from our true path. This is where spiritual intelligence comes into play. By focusing our awareness on our core (soul), we can begin to unravel the veil of the ego and see the truth that lies beyond.

Through mindfulness and self-reflection, we can liberate our core from the bondage of our ego. By cultivating a deep sense of awareness, we can begin to see through the illusions that our ego creates and connect with the deeper dimensions of our being. We can begin to recognise the voice of our soul and to live in alignment with its purpose. When we do this, we become free from the constant craving for external validation and material possessions and find true fulfilment in our lives. The process of awakening to our true nature can be a difficult one. It requires us to confront our deepest fears, doubts, and insecurities. It also requires us to be honest with ourselves about our shortcomings and limitations. However, it is a journey that is worth taking, as it leads us to a place of inner peace, joy, and purpose.

One of the most powerful tools for the development of spiritual intelligence is self-reflection and enquiry. In this context, it is important to understand what our true identity is. Our true identity is not merely a matter of who we are or what we do but, rather, a purpose-driven quest that is rooted in our core values. To truly understand our existence on this earth, we must first identify our purpose, our reason for being. This means going beyond the surface of superficial labels and roles we may assign to ourselves or be assigned by society and instead tapping into the deeper, more fundamental aspects of our being.

Knowing our true identity requires us to be in alignment with our core values, which are the principles that guide our thoughts, actions, and decisions. When we are true to our values, we experience a sense of coherence and harmony in our lives. Our values serve as a compass that guides us towards what is meaningful and fulfilling and away from what is unimportant or distracting. The creation of a state of bliss in our lives is a natural result of our being in alignment with our core values and pursuing our purpose. Bliss is not merely a fleeting emotion but a state of being that is characterised by a sense of inner peace, contentment, and fulfilment. It is a state that is independent of external circumstances or material possessions; it arises from within us.

Seeking wisdom is a crucial part of discovering and living out our true identity. Wisdom is the ability to see beyond the surface level of things, to discern what is truly valuable and meaningful, and to act accordingly. It is a lifelong pursuit that requires an openness to new ideas, a willingness to learn from our experiences and from others, and a humility founded upon the recognition that we do not have all the answers.

Living a life of fulfilment, therefore, is not about achieving external success or accumulating material possessions, but rather about aligning ourselves with our purpose and values, cultivating a state of inner bliss, and seeking wisdom to guide us on our journey. When we live in alignment with our true identity, we are able to experience a deep sense of purpose, meaning, and fulfilment in our lives.

The practice of mindfulness and meditation can help individuals become aware of their false or assumed identities and allow them to connect with their true selves. When our consciousness reflects in our *chitta*, there is an awakening that leads to enlightenment.

Ahankara is our sense of identity, which is not limited to our profession, religion, or community but goes beyond it. However, if our identity is ego-driven, it can cloud our judgement and influence our decision-making.

Chitta is our cosmic intelligence, which reflects our consciousness when it is not clouded by false identity. However, our ego-driven identity can hijack even our intellect, and our *chitta* becomes clouded by ego-driven thoughts. Spiritual intelligence encourages us to become aware of our false identity and allow pure awareness to reflect in our *chitta* through mindfulness and meditation. When we shed our ego-driven thought process, we can awaken to true knowledge and wisdom.

The process of shedding off *ahankara*, or ego-driven thought processes, is crucial for spiritual growth and development. It involves recognising the limitations of our identities and opening ourselves to the infinite possibilities that exist beyond them. This shift in perspective allows us to let go of our attachment to material possessions, negative emotions, and toxic relationships, leading to greater peace, happiness, and fulfilment. Mindfulness and meditation hold the key to developing spiritual intelligence. By becoming more aware of our thoughts, emotions, and behaviours, we can identify our ego-driven tendencies and take steps to overcome them. Through meditation, we can connect with our inner self and the universal consciousness, leading to greater clarity, wisdom, and insight.

Your Inner Voice is Your Guru

When we are faced with conflicts or important decisions, we often seek the opinion of others. While seeking advice is not wrong, spiritual traditions emphasise that we are best-equipped to find our own solutions, as all the resources are within us. Our inner voice is the intuitive power that guides us. However, our inner voice can often be clouded by confusion, doubts, anxiety, fear, and the dominance of our 'I' sense or ego.

To listen to our inner voice, we need to remove the cloud of these negative emotions. Mindfulness and meditation can help with this and reveal to us multiple options that can be converted into opportunities. When we consult others, we may get a different perspective that we had not considered. However, it is important to reflect on why our inner voice did not discover that option. We should not simply accept the suggested option without evaluating it and filtering it through our internal dialogue.

When we listen to everyone around us but do what we feel in our core, we can ascertain and firm up ownership and accountability. We can then go ahead with an execution plan. We should listen to everyone around us, but we should do what we feel is right only when we have conviction. When we listen to our inner voice, we can awaken to true knowledge and wisdom.

Trusting Your Inner Voice

One of the key components of spiritual intelligence is the ability to trust our own inner guide, rather than relying on external sources for validation or direction. Over time, many of us have come to rely on the opinions of others to help us make decisions and guide our actions. We seek the advice of friends, family members, and experts, hoping that they will be able to provide us with the answers we need. However, relying too heavily on external sources of guidance can leave us feeling vulnerable and uncertain.

The truth is that no one knows us better than we know ourselves. Others may offer us advice based on their own experiences and beliefs, but ultimately, we are the only ones who can truly know what is best for us. This is where spiritual intelligence comes in. When we learn to trust our own inner guide, we are able to tap into a deep well of wisdom and insight that is uniquely our own. Trusting our inner guide means being willing to let go of the opinions and judgements of others. We must learn to recognise that their feedback is simply that—feedback. It does not reflect our worth or our abilities. When we are able to detach from the opinions of others, we can begin to trust our own instincts and make decisions based on what feels right for us.

In the modern world, spiritual emptiness is a universal disease. Achieving mindfulness and spiritual intelligence requires us to confront this disease. Emptiness is a void within us, a gap between our aspirations and our sense of fulfilment, leading to a sense of loneliness, despair, and dejection. People try to escape their emptiness by getting involved in other activities to keep their minds busy. This void communicates with us. This emptiness is actually a calling, inviting us to connect with our core values and true purpose. While this may seem like a sad state of affairs, it actually holds great potential for growth and transformation.

The feeling of emptiness that you're experiencing suggests that there's a yearning within your soul for something more. Your soul is crying out, signalling that you require spiritual alignment with a deeper connection to your core values. There's a gap between what you're currently doing and what you need to do, which is your true calling. It's important to listen to this inner voice, as it has the power to transform your life. By heeding this message and aligning with your calling, you can find a sense of purpose and fulfilment that may have been missing before. By listening to the song of your soul and gaining clarity on your purpose, you can realign with your core and be filled with momentum and drive. Meditation can provide you with the power to achieve this clarity and take the necessary steps to move forward. Once you discover your true calling, you will pursue it with passion.

By listening to that inner silence, we can unfold a new version of ourselves that is richer, more meaningful, and more fulfilling. It is in this state of emptiness that we can recognise our true potential and start to access and manage it. We must recognise and understand that it is an invitation to evolve spiritually. Through meditative practices, we can discern and work on our spiritual needs to overcome this void and lead a life of fulfilment.

It's important to note that the psychological experience of emptiness or void should not be mistaken for the Buddhist concept of emptiness or *shunya*. While both may involve a sense of emptiness, the two are fundamentally different. The psychological condition of emptiness is a conscious state that can be distressing and disorienting, whereas the Buddhist concept of emptiness refers to a profound meditative state of consciousness. Conflating the two can lead to confusion and misunderstandings about Buddhism and its practices. The state of emptiness in Buddhism is a central feature of the path to enlightenment, and it is characterised by freedom from attachment and a deep understanding of the nature of reality. In contrast, the psychological experience of emptiness is often associated with feelings of loneliness, boredom, or a lack of purpose. By understanding the difference between the two, we can better appreciate the transformative power of Buddhist practice and support those who may be struggling with the psychological experience of emptiness.

Developing spiritual intelligence requires a willingness to cultivate self-awareness and to listen deeply to our inner voice. We must be willing to take the time to reflect on our values, beliefs, and goals, and to align our actions with these principles. This may require us to make difficult choices and to stand up for what we believe in, even when it is unpopular or goes against the advice of others. At the same time, we must also cultivate compassion and understanding for others. Just as we seek to trust our own inner guide, we must also recognise that others are on their own unique paths. We cannot control their opinions or judgements, but we can choose how we respond to them. When we are able to approach others with kindness and understanding, we create space for deeper connections and greater understanding.

Perception is Not Reality

Spiritual intelligence entails the ability to see the reality beyond surface-level perception. It is the power to recognise that our perceptions are not the absolute truth and that our beliefs and perspectives can be altered by changing our perception. This ability is critical to understanding oneself and the world.

Perception is not reality. It is a modification and fabrication of the mind based on what we sense through our representational system. We have already seen above that our perceptions are formed based on our beliefs, values, and experiences, which make up our model of the world. However, our model of the world is not a universal truth; rather, it is a subjective reality that we create for ourselves. Changing our perspective can alter our perception of reality. When we change our perspectives, we open ourselves up to different possibilities. This openness to learning and exploring new dimensions of life enables us to form an empowering belief system, which results in elevation and emancipation. Through this process, we learn to accept different perspectives and we become more accepting and tolerant of others.

Reality is perceived only through direct evidence. Information that is processed through assumptions, inferences, hypotheses, or comparisons can be misleading. Therefore, what we believe based on our perception may be entirely accurate, partially accurate, partially incorrect, or entirely wrong. When we put our perspectives through these four filters of scrutiny, we become open to different viewpoints, which can expand our minds and broaden our understanding of the world. We have already dwelt on these aspects in the discussions on Pantajali's *vrittis* of mind and more specifically on *pramana*.

Spiritual intelligence is about being mindful of our perceptions and beliefs and being open to changing them when necessary. By doing so, we can reduce intrapersonal and interpersonal conflict and create harmony in our relationships with ourselves and those around us. Another way to develop spiritual intelligence is by learning about different spiritual traditions and beliefs to broaden our perspective and deepen our understanding of others. Very often, we tend to dismiss others' opinions if they do not match our own. We may believe that our way of thinking is the only right way, and we may be closed off to different perspectives. However, if we are open to different perspectives, we can expand our experience and the horizon of what we see.

The number 9 is a simple and a good example of how tricky perspectives can be. When viewed from the top, it looks like the number 6, and when viewed from the bottom, it looks like the number 9. Similarly, in many life situations, people come up with diverse views, and each of them is right from their perspective. This is because each person's internal model of the world and their experiences shapes their perspective. Therefore, there is nothing inherently right or wrong about any particular perspective. Our perspective makes it so. The moral of this is that, unless we learn to see things from different positions and understand others' points of view, we will never know the truth.

Diving into *Anekantavada* Theory: Embodying the Multifaceted World

The theory of *anekantavada* holds that reality is not fixed or absolute but is constantly changing and evolving. It suggests that there are multiple perspectives or viewpoints that can be used to understand and interpret reality. Each perspective is partial and incomplete and can only provide a limited understanding of the truth. The Jain concept of *anekantavada* is closely related to the idea of *syadvada*, or the doctrine of conditioned viewpoints. *Syadvada* holds that every statement about reality is true only from a certain perspective and that it may be false or incomplete from other perspectives. Therefore, Jainism emphasises the importance of considering multiple viewpoints and being open to new ideas and perspectives.

The theory of *anekantavada* has many practical applications in Jainism. It encourages individuals to be tolerant and respectful of different beliefs and opinions and to avoid dogmatism and absolutism. It also promotes the practice of non-violence and compassion, as it recognises the inherent value and dignity of all.

Jainism relies on the following arguments to support the idea of accepting different or multiple perceptions:

- Every individual has their own unique experiences and perspectives, which shape their understanding of reality.
- Language and concepts are limited and cannot fully capture the complexity of reality.
- Reality is constantly changing and evolving, so no single perspective can provide a complete and unchanging understanding of it.
- Different perspectives can complement and enrich each other, leading to a deeper and more comprehensive understanding of reality.
- Respecting and acknowledging different perspectives can promote tolerance, compassion, and non-violence towards others.

There are also arguments for discounting certain perceptions:

- Some perceptions may be based on limited or false information and, therefore, may not accurately reflect reality.

- Perceptions can be influenced by personal biases, emotions, and prejudices, which could be shaped by cultural and societal norms and can distort one's understanding of reality.

The *anekantavada* theory encourages individuals to approach reality with a sense of humility and openness, recognising that their understanding of reality is limited and partial. It emphasises the importance of considering different perspectives while also being critical and discerning in evaluating them. By embracing this multifaceted approach to truth, Jainism seeks to promote harmony, tolerance, and compassion in the world.

The Story of the Blind Men and the Elephant

The story of the blind men and the elephant is a famous parable that has been told in many cultures and religions, including Jainism. In this story, six blind men are asked to describe what an elephant is like, but each man can only touch one part of the elephant. The man who touches the elephant's leg thinks it is like a pillar, the one who touches the tail thinks it is like a rope, the one who touches the trunk thinks it is like a tree branch, the one who touches the ear thinks it is like a fan, the one who touches the belly thinks it is like a wall, and the one who touches the tusk thinks it is like a spear.

The point of this story is to illustrate the concept of *anekantavada*. The truth is multifaceted and cannot be captured by any single perspective; this is why the blind men in the story are unable to describe the elephant accurately. Each one has a limited perspective and is only able to describe a small part of the whole. In Jainism, embracing *anekantavada* is considered essential to achieving spiritual enlightenment, as it encourages individuals to be open-minded, tolerant, and compassionate towards others.

It is often said that nobody is an expert on life. This is true because every individual has their own unique experiences, beliefs, and perspectives that shape their understanding of the world. The only person who can truly understand and handle your life well is you. Others can provide objective views, but ultimately, you are the subject and the only person who can make decisions that align with your values and purpose.

The first step towards taking control of your life is to become aware of what you love the most, the aspirations that give you a sense of fulfilment. This requires taking time to reflect on your experiences, values, and goals. By doing this, you can gain clarity on what matters to you and what you want to achieve in life. Once you have clarity on your purpose, the next step is to pursue it with passion and love. You don't need complex strategies or processes to achieve your goals. Instead, you need to let your passion guide you, and your inner wisdom will take care of the rest. This intrinsic motivation will drive you towards your vision without the need for external triggers or incentives.

As you embark on this journey, it is important to keep in mind that the concept of survival of the fittest is no longer applicable in today's world. Instead of focusing on competition, we should shift our focus to contribution. By doing so, we can create a win-win situation for everyone and empower ourselves to live creative lives. By becoming aware of what matters to us, pursuing our goals with passion, and cultivating practices that nurture our spiritual growth, we can unlock our full potential and make a positive impact on the world. Remember, you are the expert in your life and you have the power to make it the best it can be.

Long before the concept of the computer was even thought of, human beings refreshed, rebooted, recycled, reconnected, reprogrammed, and reaffirmed themselves. While using these functions to upgrade machines, unfortunately, we neglect to mindfully use them to realise the immense possibilities within us. Your inner voice and inner intelligence, in the forms of instinct and intuition, will guide you. You must institute a system and put a process in place through mindfulness or meditation, using the above faculties to seek guidance from the inner voice and intelligence within and thereby realising true knowledge and wisdom.

What's not serving us or blocking our energy must be recycled. Periodically, we must refresh and reconnect to new knowledge spaces. We also need to re-energise and perform reprogramming to align with the aspirations that arise from our core values, which gives us a sense of fulfilment. These faculties can be sensibly put to optimum use to realise our true potential.

Spiritual intelligence enables us to explore the mysteries of life beyond our immediate physical reality and find a deeper sense of fulfilment and satisfaction. However, developing spiritual intelligence is not an easy task, as it requires us to challenge many of our preconceptions and beliefs about the world and ourselves. One of the critical aspects of this process is unlearning—letting go of our existing notions and beliefs to create space for new insights and ideas to emerge. An empty mind is a receptive mind, and, to learn, we must first recognise our limitations and embrace an attitude of humility and openness. This attitude allows us to be curious and receptive to new ideas, which can then lead to true learning and growth.

One of the key insights of spiritual intelligence is the recognition that the knowledge we have acquired through reading or listening to others is borrowed knowledge. While it may be valuable, it is not truly ours until we have experienced it for ourselves and verified it through evidence or *pramana* (direct evidence or experience). This is why it is essential to challenge, discount, and reject any knowledge that does not resonate with our inner truth, as it may be a misconception or misjudgement. Only by experiencing the truth for ourselves can we truly understand it and incorporate it into our lives.

It is also crucial to recognise that we are finite beings attempting to comprehend the infinite. Our senses and intellect can only grasp a limited portion of the vastness of knowledge and truth. Therefore, we must be humble and receptive to the possibility that there may be aspects of reality we cannot comprehend fully. The ego or *ahankara* can hijack our intellect and cloud our mind, preventing us from experiencing the deeper aspects of our being. When the clouds of thoughts or *vrittis* in our mind are clear, we can begin to see beyond the limited ego self and connect with the consciousness or soul that is our true nature.

One of the essential skills required to develop spiritual intelligence is the ability to convert loneliness to solitude. This art requires understanding the thin lines between loneliness, emptiness, and solitude. Loneliness is the state of feeling isolated or cut off from others. It is a negative emotion that can be caused by various factors, such as social isolation, loss of a loved one, or lack of connection. Emptiness, on the other hand, is the feeling of an inner void or hollowness. It can arise from a lack of purpose, meaning, or fulfilment in life. Solitude is the state of being alone but not feeling lonely. It is the positive and peaceful experience of being with oneself.

When we experience emptiness or loneliness, the most common response is to look for ways to avoid it. We may distract ourselves with activities or behaviours that make us feel better temporarily. This approach is called escapism, and it only masks the underlying issues. However, feeling empty or lonely is a positive sign, a sign that our intuitive power is trying to communicate something profound. It is a perfect time to connect, read about, and understand the phenomenon of emptiness. The feeling of emptiness is a message from within that we are incomplete and unfulfilled. It is an invitation to explore our inner selves, values, and beliefs. It is an opportunity to reconnect with our true purpose and meaning in life. By being mindful of this phenomenon, we can learn to listen to our inner voice and inner calling. We can focus on this silence and find wisdom in it.

The feelings of loneliness and emptiness may appear to be alarming and depressive, but they can lead to realisation and enlightenment. By embracing solitude and being present with ourselves, we can discover new insights, perspectives, and truths. We can develop a deeper understanding of ourselves and the world around us.

Three Dimensions of the Mind: Insight, Instinct, and Intuition

We are all blessed with three faculties: insight, instinct, and intuition.

Insight is the ability to see something extraordinary in the available information, resulting in a sudden and profound understanding or realisation. It involves connecting seemingly unrelated pieces of information to arrive at a new and meaningful understanding, often in a creative way. Insight can be helpful in developing intelligence by allowing individuals to identify patterns and connections that others may overlook and to come up with creative solutions to problems.

Instinct is a natural sense that guides us, surfacing in our consciousness and helping us determine whether something is right or wrong. We must have faith in our instincts, as they can provide us with fast and reliable information about our environment. For example, animals rely on their instincts to survive in the wild, and humans can also use their instincts to make quick decisions and avoid danger. Instincts are innate and automatic behavioural responses that have evolved over time to ensure survival and adaptation. They offer a glimpse into the core of our being, providing a deeper understanding of the complexities of human and animal behaviour. Leveraging instincts can be a powerful tool for personal and professional growth. Instincts often manifest as gut feelings or intuitive hunches. Learn to recognise and trust these signals, as they can provide valuable insights and guide your decision-making process. Pay attention to your instinctual responses in different situations. By becoming more aware of your instincts, you can better understand your motivations, strengths, and weaknesses. This self-awareness can help you make more informed choices aligned with your true nature.

Pay attention to the feedback you receive from others. Sometimes, people around you may notice patterns or behaviours that you might be unaware of. Listening to their observations can provide valuable insights into your instinctive tendencies and how they impact your interactions and relationships. Instincts often emerge when we are faced with uncertain or risky situations. While it's important to assess risks and make informed decisions, being open to calculated risks can help you tap into your instincts and discover new opportunities for growth and success.

Intuition is a magical power that we have within us, guiding us and providing signals through someone, a situation, an event, or even a dream. Its process is less clearly defined than those of insight or instinct. Intuition is usually used to refer to a feeling or sense that something is true or important, even if there is no clear evidence to support it. Intuition can be useful in developing intelligence by providing individuals with a different perspective or angle on a problem that they may not have considered before. It can also help individuals make decisions based on their emotional intelligence and gut feelings, rather than purely logical or rational thinking.

Intuition is a phenomenon characterised by the immediate understanding or knowledge of something without the need for conscious reasoning or logical analysis. Like instinct, it is often described as a 'gut feeling' or a sense of inner knowledge. It can manifest in various forms—hunches, insights, or flashes of inspiration. Unlike conscious thought processes, which involve deliberate evaluation of information and logical deductions, intuition operates at a subconscious level. It draws upon accumulated knowledge, past experiences, and patterns stored in the mind, allowing individuals to quickly assess a situation and make decisions based on their inner guidance.

Intuition plays a vital role in decision-making, problem-solving, and creativity. It can provide valuable insights and alternative perspectives that may not be immediately apparent through rational analysis alone. Many successful entrepreneurs, artists, and leaders credit their intuition with playing a crucial role in their achievements. While intuition can be a valuable tool, it is important to note that it is not infallible. Sometimes, intuitive feelings can be influenced by biases or emotions, leading to errors in judgement. Therefore, it is advisable to combine intuition with critical thinking and empirical evidence to arrive at well-informed decisions.

Cultivating and harnessing intuition can be achieved through practices such as mindfulness, self-reflection, and trusting one's instincts. By paying attention to our inner signals and being open to intuitive insights, we can tap into this innate ability and benefit from its wisdom in various aspects of our lives. Leveraging intuition effectively involves recognising its presence, trusting it, and integrating it with other forms of decision-making. Be attuned to your thoughts, feelings, and bodily sensations. Pay attention to moments when you have a strong sense or gut feeling about something. Developing self-awareness helps you recognise and distinguish intuitive signals from other thoughts and emotions. Reflect on instances in which your intuition proved to be accurate in the past. Recognise patterns and commonalities in those experiences. This validation can build trust in your intuition and provide confidence in future intuitive judgements.

Intuition often emerges when the mind is relaxed and not preoccupied with analytical thinking. Set aside time for quiet reflection, meditation, or activities that promote relaxation, such as walking in nature or engaging in creative pursuits. These practices can help quiet the mind and create space for intuitive insights to surface. When faced with a decision or problem, pay attention to your initial instinctive response. Trust that your intuition may be providing you valuable information. However, remain mindful of biases or personal preferences that might influence your intuition. Intuition is most powerful when combined with analytical thinking. After you have a gut feeling or intuitive insight, engage in rational analysis to evaluate the situation objectively. Consider gathering relevant information, weighing pros and cons, and examining potential risks and consequences. Integrating both intuition and logical reasoning can lead to well-informed decisions.

Developing these three cognitive processes can help individuals become more intelligent and better problem-solvers. Insight, instinct, and intuition all have their unique strengths and weaknesses, and learning to use them effectively can help individuals become more adaptable and resilient in the face of challenges. However, developing spiritual intelligence through these three elements requires us to cultivate a deep trust in our own inner guide. We must learn to detach from the opinions and judgements of others and to trust ourselves. This requires us to cultivate self-awareness and to align our actions with our values and beliefs. When we are able to trust ourselves in this way, we are able to live a purposeful and fulfilling life, guided by the wisdom and insight of our own inner guru.

Transcending Boundaries: Embracing *Neti Neti* as a Spiritual Guide

The *neti neti* concept is from the Brihadaranyaka Upanishad, one of the major Upanishads. *Neti neti* is a Sanskrit term that means 'not this, not this.' It is a concept often used in Hinduism and Advaita Vedanta to describe a process of negation or elimination. The idea is that, in order to gain true knowledge or wisdom, one must strip away all that is not essential or true until only the ultimate reality remains.

The term *neti neti* is used to negate any identification of the self with anything that is not the true self. It is a powerful tool for self-enquiry, which involves a process of negation or elimination of all that is not the self. It involves questioning our beliefs, assumptions, and perceptions about ourselves and the world around us. We start by identifying the things that we are not, such as our thoughts, emotions, physical sensations, and even our identity. By doing so, we begin to recognise that these things are impermanent and subject to change and that they are not the ultimate reality.

This process of negation is used to separate the self from the external world and the ego. By acknowledging what one is not, one can come closer to understanding what one truly is. For example, if one were to say, 'I am not my body, I am not my thoughts, I am not my emotions,' eventually only the true self—pure consciousness or awareness—would remain.

The practice of *neti neti* is particularly relevant to improving spiritual intelligence because it encourages individuals to question their preconceived notions about reality and to go beyond the superficial aspects of life. It helps people develop a deeper understanding of themselves and the world around them. In order to practise *neti neti*, one must first identify the things that are not essential or true. This may include physical possessions, emotions, thoughts, beliefs, and even one's own identity. Then, one must let go of these things and focus on the ultimate reality, which is often described as pure consciousness or awareness.

By practising *neti neti*, individuals can develop a greater sense of self-awareness and self-realisation, which can lead to a deeper understanding of their own spirituality. It can also help individuals develop a greater sense of empathy and compassion for others, as they begin to recognise the interconnectedness of all things. *Neti neti* is a powerful tool for acquiring wisdom and improving spiritual intelligence. By stripping away all that is not essential or true, individuals can gain a deeper understanding of themselves and the world around them and ultimately come closer to realising their true nature.

Moreover, the practice of *neti neti* can help us overcome attachment and identification with our thoughts, emotions, and identity. These attachments can create a sense of limitation and separation and can prevent us from experiencing the true nature of reality. By letting go of these attachments, we can become more open and receptive to the present moment and to the ultimate reality that lies beyond our perceptions.

The Upanishads teach that the true self, or *atma*, is not the body, mind, senses, or any of their attributes but is beyond all of these. You may wonder how this is relevant to a layman. The relevance of the *neti neti* concept to a layman or a person living in the materialistic world stems from the fact that it is a practical tool for self-enquiry and self-awareness. In our daily lives, we often identify ourselves with external factors such as our jobs, possessions, relationships, and social status. However, these external factors are temporary and subject to change. When we identify ourselves with them, we often experience insecurity, anxiety, and dissatisfaction. The *neti neti* concept encourages us to look beyond these external factors and discover our true essence, which is beyond all forms and attributes. It invites us to ask ourselves 'Who am I really?' and to keep negating all that is not the true self until we arrive at a state of pure awareness.

While this process may seem abstract or complex, it can be practised in daily life through simple techniques such as meditation, mindfulness, and self-reflection. By practising these techniques, we can gradually detach ourselves from our identifications with external factors and experience a deeper sense of peace, clarity, and fulfilment.

Chapter 7

Self-Enquiry

Spiritual intelligence is the ability to understand and utilise spiritual concepts to navigate life effectively. It is a way of thinking and behaving that goes beyond materialistic pursuits and worldly success. To attain spiritual intelligence, one needs to go beyond external sources of knowledge and tap into the wisdom within.

Understanding 'Seer' and 'Knower'

'Seer is different from seen. Seer can see the Seen but Seen cannot see the Seer. The Knower knows the Known. But the Known does not know the Knower. The Knower is different from Known.' – the Upanishads

Advaita Vedanta proposes a distinction between the 'Seer' and the 'Seen' and the 'Knower' and the 'Known.' 'Seer' refers to the part of us that perceives things, while 'Seen' refers to what we perceive. For example, our eyes are the 'Seen' and our mind is the 'Seer.' The mind can perceive what the eyes see, but the eyes cannot perceive the mind. This is because the mind is a subtle and internal organ, while the eyes are external and physical.

Similarly, the 'Knower' is the part of us that understands things, while the 'Known' is what we understand. The Knower can know the Known, but the Known cannot know the Knower. This is because the Knower is a subjective and internal experience, while the Known is an objective and external phenomenon. The self is the ultimate Knower. This self is beyond the mind, and the mind is just a tool that helps us understand it. In other words, the self is the ultimate reality, and the mind is just a means of accessing and experiencing it. The self is not limited by the mind or any other aspect of the individual personality; rather, it is an eternal and unchanging essence that transcends individual identity.

This is a philosophical perspective that emphasises the importance of subjective experience and internal awareness while recognising the limitations of external perception and objective knowledge. By cultivating an understanding of the self as the ultimate Knower, one can gain a deeper appreciation for the nature of reality and the interconnectedness of all things. Knowing the knower emphasises the importance of subjective experience and internal awareness. It suggests that we should cultivate an understanding of the self as the ultimate Knower, beyond the limitations of our external perception and objective knowledge. By recognising the distinction between the Seer and the Seen, and the Knower and the Known, we can gain a deeper appreciation for the nature of reality and the interconnectedness of all things.

We can glean from the above that our minds and senses can only provide us with a limited understanding of the world around us. We may be able to observe and analyse the external world through our senses and reason, but there is also an internal world that we can access only through introspection and meditation. By becoming more aware of our own thoughts, feelings, and experiences, we can develop a deeper understanding of ourselves and the world around us.

This also suggests that we should strive to recognise the ultimate reality beyond our individual identity. This means recognising that our sense of self is not limited to our thoughts, emotions, and the physical body but also includes an eternal and unchanging essence that transcends individual identity. By cultivating a sense of connection with this ultimate reality, we can develop a greater sense of purpose and meaning in our lives. This understanding encourages us to look beyond the limitations of our external perception and objective knowledge and to cultivate a deeper awareness of our internal experiences and the ultimate reality beyond our individual identity.

By recognising the limitations of external perception and objective knowledge, individuals can become more aware of their internal experiences and develop a greater sense of introspection and self-awareness. This can lead to a deeper understanding of their own values, beliefs, and sense of purpose, which are important aspects of spiritual intelligence. Additionally, recognising the ultimate reality beyond individual identity can help individuals develop a greater sense of compassion and empathy for others.

It's crucial to understand not only the objects that we perceive but also the subjects who do the perceiving. Unfortunately, we tend to focus solely on the objective world, forgetting the importance of the subjective world. The objective world includes everything that can be perceived through our senses, such as sights, sounds, smells, tastes, and touch. These objects are external to us and are experienced as separate from the self—the 'Knower.' However, our sensory perception of reality is limited, and there may be more to reality than what we can perceive through our senses.

This realisation invites us to consider the nature of consciousness and the relationship between the subjective and objective aspects of reality. It raises questions. What is consciousness, and how does it relate to the objects that we perceive? Is the subjective experience of the self merely an illusion, or is it an essential part of reality? Can we truly understand reality without considering both subjective and objective aspects of it? By exploring these questions, we can deepen our understanding of the world around us and gain a more holistic perspective on reality. We can also learn to appreciate the importance of both the subjective and objective worlds and recognise the limitations of our sensory perceptions.

This true self that lies beyond the mind is often described in spiritual and philosophical traditions as a state of pure consciousness or awareness that is unchanging and eternal. According to this perspective, the mind is a limited aspect of the self that is conditioned by the experiences and perceptions of the physical body and the external world. The mind is bound by time, space, and the limitations of sensory perception and interpretation. The mind minus thoughts is equal to pure consciousness, a concept that is often associated with the teachings of Advaita Vedanta, which emphasises the unity of all existence and the non-dual nature of reality. According to Advaita Vedanta, the true self or consciousness is identical to the ultimate reality or *brahman*, which is beyond all limitations and is the source of all existence.

This idea suggests that there is a deeper reality beyond the physical world that can only be experienced through spiritual practice and self-realisation. The following are some ways to get closer to this reality:

Experiential knowledge. No university, books, or teachings can impart real/true knowledge, as profound concepts are experiential. While books and teachings can serve as guiding principles, they are third-person perspectives and cannot replace the profound knowledge that comes from within through realisation. To gain true knowledge, one needs to experience it for oneself.

The university of wisdom within. The true source of wisdom lies within each of us. We all have the potential to tap into our inner wisdom and connect with the universe of knowledge within. By being a seeker and embarking on the process of initiation and invocation of this profound knowledge, we can unlock our potential for spiritual intelligence.

Seeking the truth. Being a seeker means actively pursuing the truth and not settling for superficial knowledge. It involves questioning everything and being open to the unknown. The seeker seeks not only external knowledge but also the internal wisdom that lies within. Through self-reflection, introspection, and meditation, one can unlock the secrets of the inner self and gain spiritual intelligence.

Initiation and invocation. The process of initiation and invocation is the key to unlocking the inner wisdom within. It involves taking the first step towards self-discovery and actively seeking the truth. This process requires dedication, discipline, and the willingness to explore the unknown. By embracing the unknown and confronting our fears, we can tap into the profound knowledge that lies within.

While true knowledge comes from within, books and teachings can put seekers on the path of spiritual intelligence with guiding principles. These external sources can provide insight and inspiration, but they cannot replace the wisdom that comes from direct experience. The seeker must take the initiative and actively seek the truth.

Kabir emphasised the importance of inner knowledge over outer knowledge. According to him, true knowledge comes from within and can only be attained through self-realisation and introspection.

'Jaise til mein tel hai, jyon chakmak mein aag,

Tera sayeen tujh mein hai, tu jaag sake to jaag'

(Just as oil is present in the sesame seed, and fire is present in the flint,

Your Master is within you, if you can awaken, then awaken.)

Self-Reflection and Enquiry

Self-reflection is a faculty of self-enquiry. It is the process of looking inward and examining our thoughts, feelings, and actions. It involves stepping back from our daily routines and concerns and taking time to be present with ourselves. In this state of heightened awareness, we can observe our thoughts and emotions without judgement and gain greater insight into our inner world. Meditation is one of the most powerful tools for cultivating self-reflection and enquiry. By sitting in stillness and focusing on our breath, we can quiet the mind and create a space for self-enquiry. As we observe our thoughts and emotions, we can begin to identify patterns and themes that may be holding us back or causing us distress.

Enquiry, on the other hand, is a process of asking questions and seeking answers. It involves a sense of curiosity and inquisitiveness and a willingness to explore the unknown. When we engage in self-enquiry, we are seeking to understand ourselves at a deeper level, to uncover our true nature and potential, and to find ways of aligning our lives with our highest values and aspirations.

As we engage in self-reflection and enquiry, we become more open to suggestions or 'programming.' This does not mean that we are passively accepting external influence; rather, we are opening ourselves up to new ideas and perspectives. We are willing to consider alternative viewpoints and to challenge our own assumptions and beliefs. At the same time, we recognise that our own consciousness is the ultimate guide and teacher. Through self-reflection and enquiry, we can tap into the wisdom and intuition that resides within us and use this knowledge to guide our actions and decisions.

The process of self-reflection and enquiry can lead to a greater sense of clarity and purpose in our lives. As we become more aware of our true nature and potential, we can align our lives with our highest values and aspirations. We can clarify our goals and priorities and find ways to use our talents and abilities to serve others. Through this process, we also experience a greater sense of fulfilment and well-being. When we live in alignment with our highest potential, we feel a deep sense of satisfaction and contentment. We face challenges with greater resilience and adaptability and find meaning and purpose in even the most difficult situations.

Human beings are complex individuals with a wide range of emotions and experiences. At times, we all face challenges and difficulties that can cause emotional distress, but it is important to remember that we are not broken pieces that need to be fixed. Instead, we have the innate ability to dig deep within ourselves and overcome these challenges. This is where spiritual intelligence comes into play. Spiritual intelligence involves understanding and connecting with our inner selves and others at a deep level. When we face challenges, it can be easy to turn to others for advice and sympathy. However, this approach is often not helpful, as it can limit our ability to tap into our own internal resources and strengths. Instead, we should focus on exploring our inner selves and the innate resilience that lies within each of us. Through reflection and self-exploration, we can tap into our own internal resources and strengths to find a way forward. This means that advice and sympathy are often the last things we need. Instead, we should look for partners who can provide motivational support by connecting with us and showing empathy. When someone is willing to be a partner in our process of reflection, we are more likely to shift our state of being. This means that we can access a deeper level of understanding and connect with our inner selves to find the answers we need. By having someone to listen to us and be empathetic, we can begin to see things from a different perspective, which can help us find solutions and overcome our challenges.

Collaborating with the Self in the Journey of Self-Exploration

Self-enquiry involves developing a collaborative and curious relationship with oneself in order to explore and uncover unknown aspects of the self. Through this process, we are able to reinvent and realign ourselves with our core values, purpose, and true identity. It requires a willingness to ask ourselves tough questions and to explore our thoughts, emotions, and beliefs without judgement.

This process of self-discovery can be transformative, leading to a greater sense of clarity, self-awareness, and self-acceptance. Self-enquiry helps us become more authentic and aligned with our true selves. It is possible for us to establish collaborative relationships with others and assist them in discovering their true selves too, just as they can do the same for us.

Human beings are social creatures and we thrive in environments where we can connect with others and form collaborative partnerships. These partnerships can take many forms, such as friendships, romantic relationships, professional collaborations, or mentor–mentee relationships. When we engage in collaborative relationships, we have the opportunity to not only benefit from the insights, experiences, and perspectives of others but also to contribute to their growth and development. One way we can do this is by helping them explore and discover their true selves.

Each person has a unique set of experiences, talents, interests, and values that make them who they are. However, sometimes it can be difficult for individuals to fully understand and appreciate their own selves. This is where collaboration with others can be helpful. By engaging in meaningful conversations, sharing experiences, providing feedback, and offering support, we can help others gain insight into their true selves and uniqueness.

Similarly, when we open ourselves up to collaboration with others, we also gain the opportunity to learn more about ourselves. By engaging in discussions and activities with others, we get exposed to new perspectives, challenge our assumptions, and discover new aspects of our own personalities. Thus, forming collaborative partnerships with others can be a mutually beneficial experience that allows us to explore and discover our true selves and contribute to the growth and development of those around us.

However, when we help others explore their true selves, it's important to do so without being prescriptive or imposing our own ideas on them. Instead, we can facilitate the process of self-discovery by encouraging them to connect with their own inner resources and guiding them towards new perspectives and experiences. It's essential to recognise that everyone has the ability to discover and tap into their own inner resources. As collaborators, our role is not to take over or undermine their capabilities but, rather, to provide a motivating and supportive environment that allows them to explore their true selves. One way to do this is by actively listening and asking thoughtful questions. By engaging in empathic dialogue, we can help others clarify their own thoughts and emotions and gain a deeper understanding of their values and motivations.

We can also provide resources, such as books or articles, that might be helpful in their journey of self-discovery. Ultimately, our goal as collaborators should be to empower others to take ownership of their own growth and development and to support them as they navigate the process of self-discovery. By doing so, we can help others unlock their full potential and lead more fulfilling lives.

Be Your Own Light

During Buddha's last attempt at attaining nirvana, his disciples were filled with a sense of anguish and despair at the thought of being left without his guidance. They believed that darkness would descend upon them in his absence, and they were anxious about who would show them the light of life. When Buddha heard their concerns, he smiled and replied, *'Aatm deepo bhav,'* which translates to 'Be your own light.'

Buddha's response emphasises the importance of finding one's own path and relying on the light within oneself to guide the way. While many people may find this a daunting task, it is crucial to understand that mentors, peers, and teachers can only provide tips and guidance; the journey must ultimately be taken by oneself. The responsibility of discovering one's path and illuminating it lies solely with the individual.

In today's world, we are constantly bombarded with external stimuli and influenced by the opinions of others, and it can be challenging to tap into our inner light and find our true calling. However, by embracing Buddha's philosophy of being our own light, we can gain the confidence to embark on our journey of self-discovery and make the choices that align with our innermost desires and values. *Aatm deepo bhav* is a powerful reminder that we have the power to create our destiny and the key to unlocking that power lies within us. By learning to trust our inner voice and finding the courage to follow our own path, we can lead fulfilling and purposeful lives that are true to our authentic selves.

Developing spiritual intelligence is a process. This process is an invitation to engage in reflective thinking about one's beliefs, their impact on oneself and others, and their alignment with higher values and aspirations. Spiritual intelligence involves the ability to question and transcend one's limited ego-based identity and connect with a broader sense of purpose and meaning. By reflecting on our beliefs, we can become aware of their underlying assumptions, biases, and limitations and open ourselves to new perspectives and insights. This process of self-enquiry requires courage, curiosity, and humility, as we challenge our own biases and seek to expand our understanding of reality.

Spiritual intelligence also involves the ability to discern which beliefs and practices are serving us and which ones need to be edited or deleted to ensure that we are able to align with our higher goals and values. This process of self-transformation involves letting go of old habits, patterns, and beliefs that no longer serve us and cultivating new ones that promote our growth and well-being. This emphasises and highlights the importance of reflection, self-enquiry, and self-transformation in the context of spiritual intelligence. By engaging in these practices, we can cultivate greater self-awareness, wisdom, and compassion and become more aligned with our true nature and purpose.

It is important to recognise and cultivate the power of imagination and visualisation to manifest our creative potential. Spiritual intelligence involves the ability to tap into our inner resources and connect with the creative intelligence that animates the universe. By using our imagination and visualisation, we can transform our thoughts and ideas into tangible forms that can be shared with the world. This process of manifestation requires clarity of intention, focus, and alignment with our values and purpose.

Spiritual intelligence also involves recognising that all creations begin in the mind and that we have the potential to manifest our dreams and aspirations. This requires developing a positive mindset, cultivating resilience, and overcoming limiting beliefs and doubts. By using our powers of imagination and visualisation, we can tap into our creative potential and manifest our aspirations. By developing our spiritual intelligence, we can cultivate a deeper connection with the creative intelligence of the universe and become co-creators of our own destiny.

There is no way of tangibly measuring how good we are as humans; assessing our current state and potential for growth requires reflection and self-enquiry. In reflection mode, we can ask two fundamental questions: what am I right now as a person, and what do I want to become? To bridge the gap between the two, we need to align our goals with our core values and character and put processes in place to reach the pinnacle of our potential.

Leveraging the Johari Window for Self-Exploration

The Johari Window is a useful tool that was first introduced by psychologists Joseph Luft and Harry Ingham in 1955. It is a framework that helps individuals better understand their relationships with others and themselves.

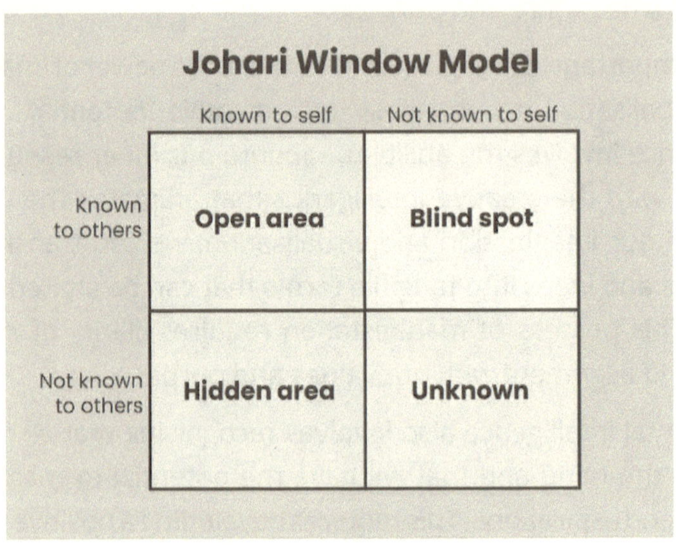

Figure 15

The window is divided into four quadrants, each representing different aspects of the self: the open, blind, hidden, and unknown selves.

The first quadrant of the Johari Window is the open self. This represents what we know about ourselves and what others know about us. In the context of spiritual intelligence, the open self can include the beliefs, values, and experiences that we openly share with others. This can help us better understand how our spiritual beliefs and values align with those of others and can be a starting point for building deeper connections with others.

The second quadrant is the blind self. This represents what others know about us that we are unaware of. In the context of spiritual intelligence, the blind self can represent how our behaviour or attitudes may impact others or how others may perceive our beliefs, values, and actions. This quadrant can be particularly important for spiritual growth, as it allows us to gain feedback from others on how our actions align with our spiritual beliefs and values.

The third quadrant is the hidden self. This represents what we know about ourselves but others do not know about us. In the context of spiritual intelligence, the hidden self can include the innermost beliefs, values, and experiences that we may not share with others. This can be a valuable area to focus on during self-reflection and exploration, as we can delve deeper into our spiritual beliefs and values and better understand what drives us. We can then express and demonstrate them through our behaviour and actions for others to see and experience it.

The fourth quadrant is the unknown self. This represents what we and others do not know about ourselves. In the context of spiritual intelligence, the unknown self can represent unexplored or undeveloped aspects of our spirituality. This quadrant can be an opportunity for growth, as we can explore new spiritual practices or beliefs and develop a deeper understanding of ourselves and our place in the world.

The Johari Window's fourth quadrant, also known as the unknown or unconscious quadrant, is believed to be the window of immense potentiality. The unknown quadrant represents the aspects of an individual's personality that are not known to the individual concerned or others. These aspects may include hidden talents, repressed emotions, or unconscious behaviours. The unknown quadrant is often considered the most interesting and mysterious quadrant of the Johari Window because it is the least-explored aspect of an individual's personality.

The unknown quadrant is believed to hold immense potential because it represents the untapped resources of an individual's personality. These resources can only be accessed through self-exploration and introspection. It is only by exploring our unconscious that we can discover our hidden talents and abilities. The process of exploring the unknown quadrant requires a willingness to step out of our comfort zone and try new things. It requires us to take risks and embrace uncertainty. By doing so, we can develop our potential and become more self-aware.

It is important to note that exploring the unknown quadrant is not always easy. It can be a challenging and uncomfortable process, as it often requires us to confront our fears and insecurities. However, the rewards of exploring our unconscious are significant. By tapping into our hidden potential, we can discover new passions, develop new skills, and achieve our goals.

Furthermore, the process of exploring the unknown quadrant can help us identify areas where we need to improve. By becoming more self-aware, we can recognise our weaknesses and work on developing them. This can open up opportunities for personal growth and development and improve our chances for success in various areas of our lives. Exploring the unknown quadrant can lead to greater creativity and innovation. By tapping into our unconscious mind, we can access new ideas and perspectives that we may not have considered before. This can lead to new opportunities for problem-solving, innovation, and creativity in our personal and professional lives.

Mapping Your Spiritual Growth: The Life Scale Assessment

One of the most useful and simple tools for assessing and measuring progress in life is the life scale. Using this scale involves first reflecting on the positives and negatives that we experience in our daily lives. Positive traits include compassion, forgiveness, the ability to let go, righteousness, resourceful, courage, confidence, activeness, perseverance, acceptance, being supportive and empowering, etc, and negative traits include anger, lust, greed, self-centredness, lethargy, impatience, egoism, laziness, passivity, cowardice, etc. One can then measure the score on this scale.

Assigning points to qualities on the life scale assessment tool is a subjective task, and it ultimately depends on your personal values and beliefs. The range of the life scale is 0–1,000, and the value of each parameter can be decided by adding some more qualities. There are general guidelines that can help you assign points. To begin with, you need to divide the total range between the positive and negative qualities. For example, you can assign 500 points to positive qualities and 500 points to negative qualities. Distribute the allocated points among the positive qualities based on their importance to you. Think about which qualities are most important to you and allocate a larger number of points to those qualities. If personal growth and development are important to you, you may want to assign more points to qualities that are associated with growth, such as resilience, learning, self-reflection, and open-mindedness. This will reflect their significance in your life and allow you to give them higher weightage in your overall score. For example, you might assign 100 points to empathy, 80 points to kindness, 70 points to acceptance, and so on. Similarly, distribute the allocated points among the negative qualities, such as anger, hatred, greed, unkindness, and self-centredness. Again, consider the significance of each negative quality and assign points accordingly. For instance, you could assign 100 points to anger, 80 points to hatred, 70 points to greed, and so forth.

Once you have assigned points to both positive and negative qualities, you can calculate your overall score. Add up the points assigned to positive qualities and subtract the points assigned to negative qualities. This will give you a numerical value that represents your overall score on the life scale assessment tool. Remember that this is just a general guideline, and you have the flexibility to adjust the point allocation based on your personal preferences. The key is to reflect on the importance of each quality and assign points accordingly to create a meaningful assessment for yourself. You may aim for a balanced approach when assigning points. While it's important to acknowledge and reward positive qualities, it's also essential to recognise and work on areas that need improvement. Strive for a fair allocation of points between positive and negative qualities to maintain a holistic perspective.

You may also seek inputs from others. Sometimes, it can be helpful to seek out different perspectives. You could ask trusted friends, family members, or mentors for their inputs on the assignment of points. Their insights and feedback may offer valuable perspectives that you hadn't considered before. It's a good idea to periodically reassess and adjust your assignment of points. As you grow and evolve as a person, your priorities and values may change. Revisiting the scale and adjusting the points allocation can ensure that it remains aligned with your current beliefs and aspirations. This will encourage you to focus on positive qualities and track your progress over time.

Remember that the life scale assessment tool is a personal tool for self-reflection and growth. The goal is to create a framework that resonates with you and helps you assess your progress and development over time. By assessing our scores on the life scale, we can know where we stand currently and what we need to do to improve. If our self-assessed score is less than 200, we are in the danger zone, leading to stagnation, which is equivalent to death. Therefore, it is essential to develop our spiritual intelligence by cultivating positive traits, letting go of negative ones, and aligning our goals with our core values and character.

Spiritual intelligence is a powerful tool that can help us transform our inner world and ultimately change our outer world as well. Many of us spend our lives trying to fix the outer world, assuming that external success and achievements will bring us happiness and fulfilment. However, true happiness and fulfilment come from fixing the inner world first. It is only by taking the time to reflect on our thoughts, emotions, and beliefs that we can begin to understand who we truly are and what we want out of life. This process of self-reflection and introspection requires mindfulness, which means being fully present in the moment and aware of our thoughts and feelings without judgement or criticism.

Through mindfulness, spiritually aligned people are able to gain a sense of control over their life. Instead of being controlled by external circumstances and events, they are able to take control of their thoughts and emotions and steer their life in the direction they want it to take. This sense of control and self-awareness helps them become better versions of themselves. They have been able to learn from their experiences and use that knowledge to rebuild themselves, becoming stronger, more resilient, and more compassionate in the process.

The ups and downs of life are all part of their churning process. In other words, the challenges and difficulties they face are not setbacks but opportunities for growth and transformation. By embracing these challenges and using them as learning opportunities, they are able to gain valuable insights into themselves and the world around them.

By focusing on the inner world and developing self-awareness, mindfulness, and compassion, we can transform ourselves and our lives in powerful and meaningful ways. It is a journey that requires dedication and effort, but the rewards are truly life-changing. Spiritual intelligence is a way of knowing oneself and others more profoundly. One of the key aspects of spiritual intelligence is the recognition that the purpose of life is to lead it meaningfully and derive joy from living. The purpose of life is unique to each individual, and it is essential to find it to live a fulfilling life. When one understands the purpose, passion is born out of it, which is a fire that drives the purpose. Vision and mission are the natural fallouts of purpose and passion. One needs to connect with oneself and be aware of the inner voice to understand the purpose of life. It cannot be dictated by others.

We are all born with the innate quality of being joyous, but as we grow up, we condition our state of mind by associating our feelings/ emotions with experiences of hurt, fear, sorrow, and depression. These experiences form our subconscious memories, and we keep experiencing the same feelings until we recondition or reprogram ourselves to disassociate from them. This disassociation will happen only when we superimpose another desirable experience of emotions upon our subconscious. Memories and the feelings associated with them in the subconscious are part of a cyclical activity. Unless we break this cyclical activity through a new pattern, our subconscious will not change.

In the state of mindfulness, we can understand this phenomenon of compulsive thinking and turn on our reprogramming mode. Mindfulness helps in identifying the patterns of thinking and behaviour that are not serving us and helps reprogram them. This process requires a lot of self-reflection and introspection. The Chinese general Sun Tzu, in his famous book *The Art of War*, recognised the importance of knowing ourselves and others in achieving success. He wrote: 'If you know the enemy and know yourself, you need not fear the result of a hundred battles. If you know yourself but not the enemy, for every victory you will also suffer a defeat. If you know neither the enemy nor yourself, you will succumb in every battle.'

In the context of spiritual intelligence, Sun Tzu's advice can be interpreted in many ways. The 'enemy' can be understood as our own negative patterns of thought and behaviour or as the challenges and obstacles we face in life. By knowing ourselves, we can understand and overcome these challenges and develop the resilience and strength needed to succeed. Similarly, knowing others can help us build alliances and support networks and collaborate with others towards common goals. Moreover, by knowing ourselves and our own minds, we can overcome the spiritual emptiness that plagues so many of us and create a more fulfilling and meaningful life for ourselves and those around us.

Spiritual intelligence is about cultivating a deep awareness of ourselves and the world around us. It is about developing the wisdom and insight needed to navigate life's challenges with grace and compassion, and to build a more harmonious and connected world. By knowing ourselves and others, we can develop the skills and mindset needed to achieve our goals and make a positive impact in the world.

Assessing Spiritual Intelligence Through Psychometric Tools

Psychometric tools for measuring spiritual intelligence are designed to assess an individual's level of spiritual awareness and understanding and the integration of this awareness and understanding into their daily life. While the concept of spiritual intelligence is still evolving, there are a few psychometric tools that have been developed to measure this construct, one of them being Spiritual Intelligence Self-Report Inventory (SISRI) developed by David King. The SISRI is a self-reporting questionnaire consisting of items that measure various aspects of spiritual intelligence, such as the abilities to transcend the ego, to behave with compassion, and to act with wisdom and discernment. Respondents rate each item on a Likert scale, indicating the extent to which they agree or disagree with the statements. The SISRI assigns scores to different dimensions of spiritual intelligence and an overall spiritual intelligence score.

The SISRI assesses five dimensions of spiritual intelligence: critical existential thinking, personal meaning production, transcendental awareness, conscious state expansion, and heightened altruistic engagement.

Critical existential thinking: This dimension assesses an individual's ability to reflect on existential questions such as the meaning of life, death, and suffering.

Personal meaning production: This dimension assesses an individual's ability to create meaning in their life through their values, beliefs, and sense of purpose.

Transcendental awareness: This dimension assesses an individual's ability to connect with something greater than themselves, such as nature, a higher power, or the universe.

Conscious state expansion: This dimension assesses an individual's ability to experience altered states of consciousness, such as those that emerge through meditation or prayer.

Heightened altruistic engagement: This dimension assesses an individual's ability to act in a way that benefits others, even if there is no immediate benefit to themselves.

The SISRI is relevant because it provides a structured way of assessing an individual's level of spiritual intelligence, which can be useful in personal and professional development. By identifying areas where one may be strong or weak, individuals can focus on developing their spiritual intelligence in specific areas, which can lead to increased well-being and fulfilment. In addition, the SISRI can be used in leadership development, as spiritual intelligence is increasingly recognised as an important trait for effective leadership in a rapidly changing world.

SQ21 (Spiritual Intelligence 21) is another psychometric tool designed to measure spiritual intelligence. It was developed by Cindy Wigglesworth and is based on her model of spiritual intelligence, which she describes as 'the ability to behave with wisdom and compassion while maintaining inner and outer peace (equanimity) regardless of the situation.'

SQ21 is a comprehensive assessment tool designed to evaluate an individual's spiritual intelligence. It assesses 21 distinct skills and competencies, thoughtfully grouped into four meaningful quadrants:

1. Self-awareness: your journey within.
2. Universal awareness: connecting with the world around you.
3. Self-mastery: cultivating your inner strength.
4. Social mastery/spiritual presence: nurturing harmonious relationships and spiritual presence in society.

Each of these categories contains specific competencies that provide a detailed view of a person's spiritual intelligence. SQ21 is typically administered as a self-assessment, with individuals rating themselves on a scale for each competency.

It's worth noting that SQ21 is one of the better-known tools for measuring spiritual intelligence and is often used in organszational and leadership development contexts to help individuals and teams explore their spiritual intelligence and its impact on their work and relationships. However, like other tools in this field, its use and interpretation should be approached with care and consideration for the broader context in which it is applied.

It's important to note that the concept of spiritual intelligence is still debated among researchers, and psychometric tools to measure it are still being researched and improved. Although these tools can be useful in understanding an individual's level of spiritual intelligence and identifying areas for personal growth and development, it is essential to note that spiritual intelligence is a complex construct and cannot be fully captured by any single measure or instrument. Therefore, it is important to use these tools in conjunction with other forms of assessment and the exploration of an individual's spiritual beliefs, practices, and experiences.

Assessing spiritual intelligence can be a complex process as it involves subjective experiences and beliefs. There are no universally accepted or tangible ways of measuring spiritual intelligence, but there are some ways of gaining an insight into your own spiritual intelligence level and that of others:

1. **Reflect on your own spiritual experiences.** Take some time to reflect on your spiritual experiences and beliefs. Consider how they have influenced your life and how they contribute to your sense of meaning and purpose.
2. **Self-assessment tools**. Individuals can utilise existing psychometric tools to scientifically assess their own level of spiritual intelligence, should they desire to do so. You may try measuring your spiritual intelligence using the life scale, as described above, although it is a subjective assessment.
3. **Seek feedback from others.** You can also seek feedback from others that you consider spiritually intelligent. Ask them about their beliefs and experiences and how they incorporate spirituality into their lives. This can give you a better understanding of what spiritual intelligence looks like in practice.
4. **Observe behaviours.** Observe the behaviours and actions of individuals that you believe possess high levels of spiritual intelligence. Look for qualities such as empathy, compassion, gratitude, humility, and a sense of interconnectedness. Emulate your role models.

It's important to remember that spiritual intelligence is a deeply personal and subjective experience. While these methods can give you some insight, the best way to understand your own spiritual intelligence and that of others is through self-reflection, self-enquiry, observation, and open-mindedness.

Our Conscience Serves as Our Internal Advocate

Spiritual intelligence is not just about possessing a knowledge of spiritual practices; it is also about having the wisdom to incorporate those practices into our daily lives. The idea of having a 'wise advocate' within us to monitor us is an important aspect of spiritual intelligence. The wise advocate can be understood as our inner guide, the voice of our conscience that helps us navigate life's challenges. It is this voice that reminds us of our values, beliefs, and principles and helps us make decisions that align with them. It is the attentive brain that is rooted in our value-based conscience. On the other hand, our deceptive brain can be seen as the voice of our ego, which often tries to persuade us to do things that are not in our best interests or contradict our values. The deceptive brain is dominant and can easily overwhelm the attentive brain, making it difficult for us to make wise decisions.

Our conscience serves as our internal guardian, constantly monitoring our thoughts, behaviours, and actions. It is shaped by our principles, beliefs, and values, which form the foundation of our consciousness. Our conscience acts as an advocate and judge, observing all our actions and providing judgement. When our actions go against our conscience, it is as if our conscience is witnessing its own violation. Hence, it is crucial to prioritise our conscience in every action we take.

Spiritually intelligent individuals ensure that their conscience remains pure and untainted by corruption. They recognise the significance of upholding their conscience as a guiding force in their lives, like a moral compass. It is our responsibility to keep our conscience pure and uncorrupted. By doing so, we can strive towards living a morally upright and spiritually fulfilling life.

A strong character is built on a well-developed and morally upright conscience. When we listen to our conscience and act in alignment with our principles and values, we cultivate a character that is grounded in integrity, honesty, and ethical conduct. Our conscience helps us make wise decisions, treat others with respect, and uphold moral standards even in challenging situations. This builds a foundation of trust and respect in our relationships and reflects our inner strength and resolve.

On the other hand, a weak character can arise from ignoring or disregarding the conscience. When we fail to heed the guidance of our conscience and act in conflict with our principles and values, our character may become compromised. This can lead to unethical behaviour, inconsistency, and a lack of moral integrity. Ignoring our conscience can also result in inner conflict, guilt, and a sense of disconnect from our true selves.

Resolving the Conflict Within

The phrase 'to be or not to be' from Shakespeare's *Hamlet* sums up the conflict that many of us experience within ourselves. This constant battle can cause mental and emotional agony and can become a source of pain and discomfort in our lives. The real enemy, in this case, is within us, and it causes constant pain and suffering.

One of the best ways to deal with this disturbing and devastating phenomenon within us is to disassociate from it and just be an observer. By being a neutral observer, we can edit and delete what's not desirable or serving our interests. This is a powerful management lesson from the Bhagavad Gita, which teaches us to be *sthitpragya* (neutral/an observer). By doing so, we can sensibly and rationally edit and delete the thoughts, feelings, and emotions that are not empowering us.

The advantage of disassociating from our thoughts, feelings, and emotions is that we can observe them without getting emotionally affected. In spiritual parlance, it is called being *sakshi* (a witness or observer). This allows us to see things from a neutral perspective and make decisions based on what is best for us. By disassociating ourselves, we can be in a better position to choose our thoughts, feelings, and emotions, instead of being controlled by them.

Creating Reality Through Observation

It is said that reality doesn't exist without an observer. It is the observer who creates their own reality. By being an observer of our thoughts, feelings, and emotions, we can choose what to focus on and what to ignore. This enables us to create a reality that is empowering and serves our interests. The conflict within us can cause mental and emotional agony, but by disassociating ourselves, we can observe our thoughts, feelings, and emotions without being emotionally affected. This enables us to choose our thoughts, feelings, and emotions and create a reality that is empowering and serves our interests. By being an observer, we can develop our spiritual intelligence and lead a fulfilling life. Aligning one's thoughts, actions, and goals with their higher purpose means liberating oneself from old patterns that are neither empowering nor serving one. Liberation is nothing but being released from our own captivity. Our psychological and social conditioning, which has been performed over a period of time, traps our soul (true self) in this captivity. The moment we release and free ourselves from this conditioning, we get a sense of immense joy. In the context of spiritual intelligence, liberation is about freeing ourselves from our mental and emotional limitations, which prevent us from achieving our full potential.

Establishing Credibility: Walk the Talk

One of the key aspects of spiritual intelligence is leading by example. People take notice of the credentials of a person who is talking, and if they see the person living by their values, they are more likely to listen and follow.

The phrase 'walk the talk' is often used to describe the importance of aligning one's actions with their words and values. It is a call to be authentic and true to oneself and to act in a way that is consistent with one's beliefs and principles. In order to be authentic and acceptable to society, it is essential to not only talk about one's values and beliefs but also to live by them. This means that individuals must be willing to take action and make decisions that reflect their true selves, even when it is difficult or uncomfortable to do so.

Walking the talk requires honesty, integrity, and a willingness to be vulnerable. It means being willing to admit when one has made a mistake or acted in a way that is inconsistent with one's values and taking steps to make amends and improve in the future. When individuals walk the talk, they inspire others to do the same. They become role models for authenticity and integrity and they help create a culture in which being true to oneself is valued and respected.

Spiritual intelligence can help develop a 'walk the talk' attitude by providing individuals with a deeper understanding of their values, beliefs, and purpose in life. When individuals are connected to their spiritual selves, they are more likely to act in a way that is consistent with their beliefs and values. Spiritual intelligence helps individuals cultivate self-awareness, which is essential in the development of a 'walk the talk' attitude. Self-awareness allows individuals to recognise their true intentions and motivations, which can help them align their actions with their values and beliefs. By becoming more self-aware, individuals are less likely to act in a way that is inconsistent with their values and are more likely to act in a way that is authentic and true to themselves. When individuals are connected to their spiritual selves, they are more likely to recognise the interconnectedness of all beings and to act in a way that benefits the greater good. This can inspire individuals to even make sacrifices or take risks if required.

Core values are the guiding principles that reflect the true character of a person. They are the foundation of a person's moral compass, and they guide our decisions, actions, and interactions with the world. Developing and living by core values is an essential aspect of spiritual intelligence. It is about aligning our actions with our values and using our values as a guide for how we live our lives. Personality and character are two identities that are often used interchangeably, but they actually refer to different aspects of a person's behaviour and traits. Personality refers to the combination of thoughts, emotions, traits, behaviours, and characteristics that make up an individual's unique patterns of thinking, feeling, acting, and self-presentation. It is influenced by a variety of factors, including genetics, upbringing, and life experiences. Personality is typically considered more surface-level and may change over time, as individuals are exposed to new experiences and learn new behaviours. It is a subset of individuality, as it focuses specifically on the psychological aspects that define a person, while individuality encompasses the broader range of characteristics that make each person distinct and different from others. Life experiences, personal growth, and various external factors can all contribute to changes in one's personality. However, it's important to note that personality change is a gradual process and may vary from person to person.

Character, on the other hand, refers to a person's moral and ethical values, beliefs, and principles. It is the set of traits that defines a person's sense of right and wrong and their ability to act in accordance with these values. Character is considered deeper and more enduring than personality, as it is based on a person's core values and beliefs, which are less likely to change over time.

Meanwhile, individuality refers to the distinctiveness of a person's personality and behaviour. It is the unique set of traits and characteristics that make an individual different from anyone else or stand out from the crowd. Individuality is influenced by personality, but it is also shaped by a person's life experiences, cultural background, and personal values. While personality is a relatively stable set of traits and characteristics, individuality can be a more dynamic and adaptable concept that recognises the multifaceted nature of each person's identity. Personality focuses on the consistent patterns of traits and behaviours that define a person, while individuality embraces the entire range of distinctive attributes that contribute to a person's uniqueness. Personality is just one part of a person's individuality, which encompasses a broader and more diverse set of characteristics.

Both personality and character play important roles in walking the talk, but character is generally considered more important, because character is based on the moral and ethical values that guide behaviour and decision-making. If a person's behaviour is not aligned with their values, it can lead to a sense of inner conflict and cognitive dissonance. This is not to say that personality should be discounted. For example, if a person is naturally outgoing and assertive, they may be more likely to speak up and take action in situations that threaten to compromise their values. On the other hand, if a person is more introverted and reserved, they may need to work on building their assertiveness to follow through on their values and beliefs.

A deeper analysis will reveal a difference between personality and character. Personality is a set of traits that we use to conform to societal expectations, which may not necessarily align with our core values and moral principles. On the other hand, character represents the set of core values and moral principles that we want to nurture. The clash between personality and character sometimes gives rise to a duality or double standard. For example, a person may have a dishonest and deceitful character, but they may project a moral and honest personality to conform to societal expectations. This mismatch between personality and character can reflect a lack of authenticity and create a sense of inner conflict.

When personality and character are in sync, there is no duality or double standard. It is only when a person walks the talk and demonstrates their true character that they can be considered genuine and authentic. Spiritual intelligence can help align a person with their core values and moral principles and thus bridge the gap between personality and character.

In today's busy and fast-paced world, people want everything instantly. They expect quick fixes and immediate gratification. However, not all great things can be achieved instantly. Achieving a true sense of fulfilment requires self-discipline and perseverance. It is important to understand that the ill effects of this instant sense of fulfilment can have lasting consequences. Therefore, it is crucial to develop patience and an appreciation for the process of personal growth and development. True fulfilment and personal growth cannot be achieved overnight. Seeking instant gratification can have negative consequences.

Chapter 8

Character-Building

Spiritual intelligence involves being mindful of one's thinking patterns, as they shape one's beliefs, which, in turn, create experiences. Our thoughts and beliefs impact our actions and behaviour. Therefore, it is essential to cultivate positive thinking patterns that promote empowering beliefs and actions. Negative thinking patterns and beliefs can lead to destructive actions, such as anger, greed, lust, and revenge.

In Hindu philosophy, the three *gunas—sattva*, *rajas*, and *tamas*—are believed to be the fundamental qualities that also make up the universe. These qualities are present in all aspects of our lives, including our thoughts, actions, and emotions. They are inherent attributes of our personality. Every person has a unique proportion of these attributes. The challenge is to identify which emotions serve us and let go of those that do not.

The Impact of Three *Gunas* on Spiritual Intelligence

Sattva Guna (Purity)

Sattva guna is the quality that encompasses purity, harmony, balance, clarity, peace, goodness, and righteousness. It uplifts the mind, leading to spiritual growth and inner transformation, and promotes a sense of calmness, serenity, and joy, allowing individuals to experience higher states of consciousness. In the realm of *sattva*, one's actions and thoughts are guided by selflessness, compassion, and truth. This *guna* fosters the development of wisdom, intuition, and a deep connection with the divine. By cultivating *sattva guna*, individuals can attain a harmonious existence, aligning their lives with higher principles and nurturing their spiritual journey.

Sattva guna involves the ability to cultivate inner peace, clarity, and wisdom. It requires a deep commitment to spiritual practices such as meditation, yoga, and self-reflection. These practices help purify the mind and body, allowing us to connect with our inner self and the world around us. Individuals who possess *sattva guna* are known for their wisdom and the ability to make choices that are aligned with their higher purpose. They are often viewed as spiritual leaders and are highly respected in their communities.

Rajas Guna (Activity)

Rajas guna is a quality that encompasses activity, passion, ambition, desire, and enthusiasm. It represents a state of dynamic energy and restlessness and drives individuals towards action, achievement, and the pursuit of goals, fuelling productivity and determination in various spheres of life. However, if unbalanced, *rajas guna* can lead to excessive attachment, restlessness, and a tendency to get caught in the cycle of desires and cravings. It is essential to channel the energy of *rajas guna* in a constructive and mindful manner, using it to propel personal growth, self-improvement, and the pursuit of noble endeavours. By cultivating awareness and balance within the realm of *rajas*, individuals can harness their passions effectively and lead purposeful lives.

Individuals who possess *rajas guna* are often driven and ambitious. They are known for their ability to take risks and pursue their dreams with passion and determination. However, they must be careful not to become too attached to their desires and lose sight of their spiritual path.

Tamas Guna (Apathy)

Tamas guna is a quality that encompasses inertia, darkness, laziness, ignorance, and delusion. It embodies a state of heaviness, ignorance, stagnation, and resistance to change and can manifest as a lack of motivation, confusion, and a tendency to indulge in negative habits or behaviours. *Tamas guna* obstructs progress, hampers clarity, and limits one's potential for growth. It is crucial to recognise and transcend the influence of *tamas guna* through conscious effort and self-reflection. By cultivating awareness and actively seeking positive transformation, individuals can overcome inertia, embrace light, and awaken to higher levels of consciousness. Breaking free from the grip of *tamas guna* opens the door to vitality, clarity, and a life filled with purpose and fulfilment.

Overcoming *tamas guna* involves the ability to overcome our negative tendencies and cultivate a sense of inner peace and clarity and requires a deep commitment to self-awareness and personal growth. Individuals who possess *tamas guna* may struggle with addiction, depression, and other mental health issues. However, with the help of spiritual practices such as meditation and yoga, they can begin to see the truth and connect with their inner self.

Achieving the Right Balance of *Gunas*

As evidenced by the philosophy of yoga, all material in the universe arises from a fundamental substrate known as *prakriti*. The three primary *gunas* emerge from this ethereal *prakriti*, creating the essential aspects of all nature, including energy, matter, and consciousness. Understanding and consciously manipulating these three *gunas* can be a powerful way of reducing stress, increasing inner peace, and leading one towards enlightenment.

Self-reflection allows us to delve into the depths of our being and unravel the intricate tapestry of the three *gunas* residing within us. Each one of us possesses a unique amalgamation of these qualities, yet it is through the lens of mindfulness and introspection that we can truly discern our dominant *gunas*. By embarking on this profound journey of self-discovery, we pave the way for the eradication of *tamas*, the suppression of *rajas*, and the ascendance of *sattva* as our prevailing essence.

In the realm of yoga and ayurveda, a *guna* is a *tattva*, or element of reality, that can influence our psychological, emotional, and energetic states. Although initially conceived as an essential component of Sankhya philosophy, the *gunas* are now a major concept in most schools of Indian philosophy. The interplay of these three *gunas* is constantly changing. They interact with one another in a playful state of illusion known as *maya*. *Prakriti*, the external world, is veiled in *maya*. As you perceive this illusory world through the lenses of your senses, so too does your *guna*, which influences your very nature. The patterns that emerge from this interplay can define the essential qualities of individuals or things and significantly impact the path and progress of life. For yoga practitioners, awareness of the *gunas* provides a guide to being more balanced, peaceful, and harmonious both on and off the mat. Developing the ability to identify and understand the nature of the *gunas* brings one closer to perceiving the universal truth of oneness.

While all three *gunas* are always present in all beings and objects around us, their relative amounts vary. Humans have the unique ability to consciously alter the levels of the *gunas* in their bodies and minds. Although it is not possible to remove a *guna*, it is possible to consciously act to increase or decrease its presence. One can achieve this through external objects, lifestyle practices, and thoughts.

The psychological qualities of the mind are highly unstable and can easily fluctuate. The predominant *guna* of the mind acts as a lens that influences our perceptions of and perspective on the world around us. If the mind is in *rajas*, it will experience events in the world as chaotic, confusing, and demanding. As a result, it will be marked by the tendency to continue reacting to events in a *rajasic* way. To make progress along the path of yoga, one must practise self-observation and discernment to witness the activities of the *gunas* without reacting to them. One must also have the inner strength and willpower to consciously shift thoughts and actions away from *tamas* and *rajas* and towards *sattvic* balance and purpose.

To achieve a state of *sattva*, yogic practice focuses on reducing both *tamas* and *rajas* and embracing *sattvic* foods, activities, and environments, which produce joy and positive thoughts. Whole grains, legumes, and fresh fruits and vegetables that grow above the ground are some examples of *sattvic* foods. To reduce *tamas*, one must avoid *tamasic* foods, oversleeping, overeating, inactivity, passivity, and fearful situations. *Tamasic* foods are those that are considered heavy and drab and may have a negative impact on the mind and body. Some examples of *tamasic* foods include alcohol and other intoxicants, overripe or spoiled food, food that is excessively bitter, sour, astringent, pungent, or oily, food that is heavily processed or refined (such as white flour or sugar), and food that is artificially flavoured or coloured, which can lead to lethargy, inertia, and sense of heaviness.

It is believed that consuming too much *tamasic* food can lead to feelings of lethargy, laziness, and even depression. Therefore, it is recommended that one should consume a diet that is primarily made up of *sattvic* foods, which are considered to be pure, light, and nourishing for the mind and body. On the other hand, to reduce *rajas*, one must avoid *rajasic* foods, over-exercising, overwork, loud music, excessive thinking, and over-consumption of material goods. *Rajasic* foods are stimulating and energising, but they are very rich and can lead to harmful effects in the long run. Fried food, spicy food, and stimulants are some examples of *rajasic* food.

It's important to note that all three *gunas* create attachment, which can bind one's self to one's ego. Thus, the ultimate goal of a person is to transcend the misidentification of their self with the *gunas* and be unattached to both the good and the bad, the positive and negative qualities of all life. While practising yoga and leading a yogic lifestyle strongly cultivates *sattva*, the ultimate goal is to move beyond the *gunas* and attain enlightenment.

Being mindful of these tendencies is crucial to achieving balance in life. Spiritual intelligence involves balancing between letting go of negative emotions and cultivating positive emotions that empower us. Balancing these tendencies enables individuals to experience spiritual growth and achieve greater emotional intelligence. Spiritual intelligence is a vital aspect of emotional intelligence that involves connecting with the divine, comprehending the deeper meaning of existence, and relating to others with empathy and compassion. It requires cultivating positive thinking patterns and beliefs, being mindful of the three *gunas*, and balancing tendencies to achieve a state of inner peace and growth.

In the context of the three *gunas*, spiritual intelligence requires a deep commitment to spiritual practices such as mindfulness, meditation, and self-reflection. By cultivating inner peace and clarity, we can overcome our negative tendencies and lead a fulfilling life that is aligned with our higher purpose. The *gunas* are believed to influence not only the individual's personality and behaviour but also the environment and the world at large. For example, a predominantly *tamasic* environment may be characterised by decay, desolation, and destruction, while a predominantly *sattvic* environment may be characterised by harmony, balance, and growth.

It's important to note that the influence of the *gunas* on creation is not direct or tangible in the conventional sense. Rather, it's believed to be a subtle, underlying force that shapes the nature and qualities of creation. Moreover, the concept of *gunas* is not unique to Hinduism but is found in other philosophical traditions as well, such as Buddhism and Jainism. In these traditions, the *gunas* are referred to by different names but are believed to have similar qualities and influences on the individual and the world. While it may be difficult for some people to grasp how *gunas* influence creation, it's worth exploring this philosophy further to gain a deeper understanding of the nature of reality and the interconnectedness of all things.

The Bhagavad Gita teaches that the path of self-realisation can be followed by the practice of yoga. All the *gunas* are described in the Bhagavad Gita as they have been described above, and while it is true that the development of *sattva guna*, which is associated with purity, goodness, and moral values, is considered desirable, the ultimate goal is to go beyond all the *gunas* and to attain the state of pure consciousness or self-realisation: 'When one rises above the three *gunas* that originate in the body, one is freed from birth, old age, disease, and death, and attains enlightenment.' This entails cultivating a sense of detachment and equanimity towards them.

The development of *sattva guna* is certainly an important aspect of spiritual practice, as it helps us cultivate virtues such as compassion, generosity, honesty, and self-control. However, the Bhagavad Gita emphasises that even *sattva guna* is a product of nature and is subject to change and transformation. The ultimate goal of the Bhagavad Gita is to attain liberation from the cycle of birth and death by realising the true nature of the self and the ultimate reality, which is beyond all qualities and attributes.

Buddhism, too, acknowledges the concept of the three *gunas*, although it is more commonly associated with Hindu philosophy. In Buddhism, the emphasis is often placed on the Three Marks of Existence, which are impermanence (*anicca*), suffering (*dukkha*), and non-self (*anatta*). While the concept of the three *gunas* is not explicitly discussed in Buddhist teachings, some Buddhist practitioners may acknowledge their existence and recognise their influence on the human mind and behaviour. However, it's important to note that Buddhism generally places more emphasis on the Four Noble Truths, the Eightfold Path, and other core teachings than on the specific categorisation of qualities or energies like the *gunas*.

While Jainism does not explicitly discuss or emphasise the three *gunas*, it does recognise the influence of mental states and emotions on one's spiritual progress. Jain scriptures discuss various mental qualities and states of consciousness that can hinder or support spiritual growth. Jain philosophy focuses more on the concepts of *karma*, non-violence (*ahimsa*), and the path to liberation (*moksha*), primarily emphasising the three jewels of right belief, right knowledge, and right conduct. It teaches the importance of practising non-violence, truthfulness, non-attachment, and other ethical virtues that can be associated with the *gunas*. Jain philosophy places great emphasis on the idea of *karma*, which refers to the accumulation of actions and their consequences. The goal in Jainism is to reduce and eventually eliminate karmic bondage through ethical conduct, ascetic practices, and spiritual purification, with the ultimate aim of purifying one's soul (*jiva*), eliminating *karma*, and achieving liberation from the cycle of birth and death. It encourages individuals to lead a disciplined and ethical life, minimise harm to living beings, and practise self-control.

Understanding *Gunadharma*

The particular combination of the three *gunas* in any entity is that entity's *gunadharma,* and it is specific to each entity. For example, an individual who is dominated by *sattva guna* may have a *gunadharma* that is characterised by wisdom, knowledge, and peacefulness. They may be naturally drawn to spiritual practices and have a strong sense of morality and ethics. An individual with a dominant *rajas guna*, on the other hand, may have a *gunadharma* that is characterised by ambition, passion, and activity. They may be driven to achieve success and may be more focused on worldly pursuits.

Gunadharma is influenced by various factors, such as genetics, upbringing, environment, and personal experiences. Thus, while *gunas* refer to the three fundamental qualities that pervade all things in the universe, *gunadharma* refers to the unique nature and characteristics of each entity. The *gunas* provide a framework for understanding the nature of things, while *gunadharma* provides insight into the actions and reactions of specific entities. It can also be seen as a combination of personality, character, and individuality.

It's important to note, however, that an individual's *gunadharma* is not fixed or rigid. It can be influenced by various factors. With self-discipline and spiritual growth, an individual can work to balance and transform their *gunas*, leading to a transformation of their *gunadharma*. The first step towards this is to become aware of one's dominant *gunas* and how they influence one's thoughts, behaviours, and emotions. This self-awareness can be developed through meditation, introspection, and reflection on one's actions and experiences.

Once aware of one's dominant *gunas*, the aim should be to work towards balancing them, rather than completely changing or eliminating them. This means developing the positive qualities associated with each *guna* while minimising the negative ones. For example, an individual with a dominant *rajas guna* can work to cultivate qualities such as ambition and passion while minimising restlessness and impulsiveness. Ultimately, the goal is to transform one's *gunadharma* in a positive way, guided by principles such as compassion, selflessness, and spiritual growth. This involves cultivating positive character traits, such as honesty, integrity, and empathy, while letting go of negative habits and tendencies. Therefore, the focus should be on transforming one's *gunadharma* by balancing and cultivating the positive qualities associated with each *guna*. This can be done through spiritual practices, self-awareness, and self-discipline, leading to personal growth and spiritual evolution.

The *gunas* are considered subtle energies or forces that underlie all of creation. If we remain unconcerned about the three *gunas* or *gunadharma*, then we will continue to live life as we currently do, without any conscious effort to transform our thoughts, behaviours, and emotions. It's important to understand that the three *gunas* and *gunadharma* play an important role in shaping our personality, character, and overall well-being. By ignoring these concepts, we may miss out on opportunities for personal growth and spiritual evolution.

Moreover, imbalanced *gunas* or negative *gunadharma* can lead to various problems, such as stress, anxiety, depression, and relationship issues. By working towards balancing and transforming your *gunas*, you may be able to mitigate these issues and lead a more fulfilling and meaningful life. It's ultimately up to you to decide whether or not to take these concepts seriously. However, it's worth considering the potential benefits of doing so and exploring spiritual practices that can help you achieve a balanced and positive *gunadharma*.

As every individual has a unique set of characteristics or *gunadharma*, we should not judge or label people based on one isolated act or trait, as it could be a misleading perception. Instead, we should strive to understand and appreciate the complexity of each individual and their unique journey towards self-discovery and spiritual growth. By embracing the principles of *dharma*, developing spiritual intelligence, and practising non-judgemental awareness, we can create a more harmonious and compassionate world.

Breaking Free from *Kleshas*: A Path to Inner Peace and Happiness

The *kleshas*, which we have discussed earlier, are negative mental states or psychological afflictions that are described in Patanjali's Yoga Sutras. These *kleshas* are considered the root cause of human suffering and the main obstacle to achieving spiritual liberation or enlightenment. The equilibrium of consciousness can be disturbed by five kleshas:

1. ***Avidya* (Ignorance).** The first *klesha* is *avidya,* which is the fundamental *klesha* that gives rise to all the other *kleshas*. *Avidya* refers to spiritual ignorance or delusion, which causes us to mistake our true essence for something else. It can also be translated as 'lack of insight.' This *klesha* makes us identify with our ego, body, and mind, leading to a sense of attachment to material things. It creates an illusion that makes us see the world as something separate from ourselves. *Avidya* can manifest as confusion: confusing the impermanent with the permanent, the impure with the pure, pain with pleasure, and the false self with the true self (*purusha* or *atma*).
2. ***Asmita* (Egoism).** The second *klesha* is *asmita,* which refers to identification with the ego or the sense of self that is formed by the narrative of our lives, our habits, opinions, and thought patterns. *Asmita* is the belief that we are separate from others and the universe, leading to a sense of superiority, inferiority, or competition. This *klesha* makes us crave recognition, success, and power, leading to anxiety, stress, and disappointment.
3. ***Raga* (Attachment).** The third *klesha* is *raga,* which is the attachment to pleasure and the desire to possess or enjoy things. *Raga* is the tendency to cling to experiences, people, and objects that bring us pleasure or satisfaction. This *klesha* leads to the craving for sensory pleasures, such as food, sex, and entertainment, and creates an insatiable desire that can never be fulfilled. We already have the tools to create true happiness within us. Being mindful of this will help keep us from depending too heavily on external factors or material things for our happiness.
4. ***Dvesha* (Aggression or Anger).** The fourth *klesha* is *dvesha,* which is the avoidance or rejection of pain or unpleasant experiences. *Dvesha* is the tendency to resist, reject, or

escape from things that we perceive as uncomfortable or threatening, based on the presumption that external causes are responsible for the emotions of pain and suffering. This *klesha* leads to fear, anger, and hatred, and creates a sense of separation and conflict with others.

5. ***Abhinivesha* (Fear and Anxiety).** The fifth *klesha* is *abhinivesha*, which is the fear of death and the attachment to life. *Abhinivesha* is the belief that our existence is limited to the physical body and that death is the end of our identity and consciousness. *Abhinivesha* is also the fear of the ego's extinction and the desire to maintain the status quo. This *klesha* creates a sense of insecurity and attachment to the material world, leading to the fear of loss, change, and uncertainty.

These *kleshas* affect us in various ways, creating mental and emotional disturbances that prevent us from experiencing peace, joy, and fulfilment. They cause us to identify with the limited self, leading to suffering. By understanding and overcoming these *kleshas*, we can attain spiritual liberation and realise our true nature as pure consciousness.

According to Patanjali's Yoga Sutras, there are several steps or practices that can help us overcome the *kleshas* and achieve a state of liberation or enlightenment. These practices are collectively known as *ashtanga* yoga, or the eight-limbed path of yoga, which we have already discussed in the previous chapter.

Buddhism also believes in *kleshas*. In Buddhist philosophy, *kleshas* are the negative mental states or afflictions that make the mind cloudy, lead to unwholesome actions, cause psychological and emotional suffering, and hinder spiritual growth. While the concept encompasses a range of emotions, like anxiety, fear, anger, jealousy, and depression, among others, the three *kleshas* of ignorance, attachment, and aversion are considered the fundamental or primary causes of all the other *kleshas* in both the Mahayana and Theravada Buddhist traditions. They are known as the 'three poisons' in Mahayana Buddhism, while in Theravada Buddhism, they are referred to as the 'three unwholesome roots.' Ignorance refers to a lack of understanding or awareness of the true nature of reality, attachment refers to clinging to or craving things that are impermanent, and aversion refers to a strong dislike for or avoidance of things that are unpleasant. By recognising and addressing these three root *kleshas*, individuals can work towards overcoming the other *kleshas* and achieving liberation or enlightenment.

Attaining enlightenment can be challenging because of the *kleshas*. If a person is consumed by anger, they may act in harmful ways towards others, leading to negative consequences for themselves and others. By practising mindfulness, Buddhists aim to reduce the influence of the *kleshas*.

The philosophies of both Patanjali and Buddhism share a similar notion: that *avidya*, or ignorance, is the root cause of suffering (*dukkham*). While this statement may sound pessimistic, it is actually empowering because it suggests that suffering can be overcome through awareness and self-realisation. By recognising the detrimental effects of negative emotions (*kleshas*) and the illusory nature of the world, one can connect with one's inner being and embark on a spiritual journey towards self-discovery. Through wisdom and practice, individuals can break free from the attachments that lead to suffering and realise their true essence. Ultimately, these distractions are fleeting and do not define our existence.

It is essential for individuals to strive towards dispelling *avidya*. The following Tao Te Ching quote describes the concept of *avidya* (ignorance) most appropriately: 'When a superior person hears of the Tao, she diligently puts it into practice. When an average person hears of the Tao, she believes half of it, and doubts the other half. When a foolish person hears of the Tao, she laughs out loud at the very idea. If she didn't laugh, it wouldn't be the Tao.' Tao (also spelled 'Dao') is a fundamental concept in Taoism that literally means 'the way' or 'the path.' It refers to the natural order or flow of the universe, which Taoists believe is the ultimate reality (as discussed earlier). The quote highlights the importance of being open to new ideas and perspectives and how one's level of wisdom and understanding can impact how one perceives and interacts with the world. Dispelling the ignorance within is the way forward.

Although the five *kleshas* mentioned above are considered the primary *kleshas*, there are other negative mental states or passions of mind that are also seen as subsidiary *kleshas*—*kama*, *krodha*, *lobha*, *moha*, and *matsarya*—and are sometimes grouped together as secondary *kleshas*.

1. ***Kama* (Desire).** *Kama* is the desire for sensory pleasure and gratification. It is the craving for pleasure through the senses, such as sight, sound, taste, touch, and smell. *Kama* is related to *raga*, the *klesha* of attachment, as it creates a strong attachment to sensual pleasures and material objects. It is used interchangeably with lust, the excessive desire for sensual pleasure or worldly possessions. It is a powerful force that can distract us from our spiritual goals and cause us to become attached to the material world. The pursuit of pleasure can become an addiction, leading to suffering and negative consequences.
2. ***Krodha* (Anger).** *Krodha* is the emotion of anger or resentment. It is the reaction to a perceived threat or injustice and can manifest as irritation, frustration, or rage. *Krodha* is related to *dvesha*, the *klesha* of aversion, as it leads to a desire to avoid or eliminate what is causing the anger. It is a destructive force that can harm us and others. When

we are angry, we are unable to think clearly and may act impulsively, leading to regrettable actions.

3. ***Lobha* (Greed).** *Lobha* is the desire for material gain or wealth. It is the craving for possessions or money, and can lead to a sense of entitlement, envy, or jealousy. *Lobha* is related to *raga*, as it creates a strong attachment to material wealth and possessions. It can lead to a relentless pursuit of material gain, which can become an obsession. Greed can lead to selfishness, dishonesty, and corruption.
4. ***Moha* (Delusion).** *Moha* is the state of confusion or illusion. It is the inability to distinguish reality from fantasy and can lead to mistaken beliefs or perceptions. *Moha* is related to *avidya*, as it arises from a lack of understanding regarding our true nature and the nature of reality. It is a desire for things to remain as they are, which can hinder our spiritual growth. Attachment can cause us to hold on to things that are no longer serving us or prevent us from moving forward.
5. ***Madha* (Pride).** *Madha* or ego is the fifth *klesha*, which refers to our excessive pride or sense of self-importance. It can cause us to overestimate our abilities, become arrogant, and disregard the needs and feelings of others. Ego can create an illusion of separation, leading to feelings of isolation and loneliness. It is closely related to *asmita klesha*.
6. ***Matsarya* (Envy).** *Matsarya* is the emotion of envy or jealousy. It is the feeling of resentment or dissatisfaction that arises in response to others' achievements, qualities, or possessions. *Matsarya* is related to *asmita*, the *klesha* of egoism, as it arises from a sense of insecurity or inferiority in comparison to others, leading to negative emotions such as envy, resentment, and bitterness. Jealousy can cause us to compare ourselves to others, leading to dissatisfaction and discontentment.

These secondary *kleshas*, like the primary *kleshas*, can create mental and emotional disturbances that prevent us from experiencing peace, joy, and fulfilment. By recognising and overcoming these *kleshas*, we can cultivate a more balanced and peaceful state of mind and move towards spiritual liberation. Our thinking patterns, behaviours, actions, and experiences are all outcomes of these *kleshas* within us. Expressions of these determine our characteristics and go on to build our character.

All of these *kleshas* can act as obstacles to our spiritual growth and development. They can lead to negative thoughts, emotions, and behaviours, causing us to become stuck in negative patterns. To overcome the *kleshas*, we must cultivate awareness, mindfulness, and self-reflection. We must learn to recognise when these *kleshas* arise within us and work to overcome them. The Bhagavad Gita offers powerful insights and guidance on how to overcome these *kleshas* and cultivate a more positive and enlightened mindset. By embracing the teachings of the Bhagavad Gita, we can reduce the influence of the *kleshas* and live a more fulfilling and meaningful life.

The first step towards overcoming the *kleshas* is to practise detachment. Krishna emphasises the importance of letting go of our attachments to outcomes and focusing on our duties without expecting anything in return. By practising detachment, we can break free from the cycle of desire and reduce the influence of *kama*, *moha*, and *lobha*.

The second step is to develop self-control. Krishna emphasises the importance of controlling our mind and senses. By developing self-control, we can reduce the influence of *krodha* and *matsarya* and cultivate a more peaceful and harmonious mindset.

The third step is to cultivate awareness and mindfulness. Krishna emphasises the importance of remaining constantly aware of our thoughts and actions. By cultivating awareness, we can become more attuned to the influence of the *kleshas* and work to overcome them.

The fourth step is to embrace humility. Krishna emphasises the importance of letting go of our ego and sense of self-importance. By embracing humility, we can reduce the influence of *madha* and *matsarya* and become more open to learning from others.

The final step is to seek knowledge and wisdom. Krishna emphasises the importance of constantly striving to learn and grow. By seeking knowledge and wisdom, we can overcome the influence of *moha* and cultivate a more expansive and enlightened mindset.

By following these teachings, we can overcome the *kleshas* and live a more fulfilling and meaningful life. The Bhagavad Gita's teachings are relevant not only to those on a spiritual path but to anyone seeking to cultivate a positive and constructive mindset.

In Jainism, the concept of *kleshas* does not exist in the same way as in other Indian philosophical systems, such as Hinduism and Buddhism. However, a similar concept in Jainism is that of the *kashayas*, which are the passions or negative emotions that bind the soul and perpetuate the cycle of birth and death. The internal impurities or afflictions that hinder spiritual progress and contribute to human suffering in Jain philosophy are:

1. ***Mithya Drishti* (False Belief or Wrong Perception)**. This arises when a person holds false or distorted beliefs and perceptions about the world, leading to attachments and aversions that hinder spiritual growth.

2. ***Avirati* (Lack of Control Over the Senses).** This arises when a person lacks self-control over their senses and engages excessively in sensual pleasures, leading to attachment and addiction, and preventing spiritual progress.
3. ***Pramada* (Carelessness or Negligence)**. This arises when a person is careless and negligent in their spiritual practices and fails to cultivate mindfulness and awareness. This carelessness leads to ignorance and delusion, hindering spiritual advancement.
4. ***Kasaya* (Passion)**. This arises when a person is overcome by intense emotions such as anger, greed, jealousy, and lust. These passions create suffering and generate negative *karma*, obstructing spiritual purity.
5. ***Yoga* (Attachment or Clinging).** This arises when a person becomes excessively attached or clings to people, possessions, or ideas. This attachment leads to bondage and delusion, hindering spiritual liberation.

The Jain path emphasises the need to overcome these passions through practices such as ethical conduct (righteousness), meditation, introspection, self-discipline, self-control, and the cultivation of virtues such as forgiveness, generosity, humility, and honesty. While there may be some similarities between the *kleshas* in other Indian philosophies and the *kashayas* in Jainism, it is important to note that Jainism has its own unique terminology and approach to understanding negative emotions.

Spiritually intelligent people understand that the behaviour of an individual is merely a manifestation of their external personality, arising from *kleshas*. They recognise that the inner self of a person is far more complex and multifaceted than what is visible on the surface and that the actions of an individual are often influenced by the *gunas* or qualities that govern their consciousness, namely *rajas* and *tamas*. Those who possess spiritual intelligence are aware that ignorance and a lack of self-awareness can cause individuals to behave in a manner that is not in line with their true nature. Thus, they approach people with compassion and understanding, knowing that every individual has the potential to transform and evolve. By looking beyond the surface-level behaviour of individuals, spiritually intelligent people can connect with others at a deeper level and facilitate growth and healing in themselves and others.

As we work to remove *kleshas*, we open ourselves up to greater levels of spiritual insight, wisdom, and understanding. We become more fully present in each moment and more attuned to the deeper currents of life that are always flowing within and around us. Ultimately, this process of spiritual growth and development can lead to greater happiness, fulfilment, and a more meaningful and purposeful life.

Dealing with *Tamasic* Tendencies

The best lesson for relationship management is that of attachment with detachment. We should look at all our attachments with this perspective—with mindfulness—and consciously assess where we stand on this parameter. This is more a function of spiritual intelligence than of emotional intelligence.

Detachment is a crucial component of spiritual intelligence, as it frees us from the suffering caused by attachments and expectations. Attachment with detachment is the key to joyful living. One of the vital aspects of spiritual intelligence is the ability to distance ourselves from toxic people and situations, as this can significantly enhance our peace of mind. Toxic people are those who constantly cause irritation, anger, and unhappiness in our lives. They manipulate situations to their advantage, and often have a very strong sense of self-centredness and ego. Their intelligence is dominated by *tamasic* tendencies. Dealing with such people can cause mental agony and emotional disturbance, resulting in physical damage to the body through the release of harmful chemicals like cortisol. It is important to note that toxic people are unaffected by positive and *sattvic* approaches to transforming them. The best approach is to diplomatically avoid them. This does not mean that we should become rude or mean to them; rather, we should distance ourselves from their influence and focus on our own well-being.

The art of distancing ourselves from toxic people and situations involves disassociating from the negative energy they bring into our lives. It requires us to be observers, neutral parties that can sensibly and rationally edit and delete what is not desirable, empowering, or serving our interests. Those who do not add value to our lives but detract value from it are not meant to be in our lives. When we recognise this, we can edit out the negativity and focus on the positivity that exists around us.

The benefits of distancing ourselves from toxic people and situations are significant. By removing ourselves from the negativity that surrounds us, we can enhance our peace of mind, reduce stress, and protect ourselves from the physical harm caused by cortisol release. This is why it is important to be mindful of the people we allow into our lives and to recognise when it is time to distance ourselves from those who are toxic.

Emulating Role Models with Strong Spiritual Qualities

Our ultimate aim is to elevate our spiritual qualities and moral values to become the best version of ourselves. To achieve this, we can draw inspiration and guidance from those who possess exceptional spiritual qualities. By emulating their behaviour and actions, we can strive to improve ourselves and our own character. By following their example, we can cultivate positive traits and values that contribute to our personal growth and development. By mirroring their exemplary behaviour, we can foster a profound transformation within ourselves, paving the way for a more fulfilling and purposeful life. Embracing their teachings can help us develop a deeper understanding of ourselves, enabling us to embody the virtues and values that we admire. Maintaining an awareness of such people helps in making us mindful of qualities that we relate to and wish to emulate. The following are a few examples of such people from around the world:

1. **Mother Teresa.** Mother Teresa was a Catholic nun who dedicated her life to serving the poorest of the poor in India. Despite receiving international recognition and numerous awards for her humanitarian work, she remained humble and focused on serving others. Her humility was made evident by her simple and frugal lifestyle and her choice to work with the most vulnerable people in society. Her wisdom and spiritual intelligence were reflected in her deep faith, which guided her work and inspired others to follow her example.
2. **Nelson Mandela.** Nelson Mandela was a South African anti-apartheid revolutionary and politician who served as President of South Africa from 1994 to 1999. Despite being a global icon and a Nobel Peace Prize winner, he remained humble and committed to the cause of social justice. He was known for his compassion, forgiveness, and willingness to listen to others, even those who had previously oppressed him. His humility was evident in his willingness to admit his mistakes and his commitment to learning from others. His wisdom and spiritual intelligence were reflected in his deep commitment to reconciliation and his belief in the power of forgiveness to heal wounds and build bridges between people.
3. **Malala Yousafzai.** Malala Yousafzai is a Pakistani activist for female education and the youngest Nobel Laureate ever. Despite facing threats to her life and being shot by

the Taliban for her activism, she has remained humble and focused on her mission to advocate education for girls. Her humility was made evident when she gave credit to her family and supporters for her success and by her willingness to listen to the voices of others who may not share her views. Her wisdom and spiritual intelligence are reflected in her courage to stand up for what she believed in and her belief in the power of education to transform individuals and societies.

4. **Satya Nadella.** Satya Nadella is an Indian-American business executive who is the CEO of Microsoft. Despite leading one of the largest and most successful companies in the world, he has remained humble and focused on creating value for customers and society. His humility is made evident in the way he listens to feedback from employees and customers and by his willingness to learn from others, including those who are not in leadership positions. His wisdom and spiritual intelligence are reflected in his focus on empowering people and organisations through technology and his belief in the importance of empathy and compassion in leadership.
5. **Mahatma Gandhi.** Mahatma Gandhi was an Indian nationalist leader who advocated for non-violent civil disobedience as a means of achieving political and social change. Despite being one of the most influential figures of the 20th century, he remained humble and lived in a simple manner. His compassion and love for all people were evident in his advocacy of the rights of the poor and marginalised, including untouchables and women. He emphasised the importance of selflessness, non-violence, and service to others. 'Truth is within ourselves. There is an inmost centre in us all, where Truth abides in fullness. Every wrong-doer knows within himself that he is doing wrong, for

untruth cannot be mistaken for Truth. Understand the word in a much wider sense. There should be Truth in thought, Truth in speech, and Truth in action.' This assertion made by Mahatma Gandhi effectively highlights the significant role of truthfulness as a fundamental characteristic of spiritual intelligence.

6. **Desmond Tutu.** Desmond Tutu is a South African Anglican bishop and anti-apartheid activist who won the Nobel Peace Prize in 1984. Despite facing persecution and imprisonment for his activism, he remained humble and focused on his mission to promote social justice and human rights. His compassion and love for all people were evident in his advocacy of reconciliation and forgiveness, which played a key role in South Africa's transition to democracy. He emphasised the importance of empathy, forgiveness, and generosity of spirit.
7. **The Dalai Lama.** The Dalai Lama is a spiritual leader who is highly regarded for his wisdom and teachings on compassion, kindness, and inner peace. He is the head of the Gelug school of Tibetan Buddhism and is known for promoting non-violence, religious harmony, and the preservation of Tibetan culture. The Dalai Lama has emphasised the importance of cultivating inner wisdom, which he defines as the ability to discern between what is beneficial and what is harmful. He believes that developing this kind of wisdom requires a combination of knowledge, reflection, and practice. Central to the Dalai Lama's teachings is the concept of 'interdependence,' which is the idea that all things and beings are connected and that our actions have a ripple effect on the world around us. He believes that recognising and understanding this interdependence is crucial to developing wisdom and making wise decisions. The Dalai Lama also

emphasises the importance of compassion in developing wisdom. He believes that true wisdom must be grounded in empathy and understanding for others. Through cultivating compassion, we can develop a deeper understanding of the interconnected nature of all things and the impact of our actions on others.

In 1959, when the Chinese military invaded Tibet, the Dalai Lama was forced to flee to India, where he established a government-in-exile. Despite immense political pressure and violence towards his people, he has remained committed to non-violence and the peaceful resolution of the conflict. In 1989, the Dalai Lama was awarded the Nobel Peace Prize for his efforts to peacefully resolve the conflict between Tibet and China.

The Dalai Lama is a paragon of spiritual leadership, inspiring millions to follow in his footsteps. His remarkable humility, empathy, fearlessness, and visionary leadership make him a beacon of hope for humanity. He encourages individuals to cultivate mindfulness through meditation and other practices that help us become more aware of our thoughts, emotions, and actions. In times of distress, he has shown himself to be an exceptional leader, not only to his own community but to people across the globe. His example is one to be emulated, a testament to the power of genuine compassion and enlightened wisdom.

8. **Dr. APJ Abdul Kalam.** Dr. APJ Abdul Kalam, the 11th President of India, is widely regarded as an exemplar of humility and compassion. He was an aerospace scientist who made significant contributions to India's missile development and space research programmes. However, despite his numerous achievements and accolades, Dr. Kalam remained grounded, approachable, and always ready to help others.

He once said, 'I am not a handsome guy, but I can give my hand to someone who needs help.'

9. **Martin Luther King, Jr.** Martin Luther King, Jr. was a prominent leader of the civil rights movement in the United States during the 1950s and 1960s. King's leadership was grounded in his deep spiritual wisdom, which he believed was essential for achieving justice and equality for all people. King's spiritual intelligence was unique in several ways. First, he believed that spirituality and social justice were interconnected. He saw his work as a civil rights leader as an extension of his religious beliefs, which emphasised the importance of treating all people with dignity and respect. King often referenced the teachings of Jesus Christ, Mahatma Gandhi, and other spiritual leaders to support his arguments for non-violent resistance and peaceful protest. Second, King's spiritual intelligence allowed him to connect with people of different backgrounds and beliefs. He was able to bridge the gap between different races, religions, and socioeconomic classes by appealing to their shared humanity and emphasising the common goals of justice and equality.

   King's spiritual wisdom inspired others to join the movement and work towards a better future. His powerful speeches, rooted in a deep understanding of the human condition, moved millions of people to action and helped change the course of American history. King's spiritual intelligence was not just limited to his public speeches and actions. He also practised what he preached, living a life of service and sacrifice. He was a man of great faith and prayer, and he often sought guidance from God in his work. King's unique blend of spiritual intelligence and social justice activism made him one of the most inspiring figures of the 20th century. His message of hope, love, and non-violent resistance continues to inspire people around the world to work towards a more just and equitable society.

10. **Oprah Winfrey.** Oprah Winfrey is a renowned media executive, talk show host, actress, producer, and philanthropist who has used her success to positively impact the world. Throughout her life, Oprah has been open about her spiritual beliefs and practices. She has spoken about the role of spirituality in shaping her personal and professional journey and how her faith has guided her decision-making and sense of purpose. Oprah has also spoken about her experiences with visualisation, positive thinking, and meditation, highlighting how these practices have helped her achieve success and overcome challenges.

    Oprah's spiritual beliefs centre around the idea that every individual has a purpose and is connected with others. She believes that each person has a unique contribution to make to the world and that, by connecting with others, we can create positive change. Oprah has used her platform to amplify the voices of those who are marginalised and to bring attention to issues such as poverty, education, and healthcare. Oprah's success in the media industry is unparalleled. She has won numerous awards for her talk show, including multiple Emmys, and has been named one of the most influential people in the entertainment industry. She has also been a successful businesswoman, with a media empire that includes a TV network, magazine, and production company.

    Despite her incredible achievements, Oprah remains humble and grounded. She credits her success to her spiritual beliefs and values, including authenticity, compassion, and gratitude. She has used her influence to inspire others to live their best lives and to pursue their passions, while also encouraging them to give back to their communities. Oprah's philanthropic work is a testament to her commitment to making a positive impact on the world. She has donated millions of dollars to various causes, including education, health, and the arts. She has also established her own foundation, which supports initiatives to empower women and children in the United States and around the world.

Oprah Winfrey is a powerful example of a person who has integrated spiritual intelligence into every aspect of her life and career. Her success and impact on the world are a testament to the power of living authentically, with compassion, and with a sense of purpose that transcends individual achievements.

11. **Swami Vivekananda.** Swami Vivekananda, born Narendranath Datta, was an Indian spiritual leader and social reformer who lived from 1863 to 1902. He is best known for his spiritual teachings, which emphasised the importance of self-realisation, service to others, and social justice. Vivekananda's spiritual teachings were based on the ancient philosophy of Vedanta, which emphasises the unity of all beings and self-realisation as the ultimate goal of life. He believed that spirituality was not just a matter of personal salvation but also a means of bringing about social transformation.

Vivekananda was also known for his humility and compassion. Despite his deep spiritual knowledge, he never considered himself above others and always remained approachable and accessible to people from all walks of life. He believed that service to others was the highest form of spiritual practice, and he dedicated his life to helping the poor and marginalised.

Vivekananda's connection to social justice was also a hallmark of his teachings. He believed that true spiritual practice was impossible without a commitment to social justice and the upliftment of all people, especially those who were most vulnerable. He worked tirelessly to promote education, healthcare, and other social reforms that would improve the lives of the poor and disadvantaged. Vivekananda's teachings have inspired countless people around the world to live a life of service and compassion. His message of self-realisation, social justice, and unity continues to resonate with people of all faiths and backgrounds. He is revered as a spiritual giant and a symbol of hope and inspiration for those seeking a more just and compassionate world.

Emulating such role models can help us enhance our spiritual intelligence. They are remembered or noted for remaining humble despite their great wisdom and knowledge, made evident in their interactions with people from all walks of life and their readiness to lend an ear to and go out of their way to help those in need. Common to all of them are a deep sense of compassion for others, especially for the underprivileged and marginalised sections of society, and the beliefs that there is always something to learn from everyone, which requires each of us to be open-minded and receptive to new ideas, and that education is the key to empowering people and eradicating poverty.

By practising humility, compassion, and love for all people, we can develop a deeper understanding of ourselves and others and make a positive impact on the world around us. It is important to remember that these traits are not innate but can be developed through intentional practice and self-reflection. By emulating these idols, we can become better versions of ourselves and contribute to a more compassionate and peaceful world. Their teachings and lifestyles offer valuable lessons in the importance of:

1. **Developing empathy.** By being humble, compassionate, and approachable, we can develop empathy for others and understand their needs and struggles.
2. **Cultivating gratitude.** By acknowledging the contributions of others and being grateful for our blessings, we can develop a positive outlook on life and build stronger relationships with those around us.
3. **Fostering a sense of purpose.** By dedicating our lives to a higher purpose and striving to make a positive impact on the world, we can build a strong sense of purpose and spiritual intelligence.

Chapter 9

The Wisdom Within

Spiritual intelligence is the ability to think beyond the confines of the physical world and tap into a deeper, more intuitive part of ourselves. It is a form of lateral thinking, enabling individuals to approach dilemmas in life with a sensible, impartial, and, above all, compassionate perspective. By embracing out-of-the-box thinking, those with high levels of spiritual intelligence can often find creative solutions to problems that others may overlook.

Spiritual intelligence encompasses a broad range of principles that can be applied universally to enhance one's spiritual growth. Spiritually intelligent people do not believe in providing solace and empathy alone; they believe in awakening people, helping them become more self-aware and guiding them towards a deeper understanding of themselves and the world around them. Moreover, spiritual intelligence is not limited to the realm of the individual. It also encompasses the world around us. Spiritually intelligent individuals believe that everything in the universe is interconnected and that our actions have a profound impact on the world. Therefore, awakening people also means guiding them towards a deeper understanding of their relationship with the world and encouraging them to take actions that promote harmony and balance.

There was once a saint who was renowned for his philosophical teachings, kind nature, and ability to heal people. A mischievous boy was jealous of the saint and continuously tried to find ways of embarrassing him in front of his congregation. The boy devised a plan to challenge the saint. Holding a sparrow in his hand, he asked the saint whether the bird was alive or dead. The saint understood the boy's intentions and found himself in a dilemma. If the saint said the bird was alive, the boy would crush it to death, and if he said the bird was dead, the boy would set it free, both outcomes resulting in the boy feeling triumphant. The saint reflected on the complex situation and responded, 'Son, the fate of the bird, whether dead or alive, is in our hands. So be kind and decide what you want to do. The poor and helpless bird is at your mercy.'

The saint's response demonstrated his spiritual intelligence and wisdom, his recognition of the interconnectedness of all things and the importance of kindness and compassion in decision-making. The boy realised his mistake and immediately set the bird free, seeking the saint's forgiveness and blessings, humbled by the lesson. This story also beautifully demonstrates how spiritual intelligence can help individuals navigate complex situations with kindness, empathy, and wisdom.

People with high levels of spiritual intelligence have a deep awareness of their inner selves and have realised that they are more than just their physical bodies and minds. They are not influenced by external circumstances and their responses to challenging situations come from a place of compassion and inner peace. Spiritual intelligence is lateral thinking at its finest. It allows individuals to approach life with an open mind. The ability to think beyond oneself and connect with the deeper, more intuitive part of our being is a gift that is available to everyone but can be mastered only with practice and awareness.

The Quest for Spiritual Intelligence: Learnings from Socrates' Teachings

Socrates was an ancient Greek philosopher and one of the most important figures in western philosophy. He gained recognition for admitting his lack of knowledge, often stating that the only thing he was certain of was his own ignorance. He believed that recognising our own ignorance is the initial step towards engaging in philosophical enquiry. Furthermore, he expressed the opinion that the pursuit of wisdom is a more valuable endeavour than the pursuit of wealth and status. Socrates did not impart a philosophical doctrine to his pupils and interlocutors; rather, he employed the Socratic method to scrutinise and test his own beliefs in the pursuit of truth, all the while acknowledging his own limitations in knowledge.

This implies that Socrates viewed knowledge not as a fixed or final state of understanding but as a continual process of enquiry and questioning. He believed that true knowledge cannot be fully possessed or mastered by any individual. Rather than claiming to have complete knowledge or understanding of a topic, Socrates believed in the importance of acknowledging one's own limitations and engaging in ongoing dialogue and enquiry to expand one's understanding.

Socrates believed in the importance of humility, self-awareness, and open-mindedness in the pursuit of knowledge and rejected the idea that anyone could ever fully 'master' any particular field of knowledge or area of enquiry. Nevertheless, he acknowledged that recognising one's lack of knowledge is the initial step towards wisdom.

Socrates connected the human soul to divinity, and his discussions on religion were always undertaken within the framework of his rationalism. He concluded that whoever comprehends all that is divine will gain the best knowledge of themselves. In *Euthyphro*, Socrates reaches a conclusion that deviates from the age's common practice: he deems sacrifices to the gods useless, especially when driven by the expectation of a reward in return. Instead, he emphasises that philosophy—the pursuit of knowledge—should be the primary way of worshipping the gods. By rejecting traditional forms of piety, which he connects to self-interest, Socrates suggests that people should seek religious experience through self-questioning.

Socrates suggested that several aspects of the universe, like eyelids, exhibit signs of deliberate planning, serving as evidence for the existence of an all-knowing and all-powerful divine creator. Additionally, he believed that this creator designed the universe specifically for the betterment of humanity, given that humans possess unique abilities that other animals lack. Socrates sometimes referred to a singular deity, while at other times he spoke of multiple gods, leading to the interpretation that he either viewed a supreme deity as commanding other gods or saw various gods as parts or expressions of a single deity.

As for Socrates' theory of virtue, he asserted that all virtues are fundamentally the same, since they are a type of knowledge. He claimed that people's lack of knowledge prevents them from being virtuous, as he believed that virtues are interconnected and unified. The well-known dictum 'no one errs willingly' stems from this theory. Socrates employed the example of courage to argue for the unity of virtues. He believed that the ultimate goal in life was to gain knowledge of virtue. He sought to define justice, courage, and each component of virtue, since he thought all virtues are sciences and that, once someone understands a virtue, they become virtuous.

Some of the key themes in his teachings are:

1. **The pursuit of knowledge.** Socrates believed that knowledge was the key to living a good life. He believed that true knowledge comes from within and that people should constantly question their own beliefs and assumptions to arrive at a deeper understanding of the world around them.
2. **The method of questioning.** Socrates is famous for his method of questioning, which is now known as the Socratic method. This method involves asking a series of questions

to arrive at a deeper understanding of a topic. The Socratic method is still widely used in education today.

4. **The examination of life.** Socrates believed that the most important thing in life was to examine one's own beliefs and values. He believed that people should question everything, including their own assumptions and beliefs. He concluded that whoever comprehends all that is divine will gain the best knowledge of themselves. He had a belief in the existence of the soul and likened it to a divine quality.
5. **Virtue and morality**. Socrates believed that virtue was the most important thing in life and that living a virtuous life was the key to happiness. He believed that morality could not be taught; it had to be discovered through self-examination and questioning.
6. **The importance of self-control.** Socrates believed that self-control was essential for living a good life. He believed that people had to control their passions and desires to live a life of virtue and morality.

Socrates' teachings can be treated as guidelines for the development of spiritual intelligence, which involves seeking knowledge, self-examination, and the cultivation of virtues such as compassion and self-control.

The Pursuit of Fulfilment: Moving Beyond Mere Accomplishments

Many individuals often confuse the feeling of accomplishment with that of fulfilment, although the two words have different meanings and implications. Accomplishment tends to be short-lived, while fulfilment has a lasting effect. A sense of accomplishment is the feeling that arises when you successfully complete a task or achieve a goal. It can be a short-term feeling of satisfaction, like that associated with finishing a project or crossing off items on a to-do list. This feeling is often linked to external validation, such as praise from others, recognition, or rewards. On the other hand, fulfilment is a more profound and long-lasting sense of satisfaction that comes from living a meaningful life. It involves finding purpose and meaning in your actions and experiencing a sense of inner satisfaction and contentment. Fulfilment is often associated with personal growth, helping others, making a difference in the world, and contributing to something greater than oneself. Unlike a sense of accomplishment, fulfilment is more internally driven and doesn't depend on external validation.

The concept of eudaemonia is relevant in this context. Eudaemonia is a Greek concept that refers to the ultimate goal or highest good of human life—the state of living well and fulfilling one's potential. It is the realisation of human excellence, which Aristotle believed could be achieved through the cultivation of virtues and the pursuit of reason. Eudaemonia involves a sense of fulfilment, purpose, and overall well-being that arises from living in accordance with one's virtues and leading a virtuous life. It is not a fleeting emotion or momentary pleasure but a lifelong state of well-being that encompasses the overall quality of one's life. It is not dependent so much on external circumstances or material possessions as on the development of one's character, moral virtues, and the exercise of practical wisdom. According to Aristotle, eudaemonia is the ultimate aim of human actions; all other pursuits, such as wealth, power, or pleasure, are merely a means to achieve this ultimate goal. He believed that eudaemonia is achieved through the practice of virtues, which are habits of character that promote human flourishing. These virtues include qualities like courage, justice, wisdom, temperance, and generosity.

Eudaemonia and a sense of fulfilment are intertwined because they are both concerned with living a meaningful life and experiencing well-being. When individuals are engaged in activities that align with their values, contribute to personal growth, and provide a sense of purpose, they are more likely to experience a deep sense of fulfilment. Eudaemonic activities, such as cultivating meaningful relationships, engaging in personal development, contributing to society, and pursuing goals that align with one's values, can lead to a sense of fulfilment. By focusing on personal growth, meaning, and purpose, individuals can cultivate a greater sense of fulfilment in their lives.

It is important to note that the experience of eudaemonia and fulfilment is subjective and can vary from person to person. What brings fulfilment to one individual may differ from what brings fulfilment to another, as it is influenced by personal values, interests, and goals. However, the pursuit of eudaimonia, characterised by living a meaningful and purposeful life, can contribute to a deeper sense of fulfilment for many individuals.

Exploring Spiritual Intelligence: Insights from Nachiketa's Journey

Nachiketa is a prominent character in the Katha Upanishad. Nachiketa's is a tale of spiritual seeking and the search for wisdom and enlightenment. The story teaches us about the importance of seeking knowledge beyond the superficial and cultivating qualities such as curiosity, open-mindedness, and persistence.

The story of Nachiketa is often interpreted as a metaphor for the spiritual journey, with Nachiketa representing the seeker of truth and Yama representing the obstacles and challenges along the way. The story also emphasises the importance of perseverance, determination, and the willingness to take risks in the pursuit of spiritual knowledge. Due to Nachiketa's perseverance and hunger for knowledge, Yama, the death god, imparted teachings to him on self-knowledge, the *atma* (soul), and the *brahman* (ultimate reality). Nachiketa is renowned for his renunciation of transient material desires and unwavering dedication to the pursuit of attaining *moksha*.

The story begins with Vajashravas initiating a series of offerings to God in order to receive a gift in return. His son, Nachiketa, notices that Vajashravas is only donating old, barren, blind, or lame cows, which will neither benefit the recipients nor earn the donor a place in heaven. Desiring the best outcome for his father and feeling frustrated with such offerings, Nachiketa asks, 'To which God will you offer me?'

Initially, Vajashravas ignores this, but when his son persists, he angrily replies, 'I give you unto Yamaraja (Death God) himself!'

Despite his father's regret at his outburst, Nachiketa interprets these words to have a divine meaning and goes to Yamaraja's home. Yama is not at home, so Nachiketa waits there for three days without food and water. When Yama returns, he is sorry to learn that a Brahmin guest has been waiting at his doorstep for so long without hospitality. To make up for this, Yama offers Nachiketa three boons. Nachiketa asks for peace for himself and his father and knowledge of the sacred fire sacrifice and what comes after death.

Yama is initially hesitant to grant Nachiketa's request for knowledge about what comes after death, as this is a highly esoteric and dangerous topic. He attempts to dissuade Nachiketa by offering him abundant wealth, longevity, and beautiful companions. But Nachiketa is very firm and terms these offerings impermanent and of no use in leading a life of fulfilment. Seeing the resolve of the boy, Yama eventually relents and reveals to Nachiketa the nature of the soul, the impermanence of the body, and the importance of seeking spiritual knowledge.

Yama teaches Nachiketa about the nature of the self and the path to liberation. Having learnt the wisdom of *brahman* from Yama,

Nachiketa returns to his father as a *jivanmukta* (someone who has achieved spiritual liberation while alive).

Nachiketa's Key Learnings

3. **The nature of the self.** Yama tells Nachiketa that the self is not the body, mind, or senses, but rather an eternal and indivisible essence that pervades all of existence, is beyond birth and death, and is not affected by pleasure or pain, which are subjects and functions of the mind and senses. Yama explains that the path to liberation is through knowledge of the self. By realising that the self is distinct from the body and mind, one can transcend the limitations of worldly existence and attain eternal bliss. This knowledge helps Nachiketa understand that the fear of death arises from the identification with the body and the belief that the self is mortal. (The eternal nature of soul is also described in the Bhagavad Gita.)
4. **The impermanence of the world.** Yama explains to Nachiketa that the world is impermanent and constantly changing. Everything in the world, including the physical body, is subject to decay and death. This knowledge helps Nachiketa realise that the pursuit of material possessions and pleasures is futile, as they are temporary and do not bring lasting happiness.
5. **The importance of spiritual practice.** Yama emphasises the importance of spiritual practices, such as meditation and self-enquiry. He teaches Nachiketa that only through spiritual practice can one overcome the limitations of the physical body and mind and attain liberation. When Nachiketa asks about the path to liberation, Yama teaches him that the path to liberation is through detachment from worldly desires and attachment to the self. Through meditation, self-discipline, and devotion to the self, one can attain the ultimate goal of liberation.

6. **The nature of the afterlife**. Yama tells Nachiketa that the wise person who has realised the self transcends death and attains eternal happiness. He explains that those who perform good deeds and follow the path of righteousness attain the realm of the gods, where they enjoy happiness and bliss for a certain period of time. However, even the realm of the gods is impermanent, and, eventually, the soul returns to the cycle of birth and death. Yama then reveals the path of knowledge, which leads to the realisation of the true self and liberation from the cycle of birth and death.

The relevance of the story of Nachiketa to spiritual intelligence lies in its emphasis on the importance of seeking wisdom and knowledge beyond the material world. The story highlights the impermanence of the physical body and the eternal nature of the soul, reminding us that true fulfilment and happiness come from spiritual growth and understanding. By embodying the qualities of determination, patience, and a thirst for knowledge, we too can embark on the journey of spiritual seeking and uncover the wisdom that lies within. This knowledge can help one overcome the fear of death and the limitations of the physical body and mind and attain liberation from suffering.

It also highlights the importance of curiosity and the desire to seek knowledge beyond the mundane and superficial. Nachiketa was not content with his father's offerings, and his curiosity led him to seek knowledge about the afterlife, which was a topic that had mystified many. He demonstrated a willingness to go beyond the surface level of existence and explore the deeper mysteries of life. This teaches us the importance of open-mindedness and a willingness to learn. When Death arrived, Nachiketa did not judge him or fear him; he approached him with an open mind and a desire to learn. He was not afraid to ask questions, even when Death initially seemed reluctant to grant him knowledge.

The story of Nachiketa underscores the importance of persistence and determination in pursuing one's goals. Nachiketa was determined to seek knowledge, and he waited for three days until Death arrived to teach him. He did not give up on his quest, even when it seemed like he would not get what he wished for. The story also teaches us about the transformative power of spiritual knowledge. Nachiketa gained a profound understanding of the nature of existence and the self through his encounters with Death. He emerged from this experience a wise and compassionate individual with a deeper understanding of the world around him.

Interfaith Insights into the Nature of the Soul

As explained earlier, in Jainism, the terms *jiva* and 'soul' are often used interchangeably to refer to the individual conscious entity that inhabits a living being. According to Jainism, each *jiva* is eternal and uncreated and is responsible for its own actions and consequences. The *jiva* is believed to be separate from the physical body and mind and can exist in various states of consciousness, depending on the level of spiritual development it has achieved. Jainism also teaches that the ultimate goal of the *jiva* is to attain liberation, or *moksha*, which is achieved through the removal of karmic bondage and the realisation of its true nature.

Jainism emphasises the importance of right faith, knowledge, and conduct in purifying the *jiva* and attaining liberation from the cycle of birth and death. Every *jiva* has the potential to attain this state of pure consciousness and become a liberated soul, regardless of their past actions or present circumstances. The potential for enlightenment is seen as inherent in every *jiva*, and it is up to the individual to cultivate the qualities and practices that will allow them to realise this potential. By practising right faith, right knowledge, and right conduct, individuals can achieve spiritual growth and ultimately attain *kevala jnana*, the state of pure consciousness and ultimate liberation (*moksha*). From the point of view of spiritual intelligence, we can recognise the immense potential of a *jiva* to elevate itself and attain the higher state of consciousness. This can alleviate suffering and lead to personal growth and a life of fulfilment.

In Hinduism, the body is seen as a temporary vessel for the *atma* or soul, which is considered the true self. The body is subject to birth, ageing, disease, and death and is seen as a source of attachment and suffering. According to Hinduism, the ultimate goal of life is to attain liberation (*moksha*) from the cycle of birth and death by realising the true nature of the self, which is identical to *brahman*, the ultimate reality.

In Hinduism, *jiva* and soul are often used interchangeably to refer to the individual self or *atma* that is believed to be eternal and unchanging and is seen as identical to the ultimate reality known as *brahman*. The soul or self is said to interact with the external world through the ten senses (five external senses and five internal senses) and the four inner faculties (*manas*, *chitta*, *ahankara*, and *buddhi*). These senses and faculties enable the soul to perceive, think, reason, and form judgements about the world.

The goal of Hindu spirituality is to realise the identity of *atman* and *brahman* through practices such as yoga, meditation, and self-realisation. The *jiva* is believed to be immortal, formed of consciousness, and residing within the heart space. It interacts with the world through the senses and inner faculties and is distinct from the physical body. The concept of the soul residing in the heart space is based on the idea that the heart is not just a physical organ but also a spiritual centre in the body. It is considered the seat of the individual soul and the source of emotions, feelings, and consciousness.

In Christianity, the idea of gaining wisdom and evolving as an individual is closely tied to developing a relationship with God and following his teachings. Christians believe that wisdom comes from God, and that, through prayer, reading the Bible, and attending church, individuals can gain a deeper understanding of God's will and purpose for their lives. Christians also believe that, by living according to God's teachings, they can cultivate virtues such as love, compassion, forgiveness, and humility, which are essential for personal growth and spiritual evolution.

In Christianity, the concept of the soul refers to the immaterial, eternal essence of a human being that is believed to be created by God and destined for either heaven or hell after death. The soul is considered the seat of a person's consciousness, personality, and will, the part of a person that allows them to have a relationship with God and to experience spiritual life, and the source of a person's moral and ethical decision-making. The Christian concept of the soul is closely tied to the belief in the resurrection of the dead, which holds that the body and soul will be reunited at the end of time for judgement. This belief is based on the teachings of Jesus Christ, who claimed that he would rise from the dead after being crucified. Overall, the Christian concept of the soul emphasises the eternal nature of human existence and the importance of spiritual life to achieving salvation.

In Islam, the concept of soul is known as *ruh* or *nafs*. According to Islamic beliefs, the soul is a spiritual entity that is created by Allah (God) and is breathed into every human being at the time of their creation. The Quran describes the soul as the essence of life within every human being and what animates the body and gives it consciousness and purpose. It is believed that the soul is the source of all human emotions, thoughts, and intentions and that it is what makes each individual unique.

In Islam, the soul is considered immortal; it continues to exist even after the physical body has died. The destiny of the soul in the afterlife is determined by Allah based on the person's actions and deeds during their lifetime. Islamic teachings emphasise the importance of taking care of one's soul through various spiritual practices, such as prayer, fasting, charity, and performing good deeds. By doing so, one can purify their soul and attain a higher level of spiritual awareness and closeness to Allah.

In Islam, the idea of gaining wisdom and evolving as an individual is closely tied to developing a relationship with Allah and following his teachings, as revealed in the Quran and *hadith*. Muslims believe that wisdom comes from Allah and that, by submitting to his will, individuals can gain a deeper understanding of their purpose in life and the nature of the world around them. Muslims also believe that, by living according to Allah's teachings, they can cultivate virtues such as sincerity, patience, humility, and gratitude, which are essential for personal growth and spiritual evolution.

In both Christianity and Islam, the pursuit of wisdom and personal evolution is seen not as a solitary endeavour but rather as a communal one. Both religions emphasise the importance of participating in religious communities and engaging in acts of charity and service as a means of developing one's relationship with God and evolving as an individual. Christianity and Islam both view the pursuit of wisdom and personal evolution as essential components of a fulfilling and meaningful life and both emphasise the importance of developing a strong connection to God as a means of achieving these goals.

In Greek philosophy, the idea of gaining wisdom is central to the concept of the self and its ultimate goal. The Greeks believed that wisdom could be obtained not through the accumulation of knowledge or information but through a process of contemplation and introspection. The Greek philosopher Plato believed that wisdom was attained through the pursuit of eternal and universal truths. Plato believed that the physical world was a mere reflection of the true world of forms and ideas and that true wisdom could only be achieved through contemplation of these eternal truths. Aristotle believed that wisdom was the result of a life of virtue and practical experience. It was not only a matter of intellectual understanding but also required a practical understanding of how to live a good life. The Greek idea of gaining wisdom emphasised the importance of self-examination, the pursuit of knowledge, and the cultivation of virtues as essential components of a life well-lived.

Chapter 10

Everything in the Universe is Interconnected

Before we explore the Vedanta concept of non-duality, let's look once again at Taoism, which teaches that the self is not separate from the universe but an integral part of it. The goal of Taoist practice is to cultivate a deep awareness of this oneness and to live in harmony with the natural flow of the universe. Taoism also emphasises the importance of cultivating inner stillness and quieting the mind in order to connect with the deeper aspects of the self. This can be achieved through practices such as meditation, contemplation, and mindfulness. Furthermore, Taoism teaches that the self is not fixed or permanent but is constantly evolving and changing. Therefore, there is no single 'true self' that can be discovered or attained; rather, the self is a dynamic and ever-changing process.

Taoism does not place as much emphasis on the individual self or soul as other spiritual traditions. Instead, it teaches that the self is an integral part of the interconnected whole of the universe. The goal of Taoist practice is to cultivate a deep awareness of this oneness and to live in harmony with the natural flow of the universe.

Despite their conceptual differences, Taoism and Vedanta share this belief in the interconnectedness and oneness of the individual and the universe.

The Path of Oneness: Exploring Non-duality and Advaita

The concept of non-duality, or *advaita*, is central to the Hindu spiritual tradition, and is often associated with the teachings of Vedanta philosophy. The idea of non-duality is based on the principle that the ultimate reality, known as *brahman*, is the same as the true nature of the self, or *atman*. This means that there is no separation between the individual self and the ultimate reality; they are one and the same. There is no dichotomy. According to Vedanta, the body-mind complex is not the true self, but rather a temporary and changing manifestation of the true self. The true self, or *atman*, is a pure and unchanging consciousness that exists beyond the body-mind complex. This pure consciousness is the same as *brahman*, the ultimate reality that pervades all of creation.

The idea of non-duality can be difficult to understand because it requires us to let go of our identification with the body-mind complex and to recognise the true nature of the self as pure consciousness. This can be a challenging task, as we are conditioned to identify with our thoughts, emotions, and physical sensations. To help us understand the concept of non-duality, Vedanta suggests various practices and techniques that can be used to cultivate an awareness of the true self. One such technique is self-enquiry, which involves asking oneself the question 'Who am I?' and directing one's attention inward, towards the true nature of the self. Through this practice, we can begin to detach from our identification with the body-mind complex and to recognise the true self as a pure and unchanging consciousness.

Meditation is another important practice in Vedanta. It can help quiet the mind and cultivate a deeper awareness of the true self. By turning our attention inward and focusing on the present moment, we can begin to connect with the pure consciousness that exists beyond the body-mind complex.

The Relationship Between the Individual and the Cosmos

पूर्णमदः पूर्णमिदं पूर्णात्पुर्णमुदच्यते।

पूर्णस्य पूर्णमादाय पूर्णमेवावशिष्यते॥

(This is full, and that is full. From the fullness, the fullness arises. Taking the fullness from the fullness, the fullness remains.)

The above verse, the *purnam idam* verse, is a profound statement from the Isha Upanishad about the nature of reality and the relationship between the individual and the cosmos. In it, the word 'this' refers to the entire universe, including all living and non-living things. The verse suggests that the universe is whole and complete in itself, and there is nothing that can be added to it or taken away from it. The universe is perfect as it is, and it is a manifestation of the divine. It also suggests that everything in the universe is interconnected and interdependent, and that any attempt to separate one thing from another is ultimately futile.

This verse is often interpreted as a statement about the eternal nature of the universe and the ultimate reality that underlies it. This idea is important in the context of the Vedanta spiritual tradition. It suggests that there is a deeper reality beyond the everyday world of appearances, and that this reality is ultimately more real and more enduring than anything in the physical world. Understanding this idea is seen as crucial for the emancipation of human beings, as it can help us overcome our attachment to the transient and impermanent nature of things in the external materialistic world and find lasting happiness and fulfilment. By recognising the ultimate reality that underlies all things, we can begin to see through the illusions and delusions that keep us trapped in suffering and ignorance and move toward a deeper and more profound understanding of ourselves and the world around us.

The verse emphasises that each individual is an integral part of the universe. They are not separate from the universe but a part of it. The *purnam idam* verse suggests that 'I am an individual who is mortal but I am part of that whole which is eternal.' This means that, even though we, as individuals, are mortal and subject to the cycle of birth and death, we are part of something larger that is eternal and infinite. Furthermore, the verse suggests that seeing oneness in everything gives us the wisdom and intelligence to understand the world and deal with it for our emancipation and enlightenment.

When we realise that we are not separate from the universe but a part of it, we can develop a sense of unity and interconnectedness with all things. This can lead to a sense of inner peace and harmony, which can help us navigate the challenges of life with greater ease. When we see the oneness in everything, we can gain the wisdom and intelligence to understand the world through altogether different perspectives. We are beginning to understand that all things are part of a larger whole and that this wholeness is maintained even as individual parts come into being and pass away. From a practical perspective, the verse encourages us to recognise and honour the interconnectedness of all things.

It reminds us that every action we take, no matter how small, has an impact on the world around us. By acknowledging this fact, we can begin to act more mindfully and with greater awareness of our place in the larger scheme of things. The verse suggests that we can find a sense of wholeness and completeness by recognising our connection to the larger whole; we begin to see others as extensions of us. By cultivating a sense of unity with the world around us, we can find a deeper sense of meaning and purpose in our lives.

This understanding can be incredibly empowering and inspiring, as it means that we are not limited by our past experiences, our current circumstances, or any external factors. We have the ability to tap into the limitless power and wisdom of the universe and create the life we desire. By embracing the belief that we are infinite and unlimited beings, we can let go of fear, self-doubt, and limiting beliefs that hold us back. We can access our true power and live a life of purpose and fulfilment.

Beyond the Physical: The Mystical Nature of *Brahman*

Brahman is a concept in Hindu philosophy that refers to the ultimate reality or the absolute truth. According to the Upanishads, *brahman* is the supreme and eternal consciousness that underlies and permeates all existence. It is the source of all creation, sustenance, and dissolution, and is beyond time, space, and causation. The Upanishads describe *brahman* as being formless, limitless, and indivisible. It is beyond human comprehension and can only be realised through direct experience or self-realisation. The Upanishads also describe *brahman* as being the essence of everything that exists, including the individual self or *atma*.

The term *brahman* is derived from the Sanskrit root *brha* or *brhi*, which denotes knowledge, expansion, and all-pervasiveness. *Brahman* is the ultimate reality, which exists eternally and is not subject to death, decay, or decomposition. It signifies omnipresence and oneness. One of the most famous passages in the Upanishads describes *brahman* as follows: 'Verily, all this universe is *brahman*. From *brahman* all things originate, in *brahman* they exist, and unto *brahman* they return. *Brahman* alone is real; the world is unreal; and the individual self is *brahman*.' This passage emphasises the unity of all existence and the idea that everything in the universe is ultimately one with *brahman*, the single binding unity behind all the diversity. Being self-existent, *brahman* does not need any support for existence. Though described in the Upanishads in negative terms (*neti, neti*: not this, not this) *brahman* is not a negative concept. It is not synonymous with emptiness; it is the fundamental truth underlying all of creation, encompassing every phenomenon. It symbolises wholeness, fullness, and completeness, as, upon realisation of Brahman, nothing remains to be known or understood.

Brahman should not be confused with Brahma, one of the three faces of the Hindu Trinity. *Brahman* is the unchanging truth behind the constantly changing world, the divine energy that brings bliss and is responsible for creating the universe. All beings are born from *brahman*, live because of *brahman*, and return to *brahman* when departing. *Brahman* is the essence of everything that exists, the indivisible pure consciousness that permeates everything, also known as *paramatma*, the Supreme Self. *Brahman* is beyond the limitations of time and space but supports the cosmic manifestation within them. *Brahman* does not act, but everything that happens in the world is a result of *brahman*, which causes all changes but is beyond any change and remains unaffected by cosmic experiences.

The Nature of the Ultimate Reality: *Sat Chit Ananda*

Sat chit ananda is a Sanskrit phrase that is used in the Taittiriya Upanishad to describe the nature of the ultimate reality or *brahman*. It is composed of three words: *sat*, *chit*, and *ananda*. *Sat* means 'truth' or 'existence': the absolute reality or the ultimate truth that underlies all existence. *Chit* means 'consciousness': the pure awareness that is beyond the limitations of the individual self or ego. *Ananda* means 'bliss' or 'eternal happiness': the experience of infinite joy and contentment that arises from realising one's true nature as identical with *brahman*. Together, these three words describe the nature of *brahman* as the ultimate truth, consciousness, and bliss. They also represent the essential qualities of the human being.

Chit refers to the essence of the soul, which includes both knowledge and vision; this can be impure or pure. In terms of decision-making, the mind presents ideas while the *chit* provides a more accurate picture of reality. The intellect then evaluates the information, the ego confirms it, and then action is taken. Therefore, the idea is to purify the *chit*, which includes purifying one's knowledge and vision. This can lead to greater clarity and accuracy in decision-making and a deeper understanding of oneself and the world.

The core of our being, our authentic identity, must be recognised; once that happens, we become free from all the various personalities we possess. Essentially, we are pure existence, consciousness, and bliss. With this realisation, we can embrace our different roles and fulfil our duties as indicated in the Isha Upanishad.

There is a true essence of the self that needs to be realised in order to be free from the various personalities or assumed identities that one possesses. Once this true identity is realised, one becomes free from the limitations of the ego and attains a state of pure existence, consciousness, and bliss. This realisation allows individuals to continue performing their duties and fulfilling their roles in life. In other words, by understanding and embodying this true nature of existence, individuals can navigate their lives and interact with the world around them while remaining grounded in their true nature.

Based on the above information, it becomes clear that one must try to gain *atmagyan* (self-knowledge) and *brahmajnana* (knowledge of the ultimate reality). These are two related but distinct concepts in Hindu philosophy. Understanding the difference between the two is important for anyone interested in exploring the deeper aspects of spirituality and self-realisation.

Atmagyan refers to the process of understanding and realising one's own true nature. It involves introspection, self-enquiry, reflection, and contemplation of the nature of the self. Gaining *atmagyan* is a step-by-step process that involves first recognising the limitations of the ego or the individual self and then gradually moving towards a deeper understanding of the true nature of the self. *Atmagyan* aims to dispel the ignorance (*avidya*) that causes individuals to identify with their physical body, senses, and ego and thus perceive their *atma* as separate from *brahman*. Appreciating the idea that everything is connected and that we are part of the wholeness of the universe is a crucial first step towards developing *atmagyan*. When we realise that we are connected to everything in the universe, we understand that our actions have a ripple effect on everything around us and we start to feel a sense of responsibility towards the world and its inhabitants. We see that we are not separate from the universe but rather a part of it and that our individuality is just an illusion. This realisation helps us let go of our ego and cultivate a sense of humility and gratitude towards the universe. When we are in sync with the wholeness of the universe, we can tap into its vast wisdom and power. We can use this connection to access our own inner wisdom and creativity and to live a more fulfilling and purposeful life.

Atmagyan is often pursued through various spiritual practices, such as meditation, self-enquiry (*jnana* yoga), contemplation, and the study of sacred texts like the Upanishads and Bhagavad Gita. These practices help individuals transcend the limitations of the mind and gain direct insight into their true nature. Attaining *atmagyan* is considered a significant milestone along the spiritual path in Hinduism. It is believed to lead to liberation (*moksha*) from the cycle of birth and death (*samsara*) and to bring profound inner peace, freedom from suffering, and a deep sense of connection with all beings. However, the concept of *atmagyan* is not limited to Hinduism alone. Similar notions of self-realisation and the true nature of the self exist in other spiritual traditions and philosophies as well.

Brahmajnana, on the other hand, refers to the highest knowledge or realisation of the ultimate reality or *brahman*. This realisation is said to bring about a state of pure consciousness or pure awareness, which is beyond words and concepts. It is often described as a state of enlightenment or self-realisation, whereby one experiences the ultimate truth directly and becomes one with it. It is the culmination of the spiritual journey and the goal of all spiritual practices. *Atmagyan* and *brahmajnana* represent different stages of spiritual realisation. *Atmagyan* is the foundation upon which *brahmajnana* is built. Without a deep understanding of the true nature of the self, it is not possible to realise the ultimate reality or *brahman*.

At the same time, it is important to recognise that *atmagyan* and *brahmajnana* are not separate or distinct from each other. They are different stages in the same journey towards self-realisation. *Atmagyan* is the means to achieve *brahmajnana*, and *brahmajnana* is the culmination of *atmagyan*.

In this context, it is worth discussing the *mahavakyas* from the Vedas that have the power to transform our understanding of ourselves and the world around us. *Mahavakyas* are literally the 'great sayings' or 'great sentences' of the Upanishads. These teachings offer profound insights into the nature of reality and can help us develop a deeper sense of spiritual intelligence and awareness. The Upanishads contain four *mahavakyas* that reveal the nature of *atma* and *brahman*, each approaching *brahman* from a different perspective while addressing the non-distinguishability of *atman* and *brahman*.

1. ***Aham Brahmasmi.*** *Aham brahmasmi* is a phrase from the Brihadaranyaka Upanishad, which translates to 'I am *brahman*.' It represents the realisation that the individual self is not separate from the universal consciousness and the recognition that the true nature of the self is not limited to the physical body, mind, or ego, but is instead boundless and eternal. This realisation can lead to a profound shift in perspective, freeing us from the limitations of the ego and enabling us to see ourselves and the world around us in a new light. It can help us develop a deeper sense of compassion, love, and interconnectedness with all beings. The practices of meditation, self-enquiry, and contemplation are some of the ways in which we can deepen our understanding of *aham brahmasmi*. By turning

our attention inward and focusing on the true nature of the self, we can gradually dissolve the illusions of separation and ego and experience the oneness that underlies all of creation. The phrase is often misinterpreted to mean 'I am God.' God is not within the individual; rather, the individual exists within God. As mortal beings, our bodies and minds are finite, whereas God is infinite, eternal, and immortal. It is impossible for us to be so. However, this does not mean that we are completely separate from God. Beyond the body, mind, and intellect lies the true self, also known as the pure consciousness or soul. This self is eternal and immortal, and it is through understanding this essence of the self that we can comprehend our interconnectedness with *brahman*. Therefore, *aham brahmasmi* should be understood not as a proclamation of individual divinity but as an acknowledgement of the infinite and eternal nature of the self, which is connected to the infinite and eternal reality of *brahman*.

In verse 12 of Chapter 7 of the Bhagavad Gita, Lord Krishna says, 'Know that all states of being—be they of goodness, passion, or ignorance—are manifested by My energy. I am, in one sense, everything—but I am independent. I am not under the modes of material nature, for they, on the contrary, are within Me.' This suggests that God exists beyond the material world and is the ultimate source of all creation.

In verse 4 of Chapter 9, Lord Krishna explains, 'By Me, in My unmanifested form, this entire universe is pervaded. All beings are in Me, but I am not in them.' This indicates that God is all-pervading and that everything exists within Him, but He is beyond everything.

The teachings of the Bhagavad Gita have important implications for human evolution and emancipation. The state of union with divinity occurs when the ego, which encompasses all identifications with objects and titles, is eliminated. This state is known as yoga, characterised by integration and union. The annihilation of the ego results in the integration (union) of *atma* and *brahman*: the individual self and higher self merge into one. The self dissolves completely into the universal consciousness and cosmic intelligence, unifying the creator and creation. The realisation that 'I am the truth' marks the ultimate point, exemplifying the beauty of *advaita*: non-duality. The declaration *aham brahmasmi* expresses the internal experience of realising one's true identity with *brahman*, transcending the separation between observer and observed.

Ana 'i-haqq is a Persian phrase that means 'I am the Truth' or 'I am God' in English. This phrase is often associated with the Sufi mystic Mansur Al-Hallaj, who was executed in the 10th century for his unorthodox views on the nature of God and the relationship between the individual and the divine. In Sufism, *ana 'i-haqq* represents the ultimate realisation of the unity of all existence and the union of the self with the divine. It emphasises the idea that the essence of the individual self is not separate from the essence of God or ultimate reality but is identical to it.

Ana 'i-haqq and *aham brahmasmi* share similarities, despite originating thousands of years apart in cultures that had no apparent connections or lines of communication with each other. It's remarkable how the underlying ideas of these two distinct belief systems align with each other, reflecting a universal and homogeneous way of thinking, a testament to the wisdom of enlightened masters who transcended the barriers of caste, creed, and religion.

2. ***Ayam Atma Brahma.*** *Ayam atma brahma*, from the Mandukya Upanishad of the Atharva Veda, can be translated to mean 'This self is *brahman*' or 'This individual soul is the ultimate reality.' This phrase highlights the central teaching of the Upanishads, which is the idea that the true nature of the self (*atman*) is identical with the ultimate reality (*brahman*), like the wave and the ocean, which may appear distinct at first but ultimately merge into a single entity. Just as the wave is an expression of the vastness of the ocean, the *atman* is a spark of consciousness that is an inseparable part of the universal consciousness, *brahman*. Therefore, let us awaken to the truth of our interconnectedness with the universe and embrace the infinite potential that lies within us. When we say *ayam atma brahma*, we affirm this oneness between the individual self and the ultimate reality and acknowledge that our true nature is not limited to the body and mind but is a part of the infinite and eternal consciousness that pervades the universe.

3. ***Tat Tvam Asi.*** *Tat tvam asi* is a phrase from the Chandogya Upanishad. The phrase translates to 'That thou art,' which means that the individual self (*atma*) is identical to the ultimate reality (*brahman*). It represents the realisation that the true nature of the self is not separate from the divine consciousness but is an expression of it, that we are not isolated beings but a part of the larger cosmic whole.

   Tat tvam asi is a part of conversation between two individuals, i.e. teacher and a disciple, wherein the teacher is pointing at the disciple and declaring that the very essence of his being is the absolute reality, *brahman*. It's not just a philosophical concept, it's who we truly are at our core. This revelation is like a wave that is not separate from the ocean but an inseparable part of the ocean itself. Let us embrace this profound truth and experience the blissful unity of existence. This profound teaching of the Chandogya Upanishad demands action in terms of contemplation. Take a moment to turn inward and direct your attention towards the core of your being, possibly towards your heart centre. As you contemplate the essence of this truth, let go of the false identities that are only temporary and relative. Point your finger at yourself and declare with conviction, 'That is who you are!' As you reflect on the supreme knowledge of *brahman*, shift your focus towards your own spiritual nature and repeat, '*Tat tvam asi*; that you are!' Embrace the feeling that arises from this realisation and experience the transcendental joy of your true nature, beyond the limitations of your mind and body.

4. ***Prajnanam Brahma.*** *Prajnanam brahma* is a profound statement from the Aitareya Upanishad, a part of the Rig Veda. *Prajnanam* means knowledge and *brahma* is the same as *brahman*. Therefore, the phrase can be translated to mean 'knowledge is *brahman*' or 'consciousness is the ultimate reality.' This means that all other types of knowledge stem from and are part of a higher knowledge, with the exception of the absolute knowledge, which is the highest form of knowledge and is not dependent on anything else. The supreme knowledge is the foundation from which all other knowledge and experiences grow, and it is represented by the concept of *brahman*, which is the oneness of universal consciousness. Although it is difficult to articulate this concept in words, people have used numerous metaphors to describe it over time. In essence, this *mahavakya* reminds us that, as we ascend the ladder of knowledge, we will find this higher knowledge at the level of *brahman*.

When attempting to contemplate the nature of supreme knowledge, the mind may become filled with memories, sensations, emotions, and other forms of knowledge. It must be remembered that, although they are undoubtedly forms of knowledge, they are not the highest knowledge. Take a moment to observe your patterns of thought and ask yourself, 'Is this higher knowledge?' Upon reflection, you will find that these patterns are not higher knowledge; they are lower forms of knowledge. This process of contemplation creates a sense of calmness that allows the intuition of higher knowledge to emerge. This intuition is strengthened with regular practice. The calmness it brings about is not the calmness of inactivity or apathy but the calmness of clarity and receptivity. As the field of knowledge gradually expands, a smile will appear on your face and in your heart.

Prajnanam brahma carries a deep spiritual significance and has profound implications for our understanding of the nature of reality and our place in it. It suggests that the ultimate reality is not abstract or inaccessible; it can, in fact, be realised through the cultivation of knowledge and consciousness. It also highlights the importance of knowledge in spiritual practice. Knowledge is not simply information or intellectual understanding. Rather, it is a deeper, more intuitive understanding that arises from direct experience and realisation. It transcends the limitations of the mind and the senses and connects us with the divine. In Hinduism, knowledge is seen as a means of liberation from the cycle of birth and death and attainment of *moksha* or spiritual liberation. By recognising that knowledge is synonymous with the ultimate reality, one can cultivate a deeper understanding of the nature of reality and the self.

The crux of these *mahavakyas* is that, when one recognises and comprehends the connection between *atman* and *brahman*, one realises that one is not merely a body and mind but an integral part of the ultimate reality. Although one may be limited and bound by their physical and mental constraints, once one unites with *atman* and *brahman*, one becomes boundless. This notion alone is astounding and motivating, prompting liberation from limitations and allowing the realisation of the vast potential within oneself, leading to a fulfilling life. It is crucial to acknowledge that one's perceived identity or ego stems from *avidya* (ignorance). By dispelling this ignorance, one can follow a path illuminated by the radiant soul within.

Each of the *mahavakyas* offers a unique perspective on the same underlying reality, like gaining different points of view from different vantage points. These perspectives gradually converge to provide a holistic understanding of the absolute reality, as if looking at different reflections of the same truth in a mirror. This integrated flash of insight reveals the true meaning of the word *brahman* and enables us to embrace the interconnectedness of all things.

These teachings offer a powerful framework for developing spiritual intelligence and awakening to the deeper truths of existence. *Prajnanam brahma* emphasises the role of consciousness as the fundamental essence of reality. It highlights the idea that consciousness is not just an attribute of the self but is the very basis of all existence. *Ayam atma brahma* focuses on the self as the ultimate reality. It suggests that the individual self is not different from the universal self, and the realisation of this truth leads to liberation from the cycle of birth and death. *Tat tvam asi* stresses the idea of identity between the individual self and the universal self. It asserts that the true nature of the self is identical to the ultimate reality of *brahman*. *Aham brahmasmi* conveys the idea that the individual self is not separate from *brahman* but is, in fact, identical to it. It suggests that the realisation of this truth leads to the dissolution of the ego and the attainment of ultimate liberation or *moksha*.

The *mahavakyas* remind us of the impermanent nature of worldly objects and of the existence of an eternal nature that is not subject to change. They offer a powerful framework for developing spiritual intelligence, cultivating compassion and wisdom, and experiencing a deeper sense of inner peace and connection to the divine. By integrating these teachings into our lives, we can awaken to the deeper truths of existence and experience the transformative power of spiritual intelligence.

Mahavakyas and Contemplation

Mahavakyas are not just words. They are the very essence of our being. To truly understand and experience their significance, we must engage in contemplation. Through this process, we can undertake a transformational journey towards realising the meaning and purpose of our existence. It is not a mere intellectual exercise, but a spiritual one that requires stillness and reflection. The truth of *mahavakyas* can only be grasped through intuitive flashes that become progressively deeper with practice. Metaphors may aid in explaining the principles, but the real key to unlocking their power lies in the inner workshop of contemplation and meditation. One may experience oneself as being like gold or clay, or like a wave in an ocean of bliss. All these metaphors are used only as tools of explanation. After engaging in thinking, we must enter a state of contemplative insight. Initially, the insights may arise in a manner similar to the creative process, wherein we reflect and ponder until we finally let go and enter a state of silence. In this state, the solution to a problem or a profound idea may suddenly emerge. Contemplating the *mahavakyas* follows this pattern initially, but as we progress, it becomes a deeper form of meditation.

The insights that arise from contemplating the *mahavakyas* will be unique to each individual and their cultural and religious background. The metaphors used to explain the principles are simply tools, and the insights gained will not seem foreign or unnatural. In fact, one's religious values will be affirmed rather than violated. Through contemplation, we can discover the profound truth of the *mahavakyas* within the context of our own lives.

The *mahavakyas* are to be taken not as mere statements of truth to be blindly believed but as invitations to direct experience. The sages advise against relying solely on hearsay or written texts and instead encourage individuals to test the validity of the *mahavakyas* for themselves through personal exploration. Although the experience of ultimate oneness may be universal, cultural and religious influences may colour the early stages of insight differently for each person.

Contemplating the *mahavakyas* is therefore not a mere mental exercise but a gradual journey towards profound silence and direct experience of reality. It is not about chanting mantras or programming the mind with affirmations but about moving systematically towards the highest level of understanding. Contemplation of the *mahavakyas* and the question 'Who am I?' are not mutually exclusive practices; they complement each other in a unified pursuit of truth. It is a process that leads towards the direct realisation of the meaning of the *mahavakyas* rather than acceptance of them as intellectual concepts.

The pinnacle of contemplation is known as *sakshatkara* (enlightenment), a state in which perception and conceptualisation are fully aligned and all doubts from various levels of understanding are eliminated permanently. At this stage of enlightenment, the truth reveals itself to the seeker, and they achieve the ultimate realisation: 'I am *atman*—I am *brahman*.' This state of *advaita* (non-duality) can be attained through contemplation, while meditation has a different role, aiding the aspirant in focusing their mind, turning it inward, and keeping it steady.

Stillness and steadiness are prerequisites for meditative practice. The subsequent stages of sitting, breathing, concentrating, and allowing the uninterrupted flow of the focused mind to help expand one's capacity enable contemplation without any distractions. The realisation of the *mahavakyas* is a gradual process that occurs in stages. Initially, we attain a cognitive understanding of their meaning. However, as we delve deeper through contemplation, intuition begins to unveil their deeper meanings. Ultimately, the experience of merging with the direct realisation of the *mahavakyas* is achieved. This experience is akin to travelling upwards, although there was never any separation between us and the *mahavakyas* in the first place.

The Upanishads have also provided a systematic framework for learning and contemplating spiritual knowledge through *shravan* (hearing the truth), *manana* (contemplating the truth), and *nididhyasana* (living and breathing the truth).

1. ***Shravana***, the first stage, involves actively listening to the teachings of a guru or qualified teacher and engaging in a deep study of the *mahavakyas*. The purpose of *shravana* is to gain an intellectual understanding of the *mahavakyas*, the foundational knowledge necessary for the journey ahead.
2. ***Manana***, the second stage, involves reflecting and contemplating on the teachings of the guru. Through deep analysis and introspection, the disciple gains a deeper understanding of the teachings and a stronger conviction in their truth. After gaining an intellectual understanding of the *mahavakyas* through *shravana*, the seeker engages in deep contemplation and introspection. They critically analyse and reflect upon the teachings, examining them from different angles and resolving any doubts or intellectual barriers that may arise. The goal of *manana* is to develop a clear and logical comprehension of the *mahavakyas*.
3. ***Nididhyasana***, which means 'meditation' or 'profound contemplation', is the final stage. In this stage, the seeker transcends intellectual understanding and dives into direct

experiential realisation. *Nididhyasana* involves intense meditation, with the seeker repeatedly dwelling on the *mahavakyas*, focusing their attention on the ultimate truth they convey. The aim is to transcend the limitations of the mind and intellect and directly experience the truth at a deeper level of consciousness. The seeker may employ various techniques, such as mantra repetition, breath awareness, visualisation, or self-enquiry to deepen their meditation practice. Through sustained and focused meditation, the seeker gradually transcends the dualistic nature of the mind and merges with the underlying unity of existence, realising the truth of the *mahavakyas* at a profound level. *Nididhyasana* is not merely a mental exercise but a transformative process that leads to direct experiential realisation. It goes beyond intellectual understanding and seeks to merge the seeker's awareness with the ultimate reality or the self. It is through this deep contemplation and meditation that the seeker is said to attain the state of self-realisation or enlightenment.

It's important to note that the stages of realisation may vary for different individuals and the journey of spiritual realisation is unique to each seeker. *Nididhyasana* represents the culmination of the process and is considered the gateway to profound self-realisation.

The Principle of a Single Unifying Force in Other Religions

The principles of interconnectedness and oneness that we find in Hinduism and Vedanta are also found in many other religious and philosophical traditions. In Jainism, the concept of *anekantavada*, discussed previously, is similar to the principle of non-duality, whereas in Buddhism, it is the doctrine of dependent origination or dependent arising (*pratityasamutpada* in Sanskrit). Dependent origination is a fundamental teaching in Buddhism that explains how all phenomena are dependent on multiple causes and conditions and must not be viewed as independent and self-existent entities. This principle emphasises the interdependence and interconnectedness of all things and rejects the idea of an independent and unchanging self or soul. In this sense, dependent origination can be seen as a form of non-dualism. It is intimately linked to the ultimate aim of Buddhist spiritual practice, which is to realise the emptiness (*shunyata*) of all phenomena or the fact that all phenomena lack inherent existence and are dependently originated. This realisation leads to the cessation of suffering and the attainment of *nirvana*, the state of ultimate liberation.

In Sikhism, the concept of *ik onkar* is similar to the principle of non-duality in Vedanta. *Ik onkar* is a central principle in Sikhism that affirms the unity and oneness of the divine and the universe. It emphasises that there is only one supreme reality that pervades everything in the universe, that this reality is both immanent and transcendent, and that the ultimate goal of human life is to realise this oneness and merge with the divine. In Sikhism, this realisation is achieved through the practice of meditation, selfless service, and devotion to the divine. This leads to the attainment of spiritual liberation and the merging of the individual soul with the universal soul. The concept of *ik onkar* is a powerful expression of the principle of non-duality, emphasising the unity and oneness of all things and pointing towards the ultimate goal of spiritual realisation and liberation.

In Christianity, the principle of non-duality can be found in the concept of the Holy Trinity or the triune nature of God. Christianity posits that God exists as three distinct persons: God the Father, God the Son (Jesus Christ), and God the Holy Spirit. Each aspect of the Trinity is fully God, yet they are not three separate gods but rather one God in three aspects; one in essence but three in person. Non-duality emphasises the oneness or unity of all things, including the divine. The Trinity can be seen as a metaphorical expression of this principle. Rather than viewing the Trinity as three separate persons, non-duality suggests that it represents different aspects or expressions of the same divine essence. The Father, Son, and Holy Spirit can be seen as different manifestations of the one divine consciousness or ultimate reality. The Trinity serves as a reminder that apparent distinctions and separations are ultimately illusory. It points to the underlying unity that transcends the multiplicity of forms.

The principles of oneness, compassion, and non-attachment are universal principles that can be found in many religious and philosophical traditions. They offer a powerful framework for developing spiritual intelligence, cultivating compassion and wisdom, and experiencing a deeper sense of inner peace and connection to the divine. By integrating these principles into our lives, we can awaken to the deeper truths of existence and experience the transformative power of spiritual intelligence. Rather than getting entangled in the material world, we need to see this interconnectedness to experience reality. In this context, Adi Shankaracharya's teachings on *brahma satyam jagat mithya* hold great significance.

Brahma Satyam Jagat Mithya

Brahma satyam jagat mithya is a famous saying attributed to Jagadguru Adi Shankaracharya that translates to '*brahman* (the ultimate reality) is the only truth, the world is illusory.' It means that the world is constantly changing and what we see is just its appearance. This statement reflects the belief that the material world is not ultimately real but an illusion or a temporary manifestation of the ultimate reality. However, it is important to note that this does not mean the material world is completely non-existent or that it has no value. Rather, it means that the world we experience is a subjective construction of our own thoughts as they are filtered through the lenses of our perceptions. As our thoughts and beliefs evolve over time, so does our perception of the world, leading to a constantly changing and impermanent experience. What we perceive as reality is merely an appearance or manifestation of the underlying reality of *brahman*.

In the context of seeking truth and purpose in life, the concept of *jagat mithya* can be relevant in several ways. Firstly, it encourages individuals to look beyond the material world and towards a deeper, spiritual reality. This can help individuals develop a sense of detachment from material possessions and transient experiences and focus instead on cultivating a deeper connection to the divine. Secondly, it encourages individuals to question the nature of reality and seek a deeper understanding of the world around them. By recognising the illusory nature of the material world, individuals may be more motivated to seek out the ultimate truth and purpose beyond the surface level of everyday life. However, it is important to note that the concept of *jagat mithya* can also be challenging to grasp for some individuals, as it raises questions about the nature of existence and the purpose of life. It may also be difficult for individuals to reconcile this concept with their own experiences and beliefs about the world. Therefore, it is important for individuals to approach this concept with an open mind and a willingness to engage in critical reflection and enquiry.

Brahma satyam implies that *brahman* is the ultimate reality, the source of all existence, and the divine consciousness that pervades the entire universe. This idea is significant in the context of spiritual growth because it emphasises that we are all part of the divine consciousness that pervades the universe, that the ultimate reality or *brahman* is the essence of our being and that we can connect with it through introspection and meditation. When we connect with our inner world, we can become aware of our true nature, which is not separate from the divine consciousness. By recognising this oneness, we can overcome our limitations and experience spiritual growth. *Brahma satyam* also reminds us that our true nature is beyond the physical body, emotions, and thoughts.

While the concept of *jagat mithya* can be a valuable tool for individuals seeking truth and purpose in life, it is important to approach it with care and reflection and to seek guidance from trusted spiritual teachers or mentors. A surface-level engagement with the concept may not produce a genuine understanding of its meaning.

The concepts of *mithya* and *maya* are rooted in the teachings of Shankaracharya, who believed that the finite, constantly changing material world (*jagat* or *prakriti*, made up of the three *gunas—rajas*, *tamas*, and *sattva*) is superimposed on reality. The *mithya* nature of the material world prevents us from realising and attaining the oneness of *atman* and *brahman*. In the material world, our senses keep us occupied with the names and forms of things and our experiences are constantly changing with time and the nature of things. Only when we start recognising that there is a reality beyond the appearance of this material world can we begin to understand its true nature, interconnectedness, and non-duality. This is a profound and complex concept with many possible interpretations and in-depth analyses that could fill an entire book. To truly grasp it, a background in Vedanta and a spiritual orientation are necessary. However, from a layperson's perspective or within the context of spiritual intelligence, what can be gleaned from it is that every experience we have in the material world is relative to the nature of things and is temporary. The joy or sorrow we experience is impermanent and solely a result of our perceptions. This is why the saying 'this too shall pass' holds true for all worldly experiences. The happiness we derive from worldly possessions is fleeting and short-lived. To find lasting contentment and fulfilment, we must turn our attention inward and strive to attain a higher state of consciousness. Only by delving into our higher selves can we truly understand the illusory nature (*maya*) of the material world and realise that it alone cannot provide a fulfilling life. The economic law of diminishing marginal utilities can also be applied to the pursuit of material wants and desires. As we acquire more and more of these material possessions, the pleasure and happiness derived from them tends to decrease over time. This is because our wants are abundant but our capacity for enjoyment is limited. Even wealthy individuals may find themselves feeling unfulfilled and lacking in peace despite their abundance of possessions. It is only when we shift our focus from material pursuits to spiritual growth and contribution to society that we can find a lasting sense of contentment and fulfilment. Recognising the *mithya* nature of the material world and the ultimate reality of *brahman* can help us detach from our material desires and focus on pursuits that bring lasting satisfaction and joy.

The term *jagat* refers to the world we experience. While *atman* and *brahman* are considered absolute and unchanging, *jagat* is transitory. It is subject to time and change and can be negated, which means that it is not the absolute reality like *atman* or *brahman*. Instead, it is considered a *vyavaharika* (transactional) reality, which means that it is a reality that we experience in our everyday lives. The term *asat* (unreal) is used to describe *jagat* in this context, but the world is not completely unreal or non-existent; rather, it may have some degree of reality in our everyday lives, but it is simply not the absolute reality.

Maya, or the illusory nature of the world, has the power to camouflage reality and deceive us and distract us from the true essence of our being. Buddha taught us to focus on the impermanence of this world and to recognise the fleeting nature of all things. Shankaracharya, too, emphasised that the world we perceive as real is in fact a product of our own perception and is ultimately illusory. Our ignorance is responsible for our false perception of a stable and permanent reality. While we have access to an abundance of information, we must be discerning in our acceptance of what is factual and true. The impact of recognising *maya* is transformative. It allows us to let go of our attachment to fleeting and temporary things and instead focus on that which is eternal and enduring. By recognising the true nature of our being, we can attain a state of peace and contentment that transcends the vicissitudes of the world around us.

Shankaracharya's statement '*Jivo brahmaiva naparah*' means that the realisation of the purest form of individual self (*atman*), or life energy without ego, is equivalent to realising the almighty energy or *brahman*. This belief is similar to the ancient Greek aphorism 'Know thyself,' which emphasises studying oneself to gain knowledge. To achieve the goal of *brahman*, Shankaracharya suggests the *sadhana chatushtaya*, the four-fold path of spiritual practice:

1. ***Viveka* (Discrimination).** This involves developing the power to discriminate between what is real and what is not. It requires us to distinguish between the eternal (*nitya*) and temporary (*anitya*), the self (*atma*) and non-self (*anatma*), and the divine (*siva*) and non-divine (*asiva*). *Viveka* helps us see beyond illusions and recognise the ultimate truth.
2. ***Vairagya* (Detachment).** This involves cultivating detachment from worldly desires and attachments. This detachment is not about renouncing the world (*samsara*) but developing a sense of non-attachment to avoid being caught up in the cycle of birth and death. *Vairagya* helps us focus on spiritual growth and cultivate inner peace.
3. ***Shad Sampat* (Six-fold Virtues).** This involves cultivating six virtues that are essential for spiritual progress:

3.1. *Sama* (Control of mind). This involves bringing the mind to a state of calmness and serenity by controlling it through meditation.

3.2. *Dama* (Control of senses). This involves restraining the senses and regulating their activities to avoid being distracted from spiritual pursuits.

3.3. *Uparati* (Cessation from distracting activities). This involves withdrawing from external activities that hinder spiritual growth.

3.4. *Titiksha* (Endurance). This refers to cultivating patience and forbearance to overcome difficulties on the spiritual path.

3.5. *Shraddha* (Faith). This involves developing unwavering faith in the ultimate truth and the path to self-realisation.

3.6. *Samadhana* (Concentration). This involves developing the ability to concentrate the mind on a single object of meditation to achieve deeper states of awareness.

4. ***Mumukshutva* (Desire for Liberation).** This is the final step, which complements *sadhana chatushtaya. Mumukshutva* involves cultivating a strong desire for liberation (*moksha*) from the cycle of birth and death. It is a burning commitment to spiritual growth and self-realisation, which helps us stay focused on our path and overcome any hindrances that come our way.

Similarities Between the Allegory of the Cave and *Jagat Mithya*

Plato's allegory of the cave is a fascinating philosophical concept that has captured the imaginations of countless thinkers over the centuries. This is a philosophical metaphor that describes the journey of prisoners who have been chained inside a dark cave since birth. In the allegory, they are bound in such a way that they can only see the wall in front of them. Behind them is a fire burning and between the fire and the prisoners is a raised walkway. Along this walkway, various objects and figures are carried, casting shadows on the wall that the prisoners perceive as reality.

Figure 16

The prisoners, unable to turn their heads, believe that these shadows are the only reality they have ever known. They give names to the shadows and consider them the true forms of those objects. The echoes of voices from the people carrying the objects further reinforce their perception of reality. One day, one of the prisoners is freed and forced to turn and face the fire. At first, the prisoner is dazzled by the light and struggles to understand the true nature of the objects creating the shadows. Gradually, the prisoner becomes accustomed to the light and begins to perceive the objects as they truly are.

If the other prisoners were to leave the cave, they would encounter sunlight, which represents the realm of true knowledge and ultimate reality. Initially, the prisoners could be blinded by the intense light, but as their eyes adjusted, they would see the real world, filled with the beauty of nature and the true forms of objects. The allegory of the cave symbolises the journey of a philosopher seeking knowledge and wisdom. The prisoners represent ordinary people who are unaware of the true nature of reality and rely solely on their sensory perceptions. The cave represents the material world, the realm of appearances and illusions. The shadows cast on the wall symbolise the distorted and limited understanding we have through our senses, which can be influenced by societal norms, cultural biases, and personal beliefs. The freed prisoner represents the philosopher who ventures beyond the world of appearances and seeks true knowledge through reason and philosophical enquiry.

Plato suggests that the philosopher has a responsibility to return to the cave and enlighten the prisoners about the existence of a higher reality. However, the prisoners, comfortable in their familiar illusions, may resist and reject the philosopher's teachings, clinging to their false perception of reality. According to Plato, the prisoners represent individuals who are trapped in the physical world and cannot see beyond their limited perception; their perception of reality is limited and influenced by external factors, as ours often is. The cave represents the material world that we experience through our senses, and the shadows represent the illusions and false beliefs that we mistake for reality. The allegory encourages us to question our beliefs, seek knowledge beyond appearances, and strive for a deeper understanding of the world around us.

The journey out of the cave represents the process of education and enlightenment, whereby individuals can break free from their limited perception and discover the true nature of reality. Plato believed that this journey could only be achieved through philosophy and that the ultimate goal of human existence is to attain knowledge of what he called forms or ideas, which exist beyond the material world. Plato's theory of forms, to which the allegory of the cave is linked, proposes that the true reality exists in forms or ideas rather than in the material world that we perceive through our senses. Understanding forms is considered the highest form of knowledge. Socrates says that those who aspire to become the most excellent people must engage in the highest form of study, which involves contemplating forms or what he calls 'the Good'. However, those who have attained this level of understanding should not remain isolated but return to the cave and coexist with the prisoners, sharing their struggles and triumphs. This way, they can utilise their knowledge to help others and make a positive impact on the world.

The allegory of the cave serves as a metaphor for the human condition and the importance of intellectual enquiry and philosophical contemplation in seeking the truth. Similarly, in Hindu philosophy, the concepts of brahma satya and jagat mithya are equally captivating. They suggest that the world we perceive is an illusion, and the ultimate reality lies beyond it. These ideas share a fundamental insight: that our perception of reality is limited and that the ultimate reality lies beyond our perception. However, the focus and emphasis of each concept is unique. Plato's allegory of the cave primarily addresses the limitations of human perception, while concepts such as 'brahma satyam jagat mithya' revolve around the nature of ultimate reality. Nevertheless, a common thread emerges between Plato's theory of forms and Advaita Vedanta, both asserting that the material world we perceive and identify by name, form, and nature does not accurately reflect the true nature of reality. These two philosophical concepts offer profound insights into the nature of reality and our relationship with it.By recognising the limitations of our perception, we can begin to glimpse the deeper truths that lie beyond the surface of things. Whether it is through the allegory of the cave or the concepts of brahma satya and jagat mithya, we are being invited to see the world in a new and profound way and to explore the mysteries of existence with fresh eyes and an open heart.

The Charvaka School: Exploring Indian Philosophy of Materialism and Atheism

There are numerous individuals who completely immerse themselves in the materialistic world and do not believe that there is a fulfilling life beyond it. They feel life is about enjoyment and that satisfying the senses leads to real pleasure. They may not actively pursue a spiritual path. In this context, I would like to draw attention to the mindset of the Charvaka school of philosophy, which emphasises that pleasure and the avoidance of pain are the ultimate goals of life and that there is no afterlife or spiritual realm. Examining these teachings can help those who are not on a spiritual path understand and appreciate the significance of developing wisdom or spiritual intelligence. By striking a balance between the material and spiritual aspects of our being, we can lead a fulfilling life.

Charvaka, also known as Lokayata, was a philosophical school of thought that emerged in ancient India around the sixth century BCE. The Charvaka school rejected traditional Hindu concepts such as *karma*, reincarnation, and the authority of the Vedas, and instead focused on a materialistic and atheistic worldview. The Charvaka school held that the only reality was the material world and that sensory experience was the only valid means of knowledge. Charvakas (the disciples of the school) also rejected the idea of a divine creator or any supernatural entities, arguing that everything could be explained through natural causes and physical laws. They believed that consciousness was a product of the physical brain and that there was no such thing as a soul or a self that continued after death.

Charvaka's philosophy was distinct from other Indian schools of thought, as it rejected the notion of abstaining from pleasure due to fear of pain. Rather, it celebrated hedonism and believed that the enjoyment of life lay in indulgence: delicious food, the company of young women, fine clothes, perfumes, garlands, etc. Charvaka considered death the ultimate liberation from life and thus rejected the idea of striving for spiritual enlightenment. According to Charvaka, only foolish individuals waste their time with penances and fasts, while chastity and other such practices are imposed by weak-minded people.

Despite being an ancient school of thought, the ideas of the Charvaka school continue to be debated and studied today, and they have influenced many later philosophical and religious movements in India. While many of their ideas were considered heretical at the time, the Charvakas played an important role in the development of Indian philosophy and the ongoing search for truth and meaning in life.

The key teachings of the Charvaka school are as follows:

- **Materialism.** Charvaka believed that matter is the only reality and that everything else, including consciousness and the soul, is a byproduct of matter. The Charvaka philosophy holds that the universe is made up of four elements: earth, water, fire, and air. It denies the existence of any supernatural power or divine being and asserts that the world is not governed by any divine law or moral code.
- **Inferred knowledge is conditional.** Charvaka philosophy rejected the use of inference to establish universal truths and metaphysical certainties. This means that any truth inferred from observations or premises should be regarded with doubt, as inferred knowledge is always conditional.
- **Rejection of authority.** Charvaka rejected authority and religious texts, arguing that knowledge should be based on personal experience and sensory perception. The Charvaka philosophy is also critical of other schools of thought in ancient India, including the Vedic tradition and Buddhism. It is particularly critical of the idea of sacrifice and the concept of *karma*.
- **Scepticism**. Charvaka was sceptical of traditional beliefs and superstitions and believed that claims about gods, the

afterlife, and the supernatural were unfounded. Charvaka rejects the idea of the afterlife, rebirth, and *karma*. It holds that death is the end of existence and that there is no existence beyond the physical world. Therefore, it asserts that one should make the most of one's life while one is alive.

- **Hedonism.** Charvaka taught that the ultimate goal of life is pleasure and that one should pursue pleasure and avoid pain. It holds that pleasure is the only intrinsic good and pain the only intrinsic evil. Therefore, the Charvaka philosophy advocates a hedonistic way of life, emphasising the importance of enjoying life to the fullest extent possible.
- **Ethical relativism.** Charvaka believed that ethical values are relative and dependent on social norms and personal preferences.
- **Rejection of the caste system.** Charvaka rejected the caste system, arguing that it was a man made construct that oppressed people and prevented them from pursuing their interests. Charvaka argues that the idea of sacrifice is an attempt by priests to control people and that the concept of *karma* is a way of justifying social inequality.
- **Critique of asceticism.** Charvaka criticised asceticism and the renunciation of pleasure, arguing that it was unnecessary and even harmful to one's physical and mental health.
- **Importance of material wealth.** Charvaka believed that material wealth was important and that one should strive to accumulate it, as it could provide pleasure and security in life.

Some may view Charvaka teachings as hedonistic or nihilistic; however, a balanced view suggests there are aspects of their philosophy that can help in evolving and gaining wisdom while others may cause negative results. Therefore, here are some dos and don'ts based on Charvaka teachings:

Dos

Question everything. Charvaka teachings emphasise the importance of critical thinking and rationality. They encourage individuals to question everything, including beliefs, assumptions, and authority. Charvaka philosophy emphasises the importance of experience over blind faith or religious dogma. This means that one should not accept beliefs simply because they have been handed down from previous generations or because they are written in sacred texts. Instead, one should question everything and rely on personal experience to gain knowledge and understanding. This can lead to a more critical and independent mindset, which can help one evolve and gain wisdom.

Live in the present. Charvaka teachings reject the idea of an afterlife and the existence of the soul. Therefore, they emphasise the importance of living in the present and making the most of this life.

Seek pleasure. Charvaka philosophy encourages people to enjoy life and embrace pleasure. This does not mean that one should indulge in excessive or harmful behaviours; rather, it suggests that one should appreciate the good things in life and not feel guilty for enjoying them. By embracing pleasure and happiness, one can cultivate this positive mindset and a greater sense of well-being, which can contribute to overall personal growth. However, the pursuit of pleasure should be balanced with other values and responsibilities.

Reject superstition. Charvaka philosophy is sceptical of religious beliefs, superstitions, and supernatural claims. By rejecting these ideas, one can cultivate a more rational and evidence-based worldview. This can help one avoid falling prey to scams, cults, and other forms of manipulation and make more informed and responsible decisions in life.

Encourage free thinking. Charvaka philosophy values freedom of thought and expression. This means that one should be able to express one's ideas and opinions without fear of persecution or censorship. By encouraging free thinking, Charvaka teachings can help individuals develop critical thinking skills and cultivate their own unique perspectives on life.

Don'ts

Neglect social responsibility. Charvaka teachings can promote a hedonistic and selfish worldview, as they promote the belief that only the material world exists and that pleasure is the ultimate goal in life, which can lead to a diminished sense of social responsibility and concern for others.

Disregard spiritual experiences. Charvaka teachings reject the existence of any supernatural entities or transcendent experiences, which can promote a shallow and superficial understanding of life, limiting an individual's perspective and preventing them from exploring deeper and more profound questions. This can lead to a sense of emptiness and lack of fulfilment, as material pleasures alone may not provide one with a sense of meaning and purpose in life.

Ignore consequences. Charvaka teachings reject the concept of *karma* and the idea that actions have consequences beyond this life. This can encourage individuals to act recklessly and without concern for the impact of their actions on others or on future generations, thereby promoting a lack of accountability and responsibility for one's actions.

Balancing material goals and spiritual values can be a challenge in today's fast-paced, materialistic world. Charvaka teachings may not provide guidance on spiritual matters, but other eastern teachings, such as Hinduism, Buddhism, and Jainism, do offer insights into how to balance material and spiritual goals. Balancing material and spiritual goals requires a holistic approach and a sense of detachment from material possessions and achievements. By incorporating teachings from both eastern and western philosophies, one can find a balance that works for them and allows for both material success and spiritual fulfilment.

Swetketu: Paragon of Spiritual Intelligence Mastery

According to the Chandogya Upanishad, Swetketu was a young and eager student who had completed his formal education and returned home to his father, Uddalaka, who was a wise and revered sage, expecting to be praised for his knowledge and spiritual growth. But Uddalaka noticed that his son had become arrogant and proud and had not truly understood the nature of *brahman*.

To teach Swetketu a lesson and help him gain true wisdom and spiritual intelligence, Uddalaka asked Swetketu if he had learnt that which enabled him to know the unknowable, meaning the spiritual reality that lies beyond our physical senses. He also asked him whether he knew that by knowing which one knew everything. He then referred to a deeper perception, which allowed one to know that which could not be perceived through the five senses but the perception of which created a sense of complete fulfilment. This perception is wisdom, the ability to understand and access the deeper aspects of reality beyond the material world. Swetketu replied that he had not, as he assumed that he already knew everything and there was nothing more to know.

Uddalaka went on to explain that, to gain spiritual wisdom, we must know the knower, or the true self, rather than just the known or external world. By knowing the knower, we come to know the essence of everything, as this true self is connected to the universal consciousness that underlies all of creation. This knowledge of the knower is essential to relating to the objective world because it allows us to see beyond the limitations of our sensory experience and connect to the deeper essence of all that exists. Without this understanding of the self, we are limited in our ability to perceive and relate to the world around us. Gaining spiritual intelligence requires a deeper understanding of the self and the ability to perceive the universal consciousness beyond our physical senses.

Uddalaka realised that Swetketu was still seeking a deeper understanding of the world and had not yet learnt about the ultimate reality, or *brahman*. He went on to teach Swetketu about the nature of *brahman*, using analogies about the essence of butter being present in milk and the essence of a tree being present in its seed, explaining that everything in the world is a manifestation of *brahman* and that all things are interconnected. Swetketu struggled to understand this concept and asked his father to explain it further.

His father then gave him a simple task. He asked him to take a lump of salt, dissolve it in water, and then drink the water. Swetketu did as he was told, finding the water very salty. His father then asked him to take a sip from different parts of the cup, and Swetketu found that the water was less salty in some parts and more salty in others. His father then explained that, just as the salt was present throughout the water but was more concentrated in some areas, *brahman* was present throughout the world but was more evident in some things than in others.

The following dialogue between Uddalaka (U) and Swetketu (S) carries immense significance and relevance, since it clarifies the essential nature of our existence:

U: Bring a banyan fruit.

S: Here it is, sir.

U: Cut it up.

S: I've cut it up, sir.

U: What do you see here?

S: These quite tiny seeds, sir.

U: Now, take one of them and cut it up.

S: I've cut it up, sir.

U: What do you see there?

S: Nothing, sir.

U: This finest essence here, son, that you can't even see—look how on account of that finest essence this huge banyan tree stands here. Believe, my son: the finest essence here—that constitutes the self of this whole world; that is the truth; that is the self. And that's how you are, Swetketu.

Uddalaka, having asked Swetketu to cut up the banyan fruit and then one of its seeds and having elicited the observation from the student that the seed appeared to be empty, explained that the essence of the banyan tree, which allows it to grow and stand tall, cannot be seen by the naked eye. He used this observation to illustrate the idea that the finest essence, which is the self of the world and the truth, cannot be perceived through our physical senses. This teaching is meant to convey the concept of the self (*atma*) as something that is beyond our physical body and cannot be easily understood or observed.

Uddalaka's teachings to Swetketu in the Chandogya Upanishad relate to the concept of unity and the true essence of things. Some of the simple metaphors contained in this parable can be explained as follows:

- **'Ornament' is only the name—the true essence is gold.** This teaching is a metaphorical expression that illustrates the concept of the true nature of things. It means that the name or form of an object is not its true essence. For instance, a piece of jewellery may be called a ring or a necklace, but its true essence is the gold or precious metal from which it is made. In the same way, the true essence of a person is not their name or form but their innermost self or soul.

- **A drop of water, when it merges with the ocean, becomes an ocean.** This teaching is also a metaphor that emphasises the concept of unity. It means that, just as a drop of water merges with the vast ocean and becomes one with it, the individual self can merge with the universal self or *brahman* and become one with it. It emphasises the idea that the individual self is not separate from the universal self but is a part of it. Similarly, by understanding *brahman*, the ultimate reality, you too realise that you are the essence of it.
- **Everything in the universe is unity.** It is we, through our finite perceptions, who assign *naam* (name), *roop* (form), and *vyavahar* (nature); the diversity of the universe is created by our finite perceptions, whereas the true nature of things is unity. For example, when we look at a table, we identify its form and nature as those associated with a table, but the essence of the table is wood. When the table is dismantled, what remains is wood. Similarly, the true essence of a person is not their external appearance or personality but their innermost self or soul.

The above teachings helped Swetketu understand the concept of *brahman* (ultimate reality) and the essence of true living more fully. He saw that everything in the world is interconnected. As a result, Swetketu developed spiritual intelligence—the capacity to understand and connect with the deeper dimensions of existence. He understood that there is a deeper truth beyond what can be perceived by the senses and that true fulfilment comes from connecting with that truth.

Swetketu's story teaches us that true wisdom and spiritual intelligence come not just from learning but also from humility and a willingness to learn from others. Only by recognising our own limitations can we open ourselves to the infinite possibilities of knowledge and understanding. The Upanishads highlight the importance of spiritual intelligence for understanding the nature of reality beyond what is perceptible to the senses. Swetketu's story teaches us about the importance of understanding spirituality and seeking knowledge even when we think we already know a lot. Having *vyavaharik* or transactional knowledge to deal with the outer world is not enough. We must invoke spiritual wisdom to empower our intelligence. This is true knowledge—*prajnanam brahma*.

In today's world, we are often consumed by the materialistic pursuits of wealth, power, and status. In such a context, the importance of spiritual intelligence cannot be understated. Swetketu's story serves as a reminder of the importance of spiritual intelligence as a quality. It highlights the role of challenges and adversity in personal growth. It is often through difficult experiences that we are able to see our own limitations and develop the resilience and strength necessary to overcome them. The story underscores the importance of seeking out wise teachers and mentors who can guide us on our spiritual journey. No matter how intelligent or capable we may be, we can always benefit from the wisdom and guidance of those who have gone before us.

The path to wisdom and enlightenment is not a straightforward one. It requires us to be open to new experiences, to be humble in the face of our limitations, and to reflect and meditate on our self-exploratory journey. By embracing these principles, we can develop our spiritual intelligence and grow in our understanding of ourselves and the world around us.

Rumi's Concept of Unity

Jalal-ad-Din Muhammad Rumi was a 13th-century Persian poet, Islamic scholar, and Sufi mystic. His philosophy provides a framework for enhancing spiritual intelligence. This philosophy is rooted in Sufism, which emphasises the inner, mystical dimensions of Islam.

Rumi's philosophy revolves around the concept of divine love and the idea that the ultimate goal of human existence is to attain union with the divine. According to Rumi, the path to this union is through spiritual practices such as prayer, meditation, and contemplation. One of Rumi's key teachings is the idea that the human soul is inherently divine and that the separation between the individual and the divine is only an illusion. In his poetry, he often used the metaphor of a drop of water merging with the ocean to describe the union of the individual soul with the divine. This is similar to the Chandogya Upanishad's metaphor of the ocean in Swetketu's story.

Another central theme in Rumi's philosophy is the idea of surrender to the divine will. He believed that true freedom is achieved when the individual surrenders their ego and desires to the divine, allowing themselves to be guided by the will of God. Rumi also believed in the power of love as a transformative force. His poetry is filled with expressions of love and devotion to God, and he believed that love has the power to heal and transform individuals and society as a whole. In addition to his spiritual teachings, Rumi was also a proponent of inclusivity and tolerance. He believed that all religions are different paths to the same ultimate truth and that people of different faiths should come together in mutual respect and understanding.

While Rumi's philosophy and Vedanta come from different religious traditions, they share many similarities—their emphasis on unity, spiritual practice, surrender, and the transformative power of love. Both offer a profound exploration of the human soul and its connection to the divine and continue to inspire and guide spiritual seekers around the world.

Rumi's teachings can have a significant impact on improving spiritual intelligence. By emphasising the importance of connecting with the divine, cultivating inner transformation, living in accordance with one's values and beliefs, and cultivating love and compassion, Rumi's teachings provide a roadmap for individuals seeking greater fulfilment, purpose, and spiritual growth.

Chapter 11

The Theory of Causation and the Law of *Karma*

The theory of causation is a philosophical concept that attempts to explain how events are related to each other in terms of cause and effect. It is a fundamental concept in many fields, including philosophy, science, and law, and is essential to our understanding of the world around us. The theory of causation is concerned with explaining why events happen. It seeks to identify the factors that lead to a particular event and to understand the relationships between those factors, thereby providing a framework for understanding the complex relationships between events in the world around us and helping us make sense of the way that our actions and decisions can impact the world around us.

The fundamental principle of causation in philosophy asserts that every natural change is the result of a cause. This cause-and-effect relationship describes how one event, process, or object contributes to the production of another event, process, or object. To put it in the proper perspective, the cause is responsible for a part of the effect, and the effect is partially dependent on the cause. In Indian philosophy, the question of whether the effect pre-exists in its material cause is used to classify theories of causation. However, Aristotelian thought presents four types of causes—material, formal, efficient, and final—to explain the 'why' behind changes or movements in nature. Causation is a vital concept in understanding how the world works, and recognising the cause-and-effect relationship can lead to a deeper understanding of various phenomena.

Karma forms the ethical foundation of many eastern philosophical and religious traditions. It represents the sum of all the deeds one has performed through their thoughts, speech, and actions. It is a spiritual principle that emphasises the idea of cause and effect, stating that every action has a corresponding consequence that cannot be escaped. The karmic cycle governs one's life perpetually, creating a constant stream of good or bad outcomes based on one's past deeds.

The law of *karma*, a fundamental principle in many eastern philosophies and religions, is not simply a matter of cause and effect. It is concerned with the moral dimension of actions and their impact on human well-being. Unlike the law of universal causation, which deals with temporal events, the law of *karma* manifests its effects in the distant future, whether in subsequent lives or later in the same life. *Karma* is a potent force that governs our lives, reminding us that we are responsible for our actions and their consequences and that we can shape our future by being mindful of our deeds in the present.

Karma is an inescapable force that cannot be avoided, evaded, or cheated. Every deed, good or bad, carries its own rewards or punishments. The consequences of our actions may manifest in this life or in future lives, but they cannot be escaped. However, the doctrine of *karma* should not be confused with fatalism. It does not suggest that events are predetermined by a supernatural power and that humans have no control over their fate. On the contrary, the doctrine of *karma* affirms the role of personal effort in one's growth and evolution. It assures us that our material and spiritual progress is in our own hands. We are the masters of our own destiny, and our actions shape our future.

Karma is not a doctrine of despair but a path of promise. While we are born with a certain *karma* that determines our ancestry, heredity, and circumstances, we possess the power to liberate ourselves from the past by performing righteous actions with the right mindset. Today's actions pave the way for tomorrow's *karma*. By abandoning our wicked ways and resolving to do good, we can overcome grief and embrace hope.

The Bhagavad Gita offers a scientific approach to spirituality and a way of life that allows us to transcend the natural order of cause and effect. This transcendence is achieved not by arbitrary interference with the laws of nature but by breaking the chains of *karma* through the cultivation of an attitude of detachment, righteous behaviour, and an unwavering faith in the divine. By devoting ourselves to this path, we discover our unchanging self. The law of cause and effect is unyielding, universal, and impartial. However, we can rise above its grasp by realising our true nature. When we recognise ourselves to be imperishable souls, we enter a realm of reality that transcends the burden of *karma*. We reach a state of being beyond sorrow and discover the boundless potential of our existence.

The consequences of our actions will eventually catch up with us: 'What goes around comes around.' In the context of *karma*, this means that the ethical and moral choices we make result in corresponding outcomes in the future. If we engage in positive, compassionate, and virtuous actions, we are likely to experience positive outcomes in the long run. Conversely, if we engage in harmful, dishonest, or unkind actions, we may experience negative consequences later on. *Karma* emphasises the interconnectedness of actions and their consequences. It suggests that the energy or intention behind our actions creates a ripple effect that returns to us in some form or another. Therefore, by practising good deeds and cultivating positive qualities, we increase the likelihood of experiencing positive outcomes and happiness in the future.

The principle of cause and effect is a fundamental aspect of the law of *karma*: 'Every action has an equal or opposite reaction.' From a karmic perspective, this means that the choices we make and the actions we perform generate energy or *karma* that will eventually influence our lives. Positive actions generate positive *karma*, which can lead to favourable circumstances, happiness, and personal growth. Conversely, negative actions create negative *karma*, which can result in unfavourable situations, suffering, and obstacles.

While the law of *karma* is undoubtedly a causal law, it is not identical to the law of universal causation. However, we can distinguish between two kinds of effects: *phala* (fruit) and *samskara* (imprint or memory). *Phala* refers to the immediate visible and invisible effects of an action, while *samskaras* are the invisible tendencies or dispositions that influence an individual's future actions, thoughts, experiences, and interpretations. *Samskaras* represent a unique modification of the individual's being. By understanding the distinction between *phala* and *samskara*, we can better grasp the complexities of the law of *karma* and its relationship with the law of universal causation. Although reconciliation between these laws may be challenging, this differentiation provides a framework for exploring the nuances of *karma* and its effects on individuals and society. Let's look at how accumulated *karma* affects us. The specific types of *karma* that are commonly associated with *phala* and *samskara* include:

- ***Agami/kriyamana karma***. *Agami* or *kriyamana karma* refers to the actions or deeds that an individual is currently performing in the present moment. It is the *karma* that is being created or generated in the current life. It is often referred to as 'current *karma*' or 'immediate *karma*.' This concept emphasises that every action performed by an individual, whether through thoughts, words, or deeds, contributes to their present circumstances and future outcomes. *Agami karma* includes the actions and intentions that will contribute to future *sanchita karma*. It highlights the idea that individuals are responsible for their present experiences and have the power to shape their future through their current actions. Since free will guides their current actions, they have the power to modify the accumulated *karma*. Thus, it is important to perform positive actions that will result in good *kriyaman karma* and a better future.

- ***Prarabdha karma***. *Prarabdha karma* represents the portion of accumulated *karma* that has ripened and is being experienced in the current lifetime. It is considered the destiny or fate individuals are born with and is responsible for determining certain aspects of their life, such as their physical and mental constitution, family, and societal circumstances. The *phala* of *prarabdha karma* plays a role in shaping the experiences and opportunities individuals encounter in their current life.
- ***Sanchita karma.*** *Sanchita karma* refers to the accumulated *karma* from all past actions across multiple lifetimes. While the entire *sanchita karma* may not have immediate consequences, it is believed to contribute to an individual's overall karmic balance and the cycle of *samsara*. The *phala* of *sanchita karma* is believed to influence future lives and determine the conditions and situations individuals will encounter in subsequent rebirths. *Agami karma* and *sanchita karma* are distinct in their nature and implications. *Sanchita karma* represents the accumulated karmic baggage from past lives, forming a vast database of actions and consequences. On the other hand, *agami karma* refers to the actions we take in the present, which have the potential to bear fruit in this lifetime or in future ones.

Some readers may believe and some may not in the above concepts, but in the context of spiritual intelligence, the concept of *karma* and its relationship to *phala* and *samskara* provides us with the general idea that actions have consequences that can shape our present, future, and afterlife experiences. The following is a comparison highlighting the key differences and similarities between the universal law of causation and the law of *karma*:

Aspect	Universal Law of Causation	Law of *Karma*
Fundamental principle	Every effect has a cause, and every cause produces an effect.	Actions have consequences, and individuals bear the consequences of their actions.
Scope	Applies to all phenomena in the universe.	Primarily associated with the moral and ethical actions of sentient beings.
Impersonal vs. personal	Impersonal in nature, operating without regard to individuals.	Personal in nature, focusing on the individual's intentions and actions.
Temporality	Emphasises a sequential cause-and-effect relationship.	Incorporates the concept of cause and effect but extends beyond a single lifetime.
Immediate vs. delayed	Immediate—cause and effect can be observed in the present.	Effects of actions may manifest in the present life or in future lifetimes.
Reversibility	Causal events can potentially be reversed or altered.	Actions and their consequences cannot be reversed but can be mitigated through subsequent actions.

Aspect	Universal Law of Causation	Law of *Karma*
Spiritual connotations	May or may not have explicit spiritual implications.	Rooted in spiritual and religious beliefs, often associated with concepts of rebirth and reincarnation.
Moral accountability	No inherent moral judgement; focuses on cause and effect.	Inherently linked to moral accountability and the moral quality of actions.
Liberation	No specific concept of liberation or freedom from causality.	Liberation from the cycle of *karma* is seen as a spiritual goal.

One can argue that the laws of universal causation and *karma* are consistent with each other, as both make clear distinctions between the causes and effects of an action. The law of universal causation deals with the visible and invisible results, or *phalas*, that an action produces in the world. In contrast, the law of *karma* focuses on the invisible tendencies or dispositions, or *samskaras*, that an action produces in the individual who performed it. These two laws are interrelated, as the law of *karma* can be seen as an application of the law of universal causation to moral causation. Every karmic act produces *samskaras* in the agent, which ultimately influence that agent's future actions, thoughts, and experiences. Therefore, understanding the connection between these two laws can help us comprehend the complex interplay between actions, their consequences, and their impact on individuals and society.

According to the law of *karma*, every action has consequences that manifest in the cycle of death and rebirth. Good intentions result in positive *karma*, while bad intentions lead to negative *karma*. The outcome of an action also affects its karmic implications. This concept differs from the principle of pure causality found in natural sciences, as intentions and desires play a significant role in shaping *karma*. For instance, a surgeon and a murderer may perform the same action—stabbing a person—but their intentions and approach are vastly different, leading to different karmic consequences. Therefore, *karma* is not just about the action itself but also about the intention, approach, and desire of the doer, making it a powerful ethical foundation.

The ancient wisdom of *karma* reminds us that we are the masters of our own destiny. 'As a man himself sows, so he himself reaps,' goes the saying. In the rich traditions of Hinduism, Buddhism, and Jainism, *karma* is seen as a fundamental law of cause and effect. Our actions and intentions shape the course of our lives, and we are responsible for the consequences. When we act with pure intent, without expecting any particular outcome, we leave our *karma* untouched. But when we act with an expectation in mind, we accumulate *karma* that can have positive or negative effects on our lives. Good *karma* brings happiness and positivity, while bad *karma* can lead to unhappiness and suffering. And *karma* is not limited to just one lifetime; it may also impact our future incarnations. By understanding and embracing the power of *karma*, we can create a bright and fulfilling present and future for ourselves and those around us.

The concept of *karma* forms the foundation for ethics in many eastern philosophical traditions, but it is not a simple punishment-and-reward system. Rather, it is a natural law that governs the consequences of our actions. No one grants rewards or punishments; it is simply the way things are. As per many eastern philosophies, *karma* continues to influence a being even after death, determining the circumstances and quality of their next incarnation. This cycle of death and rebirth persists indefinitely, with the only escape being through a conscious attainment of release, known as *moksha*. Therefore, in eastern traditions, the repetitive cycle of birth and death, or *samsara*, is rife with anguish and likened to an inescapable prison. Unless one rids themselves of their karmic load or *samskaras*, they will be caught in this cycle indefinitely. The only means of liberation is to cleanse our *samskaras*. Actions taken devoid of desire for and expectation of personal gain do not engender *samskaras*.

From Action to Outcome: Understanding *Parinamavada* and the Theory of *Karma*

Parinamavada is a philosophical concept that explains the nature of change and transformation in the world. According to *parinamavada*, everything in the universe undergoes a real and substantial transformation. It suggests that the effect or the result (*parinama*) is a distinct entity that arises from a cause or a substance.

Satkaryavada is a related school of thought that emphasises the existence of a relationship between a cause and its effect. It states that the effect is inherent in its cause even before its manifestation. In other words, the cause already contains the potential or the seed of the effect within it. When the conditions are appropriate, the effect unfolds or manifests itself.

Vivartavada, another school of thought, on the other hand, presents a different perspective. It suggests that the apparent change or transformation we observe in the world is not real but an illusion or appearance. According to the *vivartavada* school, the effect is not a real transformation of the cause but a mere manifestation of the underlying reality.

An analogy can be used to simplify these theories. Imagine a tree and its seed. The seed represents the cause, while the tree represents the effect. The theory of *parinamavada* would contend that the seed undergoes a real and substantial transformation, resulting in the tree. It suggests that the tree is a distinct entity that emerges from the seed. The *satkaryavada* school would highlight that the tree was already potentially present within the seed. The seed contains all the necessary information and potential to develop into a tree. When the seed is provided with suitable conditions, such as soil, water, and sunlight, it grows and manifests as a tree. The *vivartavada* school, however, would argue that the apparent transformation from seed to tree is illusory. It proposes that the seed does not truly change into a tree but rather appears as a tree. The tree is merely a manifestation or appearance of the underlying reality, which is the seed. Consider another example—of water turning into ice. From the point of view of the *vivartavada* school, it would be argued that the transformation of water into ice is illusory. Instead of water actually changing into ice, the underlying reality (water) is manifesting or appearing as ice. In this perspective, the ice is not a fundamentally different entity from water; it's a temporary manifestation or appearance of the water's inherent nature.

According to *parinamavada*, the universe is not created out of nothing but emerges from *brahman* through a process of transformation. This process of transformation is believed to be driven by the power of *maya*, which is the cosmic illusion that gives rise to the perception of multiplicity and diversity in the world. *Maya* is seen as a veil that obscures the true nature of *brahman*, and it is only through the realisation of the unity of *brahman* that one can attain liberation from the cycle of birth and death.

Parinamavada is highly relevant to the theory of *karma*. In fact, the concept of *karma* is central to *parinamavada*, as it explains the workings of *karma* in the context of the constant transformation or evolution of the universe. Every action generates a particular energy or vibration, which becomes a cause for further effects, leading to a chain of causation that unfolds over time. In this way, every act influences the overall direction and evolution of the universe and contributes to the ultimate perfection towards which the universe is moving.

The consequences of our actions are already contained within the actions themselves. In other words, the results of our actions are not separate from the actions themselves but are simply the natural outcome or manifestation of the actions we have taken. It is important to note, however, that the manifestation of *karma* is not necessarily immediate or predictable. The complex interplay of various factors, such as our intentions, the context in which the actions are performed, and the actions of others can all influence the manifestation of our *karma*. Therefore, the doctrine of *karma* emphasises the importance of personal responsibility for our actions and encourages us to act in ways that are conducive to our own well-being and the well-being of others in order to create positive consequences for ourselves and for the world around us.

Foreseeing the exact effects of our actions is not always possible, as the complex interplay of various factors can influence the manifestation of *karma*. However, there are some general principles and guidelines that can help us act in ways that are likely to create positive consequences and avoid negative ones.

In Hindu philosophy, *karma* is broadly categorised into four types based on various factors such as intention, context, and timing. These categories are:

1. ***Nitya karma.*** *Nitya* means 'daily' or 'regular.' *Nitya karma* refers to the obligatory daily rituals and duties prescribed to individuals based on their caste, gender, and stage of life (*varna* and *ashrama*). It includes actions that are considered a part of one's regular duties and are to be performed without fail. *Nitya karma* is based on the concept of maintaining a disciplined and spiritually oriented lifestyle. It emphasises the importance of regularity, discipline, and the integration of spiritual practices into one's daily life. These actions are believed to help individuals to simultaneously cultivate spiritual awareness, purify the mind, and maintain a

harmonious relationship with the divine and the cosmos. It is important to note that *nitya karma* rituals may vary across different regions and sects. These include practices like daily prayers, recitation of mantras, ablutions, offerings to deities, and so on. *Nitya karma* is considered essential to the maintenance of personal and social order.

2. ***Naimittika karma.*** *Naimittika karma* refers to special duties and rituals that are performed on specific occasions or at specific events. These could include rituals performed during festivals, important milestones in life (such as birth, marriage, or death), or specific celestial events.
3. ***Kamya karma.*** *Kamya karma* refers to actions performed with specific desires or intentions, usually driven by personal desires, ambitions, or wishes for specific outcomes. These actions are undertaken to fulfil personal goals or aspirations and are not obligatory. The scriptures suggest that performing *kamya karma* can generate results corresponding to the intention behind the action. However, they also emphasise the importance of performing such actions within the bounds of righteousness (*dharma*) and without causing harm to others.
4. ***Nishkama karma.*** *Nishkama karma* refers to selfless or desireless action. It is the performance of actions without attachment to the results or outcomes. The scriptures emphasise the idea of offering one's actions and their results to a higher power, such as God or the divine. By practising *nishkama karma*, individuals aim to overcome selfish desires, cultivate detachment, find inner peace, experience spiritual growth, make positive contributions to the world, and attain spiritual growth and liberation (*moksha*).

The terms *karma*, *akarma*, *vikarma*, and *sukarma*, which refer to different concepts, can be understood in conjunction with the above categorisation of *karma*. They are also considered categories of *karma* that may fructify either in the present or in a future life.

- ***Karma.*** *Karma* refers to actions, deeds, or activities performed by individuals. It encompasses both physical actions and the intentions behind those actions. According to the law of *karma*, every action has consequences and these consequences can affect individuals in the present life or in future lives. Good actions are believed to generate positive *karma*, while negative actions generate negative *karma*.
- ***Akarma.*** *Akarma* literally means 'non-action' or 'inaction.' It refers to a state of motionlessness or the absence of any intentional action. In the spiritual context, *akarma* can be understood as performing actions without attachment to their outcomes or a sense of personal doership. It emphasises a state of detached action in which one acts selflessly, without seeking personal gain. *Akarma* is often associated with the concept of *nishkama karma*, selfless action performed without attachment to results.
- ***Vikarma.*** *Vikarma* is the work done by the five vices: *kama* (lust), *krodh* (anger), *lobh* (greed), *moh* (attachment), and *ahankara* (ego-based thoughts, speech, actions, visions, and emotions). Thus, *vikarma* refers to actions that are considered negative, harmful, or morally wrong. It implies engaging in activities that go against ethical principles, spiritual teachings, or societal norms. *Vikarma* is seen as generating negative consequences and can lead to a buildup of negative *karma*. Engaging in *vikarma* is generally discouraged in Hindu philosophy.
- ***Sukarma.*** *Sukarma* is the opposite of *vikarma* and refers to actions that are considered virtuous, righteous, or beneficial. *Sukarma* is good for the doer and for others, too.

Any godly-knowledge-based, unselfish thoughts, speech, acts, and emotions are considered *sukarma*. *Sukarma* implies engaging in activities that align with moral, ethical, and spiritual principles. It generates positive consequences and contributes to the accumulation of positive *karma*.

The understanding and application of these concepts can vary across different traditions and philosophical schools. The overarching idea is that individuals are responsible for their actions and the quality of those actions can shape their present and future experiences.

These concepts are expounded in various Hindu scriptures and philosophical texts, including the Bhagavad Gita, Upanishads, and other ancient scriptures. Each category of *karma* has its significance and plays a crucial role in shaping an individual's life and spiritual journey.

Both sets of concepts—*nitya*, *naimittika*, *kamya*, and *nishkama karma* and *karma*, *akarma*, *vikarma*, and *sukarma*—come from the same philosophy of Hinduism. They are rooted in the broader concept of *karma*, which is a fundamental principle in Hindu philosophy.

While *nitya*, *naimittika*, *kamya*, and *nishkama karma* mainly focus on the types of actions one performs based on their intent and timing, *karma*, *akarma*, *vikarma*, and *sukarma* delve into the nature and consequences of actions, highlighting the importance of righteous actions and the potential for liberation from the cycle of cause and effect.

Both sets of concepts originate from the same philosophical framework of *karma*, and they provide individuals with comprehensive guidelines for leading a purposeful and spiritually aligned life.

The scriptures provide guidelines and teachings on these various categories of actions, highlighting the importance of performing duties and rituals with the right intentions, in accordance with *dharma*, and with an understanding of the transient nature of the material world. The following are few additional tips that one can keep in mind:

- **Cultivate good intentions.** The intentions behind our actions are an important factor in determining the nature of the *karma* we generate. Therefore, it is important to cultivate good intentions through the cultivation of qualities like kindness, compassion, and generosity, so as to create positive *karma*.
- **Be mindful of the consequences.** While we cannot always predict the exact effects of our actions, we can be mindful of the potential consequences and try to act in ways that are likely to create positive outcomes.
- **Follow ethical guidelines.** There are many ethical guidelines and principles in various spiritual and religious traditions that can help us act in ways that are conducive to positive *karma*. For example, the Buddhist Eightfold Path and the Hindu concept of *dharma* provide guidance on how to live a virtuous and ethical life.
- **Reflect on past actions.** Reflecting on our past actions and their consequences can help us learn from our mistakes and make wiser choices in the future. Experience is the best teacher.
- **Seek the guidance of wise and compassionate teachers.** Seeking the guidance of wise and compassionate teachers can provide us with insights on how to act in ways that are conducive to building positive *karma*.

The Vedic theory of *parinamavada* provides a framework for understanding the relationship between the law of *karma* and the transformation and change that occurs in the material world. It emphasises the importance of taking positive actions and cultivating detachment in order to achieve positive karmic consequences and spiritual growth. The principle that every effect has a cause and that cause is inherent in the effect itself and requires a trigger to produce the effect is applicable to our mental and emotional well-being, as we often encounter people and situations that trigger negative emotions and thought patterns, which in turn can lead to mental and emotional imbalance. While external factors may trigger our responses, it is ultimately our response that produces the effect. Our responses are often based on subconscious patterns and past experiences, which can limit our ability to respond in a way that is empowering and conducive to growth.

However, by turning our attention inward and becoming more aware of these patterns, we can begin to consciously modify or delete them. This requires a willingness to examine our own thoughts and emotions and a commitment to practising new patterns of response that align with our values and goals. By doing so, we can take greater control of our internal environment and reduce the impact of external factors on our mental and emotional well-being. This is a lifelong journey that requires patience and practice, but the rewards are immeasurable. Through mindfulness and self-awareness, we can create a more structured and fulfilling life, even amidst complex and ever-changing external environments.

Leading a structured life is especially challenging when you have no control over the external environment. This environment is a very complex phenomenon, mainly consisting of people and situations that affect us. The mental and emotional imbalance that occurs within us is an effect of the external environment, which is the cause. This effect is triggered by our response to the cause. Our response is, therefore, the agent that produces the effect. Most of our responses come from the subconscious mind, where our previous experiences are stored as memories that emerge as repeated patterns. Once we develop the ability to mindfully pay attention to these patterns, we start understanding those that are not empowering us. We can then consciously modify and delete these patterns. This is a process and only through practice can we gradually master the art of producing blissful effects. Turning the mind inward is the key to it.

Purusharth: The Guiding Principle for a Life of Fulfilment

Purusharth is a Sanskrit term that refers to the four aims or goals of human life, according to Hindu philosophy. These four aims are *dharma* (righteousness or duty), *artha* (wealth or prosperity), *kama* (pleasure or desire), and *moksha* (liberation or spiritual freedom). Each of these aims is seen as important in its own way, and together they form the foundation of a complete and balanced life. In the context of spiritual intelligence, the concept of *purusharth* is important because it emphasises the need for a holistic approach to life that takes into account not just our material and physical needs but also our spiritual and emotional needs.

1. ***Dharma.*** *Dharma*, the first aim, is seen as the foundation of human life and refers to the principles of righteousness and duty that guide our actions and behaviour. In the context of spiritual intelligence, *dharma* is important because it provides a moral compass that helps us align our actions with our values and principles.
2. ***Artha.*** *Artha*, the second aim, refers to the pursuit of wealth, prosperity, and material success. While this aim is often seen as superficial or materialistic, it is important in the context of spiritual intelligence because it is founded on the recognition of the importance of material resources in fulfilling our basic needs and supporting our spiritual growth. *Artha* also means simultaneously seeking the meaning and purpose of life.
3. ***Kama.*** *Kama*, the third aim, refers to the pursuit of pleasure and desire, and encompasses love, beauty, and sensual

enjoyment. While this aim is often seen as hedonistic or indulgent, it is important in the context of spiritual intelligence because it is founded on the recognition of the importance of emotional well-being and the human need for joy, beauty, and connection. Pursuing desires while being mindful of *dharma* or ethical principles is encouraged within the *purushartha* framework.

4. ***Moksha.*** *Moksha*, the fourth and ultimate aim, refers to the pursuit of spiritual liberation and freedom from the cycle of birth and death. This aim is seen as the ultimate goal of human life and the highest achievement that a person can attain. In the context of spiritual intelligence, *moksha* is important because it is founded on the recognition of the importance of spiritual growth and the need to transcend the limitations of the ego and connect with the larger spiritual reality that underlies all of existence.

Together, these four aims provide a framework for a balanced and meaningful life that takes into account not just our material and physical needs but also our spiritual and emotional needs. By pursuing all four aims in a balanced and integrated way, we can develop greater self-awareness, empathy, compassion, and wisdom, and awaken to the deeper spiritual truths of existence.

The four ashrams of Vedic science are closely related to the concept of *purushartha*. Each ashram is associated with a specific *purushartha*:

1. ***Brahmacharya* ashram.** This stage is associated with the pursuit of *dharma* or righteousness. The emphasis in this stage is on acquiring knowledge, practising self-discipline, and developing character, all of which are necessary to live a righteous life.
2. ***Grihastha* ashram.** This stage is associated with the pursuit of *artha* or wealth. This stage is associated with the

pursuit of *kama* or pleasure. The emphasis is on fulfilling one's responsibilities towards family and society, earning a livelihood, and accumulating wealth to support oneself and one's family.

3. ***Vanaprastha* ashram.** The emphasis in this stage is on enjoying the fruits of one's labour, spending time in contemplation and reflection, and seeking inner peace and happiness. During this stage, individuals gradually withdraw from worldly responsibilities and start focusing on spiritual pursuits.
4. ***Sannyasa* ashram**. This stage is associated with the pursuit of moksha or liberation. In this final stage, individuals renounce all worldly attachments and dedicate themselves fully to spiritual pursuits, with the ultimate goal of attaining self-realisation and liberation from the cycle of birth and death.

The four *purusharth* systems and the four ashrams are interconnected and complementary. Each stage of life is a necessary step towards achieving the ultimate goal of liberation, and each *purushartha* is an important aspect of a well-rounded and fulfilling life. In today's fast-paced world, the ashram system may seem outdated, but it is no less important than it used to be. The system provides a framework for individuals to live in a fulfilling and purposeful manner at every stage of their life. It encourages individuals to prioritise their goals, responsibilities, and duties at each stage. For example, during the *brahmacharya* stage, one should focus on learning and acquiring knowledge. During the *grihastha* stage, one should take up responsibilities and duties towards family and society. In the *vanaprastha* stage, one should start to detach from worldly possessions and begin to focus on spirituality, while in the *sannyasa* stage, one should completely renounce worldly life and pursue enlightenment.

Following these stages not only helps give one a sense of direction and purpose in life, but also helps in the development of discipline, self-restraint, and fulfilment. It is essential to be mindful of the ashrams and their teachings in modern times. While the specific duties and responsibilities may differ today, the underlying principles and values remain the same.

Performing *Karma* as per *Dharma*

The scriptures tell us that we should perform *karma* as per *dharma*, which simply means that we should perform righteous actions. But what actions fit into the framework of *dharma*? The doctrine of aligning *karma* with *dharma* appears very simple on the surface, but calibrating one's actions with this doctrine is easier said than done.

Only when we nurture and build our character with virtues like compassion, non-attachment, forgiveness, acceptance, humility, kindness, etc., is *karma* in line with *dharma* possible. These virtues form the foundation of spiritual intelligence. When we embody these virtues, we naturally tend to perform actions that produce good *karma*, and the consequences of our actions are more likely to be positive. As we have seen in earlier chapters, actions categorised under *sattvic guna* can be regarded as *karma* in accordance with *dharma*.

Karma Yoga: A Guide to Life's Actions in the Bhagavad Gita

Karma yoga is one of the paths of spiritual practice described in the Bhagavad Gita. It is the path of selfless action or service, emphasising the performance of one's duties without attachment to the results. The term *karma* refers, as we know, to action, and *yoga* means union or connection with the divine. In the Bhagavad Gita, Krishna provides guidance for individuals living in the materialistic world, offering insights on how they can perform *karma* while maintaining a spiritual perspective. The following are some key aspects of *karma* yoga:

- **Selfless action.** *Karma* yoga encourages individuals to perform their actions without seeking personal gain, recognition, or attachment to the outcomes. The focus is on offering one's actions as a service to a higher power or the welfare of others. Selflessness and a sense of duty are central to *karma* yoga.
- **Detachment from results.** Practitioners of *karma* yoga learn to detach themselves from the fruits or consequences of their actions. They understand that outcomes are beyond their control and can be influenced by various factors. By relinquishing their attachment to results, individuals can maintain equanimity, reduce anxiety, and perform their actions with a calm and focused mind.
- **Dedication to the divine.** *Karma* yoga involves dedicating one's actions to a higher power or the divine. Practitioners view themselves as instruments of the divine will and offer their actions as a form of worship or devotion. This perspective helps cultivate a sense of surrender, humility, and gratitude.
- **Awareness and mindfulness.** *Karma* yoga emphasises the cultivation of awareness and mindfulness in every action. Practitioners strive to be fully present in the moment, consciously engaging in their duties and responsibilities. By being mindful, individuals can perform their actions more skilfully, with greater efficiency, and without getting carried away by distractions or negative emotions.
- **Balance and moderation.** The Bhagavad Gita promotes a balanced approach to action. It advises individuals to avoid extremes and adopt a middle path, known as the path of moderation. This path involves avoiding excessive

indulgence or negligence in one's actions and maintaining a balanced and harmonious lifestyle.

- **Unity of action and knowledge.** The Bhagavad Gita emphasises the integration of action and knowledge. It states that one should perform actions with a deep understanding of their true nature and their connection to the higher reality. Through knowledge, individuals can act with clarity, wisdom, and a sense of purpose.
- **Integration of action and spirituality.** *Karma* yoga emphasises the integration of spiritual principles into everyday actions. It encourages individuals to lead a righteous and ethical life, upholding values such as honesty, compassion, and non-violence. By aligning their actions with spiritual values, practitioners aim to purify their mind, transcend ego-driven motives, and cultivate a sense of unity with all beings.
- **Liberation through action**. *Karma* yoga teaches that, through selfless action performed with the right attitude and understanding, one can attain spiritual growth and liberation (*moksha*). By dedicating their actions to the divine and renouncing personal desires and attachments, practitioners gradually purify their consciousness and transcend the cycle of birth and death.

Karma yoga is considered suitable for individuals who are actively engaged in worldly responsibilities and professions. It offers a practical and accessible path to spiritual growth, emphasising the transformation of ordinary actions into acts of devotion and selflessness. By practising *karma* yoga, individuals can find fulfilment, inner peace, and a deeper connection with the divine in their daily lives.

Another essential teaching of the Bhagavad Gita is the concept of *bhakti* yoga, which is the path of devotion to the divine. This means cultivating a deep love and reverence for the divine and surrendering the ego and will to the higher power. By developing a sense of devotion and surrender, we can transcend our limited self and connect with our higher wisdom.

Living Mindfully with *Karma*: Buddhist Wisdom on Cause and Consequence

In Buddhism, *karma* is a fundamental concept that plays a crucial role in understanding the nature of existence and the path to liberation. The following are some key Buddhist teachings that are related to *karma*:

- **Intentional action.** Buddhism emphasises that *karma* is primarily concerned with intentional actions, both physical and mental. It recognises that our thoughts, speech, and deeds have an impact on our lives and the lives of others. Positive, wholesome actions lead to positive outcomes, while negative, unwholesome actions result in suffering.
- **Law of cause and effect.** Buddhism teaches that every action we undertake, whether big or small, creates an imprint on our consciousness. This imprint influences our future experiences, shaping the quality of our life. Actions rooted in greed, hatred, and ignorance generate negative *karma*, leading to suffering, while actions rooted in generosity, compassion, and wisdom create positive *karma*, leading to happiness and well-being.
- **Ethical conduct.** Buddhism places a strong emphasis on ethical conduct as a means of generating positive *karma*. The Five Precepts (for laypeople) and the *vinaya* (for monastics) provide guidelines for ethical behaviour, exhorting individuals to refrain from killing, stealing, sexual misconduct, false speech, and intoxication, among other things. By adhering to ethical principles, individuals can cultivate wholesome intentions and avoid actions that create negative *karma*.

- **Rebirth and continuity.** *Karma* is intimately connected to belief in rebirth or reincarnation. According to Buddhism, the cycle of birth and death (*samsara*) is perpetuated by the flow of *karma*. Our actions in this life shape our future existence, determining the circumstances and conditions of our next rebirth. The cycle continues until one attains enlightenment and breaks free from the cycle.
- **Purification and transformation.** Buddhism recognises that *karma* is not fixed or predetermined. Through mindful awareness and intentional effort, individuals can purify their *karma* and transform their lives. The practice of meditation, cultivation of virtuous qualities, and development of wisdom are essential in this process. By understanding the nature of *karma*, individuals can make choices that lead to liberation and the cessation of suffering.
- **Interconnectedness.** Buddhism teaches that all beings are interconnected and interdependent. Our actions not only affect us but also others and the world around us. Understanding this interconnectedness inspires individuals to cultivate compassion, empathy, and a sense of responsibility.

Buddhism's emphasis is on understanding the workings of *karma* and using this understanding to make choices that lead to spiritual growth and liberation from suffering. The Five Precepts that serve as ethical guidelines for laypeople are as follows:

1. **I undertake the precept to refrain from killing living beings.** This precept encourages non-violence and respect for all forms of life.
2. **I undertake the precept to refrain from taking what is not freely given.** This precept promotes honesty and discourages stealing or taking what is not offered.

3. **I undertake the precept to refrain from sexual misconduct.** This precept emphasises the importance of responsible and respectful sexual behaviour, avoiding actions that cause harm or suffering to oneself or others.
4. **I undertake the precept to refrain from false speech.** This precept encourages truthfulness and discourages lying, gossiping, or any form of harmful speech.
5. **I undertake the precept to refrain from intoxicating substances that cause heedlessness.** This precept promotes mindfulness and clarity of mind, advising against the consumption of alcohol or any other intoxicants that may impair judgement and lead to harmful actions.

Similarly, the *vinaya* is a set of rules and regulations established by the Buddha for the Buddhist monastic community. It provides guidelines for monastic behaviour, discipline, and relationships within the *sangha* (monastic community). The *vinaya* covers various aspects of monastic life, including rules on conduct, proper attire, the use of requisites, relationships between monastics, and procedures for resolving disputes or transgressions. The *vinaya* helps maintain harmony, order, and ethical conduct within the monastic community.

It's important to note that the core principles of ethical conduct and discipline remain consistent across traditions.

Understanding Jainism: *Karma* as the Governing Principle

In Jainism, *karma* is a fundamental concept that plays a significant role in shaping an individual's life and spiritual progress. According to Jainism, *karma* refers to the subtle matter that is attracted to the soul as a result of one's thoughts, speech, and actions. Every intentional action, whether mental, verbal, or physical, generates *karma*. Jainism emphasises that *karma* is not merely an external force but an actual substance that binds itself to the soul, affecting its future experiences and circumstances.

Jainism upholds the law of cause and effect, asserting that every action produces a corresponding consequence. The *karma* one accumulates in the present life will bear fruit in the future, either in the current lifetime or in subsequent ones. Jainism believes in the cycle of birth and death and that the soul is continuously reborn in different life forms based on its *karma*. Ethical conduct is emphasised as a means of mitigating the accumulation of negative *karma* and promoting spiritual growth. Jains strive to follow the principles of non-violence (*ahimsa*), truthfulness (*satya*), non-stealing (*asteya*), chastity (*brahmacharya*), and non-attachment (*aparigraha*). By practising these virtues and cultivating a compassionate attitude towards all living beings, Jains seek to minimise the generation of harmful *karma*.

Jainism also teaches that the accumulated *karma* can be purified through spiritual practices, such as meditation, self-discipline, fasting, and renunciation. By cultivating self-awareness, detachment, and a deep understanding of the nature of *karma*, individuals can minimise the effects of past *karma* and prevent the accumulation of new *karma*. However, the effects of *karma* are believed to be inevitable and inescapable until they are exhausted. The accumulation of virtuous or non-virtuous *karma* determines the conditions and species of the soul's subsequent births. The ultimate goal is to liberate the soul from this cycle through spiritual purification and the eradication of all *karma*.

Jainism categorises *karma* into various types based on its nature and impact. The two primary classifications are:

1. ***Dravya karma*.** This type of *karma* relates to the physical and material aspects of existence, including the body, senses, and the physical environment. It affects the physical well-being, appearance, and life circumstances of an individual.
2. ***Bhava karma*.** *Bhava karma* pertains to the mental and emotional aspects of existence, influencing an individual's

thoughts, emotions, attitudes, and mental states. It affects the psychological well-being, mental capacities, and overall disposition of a person.

Both types of *karma* can be further divided into subcategories based on their intensity, duration, and specific effects.

By understanding and adhering to the principles of *karma*, Jains seek to live a life of moral responsibility, spiritual progress, and compassionate engagement with the world, ultimately aiming for liberation from the cycle of birth and death. The law of causation in Jainism also emphasises the interconnectedness of all living beings and the impact of our actions on others. Jainism teaches that every action has an impact not only on the individual performing the action but also on the wider community and environment. This understanding fosters a sense of compassion and empathy towards others, encouraging individuals to act with kindness and consideration towards all living beings. By understanding the impact of their actions on others and the environment, individuals can cultivate virtues such as compassion and empathy towards all living beings, leading to a more harmonious and peaceful world.

The teachings of the Bhagavad Gita, Buddhism, and Jainism offer profound insights into the development of spiritual intelligence. Everyone is encouraged to pursue *artha* and *kama* vigorously without crossing the boundaries of *dharma* (righteousness). In this context, Vedanta urges everyone to fully indulge in the world and enjoy all the worldly pleasures without violating any ethics or morality. Swami Vivekananda concurred: 'Fulfil your desire for power and everything else, and after you have fulfilled the desire, will come the time when you will know that they are all very little things; but until you have fulfilled this desire, until you have passed through that activity, it is impossible for you to come to the state of calmness, serenity, and self-surrender.'

Interestingly, Socrates expressed a similar sentiment when he famously said, 'The unexamined life is not worth living.' He urged individuals to immerse themselves in the world so they could gain a deep comprehension of it and realise the temporary nature of worldly pleasures. Socrates himself, while walking through the marketplace, would remark on the many things he had no need for, demonstrating his wisdom and dispassion.

Purusharth highlights the importance of living a fully engaged life while remaining aware of ethical and moral boundaries. By experiencing and engaging with the world, individuals can gain a deeper understanding of themselves and their place in the world, leading to greater wisdom and dispassion. This can lead to a more fulfilling and meaningful life.

Understanding the Correlation Between *Samsara* and *Samskara*

The idea of *samskaras*, or imprints on the mind, has been extensively explored in previous chapters. However, it is worth noting that the concept of *samskaras* is relevant to the theory of *karma* too, as these imprints can influence an individual not only in their current lifetime but also in future rebirths. In the context of reincarnation and multiple births, *samskaras* refer to the impressions or tendencies that are carried over from one lifetime to another. These tendencies can be positive or negative and can influence our actions and experiences in the current life or in subsequent lives.

On the other hand, *samsara* is a Sanskrit word that refers to the cycle of birth, death, and rebirth in Hinduism, Buddhism, and Jainism. The concept of *samsara* is central to these religions and it represents the idea that our existence is perpetually trapped in a cycle of suffering and reincarnation. According to the belief, *samsara* is an eternal cycle that begins with birth and ends only with enlightenment or liberation. In this cycle, a being is born, lives a life, and dies. After death, the soul or consciousness of the being is reborn in another body, based on its *karma*. *Karma* is the accumulated result of a person's thoughts, words, and deeds, which determines their next life. It represents the idea that our existence is perpetually trapped in a cycle of suffering and reincarnation, which can only be broken through enlightenment.

Hinduism, Buddhism, and Jainism believe that *samskaras* are the root causes of suffering and bondage, as they bind us to the cycle of birth and death. Through the practice of yoga, and particularly through the cultivation of mindfulness and self-awareness, we can become aware of our *samskaras* and gradually reduce their hold on our minds. The focus is on breaking the cycle of *samsara* by eliminating the root cause of suffering, which is ignorance. The accumulated *samskaras* that are carried over from one life to another are seen as a manifestation of this ignorance and are therefore to be transcended.

The new life may be better or worse than the previous one, depending on the accumulated *karma*. If a person has accumulated good *karma*, they may be reborn in a higher realm, such as heaven or paradise, but if they have accumulated bad *karma*, they may be reborn in a lower realm, such as hell or as a lower animal form. However, the cycle of *samsara* is considered to be an endless cycle of suffering, as every rebirth is accompanied by pain and suffering, whether physical or emotional. Therefore, the ultimate goal in all of these religions is to escape this cycle of suffering and achieve enlightenment or liberation, which is known as *moksha* in Hinduism, *nirvana* in Buddhism, and *kevala jnana* in Jainism.

Samskara and *samsara* are intimately linked, as the former influences the *karma* and rebirth of an individual in the latter. By purifying the mind of negative *samskaras*, one can break free from the cycle of *samsara* and achieve spiritual liberation. This is regarded by all three religions as the ultimate goal, accomplished through various spiritual practices and the cultivation of virtuous qualities such as compassion, wisdom, and selflessness.

According to Patanjali, the goal of yoga is to calm the fluctuations of the mind, and *vasanas* are seen as the primary obstacles to achieving this state of stillness. When we are caught up in our *vasanas* (tendencies), we tend to react automatically to situations based on our past conditioning instead of responding in a conscious and deliberate manner. The effects of *samskaras* on our thinking pattern can be observed in the way we perceive and react to the world around us. For example, a person with a positive *samskara* for compassion may naturally feel empathy towards others and be inclined to help those in need. On the other hand, a person with a negative *samskara* for anger may be quick to react with hostility and aggression in certain situations.

It's important to note that positive and negative imprints are not always black and white; there can be a range of grey areas. Some actions may have both positive and negative consequences, depending on the context and intention behind them. Therefore, one must practise mindfulness, be aware of one's actions and their potential consequences, and strive towards creating positive imprints in one's life.

The development and transformation of *samskaras* is a lifelong process and can be influenced by various factors, such as upbringing, environment, and spiritual practice. By cultivating positive *samskaras* through mindful living and spiritual practices such as meditation, yoga, and service to others, we can gradually transform our thinking patterns and achieve a more peaceful and fulfilling life.

Our perception of the external world is a complex process that involves the input of information through our five senses: sight, sound, touch, taste, and smell. However, the information we receive is not always processed accurately. Our past experiences, beliefs, and values shape our perception and interpretation of the information we receive. This is where the concepts of generalisation, distortion, and deletion come into play.

- **Generalisation** refers to the process of categorising incoming information into broad categories based on our past experiences. For example, if someone has had a negative experience with dogs in the past, they may generalise that all dogs are dangerous and hostile, even if this is not the case. This can lead to a biased perception of the world and inaccurate conclusions.
- **Distortion** refers to the process of altering incoming information to fit our existing beliefs and values. This can involve emphasising certain aspects of information that support our existing beliefs while minimising or ignoring aspects that do not. This can result in a skewed perception of reality and an inaccurate understanding of the world around us.
- **Deletion** refers to the process of selectively ignoring or filtering incoming information that does not fit our existing beliefs and values. This can involve ignoring information that challenges our beliefs or dismissing information that we do not understand or do not consider important. This can lead to a limited and incomplete understanding of the world around us.

The information we perceive and store as imprints is not necessarily accurate but is filtered and processed through our individual model of the world, which is shaped by our unique experiences, beliefs, and values. This can lead to a subjective understanding of reality that may not be completely accurate. Understanding these processes of generalisation, distortion, and deletion can help us become more aware of our own biases and limitations in our perception of the world and strive towards a more objective understanding of reality.

It is important in the light of the above to understand the cycle of *samskara*, which refers to the process by which impressions, imprints, or subtle tendencies are formed in the mind as a result of past experiences, actions, and thoughts. This cycle is continuous and ongoing, and it influences our behaviour, thinking patterns, and ultimately our spiritual growth. The cycle of *samskara* consists of the following steps:

1. **Perception.** The first step in the cycle of *samskara* is perception. We perceive the world around us through our senses and interpret it based on our past experiences, beliefs, and conditioning. This interpretation creates an impression or imprint in our mind.
2. **Action.** The next step in the cycle is action. Based on our perception, we take actions that reinforce or modify the impression in our mind. For example, if we perceive a situation as threatening, we may react with fear or anxiety, which reinforces the threat perception in our mind.
3. **Reinforcement.** The third step in the cycle is reinforcement. Every time we take an action based on a particular impression, we reinforce that impression in our mind. This can lead to the formation of habitual patterns of thinking and behaviour.
4. **Incorporation into the subconscious.** The fourth step in the cycle involves the impressions being reinforced through repeated actions and thoughts and becoming part of our subconscious mind, which influences our behaviour and thinking patterns at a subconscious level. For example, the impression that snakes are a threat becomes part of our subconscious mind, leading to automatic fear or anxiety in the presence of snakes.
5. **Expression.** The final step in the cycle is expression. The impressions that are stored in our subconscious mind eventually manifest as our behaviour, thinking patterns, and attitudes towards life. This can affect our relationships, career, health, and overall well-being.

This cycle of *samskara* is a continuous process, and the impressions that we create in our mind can influence us in both positive and negative ways. Every time we perform a *kriya* (action) based on a particular *samskara*, we reinforce that *samskara* (imprint) in our mind. Repeatedly reacting with fear or anxiety to snakes, or avoiding them altogether, reinforces the *samskara* that they are a threat. By cultivating positive impressions through spiritual practices and mindful living, we can gradually transform our thinking patterns and behaviour and achieve spiritual growth and liberation. The following chart simplifies the cycle of *samskara*:

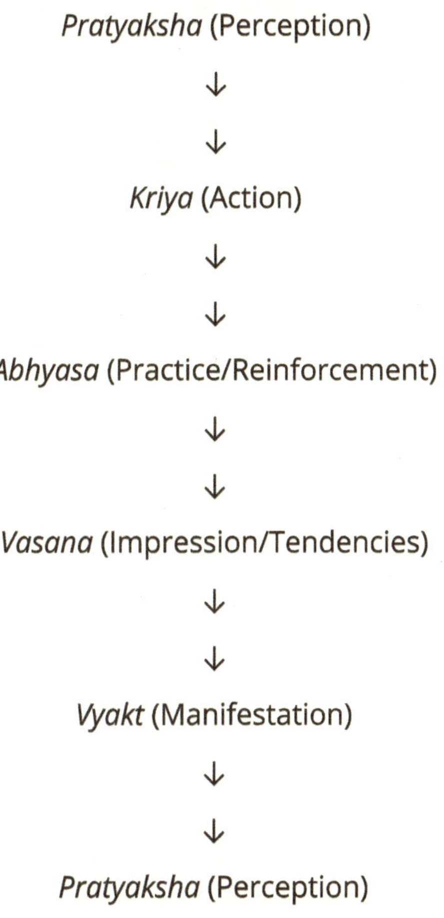

The cycle of *samskara* starts with *pratyaksha*, which refers to perception or the way we see and interpret the world around us based on our past experiences and conditioning. From *pratyaksha*, we move to *kriya*, which refers to action or the way we respond to our perceptions based on our *samskaras* or subtle tendencies. As we continue to take actions based on our *samskaras*, they become reinforced through *abhyasa*, which refers to repetition or the way our actions strengthen our *samskaras*. These reinforced *samskaras* become part of our *vasana* or subconscious mind, which influences our behaviour and thinking patterns at a subconscious level. Finally, our *vasanas* manifest as *vyakti* or expression, which refers to our behaviour, thinking patterns, and attitudes towards life. This expression in turn becomes the basis for our future perceptions or *pratyaksha*, and the cycle of *samskara* continues.

To escape the karmic cycle, there are a few things that we can do:

- **Practise mindfulness.** One way to break the karmic cycle is by becoming aware of your actions and their consequences. Practise mindfulness and cultivate awareness of your thoughts, emotions, and actions.
- **Practise self-reflection.** Reflect on your past actions and try to identify any patterns or habits that may be contributing to the nature of your karmic cycle. This can help you understand how your actions and intentions have created your current situation. Please be open to multiple perspectives.
- **Practise forgiveness.** Forgiving yourself and others can help release negative energy and create a positive shift in your *karma*. Acceptance is another quality that helps you move forward.
- **Practise compassion.** Compassion towards yourself and others can help break negative patterns and create positive karmic energy. Please see the interconnectedness, unity, and oneness in everything around you.

- **Practise good deeds.** Engage in positive actions and create good *karma* by helping others, practising kindness, and living in alignment with your values. Please refer in this connection to the spiritual teachings on righteous actions that we discussed in this chapter.

It's important to note that breaking the karmic cycle is a continuous process and requires sustained effort and awareness. It may also take time to see the effects of your actions, but practising these techniques can help create positive energy and break negative patterns over time.

The state of existence beyond death remains a mystery and lies beyond the scope and domain of our understanding. However, what we can control and influence is our present life, and it is crucial that we make the most of it. To achieve a fulfilling life, it's essential to engage in actions that lead to positive outcomes and success during our lifetime. These actions, also known as *karma*, can empower us to reach our full potential and attain a sense of contentment and satisfaction. By focusing on the present and making conscious choices that align with our values and aspirations, we can create a life that we feel proud of and that makes a meaningful impact on ourselves and others. So let us not worry about what lies beyond this life; instead, let us focus on living a purposeful and fulfilling existence while we have the chance.

From Ancient Greece to Eastern Philosophy: How Aristotle's Teachings Relate to *Karma* Theory

Aristotle tried to understand the world through logical reasoning. However, some of his teachings and ideas can immensely help enhance spiritual understanding in the context of cause and effect.

1. **The four causes.** Aristotle believed that every object or event in the world has four causes: material, efficient, formal, and final. The material cause is the physical matter of which an

object is made, while the efficient cause is the force or agency that brings an object into existence. The formal cause is the structure or organisation of an object, while the final cause is the purpose or goal for which an object exists.

This theory can be seen as a way of encouraging us to look beyond the surface level of things and seek a deeper understanding of the underlying causes and purposes of events and objects. By recognising the different causes that contribute to the existence of an object or event, we can gain a greater appreciation for the complexity and interconnectedness of the world.

2. **The doctrine of the mean.** Aristotle believed that the key to living a good life was to find the 'mean' between two extremes. For example, the virtue of courage lies between the extremes of cowardice and recklessness.

   The doctrine of the mean can be understood as encouraging us to find balance and moderation in all aspects of our lives. By striving to find the 'golden mean' between extremes, we can cultivate virtues such as compassion, generosity, and humility that can help us connect with our higher selves and live more fulfilling lives.

3. **The importance of ethics.** Aristotle believed that ethics was the key to living a good life. He believed that people should strive to develop virtues such as courage, honesty, and compassion in order to achieve eudaimonia, or a state of happiness and well-being.

   Aristotle's emphasis on ethics can be seen as encouraging us to live in accordance with our values and principles. By striving to develop virtues such as honesty, courage, and integrity, we can become more attuned to the deeper truths of the world and connect with our higher selves.

4. **The importance of observation and empirical evidence.** Aristotle believed that knowledge should be based on observation and empirical evidence. He believed that the best way to understand the natural world was through observation and experimentation.

   Aristotle's emphasis on observation and empirical evidence can be seen as encouraging us to explore and understand the natural world. By using our powers of observation and reason to explore the world around us, we can gain a deeper appreciation for the interconnectedness and complexity of the universe.

5. **The importance of logic.** Aristotle is often referred to as the 'father of logic' because of his work on syllogisms and deductive reasoning. He believed that logical reasoning was essential for understanding the world and arriving at sound conclusions.

Aristotle's emphasis on logic can be seen as encouraging us to use reason and critical thinking to understand the world. By developing our capacity for logic and deduction, we can arrive at a deeper understanding of the mysteries of the universe and connect with our higher selves.

Aristotle's teachings can thus be seen as guidelines for developing spiritual intelligence by seeking knowledge, cultivating virtue, and connecting with the deeper truths of the world. By striving to live in accordance with our values and principles and exploring the natural world with logic and reason, we can deepen our understanding of ourselves and the world around us.

Chapter 12

Spiritual Intelligence Is a Journey Through a Life of Momentum

Momentum in the context of spiritual intelligence is what ensues when we allow life to flow, unfold, and evolve. It's a process of exploring life. When this process is embraced, we become open to new ideas and concepts. Dwelling on past hurts, betrayal, guilt, and anger causes depression. Thinking about the future and worrying about it is an anxiety state. Both practices interrupt the otherwise smooth momentum of life. On the other hand, living in the present is a peaceful state. Being conscious of this state requires mindfulness, which initiates a process of exploration and evolution and creates enthusiasm, a readiness to face challenges. It facilitates and supplements your efforts to align with your purpose and value system.

Momentum is growth that builds an attitude of consistency, perseverance, and resilience. Interrupting this momentum causes stagnation, which is equivalent to death. Even if you are 24 years old but have lost momentum, you are a stagnant person; meanwhile, if a person has momentum, then, irrespective of age, he or she is an alive, active, energetic, and vibrant person. So be mindful of what you are thinking and choose to create your momentum by mindfully living a life of choice aligned with your values. The formation of a vision and mission aligned with one's core is essential to a life of fulfilment. Rather than simply going through the motions and being jerked around by the external world, one should steer a life of purpose. This can involve making deliberate choices about how we spend our time, whom we spend it with, and what we prioritise in our lives. Living with momentum also means being willing to take risks, try new things, and learn from our mistakes. We may need to step outside of our comfort zone, challenge ourselves, and push through obstacles in order to achieve our goals. Living a life of momentum means embracing the idea that growth and progress are essential to a fulfilling life. By staying engaged with our own growth and development, and by aligning our choices with our values and purpose, we can live a life that feels alive, purposeful, and meaningful.

Defining Purpose: Crafting a Clear, Inspiring Vision and Mission

Living a life of momentum and purpose involves having a clear vision and mission for our lives and aligning our daily actions with that vision. A vision statement is a declaration of our desired future state, while a mission statement is a statement of our purpose, values, and goals. Together, they can serve as a roadmap for our lives. To form a vision and mission statement, we need to reflect on our core values, passions, and strengths. We may also want to consider our unique purpose or calling in life. This process may involve journalling, talking with trusted friends or mentors, or seeking professional guidance.

Once we have a clear sense of our values and purpose, we can craft a vision and mission statement that reflects those values and goals. A vision statement should be ambitious, inspiring, and future-oriented, painting a picture of the world we want to create. A mission statement should be more concrete, outlining the specific actions we will take to achieve our vision.

With a clear vision and mission in place, we can begin to align our daily actions and decisions with that purpose. This may involve setting goals, developing habits that support our vision, and seeking out opportunities that align with our values and goals. By taking intentional steps towards our vision, we can build momentum and create a sense of forward progress in our lives. Living a life of momentum and purpose is not always easy, and we may face challenges or setbacks along the way. However, by staying true to our vision and mission, we can stay focused on what truly matters and continue to grow and develop as individuals. With time and effort, we can create a life that feels fulfilling, purposeful, and aligned with our unique purpose in the world.

A vision statement should be ambitious, inspiring, and future-oriented, painting a picture of the world we want to create. A mission statement should be more concrete, outlining the specific actions we will take to achieve our vision. This may involve setting goals, developing habits that support our vision, and seeking opportunities that align with our values and goals. By taking intentional steps towards our vision, we can build momentum and create a sense of forward progress in our lives.

Developing a clear and meaningful vision and mission that aligns with your life purpose can be a challenging task. It requires deep introspection and attentive listening to your inner calling. Your purpose is like a melody that emanates from your soul, and your vision and mission are the resulting expressions of that calling. When you tune in to your true calling, your vision and mission naturally flow from within you like poetry. They serve as a constant source of inspiration and guidance for how to live your life. Rather than relying on inspirational quotes from others, you may want to craft your own vision and mission statement, which will serve as your personal anthem and prayer, reflecting your unique path and journey.

Although others may provide guidance and mentorship, your vision and mission statement must come from within. It is the melody of your soul that only you can write and sing. While others can offer frameworks and tips to help you connect with your purpose, they cannot teach you how to be inspired and craft a statement that truly resonates with your unique journey. Ultimately, your vision and mission statement is a reflection of your innermost self and a declaration of the impact you want to make in the world. As Socrates put it, 'I cannot teach anyone anything, but I can make them think.' This statement highlights the idea that true learning and growth come from within and cannot be forced upon someone else. This is particularly true in the context of spiritual intelligence or wisdom, which involves a deep understanding of ourselves and the world around us as well as a sense of purpose and meaning in life. Spiritual intelligence cannot be implanted or taught in a traditional sense. It is a deeply personal and experiential process that involves self-reflection, introspection, and contemplation. It is about developing a sense of inner wisdom and intuition and using that wisdom to navigate the challenges and complexities of life.

To cultivate spiritual intelligence, we must be willing to engage in deep reflection and self-examination. We must be open to new experiences and perspectives and willing to challenge our assumptions and beliefs. Spiritual intelligence is a lifelong journey of self-discovery and growth. It is not something that can be taught or acquired overnight but is cultivated through ongoing practice and experience. By committing to this process of growth and self-discovery, we can develop a deeper understanding of ourselves and the world around us and lead a more fulfilling and purposeful life.

Mentoring can also be a valuable tool for developing spiritual intelligence. A spiritual mentor can offer guidance, support, and wisdom as we navigate the challenges and complexities of the spiritual journey. Mentors can help us develop a deeper understanding of ourselves, our purpose, and the world around us. Developing spiritual intelligence or wisdom requires a combination of both internal and external resources. By engaging in personal practices and seeking out the guidance and support of mentors and other resources, we can cultivate a deeper understanding of ourselves and the world around us.

Nobody born as a human being is 'spiritually dumb.' Everyone has the potential to explore and develop their spirituality, regardless of their current level of knowledge or experience. However, developing spiritual intelligence or wisdom does require a certain level of interest, openness, and curiosity about spiritual matters. For someone who is new to exploring spirituality, it may be helpful to start by reading books, attending workshops, and seeking out guidance.

However, it is also important to recognise that true spiritual growth and wisdom cannot be acquired solely through external sources. It requires a personal commitment to engaging in practices that cultivate our own inner wisdom and intuition. This may involve practices such as meditation, prayer, mindfulness, or journalling, as well as engaging in acts of service and compassion towards others. Developing spiritual intelligence or wisdom is not exclusive to those who have a certain level of knowledge or experience. It is open to anyone who is willing to explore and engage in the process of personal growth and self-discovery.

Recognising one's purpose is important because it provides a sense of direction and meaning in life. It helps individuals understand why they exist and what they hope to achieve in the long run. When an individual has a clear sense of purpose, it becomes easier to set goals, make decisions, and prioritise actions. Forming a vision and mission statement provides a roadmap for achieving one's purpose. This helps individuals stay focused and motivated and provides a framework for making decisions and planning actions.

Discovering one's purpose involves a process of self-reflection and exploring one's likes and passions. It's equally crucial to recognise what one dislikes and what is not aligned with one's calling. One should delve into one's dreams, aspirations, and unconscious mind to gain insight into their true purpose. When engaging in activities that are not aligned with one's values or purpose, it's important to observe the emotions and sensations that arise within oneself. Knowing one's calling is key to finding a career path that not only sustains a livelihood but also improves one's lifestyle.

To achieve a harmonious balance between one's purpose and professional pursuits, it's important to identify and pursue activities that align with one's calling. This approach can prevent feelings of suffocation or emptiness that often arise when living a life without purpose. Overall, discovering and pursuing one's purpose requires a deep understanding of oneself, a willingness to explore and take risks, and a commitment to aligning one's values and passions with everyday actions.

Without a clear sense of purpose, vision, and mission, individuals may find themselves feeling lost or uncertain about what they want to achieve in life. They may lack direction and focus and may struggle to make decisions or take actions that further their goals. They might be puppets, dancing to the tune of external circumstances and going through the motions of life without a sense of purpose or direction. By recognising their purpose and forming a vision and mission statement, individuals can gain a sense of clarity and purpose that can help them achieve their goals and live a more fulfilling life.

From Supervision to SuperVision: A New Leadership Paradigm

Supervision is a multifaceted concept that plays a crucial role in shaping our personal and professional lives. As individuals, we supervise our children and dependents, taking charge of their upbringing and sculpting their behaviour, attitudes, and responses. In the corporate and business world, we oversee the performance of our employees, ensuring that they meet the expected standards.

As parents, mentors, or leaders, our aim should be to perform the roles of catalyst and facilitator, assisting those who look up to us in comprehending their life's purpose and helping them in the formation of their individual vision and mission. Our collaboration with them to co-create their vision will enable them to shape their destiny and align their values and passions with it. This approach will enable them to develop virtues and sharpen their wisdom. This is the true essence of supervision—to guide, support, and inspire individuals to reach their full potential and lead a fulfilling life.

While the term 'supervision' may sound restrictive and controlling, it is, in fact, the opposite. Supervision is about empowering individuals and enabling them to reach their full potential. It is about guiding and supporting them in their personal and professional development, helping them grow and evolve. Supervision is not just about performance management or ensuring that tasks are completed on time. It is about creating a culture of growth that encourages individuals to learn, develop, and excel. It involves providing feedback, coaching, and mentoring, ensuring that individuals have the support and guidance they need to succeed.

In the context of the corporate world, supervision is often associated with micromanagement and control. However, this is a misconception. Effective supervision is about creating a culture of trust and transparency in which individuals feel empowered to take ownership of their work, are accountable for their actions, and are encouraged to take risks, innovate, and push boundaries. Moreover, it is about not only guiding and supporting individuals in their personal and professional development but also aligning their vision and mission with that of the relevant corporate or business establishment. When individuals feel that their aspirations, vision, and mission are aligned with that of the organisation, it creates a win-win situation and a sense of belonging and ownership. They become invested in the success of the organisation, which translates into increased productivity and better performance. This sense of ownership also leads to increased employee engagement, which is crucial for organisational success.

Spiritual intelligence can play an important role in the shift from the traditional archetype of management to the modern concept of 'SuperVision'. The conventional approach to management was based on control and focused on achieving specific levels of performance or productivity. However, the modern approach emphasises the importance of empowering employees and facilitating their growth and development. Those with high levels of spiritual intelligence understand the importance of connecting with others and promoting mutual growth. They recognise that the traditional model of management, with its emphasis on control, is limited in its ability to create positive outcomes. Instead, they focus on aligning their vision with that of their employees and providing support and training to help them achieve their full potential.

The concept of SuperVision also involves a shift in the relationship between supervisor and employee, from one of hierarchical authority to one of mutual respect and collaboration. Those with high levels of spiritual intelligence understand the importance of empathy and compassion in building strong relationships, and they use these qualities to guide their interactions with others. The SuperVision model of management aligns well with the principles of spiritual intelligence, which emphasise the importance of personal growth, interconnectedness, and service to others. By cultivating spiritual intelligence, supervisors can play a crucial role in promoting not only the growth and development of their employees and their organisations but also their own growth and development.

Spiritual intelligence is a vital aspect of human development that has been recognised for centuries. This wisdom flows from within and is experiential. In today's world, it is common for people to offer unsolicited advice and impose their judgements on others.

However, each person has their own mindset, shaped by their unique experiences, beliefs, and values. Therefore, it is crucial to avoid imposing our opinions and solutions on others. Instead, we must facilitate their thinking process, trigger their deliberative mind, and help them explore different perceptions and consequential options. This approach is particularly relevant in dealing with people, with the focus being on empowering individuals to find their own solutions. Encouraging individuals to tap into their creative and deliberative minds produces in them a sense of ownership and accountability. They can explore life from different dimensions and find solutions that align with their goals and aspirations.

It is important to remember that each individual has their own thought process and creative inclinations. Recognising this makes for better relationships with others, based on a deep understanding of their unique perspectives. This not only fosters excellent rapport but also helps people discover their true potential and navigate life with greater purpose. Spiritual intelligence involves respecting individual autonomy and recognising that each person has the capacity for creative problem-solving. By embracing this approach, we can help individuals reach their full potential and develop a deeper sense of fulfilment and purpose in life.

In today's management paradigm, the supervisor empowers the employee and adopts handholding to facilitate their growth and development, based on a mutual growth principle that requires vision alignment, training, mentoring, counselling, and coaching. Organisations that follow this SuperVision concept not only take care of human resources and develop them but also grow exponentially and emerge successful on many parameters.

A competent leader who is capable of instilling workplace spirituality in an organisation can yield advantages not only for the organisation's members but also for its stakeholders, who rely on being represented by the leader. The advantages include improved organisational performance, heightened job satisfaction and engagement among employees and greater returns on investments. Spiritual leadership cultivates a mindset of discernment over intervention, emphasising the value of listening instead of commanding and prioritising humility over competitiveness and expertise.

Longevity and Spiritual Intelligence: A Winning Combination

The exploratory process of gaining wisdom creates momentum that improves the quality of life. It is also a healing process. The concept of spiritual intelligence improving longevity is based on the idea that having a sense of purpose, meaning, and connection to something greater than oneself can lead to better physical and mental health outcomes. The Japanese have long exemplified the connection between a life filled with purpose, as depicted in the concept of *ikigai*, and the remarkable longevity they enjoy. When individuals have a sense of spiritual intelligence, they may be more likely to engage in activities that promote their overall well-being, such as practising mindfulness, engaging in regular exercise, and maintaining social connections. These activities can help reduce stress and promote positive emotions, which can in turn lead to a longer and healthier life.

Moreover, having spiritual intelligence or wisdom can also help individuals navigate life's challenges with greater resilience and equanimity. This can help them stay motivated and engaged in their pursuits, even in the face of setbacks or obstacles. This sense of momentum can help individuals maintain a sense of purpose and direction, which can be particularly important as they age.

The qualities that spiritual intelligence helps us develop, including empathy, compassion, self-awareness, intuition, and a sense of interconnectedness with all things, are known to cause a surge of happiness chemicals, more particularly dopamine and oxytocin, inside the body. Therefore, spiritual intelligence can not only help us lead a more fulfilling and purposeful life but also have a positive impact on our physical health and longevity:

- **Stress and anxiety reduction.** Stress and anxiety can have a major negative impact on our physical health and longevity. Research has shown that people who experience high levels of stress and anxiety are more likely to develop chronic health conditions, such as heart disease, diabetes, and cancer. Spiritual intelligence can help us reduce stress and anxiety by providing us with tools and techniques to manage our emotions and cultivate a sense of inner peace and calm. For example, meditation is a powerful practice that can help us reduce stress and anxiety by calming the mind and promoting a sense of relaxation and well-being.

  Stress-related depression has become one of the leading modern ailments, affecting individuals across all age groups, genders, and backgrounds. The pressures of daily life, including disappointments, strained relationships, and work-related challenges, have created an environment in which depression has become increasingly prevalent. Research shows that approximately one in three individuals we encounter may be experiencing some form of depression, with varying degrees of intensity. This condition can have a detrimental impact on mental, emotional, and physical health, leading to a range of negative outcomes that can ultimately lead to death. Modern-day afflictions like OCD (obsessive-compulsive disorder) and ADHD (attention deficit/hyperactivity disorder) are often the result of heightened levels of stress and a widening gap between our expectations and reality. The fear of missing out (FOMO) can create a sense of neglect, leading to feelings of anxiety and an inability to cope with the demands of daily life. In today's fast-paced and competitive world, many of us feel a constant pressure to excel in all areas of our lives, from work and school to relationships and personal goals. This pressure can be overwhelming, and when we struggle to meet these expectations, it can trigger feelings of inadequacy, self-doubt, and fear of failure.

OCD and ADHD are two conditions that can arise from this kind of stress and pressure. OCD is characterised by intrusive thoughts or obsessions that lead to repetitive behaviours or compulsions. These behaviours can provide temporary relief from the anxiety caused by the obsessions, but they can also interfere with daily functioning and cause significant distress. ADHD is a condition that affects focus, attention, and impulse control. People with ADHD may struggle to persist with a task, stay organised, or regulate their emotions, which can cause problems at work, school, or in relationships.

Both OCD and ADHD can be treated with medication, therapy, or a combination of the two. However, it's important to address the underlying causes of these conditions, which often stem from stress, anxiety, and a sense of disconnection from our true selves. By learning to manage stress, cultivate self-compassion, and align our expectations with our values and priorities, we can reduce the likelihood of developing these conditions and live a more balanced and fulfilling life. It's important to recognise that it's okay to ask for help and support when we need it, and that seeking treatment is a courageous and important step towards healing and growth.

However, there is hope for those struggling with depression. Spiritual intelligence, which encompasses a deep understanding of oneself and one's place in the world, can play a pivotal role in promoting health and longevity. By cultivating spiritual intelligence, individuals can gain a greater sense of purpose, meaning, and connection with the world around them. They can learn to navigate challenging circumstances with greater resilience, draw on inner strength, and develop a sense of inner peace that can help combat stress-related depression.

There is evidence to suggest that spiritual wisdom can have a positive impact on the placebo effect. This is because spiritual practices can help individuals develop a deeper sense of connection with their inner self as well as the world around them. This connection can lead to a greater sense of trust in the healing process, which can in turn enhance the power of the placebo effect. Another way in which spiritual wisdom can impact the placebo effect is by reducing stress and anxiety. Spiritual practices such as meditation and prayer have been shown to lower levels of the stress hormone cortisol, which can have a negative impact on the body's immune system. By reducing stress, spiritual practices can help the body function more effectively.

In addition, spiritual wisdom can help individuals develop a more positive outlook on life and to cultivate a sense of hope and optimism and develop a deeper sense of faith and trust in the healing process. This can be particularly important when an individual feels powerless or uncertain about their condition. By cultivating a sense of trust and faith, spiritual practices can help activate the body's natural healing mechanisms.

- **Promoting healthy habits.** Spiritual intelligence can also help us adopt healthier habits and lifestyle choices that can promote longevity. For example, people who have a strong sense of purpose and meaning in life are more likely to engage in healthy behaviours, such as regular exercise, a balanced diet, and good sleep hygiene. By living in alignment with our values, we can make choices that promote our physical health and well-being and help us live a longer and more fulfilling life.

- **Promoting positive emotions.** Spirituality can also promote positive emotions such as gratitude, compassion, and forgiveness. These emotions are associated with better physical health—a stronger immune system, lower blood pressure, and lower risk of chronic diseases.
- **Fostering social connections.** Social connections are an important factor in promoting longevity, as they provide us with a sense of support, belonging, and community. Spiritual intelligence can help us foster social connections by promoting qualities such as empathy, compassion, and kindness, which can help us build deeper and more meaningful relationships with others. Practising acts of kindness and generosity—volunteering, donating to charity, or simply offering a kind word to someone in need—can help us build social connections and promote a sense of community.
- **Coping with illness and disease.** Spiritual intelligence can help us cope with illness and disease in a more effective way. When faced with a health challenge, it can be easy to become overwhelmed and feel despair, which can make it more difficult to manage the condition effectively. Spiritual intelligence can provide us with tools and techniques to cope with illness and disease, such as meditation, prayer, and other forms of spiritual practice that can help us cultivate a sense of inner peace and resilience to cope with the physical and emotional challenges of illness and disease.

This can not only enhance our longevity but also improve our quality of life and sense of well-being. It is a commonly held belief that having a positive mindset can help a great deal in curing diseases and ailments. This phenomenon is attributed to the idea that individuals who believe they have a healing power within themselves can trigger this power and potentially overcome even dreaded illnesses. This is a testament to the power of the human mind and its ability to discern the workings of the body. When individuals tap into this wisdom within themselves, they can unlock incredible healing potential.

A study published in the *Journal of Psychosomatic Research* found that older adults who reported a greater sense of purpose in life had a lower risk of mortality over a five-year period than those who reported a lower sense of purpose. Another study, published in the *Journal of Behavioral Medicine*, found that meditation can help reduce stress and improve immune function, which may have a protective effect against chronic diseases. It's important to note that spirituality is a complex and multifaceted concept and its relationship with longevity is likely to be influenced by many factors. However, the available evidence suggests that spiritual intelligence can have a positive impact on health and well-being, which may contribute to increased longevity.

From Fear to Freedom: Cultivating Resilience for a Life Without Limits

Fear is a natural and instinctive feeling that is hardwired into our survival mechanism. It is not necessarily a negative feeling, as it can serve a positive purpose in our lives. Fear can be a warning signal that alerts us to potential danger, allowing us to take necessary precautions and avoid harm. However, when we allow fear to control us, we can become stuck and unable to move forward. Sometimes, people have a tendency to overreact to fearful situations. This can be problematic because it can prevent us from taking necessary risks or pursuing opportunities that may be beneficial for us. When we allow fear to limit us, we miss out on actualising our potential for growth and success.

On the other hand, it is important to strike a balance between recklessness and cowardice. Taking unnecessary risks can be just as harmful as avoiding risk altogether. Therefore, it is crucial to find a middle ground where we are not paralysed by fear but are also not acting recklessly. In certain situations, this means finding the courage to face our fears head-on and take calculated risks. By acknowledging our fears and confronting them in a thoughtful and strategic way, we can push past our limitations and achieve our goals. In the words of Robin Sharma, 'Fear we don't face becomes our limits.' Our momentum in life is affected by the fear of failure, the fear of the unknown, or the fear of rejection. As has been noted, FOMO is a modern ailment that causes stress and depression. These fears can limit us, preventing us from reaching our full potential and experiencing the richness of life. This is where spiritual intelligence comes in, helping us overcome fear and cultivate resilience.

When we face a complex situation, our mind is uncomfortable. We may feel confused, angry, or fearful. Our minds prefer familiarity, simplicity, and certainty, so when faced with something that challenges these preferences, we can become anxious and stressed. This triggers a response in our neurology; a feeling of nervousness sets in. Fear impairs our neurology, affecting our confidence, energy, and enthusiasm levels. It makes us worry, generating negative emotions and thoughts.

The amygdala is a small, almond-shaped structure located deep within the brain's temporal lobe. It plays a crucial role in regulating emotions, especially fear. When we perceive a threat, the amygdala triggers a series of physiological responses, including the release of stress hormones like adrenaline and cortisol. These responses help us prepare to fight, flee, or freeze in response to the perceived danger. However, sometimes the amygdala can become overactive, triggering fear responses in situations where there is no real threat. This can lead to chronic anxiety, which can be debilitating and can interfere with daily life. Therefore, empowering the amygdala to regulate fear is an important step towards reducing fear chemicals and unlocking one's inner potential.

The following are some tips on empowering the amygdala to regulate fear and reduce fear chemicals:

- **Mindfulness meditation.** One of the most effective ways to empower the amygdala is mindfulness meditation. This practice involves bringing your attention to the present moment and observing your thoughts and feelings without judgement. By doing this, you can learn to recognise when your amygdala is triggered and regulate your response to the perceived threat. Research has shown that regular mindfulness meditation can lead to reduced activity in the amygdala and reduced levels of stress hormones.
- **Gratitude.** Practising gratitude is another way of empowering the amygdala. When we focus on what we are grateful for, it shifts our attention away from fear and anxiety. Gratitude can also boost the production of neurotransmitters like serotonin and dopamine, which can help regulate mood and reduce stress.
- **Exercise and yoga.** Exercise and yoga *asanas* are also effective ways of regulating the amygdala and reducing fear chemicals. When we exercise, our bodies release endorphins, which are natural mood-boosters. Exercise can also help reduce cortisol levels, which can contribute to chronic anxiety.

- **Visualisation.** Visualisation is a technique that involves imagining a calming scene or situation. This can help reduce anxiety and empower the amygdala to regulate fear. By practising visualisation regularly, you can strengthen the neural connections between the amygdala and the prefrontal cortex, which is responsible for rational thinking. When faced with a situation that induces fear, visualisation can be an effective method of superimposing positive approaches and behaviours through the thinking process. This can have the dual effect of regulating the amygdala's secretions while also motivating the individual to take inspiring actions.
- **Spiritual practices.** Many spiritual practices, such as prayer, meditation, and chanting, can also empower the amygdala to regulate fear. These practices can help shift our focus away from fear and anxiety and towards inner peace and spirituality. They can also help us connect with a higher power, which can be a source of comfort and strength in times of stress.

It is possible to overcome feelings of fear and move into a state of resilience. Accepting troublesome situations as challenges and emerging as troubleshooters is what creates new experiences and learning. This is where spiritual intelligence comes in, providing a framework for us to face our fears and cultivate resilience. One way to overcome fear is to superimpose upon the mind the thought of accepting the situation as a challenge. This activates the fight mode, in which the self directs the mind instead of the mind directing the self. This puts us in a resourceful state, enabling us to move from survival mode to creative mode. This way, we protect our neurology and biology too, as the secretion of harmful chemicals such as cortisol in a fearful state can cause serious damage. Spiritual intelligence is a powerful tool for overcoming fear and cultivating resilience. When we cultivate spiritual intelligence, we can live a more fulfilling life, free from the limits of fear.

Exploring Diverse Teachings to Boost Spiritual Intelligence

The Osho Method: A Path to Spiritual Growth

Osho, also known as Bhagwan Shree Rajneesh, was an Indian spiritual teacher who gained a following in the West during the 1970s and 1980s. He offered a unique approach to spiritual growth that combined insights from traditional eastern spirituality with a modern, individualistic perspective. Some of the key and relevant teachings of Osho are as follows:

- **Meditation.** Osho placed great emphasis on the practice of meditation as a means of experiencing inner peace, silence, and enlightenment. He offered many different meditation techniques, each designed to help individuals with different aspects of their consciousness and inner being.
- **Mindfulness.** Osho believed in the power of mindfulness to transform one's life. He encouraged individuals to become aware of their thoughts, emotions, and actions in the present moment, and to live in a state of heightened awareness and consciousness.
- **Love and relationships.** Osho taught that love and relationships were essential aspects of spiritual growth. He believed that individuals could learn a great deal about themselves through their interactions with others and that true love involved a deep acceptance of oneself and others.
- **Creativity.** Osho believed that creativity was an essential aspect of spiritual growth. He encouraged individuals to explore their creativity through a variety of means, such as art, dance, music, and writing.
- **Individuality.** Osho valued individuality and encouraged individuals to express themselves freely and authentically. He believed that true spiritual growth could only be achieved

by breaking free from societal norms and expectations and embracing one's true self.

- **Mind-body connection.** Osho emphasised the importance of the mind-body connection and believed that physical health was essential for spiritual growth. He encouraged individuals to take care of their bodies through exercise, healthy eating, and other forms of self-care.

Osho's teachings have been controversial and criticised by some, but they have also had a significant impact on the spiritual landscape of the West. They offer a comprehensive approach to spiritual intelligence, combining traditional eastern spiritual practices with a modern, individualistic perspective. By following these teachings, individuals can cultivate greater inner peace, self-awareness, and purpose in their lives.

Living in Harmony: Thich Nhat Hanh's Path to Mindful Living

Thich Nhat Hanh is a Vietnamese Zen master, author, and peace activist who is widely respected for his spiritual wisdom and teachings and has been influential in bringing mindfulness and meditation practices to the West. His teachings emphasise the cultivation of mindfulness in everyday life, the practice of deep listening and loving speech, and the application of mindfulness to social and environmental issues.

Thich Nhat Hanh's teachings offer practical tools and insights for self-reflection, mindfulness, compassion, and the integration of spiritual principles into daily life:

- **Self-awareness.** Thich Nhat Hanh's teachings emphasise the practice of mindfulness, which is the foundation of self-awareness. By cultivating mindfulness, individuals become more attuned to their thoughts, emotions, and physical sensations. This awareness allows them to gain insight into their patterns of behaviour, beliefs, and motivations, leading to a deeper understanding of themselves and their spiritual journey.

- **Connection to others.** Thich Nhat Hanh's teachings promote the recognition of interbeing, the understanding that we are all interconnected and part of a greater whole. This awareness enhances our capacity for empathy, compassion, and loving kindness towards others. By cultivating a sense of interconnectedness, individuals develop a broader perspective that transcends personal boundaries and fosters a deep sense of unity and shared humanity.
- **Cultivating compassion.** Thich Nhat Hanh's teachings encourage the practice of compassion and loving kindness towards oneself and others. Compassion involves recognising and alleviating suffering, both within ourselves and in the world around us. By developing a compassionate mindset, individuals enhance their ability to respond to challenges and conflicts with empathy and understanding, fostering harmony and healing in their relationships and communities.
- **Deep listening and loving speech.** Thich Nhat Hanh emphasises the importance of deep listening and loving speech as vehicles for enhancing spiritual intelligence. Deep listening involves being fully present and attentive when others are speaking, suspending judgements and preconceptions, and offering one's full presence and empathy. Loving speech involves using words that are honest, kind, and non-violent, fostering understanding, connection, and healing in relationships. These practices enhance communication skills and promote deep connection and spiritual growth.
- **Mindful reflection.** Thich Nhat Hanh encourages individuals to engage in mindful reflection as a means of deepening their spiritual intelligence. Through contemplative practices

such as meditation, journalling, and self-enquiry, individuals gain insight into their values, beliefs, and purpose in life. Reflective practices help individuals align their actions with their spiritual values, fostering personal growth and a sense of meaning and fulfilment.

- **Transcending egoic patterns.** Thich Nhat Hanh's teachings invite individuals to recognise and transcend egoic patterns that limit their spiritual growth. Egoic patterns are driven by self-centred desires, attachments, and judgements. Through the cultivation of mindfulness and self-compassion, individuals become aware of these patterns and develop the capacity to transcend them, leading to greater spiritual clarity and freedom.
- **Integrating spiritual principles into daily life.** Thich Nhat Hanh's teachings emphasise the importance of integrating spiritual principles into daily life. The practice of mindfulness is not limited to formal meditation but extends to every aspect of life, including work, relationships, and daily activities. By bringing awareness and presence to each moment, individuals can infuse their daily lives with spirituality, deepening their connection to the sacred and enhancing their spiritual intelligence.

Sharing these principles and practices with others, providing guidance, and creating spaces for self-reflection and contemplation through workshops, retreats, discussions, and community practices, teachers can support individuals in their spiritual journey, helping them develop greater self-awareness, compassion, and connection to the interconnected web of life.

Paramahansa Yogananda's Guiding Principles

Paramahansa Yogananda was an Indian yogi and spiritual teacher who introduced the ancient practices of yoga and meditation to the western world. He founded the Self-Realization Fellowship and wrote the spiritual classic *Autobiography of a Yogi*, which has inspired millions of people worldwide. Here are some of his key teachings, along with explanations for each:

- **Self-realisation through meditation.** Yogananda emphasised the practice of meditation as a means of attaining self-realisation or direct experience of one's true nature. Meditation allows individuals to go beyond the limitations of the ego and connect with the higher self or divine consciousness within. He taught various meditation techniques, including *kriya* yoga, a powerful method for awakening spiritual consciousness. Through regular meditation, individuals can quiet their minds, turn inward, and experience a direct perception of the divine presence within themselves.

  Yogananda emphasised that meditation is not simply a technique but a way of life, encouraging practitioners to integrate mindfulness and inner awareness into every aspect of their daily routines. Through regular meditation, one can also cultivate inner peace, clarity, and a deep sense of joy.

- **Harmony of science and spirituality.** Yogananda believed in the compatibility and complementarity of science and spirituality. He encouraged individuals to explore the truths of both domains, as they ultimately converge on the quest for knowledge and understanding. Yogananda saw science as a means of understanding the physical world and spirituality as a means of understanding the underlying principles and purpose of life.

  Yogananda's teachings stressed the significance of harmonising the body, mind, and spirit. He advocated the practice of yoga postures (*asanas*) and breathing exercises (*pranayama*) as means of promoting physical health, mental clarity, and spiritual well-being. Yogananda highlighted the interconnection between the physical body and the subtle energy centres (*chakras*) within, teaching individuals how to balance and awaken these centres for spiritual evolution.

- **Unity of religions.** Yogananda taught that all religions are essentially different paths leading to the same ultimate truth. He emphasised the underlying unity of religions, highlighting that their varying practices and rituals are expressions of the same divine principles. Yogananda encouraged individuals to respect and study various religious traditions, recognising the common spiritual essence they share. He believed that the essence of every religious tradition is to guide individuals towards spiritual growth and self-realisation. Yogananda urged people to look beyond the superficial differences and dogmas of various faiths and seek the common spiritual principles that unite humanity. He envisioned a world where people of different religions could come together in harmony, recognising the underlying unity of all beings.
- **Service to others.** Yogananda advocated selfless service as a means of expressing love and compassion towards all beings. He believed that true happiness and spiritual growth can be attained by helping others and alleviating their suffering. Serving others with kindness and generosity is seen as an expression of the divine love within oneself.

  Yogananda taught that spiritual progress is not limited to seclusion or withdrawal from the world. He emphasised the importance of active engagement and service to others, encouraging individuals to find ways to contribute positively to society and promote unity, harmony, and the welfare of all beings.

- **Living a balanced life.** Yogananda's teachings revolve around the fundamental principle that the ultimate purpose of human life is to realise our true nature and experience a deep connection with the divine. He emphasised the importance of developing a personal relationship with God, or the supreme being, as the source of all existence and the ultimate truth. Yogananda emphasised the importance of living a balanced life that harmonises spiritual, mental, and physical aspects of the human experience. He encouraged individuals to cultivate spiritual awareness while also fulfilling their worldly responsibilities.

  Another of Yogananda's core teachings is the importance of cultivating self-discipline and self-control. He believed that by developing mastery over our thoughts, emotions, and actions, we can overcome negative habits and tendencies and align ourselves with higher ideals. Yogananda encouraged individuals to practise ethical behaviour, honesty, compassion, and forgiveness as means of purifying the mind and opening the heart to divine love.

- **Seeking inner happiness.** Yogananda believed that true and lasting happiness is not dependent on external circumstances or possessions but can be found within oneself through the practice of meditation and spiritual realisation. According to Yogananda, our true nature is divine, and we can experience inner happiness by establishing a deep connection with our inner self or soul. He taught that, through meditation and self-realisation, we can tap into the infinite source of joy and love that resides within us.

Living Truthfully: Embodying the Teachings of Guru Nanak

Guru Nanak's teachings offer valuable insights and practices that can help foster personal growth and deepen one's spiritual understanding. Here are some of the concepts central to Guru Nanak's teachings that can contribute to enhancing spiritual intelligence:

- **Oneness of God.** The concept of *ik onkar*, the belief in the oneness of God, cultivates spiritual intelligence by emphasising the unity of all existence. It encourages individuals to perceive the divine presence in everything and develop a sense of interconnectedness with the world.
- **Equality and brotherhood.** Embracing the principle of equality and brotherhood fosters spiritual intelligence by expanding one's compassion and empathy. Recognising the inherent worth and equality of all beings allows individuals to transcend ego-driven biases and develop a broader perspective that embraces the interconnectedness of all life.
- **Service and selflessness.** Engaging in selfless service, or *seva*, enhances spiritual intelligence by nurturing qualities such as kindness, humility, and empathy. Through acts of service, individuals develop a deeper understanding of the interconnected nature of humanity and experience a sense of fulfilment and purpose.
- **Truth and honesty.** Living a life of truth and honesty contributes to spiritual intelligence by cultivating integrity and authenticity. Embracing truthfulness in thoughts, words, and actions helps individuals align with their inner values, deepens self-awareness, and promotes inner harmony.
- **Meditation and prayer.** The practice of meditation and prayer, as advocated by Guru Nanak, enhances spiritual intelligence by facilitating self-reflection, self-discovery, and inner peace. These practices provide a means of connecting with the divine, cultivating mindfulness, and gaining insights into the nature of the self and the universe.

- **Rejecting ritualism and superstitions.** Challenging empty rituals and superstitions encourages individuals to engage in critical thinking and discernment, promoting spiritual intelligence. By focusing on the essence of spirituality rather than external practices, individuals can develop a deeper understanding of their own beliefs and connect with the divine in a more meaningful way.
- **Gender equality.** Guru Nanak's teachings on gender equality contribute to spiritual intelligence by challenging societal biases and promoting inclusivity. Recognising and honouring the inherent worth and spiritual potential of all individuals, regardless of gender, fosters a broader and more inclusive understanding of spirituality.

Walking the Path of Wisdom: Embracing Ramana Maharshi's Teachings

Sri Ramana Maharshi is a popular Indian spiritual leader who is regarded as the epitome of spiritual intelligence. Born in 1879, Ramana Maharshi is known for his teachings on self-enquiry and non-duality, which emphasise the direct path to self-realisation and liberation. Ramana Maharshi's spiritual journey began at the age of 16, when he experienced a deep inner awakening. He retreated to the sacred mountain of Arunachala in south India and spent the majority of his life there, attracting seekers from all over the world who were drawn to his presence and wisdom.

His teachings focused on the question 'Who am I?' as a means of enquiring into the nature of the self. Ramana Maharshi emphasised the importance of self-awareness and self-enquiry as a way of transcending the ego and discovering one's true nature, which he described as pure consciousness. Throughout his life, Ramana Maharshi exemplified the qualities of compassion, simplicity, and deep spiritual insight. He believed in the universal nature of spirituality, stating that all religions lead to the same truth and that the ultimate goal is self-realisation and the recognition of one's essential unity with all of creation. His teachings continue to inspire and resonate with spiritual seekers around the world. Below are some of his teachings, which can be used to cultivate and develop spiritual intelligence:

- **Self-awareness.** Spiritual intelligence involves a deep understanding of oneself and the ability to observe one's thoughts, emotions, and beliefs. Ramana Maharshi's emphasis on self-enquiry and the question 'Who am I?' helps individuals develop a heightened sense of self-awareness. By constantly questioning the nature of the self and observing one's thoughts and identifications, individuals can gain a deeper understanding of their true nature and the ego's role in shaping their experiences.
- **Transcending the ego.** The teachings of Ramana Maharshi emphasise transcending the ego and realising one's non-dual nature. Spiritual intelligence involves recognising that the ego and the limited self are not the ultimate reality. By practising self-enquiry and cultivating an awareness of the ego's patterns and attachments, individuals can gradually let go of the ego's grip and experience a broader sense of identity beyond individual separateness. This realisation expands spiritual intelligence by recognising the interconnectedness of all beings.
- **Present-moment awareness.** Spiritual intelligence involves being fully present in the moment and cultivating mindfulness. Ramana Maharshi stressed the importance of awareness and presence, teaching that true spiritual progress occurs when the mind is fully attentive to the present moment. By practising presence and mindfulness in everyday life, individuals can deepen their spiritual

intelligence, becoming more attuned to the present moment, experiencing a sense of inner peace, and gaining insights into the nature of reality.

- **Cultivating surrender.** Surrendering the ego involves letting go of attachments, desires, and the need for control. This allows individuals to develop humility, acceptance, and trust in a higher power or universal consciousness. By cultivating surrender, individuals enhance their spiritual intelligence through the recognition that there is a greater wisdom and guidance beyond their limited understanding.
- **Integration and unity.** Ramana Maharshi taught the universality of spirituality and the interconnectedness of all paths. Spiritual intelligence involves recognising the underlying unity and interconnectedness of all beings and embracing diverse spiritual traditions and perspectives. By integrating the teachings of different paths and fostering a sense of unity and compassion, individuals can expand their spiritual intelligence and develop a broader understanding of the human experience.

Kant's Philosophy: A Revolutionary Perspective on Reason and Morality

Immanuel Kant was a German philosopher who is widely regarded as one of the most important figures in western philosophy. His work has had a profound influence on many different areas of thought, including epistemology, metaphysics, ethics, political philosophy, and aesthetics.

One of the central aspects of Kant's philosophy is his attempt to reconcile the empirical, scientific approach of the Enlightenment with the limitations of human knowledge and the importance of moral values. Kant believed that knowledge was not simply a matter of collecting data through observation and experience but also required certain conceptual structures and categories that were innate to the human mind. He called these structures and categories the 'transcendental conditions of knowledge' and argued that they were necessary for us to make sense of the world around us.

Kant also believed that there are limits to what we can know about the world. He argued that our knowledge is limited to the realm of phenomena—the things we can experience through our senses. The world of phenomena, however, is distinct from the world as it actually is, or 'noumena,' which we can never know directly. Kant believed that our knowledge of the world is always filtered through our sensory experiences and that we can never know the world in itself, independent of our perceptions.

In addition to his epistemological views, Kant also developed a distinctive ethical philosophy based on the idea of the categorical imperative. According to Kant, morality was not a matter of subjective opinion or personal preference but was based on universal moral laws that applied to all rational beings. He believed that the categorical imperative was the fundamental principle of morality and that it required us to act only in ways that complied with universal laws.

Kant also emphasised the importance of reason in human life. He believed that reason is the key to understanding the world and ourselves and that it is necessary for true freedom and autonomy. He argued that we should always treat people as ends in themselves rather than as means to our own ends and that we should always strive to act in accordance with reason and moral principles.

Kant also made important contributions to aesthetics, arguing that beauty is not simply a matter of subjective taste but is based on objective principles of form, harmony, and proportion. He believed that art has an important role to play in human life and that it can help us understand and appreciate the world around us.

Kant's philosophy is complex and nuanced and has had a profound influence on many different areas of thought. His ideas continue to be debated and discussed by philosophers today and his work remains an important part of the western philosophical tradition.

Kant's philosophy can be seen as having significance for the development of spiritual intelligence. His emphasis on the importance of reason and the limits of human knowledge can be seen as relevant to the development of spiritual intelligence. By recognising that our knowledge of the world is limited to the realm of phenomena and that we can never know the world in itself, Kant encourages us to approach the world with a sense of humility and openness to the transcendent. This can help cultivate a sense of wonder and awe at the mysteries of existence and can open us up to the possibility of spiritual experiences.

Kant's emphasis on the categorical imperative and the importance of treating people as ends in themselves can also be seen as a recognition of the inherent dignity and worth of all human beings and the importance of acting in accordance with universal moral principles, encouraging us to cultivate a sense of compassion, empathy, and altruism. This can help create a deeper sense of connection and meaning in our lives and can help us transcend our own individual concerns and become more attuned to the needs of others and the world around us.

There are some similarities and resonances between Kant's philosophy and certain aspects of Hinduism, particularly in terms of their respective views on ethics, epistemology, and the nature of reality. In terms of ethics, both Kant and Hinduism emphasise the importance of moral principles and the cultivation of virtue. Kant's emphasis on the categorical imperative and the importance of treating people as ends in themselves can be seen as having resonances with Hinduism's emphasis on *dharma*, or ethical duty, and the cultivation of virtues such as compassion, non-harmfulness, and detachment from worldly desires.

Kant's distinction between phenomena and noumena and his recognition that our knowledge is filtered through our sensory experiences can be compared to Hinduism's recognition that our perceptions and interpretations of reality are often coloured by our mental and emotional states and that the ultimate reality can only be accessed through a transcendental mode of awareness. As far as the nature of reality is concerned, both Kant and Hinduism agree that the world as we experience it is not the ultimate reality and that there is a transcendental dimension to existence that is beyond our ordinary perception. Kant's recognition of the limitations of human knowledge and the importance of transcending our subjective perspectives can be seen as having resonances with Hinduism's recognition of the illusory nature of the material world (*jagat mithya*) and the importance of realising our true nature as pure consciousness.

Of course, there are also significant differences between Kant's philosophy and Hinduism, particularly in terms of their respective metaphysical frameworks and religious traditions. However, the resonances between these two perspectives have been brought up here to emphasise the universality of some concepts, which can provide a rich ground for exploring the nature of reality, ethics, and human experience.

When we examine the teachings of these esteemed masters, a common thread emerges—the importance of self-enquiry, mindfulness, meditation, and living a disciplined life guided by ethical principles. Their wisdom reveals a profound understanding of interconnectedness and unity, urging us to transcend our ego and discover our true selves. Their teachings, when embraced and applied to our daily lives, become catalysts for transformative growth and unlock the hidden treasure of spiritual intelligence within us. By integrating this form of intelligence into our day-to-day experiences, we can accelerate the process of personal transformation and embark on a fulfilling journey of self-realisation.

Spiritual intelligence is a universal, fundamental aspect of our inner being that can be cultivated and developed independently of any religious affiliation. It arises from within and is a manifestation of the inherent wisdom that already exists within each of us. While I have drawn spiritual concepts from my personal experience with Hinduism, I acknowledge that others may find similar insights and wisdom in their own faiths and belief systems.

In this context, I believe that it is highly relevant to reflect on the following quote from the Rig Veda: *ekam sat vipra bahudha vadanti*, which means 'the truth is one, but the wise speak of it in many ways.' This emphasises the unity of all religions and the idea that, while there is only one ultimate reality, it can be approached and understood in different ways by different people. It encourages people to recognise and respect the diversity of religious beliefs and practices while also recognising the underlying unity that connects them all. It reminds us that even though we may have different ways of expressing our beliefs, we are all ultimately seeking the same truth. This principle has had a significant impact on Indian philosophy and has been embraced by people of many different faiths and backgrounds as a way of promoting unity and understanding between different cultures.

Spiritual intelligence is about uncovering our true character and living in a way that is authentic and meaningful to us. By nurturing qualities like compassion, empathy, forgiveness, authenticity, and more, we can tap into our higher intelligence. While each person's journey may look different, the common thread is a commitment to seeking and embodying the qualities that arise from our higher intelligence and establishing a connection with a transcendent entity that surpasses oneself. This entity can take various forms—a higher intelligence, a higher self, divine energy, or even a deity.

While we may feel a sense of accomplishment from our perceived success in the materialistic world, true fulfilment is only achieved when we embrace spirituality, which takes us much deeper and allows us to understand the essence of our existence and the purpose of our lives. Therefore, it is crucial to reflect on how much effort we have put into developing our spiritual intelligence. It is only by nurturing all the facets of our being that we can truly evolve and progress as individuals and as a society. We must recognise that materialistic success alone is incomplete without the application of spiritual intelligence and that a fulfilling life can only be achieved by embracing spirituality as an integral part of our existence.

Many individuals find themselves feeling stressed and drained by the fast-paced modern world and often seek refuge in holistic healing centres to detoxify their body and mind, a practice that has gained popularity in recent times. Some may even attend *satsangs* or other spiritual gatherings in pursuit of inner peace and self-connection. While these practices are commendable, they only scratch the surface of true spiritual growth. To develop spiritual intelligence, one must commit to a journey of self-discovery that requires consistent effort, self-reflection, mindfulness, and meditation. It is a lifelong process that cannot be achieved through the temporary relief found in holistic healing centres or spiritual gatherings. According to Buddha, spiritual teachers serve as guides who show us the path, but it's ultimately up to us to undertake the journey. While witnessing the positive transformations of others through meditation and mindfulness may motivate us, our faith can only truly develop when we start to experience the benefits of meditation in our own lives.

Key Takeaways to Boost Your Spiritual Intelligence

As we embark on the transformative journey of expanding our spiritual intelligence, we will benefit from keeping in mind a set of essential practices that hold the power to profoundly enhance our inner growth and understanding. These pivotal steps, which lie at the core of our pursuit, are vital in nurturing and elevating our spiritual capacity. By embracing these actions wholeheartedly, we pave the way for a profound and impactful transformation:

1. **Connect with your inner self regularly.** Take time each day to connect with your inner self through practices like mindfulness, meditation, prayer, or journalling. It is important to reflect regularly on your behaviour and actions to align them with your core values and the person you aspire to be. Recognise the magical intuitive power within you to transform and heal yourself. Dedicate time to introspection, delving deep within to explore your beliefs, values, and purpose. Reflecting upon your experiences and contemplating the profound questions of existence opens doors to self-discovery and unveils hidden aspects of your spiritual being.
2. **Practise gratitude.** Focus on the positive aspects of your life and express gratitude for them. Remember that needs are limited but wants are unlimited and contentment is the key to happiness.
3. **Cultivate compassion.** Cultivate compassion towards yourself and others by practising kindness, love, empathy, and forgiveness. Being open to and respectful of diverse perspectives is also important. Practising humility and non-attachment can help change your outlook. Extend heartfelt empathy and genuine compassion to yourselves and others. Cultivating a deep understanding of the interconnectedness of all beings allows us to foster kindness, love, and understanding, nurturing our spiritual intelligence in profound ways.
4. **Seek wisdom.** Read spiritual texts, attend workshops and seminars, and seek out mentors who can guide you on your spiritual journey. Be a seeker and approach wisdom with

humility, acknowledging that one lifetime is not enough for learning. The key lies in both unlearning and learning. Explore diverse spiritual teachings, scriptures, and philosophical schools of thought. Open your mind to different perspectives, drawing inspiration from the profound insights shared by spiritual masters throughout history. Surround yourself with like-minded individuals who share your spiritual aspirations. Engaging in meaningful conversations, participating in spiritual gatherings, and seeking guidance from mentors and teachers can provide invaluable support and encouragement on your spiritual journey.

5. **Live in the present moment.** Focus on the present moment and let go of worries about the future or regrets about the past. Remember that the nature of everything in the world is impermanence, so it's essential to avoid dwelling on the past and worrying about the future. Develop a practice of present-moment awareness, engaging in each experience with a conscious and non-judgemental presence. By grounding ourselves in the present, we awaken to the beauty and richness of life, nurturing our spiritual growth in the process.

6. **Practise mindfulness.** Cultivate mindfulness by being aware of your thoughts, emotions, and actions. Observe your inner dialogue and recognise when your thoughts are negative or unproductive. Mindfulness is essential for monitoring your thoughts, words, behaviour, and actions, which can either make or break you. Incorporate contemplative practices such as meditation, prayer, or mindful thinking into your daily routine. These sacred practices provide opportunities for stillness, connection, and profound inner growth.

7. **Serve others.** Dedicate time to serving others through volunteer work or acts of kindness. Serving others will help you feel more connected to the world around you. Look for

ways to assist those in need, whether it is by volunteering at a local charity or simply being kind to those in your immediate vicinity. Remember that a mindset of giving fosters a prosperity mentality, while a mindset of taking leads to a poverty mentality.

8. **Embrace challenges.** Embrace challenges as opportunities for growth and learning. See them as chances to develop resilience and inner strength. Focus on your goal, follow the process, and give it your all without becoming overly attached to the result.
9. **Live with intention.** Establish intentions for your life and live in alignment with your values and purpose. Build a strong character. Creating a vision and mission that align with your purpose can provide you with a roadmap to follow. Every action of yours should revolve mindfully around the purpose. Align your thoughts, words, and actions with spiritual values such as compassion, gratitude, forgiveness, and authenticity. By embodying these virtues, we nurture our spiritual intelligence and create a positive impact on the world around us.
10. **Trust in a higher power.** Develop faith and trust in a higher power or universal force that is guiding and supporting you on your spiritual journey. Believing, accepting, and surrendering are the keys to this. Recognise that the truth is one.

May our journey awaken our souls, deepen our connection to the divine, and illuminate the profound wisdom that resides within us.

As I come to the end of this book, I am reminded that this is not a conclusion but rather the beginning of a journey towards discovering the reason for our existence and the essence of life itself. Each one of us has the opportunity to take away something valuable from this book, from the ancient wisdom in it, and to use it to further our evolution as individuals as well as the evolution of humanity as a whole.

Having understood the profound impact of ancient wisdom, I am acutely aware that, had I embarked on this path during my formative years in school and college, my entire being would have undergone a remarkable transformation. This transformative journey would have cultivated my spiritual intelligence, enabling me to naturally apply its principles to create a deeply fulfilling life for myself and those around me. However, I believe that it is never too late to embark on this path of self-discovery and growth. Now that I find myself immersed in the exploration of spirituality, I am astounded by the extraordinary facets of my being that were previously unknown to me.

It is with great conviction that I emphasise to readers the importance of initiating their spiritual journey early in life. By doing so, they can unlock their true potential and become the best versions of themselves. This profound inner transformation not only has the power to shape their individual lives but also has a ripple effect, leaving a lasting and positive impact on the world at large. Therefore, I encourage everyone to embark on their spiritual journey without delay.

To cultivate spiritual intelligence, it's crucial to persistently shed existing thought patterns, beliefs, and habits, and approach new perspectives, concepts, and ideas with an open mind. The key to achieving this lies in the process of unlearning and learning. The perfect example of this principle is 'The Empty Cup', a story about a zen master that I think serves as an apt conclusion for my book by conveying the message that, unless we unlearn, we cannot truly learn. Many of you may have already heard this story, but I will still narrate it, as it is particularly relevant to enhancing spiritual intelligence.

A zen master was visited by a scholar who wanted to learn about zen. The master poured tea into a cup until it was full and then kept on pouring, causing the tea to spill over the sides. The scholar asked the master to stop and exclaimed that the cup was full and could not hold any more tea. The master replied, 'Like this cup, you are full of your own opinions and ideas. How can I show you zen unless you first empty your cup?'

This story teaches us the importance of having an open mind and being willing to learn. When we are full of our own opinions and ideas, we may not be open to new perspectives and wisdom. By emptying our cup, we become receptive to new ideas and insights that can enhance our spiritual intelligence. The story also highlights the importance of humility and the willingness to acknowledge our limitations and weaknesses. When we let go of our ego and open ourselves up to learning, we can develop greater self-awareness and compassion for others. This can lead us towards a more balanced, meaningful, and fulfilling life. If we approach learning with a full cup—that is, if we think we already know everything there is to know about a subject—then we are unlikely to be receptive to new ideas and insights. Just like pouring tea into the full cup forces it to spill over, our minds can overflow with existing opinions, beliefs, and biases that obstruct the learning process. However, if we empty our cup by letting go of our preconceived notions and becoming open to new ideas and perspectives, then we can become more receptive to learning.

Through the pages of this book, I have attempted to provide insights and guidance that will enable you to tap into your spiritual intelligence and unlock your full potential. However, the journey towards spiritual enlightenment is a personal one and it is up to each of us to take responsibility for our own growth and transformation. I encourage you to reflect deeply on the ideas presented in this book and to consider how they can be applied in your daily life.

By doing so, you will be taking a powerful step towards your own personal evolution and growth. Moreover, I invite you to consider the profound impact that your personal growth can have on the world around you. As more and more individuals awaken to their spiritual intelligence and embrace their true selves, the collective consciousness of humanity shifts towards a higher level of awareness and understanding.

I have discussed notable figures and masters who have contributed to the realm of spiritual intelligence. I have also incorporated concepts from various scriptures and philosophical schools that are relevant to this subject. However, it is important to acknowledge that there are numerous other significant figures and concepts within the domain of spiritual intelligence that have not been explicitly mentioned in this book. This omission should not be interpreted as neglect or disregard for them. Rather, it is a deliberate choice made to maintain the readability of the book. Moreover, I would like to emphasise that my personal quest for knowledge and understanding in the field of spiritual intelligence is an ongoing process. The breadth and depth of this field are so immense that it is virtually impossible to fully explore every aspect within a single lifetime.

Each concept touched upon in this book deserves dedicated attention and has the potential to be thoroughly explored in its own right. Therefore, I encourage readers who wish to delve deeper into these concepts to explore related books, videos, and other resources that provide additional insights. These supplementary materials can offer a more comprehensive understanding of the diverse figures and concepts within the vast realm of spiritual intelligence.

In conclusion, I emphasise the importance of spiritual intelligence in leading a life of fulfilment and encourage you to embrace this moment as the beginning of a remarkable journey towards a life of purpose and meaning. Let this book be your guide as you navigate the path ahead. May your pursuit of spiritual intelligence be a source of joy, inspiration, and transformation to you.

Writing this book has allowed me to discover and learn many valuable things that I have excitedly shared with all of you. Along the way, I have reflected on how many of these teachings I personally relate to and practise in my own life. This self-reflection has wrought in me a newfound awareness and has paved the way for my own personal transformation. This journey has been truly wonderful, and I have enjoyed every step of it. However, it doesn't end here. I will continue to delve deeper into the subject, exploring more and expanding my understanding. I am eager to continue this exploration and share more insights with you.

I want to express my sincere gratitude to each and every reader who has joined me on this adventure. Your presence and engagement have fuelled my passion for sharing these teachings. Together, let's move forward, hand-in-hand, and explore the vast landscapes of spiritual intelligence, enriching our lives and the lives of those around us. May this journey have a profound and lasting impact on all of us. Let us approach each day with curiosity and a willingness to learn and grow. May the wisdom and practices shared in this book serve as a guiding light, leading us towards greater self-realisation and spiritual fulfilment.

www.ingramcontent.com/pod-product-compliance
Lightning Source LLC
LaVergne TN
LVHW041137150826
845673LV00001B/26

* 9 7 9 8 8 9 0 2 6 9 0 6 5 *